FRONTIER VIOLENCE WITH TWO CASE STUDIES:

THE EAST FLORIDA RANGERS

AND

THE HISTORY OF THE PONY CLUB

RAY HENDERSON

 *Lillium Press*

Frontier Violence with Two Case Studies:
The East Florida Rangers and The History of the Pony Club

ISBN 0-9628023-6-0

Front cover: 1830 Anthony Finley map of Georgia

Cover design by Rick Smith RS Creative Inc. www.recreativeinc.com

 *Lillium Press*

This book is dedicated to my father, Robyn Phillip Henderson, (1920-2000), whose efforts in WW2, Korea and Vietnam era and those of so many others, assured this book would be in English.

I would like to thank those who have help me in the researching, writing and editing and publishing of this book: John and Elaine Bailey, of Lilium Press for taking on this monster of size and dimension; for Richard Smith for the cover and to Ann Crispin for her advice when I had no idea which way was up. I want to acknowledge the role of Larry Meir of the Greater Atlanta Area Archeology Society (GAAS) for giving me the idea for this book.

Those who were always ready to help with the geneology of the club and the names of those include Diane Sanfilipo and William Lester for the York and Philpot families; Abigail Banks Dennison for William Shipley; Donna Weed for data on William G. Heard; Jerry Clark and Don Johnson for data on spoliation claims and the many many extant authors on this and related subjects without their help none of this would be possible and the data may have been lost forever.

A special thanks to the archives in various states: The Telemon Cuyler collection at the Georgia Digital Library, the Penelope Allen collection at the Tennessee State Library; the Florida PALMM digital library and the Alabama Mosaic. A special thanks goes to the personnel at the Carroll, Paulding, Douglas, Cherokee and Polk County libraries. Finally many thanks to the local digital libraries in Dekalb, Gwinnett and many other surrounding counties.

THE HISTORY OF THE PONY CLUB

Introduction:

This book began as a conversation in 1994 concerning the inhabitants of Sandtown, Georgia and the initial set of people who lived in Carroll County, Ga., in the 1820s. Speaking to Professor Larry Meier, former Cobb County, Ga. Archeologist and publisher of a series of articles for the Greater Atlanta Area Archeology Society, I learned his view that the marauders and horse thieves located at Sandtown were initially pirates and Tories associated with the disenfranchised elements of the American Revolution. They had moved up the Chattahoochee River from Florida and left their raiding bases in Appalachicola Bay, at the armed insistence of the Spanish Governor, who had suffered them as usurpers of Spanish authority for a number of years. When they reached Sandtown, opposite Carroll County, they set up operations as highwaymen and horse thieves.

Professor Meier also believed that these miscreants were the fore-runners of the outlaws of the Old West, with Doolins and Daltons and etc. being born and raised at Buzzard's Roost or Sandtown, or their parents from that infamous village. He points to records of claims made as far back as 1814 and as late as 1838 to prove the great span of their existence as well as their linkage to the Florida gangs. After running their course in Ga., the gangs were assigned to the Creek Indian nation when they finally removed to Arkansas and Oklahoma, Indian Territory.

I began research on this book really at the end of this theory, that later Indian outlaws were related to these Chattahoochee River lawbreakers. I was able to follow dozens of victims of the Fort Smith, Arkansas hangman back to the rolling hills of North Ga., and also Alabama and Tennessee. It became apparent that there was little linkage between the two places and criminal activity. At this point it became clear that I would have to start over to discover the nature of these gangs and the origin of this frontier violence.

I sought to discover the mechanisms which produced this frontier violence; reaching back to the French and Indian War, for a time when pressure to make room for new settlers was causing serious problems with the Indians of the Ohio Valley. Winning the contested valley and waterway opened vast areas for new settlers but also brought the colonists to confrontation with Imperial England. The British desire to accommodate the Indians by setting aside vast areas of Ohio as "hunting grounds" was too much for colonists to bear. Having learned how to raise an Army of 10,000 men and conduct a protracted war, the colonists fought for freedom from England, succeeding in opening up not only the Ohio Territory, but also the way into Kentucky and Tennessee. At this point, settlement and removal of the Indians were on the front page of the American Agenda.

In this book, the nature of frontier violence is examined in terms of immigration policies of Britain and its neighbors; piracy and its influence in early colonial cities and squatters and intruders on both Federal and Indian lands. The four groups of people involved in the story of settling America: Whites, Blacks, Indians and Melungeons and their contribution to the problem of frontier violence are examined as to their interplay. Why so many Americans were poor and landless is asked and answers sought. The forms of violence and the mechanisms used to create new lands for intruders and squatters are also of great interest.

With all this in mind and returning to the original premise, I set out to explore the nature of the Florida gangs and the whole Tory, runaway slave, Indian, banditti story that spans the Revolutionary War until 1818. Who were the East Florida Rangers of the loyalist effort to subdue the colonies and what were their operations against the Americans? Who were the leaders and where did they go after the end of the revolution? Finally, are the Pony Club members of later Carroll County, Ga. from these Florida Groups? All these questions were critical to the discovery of the origin of the Pony Club.

The Pony Club research carried me into uncharted territory where I don't think any man had gone before. Certainly nothing Meier had written of or spoken of would prepare me for such a vastly different set of facts. Rather than following the Florida thread I found myself in McMinn County, Tennessee watching the progress of a band of 50 or so related family members as they treked through Indian Country to come to rest at Sandtown and Buzzard's Roost on the Chattahoochee River. Instead of chronicling the progress of William Augustus Bowles' pirates, up the Chattahoochee, I was reading about the Grand Jury in Habersham County finding against several men for stealing from Bear Paw.

The journey through several states and many years of history, including that of Alabama familiarized me with the area of operation of the Pony Club. While its miscreants were centered in Georgia, its detractors seemed to spring from Alabama, where a tradition of "Captain Slick" and vigilante activity were historically headquartered. The scope of this operation is mainly known from newspaper accounts and claims made by Indians against the perpetrators from 1826-1838. The majority of victims were Cherokee Indians, though some Creeks suffered as well. The Creeks suffered a different fate at the hands of a different set of people. I could not find the linkage necessary to prove that the same people who set upon the Cherokee were the same who robbed the Creeks. As newspapers of the time note, the 1830s was not a generally lawful period of time in the South.

I struggled to find an adequate title for this book. I wasn't sure people would understand the question being asked or find the facts in support of the premise. Though the book is about the Pony Club, it is also about the East Florida Rangers. It is also about the kinds of people in America from the beginning to the time of the Indian removal. It covers many of the origins of frontier violence and explores eyewitness accounts of people and events from those times. In an academic sense it might be appropriate to call the book **FRONTIER VIOLENCE WITH TWO CASE STUDIES: THE EAST FLORIDA RANGERS AND THE PONY CLUB.** However, I felt the nature of the subject matter was just local enough to appeal more to those who have wondered all these years about that nasty group of people who troubled the frontier for so many years. So I have chosen instead to call it:

THE HISTORY OF THE PONY CLUB

WHAT IS A CRACKER?

"What cracker is this same that deafe our eares with this abundance of superfluous breath"? —- William Shakespeare, **King John**, Act II, Scene 1, 1594.

To the British Government, many things were apparent about the way America was going to be populated. Though it may have been seen as a place for religious freedom or a refuge from the harsh treatment of poor people in distant lands, countries like England saw it as a place to dump the worst of its society. A convenient way to outlaw those unwanted millions: exile them to a far away land. So, along with the millions yearning to be free were the millions yearning to be free to wander unmolested in new territory and to ravage the inhabitants of the new world and the settlers, alike. Although most penal emigrants were from debtor prison, England consistently emptied its prisons of all manner of cutthroats, malcontents and other felons and sent them to the United States well into the 1800s…yes, even after American Independence.

Much of this is mentioned by Woodiwiss (2001) who indicates as many as 600 convicts per year between 1719 and 1772 were sent to America, while 1000s more poured in from Scotland and Ireland: "Blackmailers, pimps, rapists, embezzlers and mercenary thugs" among them. So called "crimps" or kidnappers preyed on the poor in those countries, sometimes plying them with alcohol, inducing debt and then sending them from debtors prison to America.

C.E. Lester, in his 1866 *Glory and Shame of England,* makes it quite clear that this exporting of poor and criminal souls continued even after the war of 1812, despite the clamoring of state governments.

I am half tempted to give what lays at my hand, the statistics of pauper exportation to the United States by the British government. Of her exportation of criminals, secretly and clandestinely, to our shores, I need hardly speak. Ever since our government was founded this has been British policy. In multitudes of cases condemned men, indicted persons, or people who had become obnoxious or dangerous, whom the colonial authorities would not receive, have been shipped to this country--- supplying us with murderers, burglars, forgers and thieves; while of the pauper class the number has amounted to tens of thousands. We all know that this mean, unfriendly and contemptible conduct of the British government went so far, that our general and State Governments had to resort to laws of self protection, when the most earnest and repeated protests and expostulations had failed. The records of our criminal courts in every state of the union show the enormous excess imported over native pauperism and crime. It is also well known from authentic sources, that by far the larger share of imported paupers was of the class sent away by the authority or money of the government or both (page 289).

Another source for this is the Encyclopedia Americana (1920), which put the number of British convicts coming to America at 10,000 from 1717 - 1775. It mentions also that Maryland had 20,000 criminals from Britain, half since 1750 (341). Lester, (1866: 289), chronicled the continuation of shipments of British paupers to America in the 1800s:

...In one year, between June of 1835 and July of 1836, the Poor Law Commissioners of England reported that 7,075 paupers were expatriated at the cost of £39,340, or about $196,000. A more brutal deed was never justified by a civilized nation. Whenever a good opportunity offered itself, these paupers, old and infirm, were shipped off like cattle, in vessels hired to convey them to other countries, where there miserable food and miserable burial would not be charged to the government. Is not this more inhuman than shipping off slaves to New Orleans or the Georgia plantations...

Many Americans are indeed unaware of this British, Irish and Scotch effort to rid themselves of criminals by sending them to America. Many uneducated, in our Federal Government, still talk about how Georgia was a "penal colony," though no one in America considered debtors as criminals (see Dixon and Galan, 1990). Many Americans reached the colonies as indentured servants and worked off the cost of their passage to America. Before slavery was rife, most Americans working here were indentured.

By the time of the Revolutionary War, indentured servitude had been a common practice in the United States for 150 years.

...Redemptioners paid their passage to America by binding themselves as servants for terms of from two to seven years. In the seventeenth century most of the servants were English; in the eighteenth century most of them were Germans, Swiss, Scots, Scotch-Irish, and Irish. Victims of kidnappers and convicts sentenced to transportation by English courts supplemented this flow of unfree labor. Probably more than half of the immigrants to the thirteen English colonies in North American came as bondsmen. (Stampp 1956: 16).

Another problem was the colonists saw no problem in allowing pirates to use American ports.

There was little stigma attached to piracy in early British America for more than a century after Drakes exploits. As the colonies developed, stolen wealth often boosted the fortunes of hard pressed local economies. Port officials in Rhode Island, New York, Virginia Maryland and the Carolinas were prepared to offer safety and security to pirates in return for a share in the plunder. Even Governors, such as Benjamin Fletcher of New York, accepted "gifts" of money, goods and jewelry from a number of particularly ruthless pirates (Woodiwiss 2001: 29)...

This New World was occupied by millions of Indians. Already disease from De Soto's and Columbus' Expedition made its way via trade goods from Cuba as far North as the Great Lakes, before the first settlers arrived in Virginia. The death of 99% of Southern Indians left the surviving aboriginals with no oral history and no idea who had built those huge mounds and earthworks at Macon, Kahokia, Poverty Point and another 100 Indian cities. Studies have shown drastic population reduction throughout the East and South from 1540-1600. When the Mound Builders died out other tribes came in: The Cherokee reached North Georgia by 1650; Souixian groups like the Nanticoke and Saponi were as far east as Virginia and the Shawnee ranged from the great lakes to the Tennessee Valley.

In Florida and the Deep South were the Spanish, who brought with them Moors, Sephardic Jews and other North Africans. Spanish settlements and missions proceeded up the East Coast beyond South Carolina and all these peoples found their way into the local Indian gene pool. In 1619, the first boatload of Angolans arrived aboard the White Cloud and soon melted into the population of the new colonies. The New World had become a huge cauldron of émigrés: those with great hopes of new wealth and the profligate.

Many who made it to America had been on the run from the Spanish inquisition; these conversos, Moors and Sephardic Jews left Spain and radiated throughout Europe and the British Isles. There were Angolans from a civil war; Scots from a border conflict with England that had gone on for centuries and Irish from their war with England. Many of the horrors of war were exported to America; attitudes and forms of villainy poured off the boats.

The aristocracy and even the middle class in England called these people "lubbers," idlers, braggarts, trespassers on their land and common criminals. By lubber I mean as in "land lubber," not land lover as many think it. A lubber was an idle profligate trespassing and poaching and under the constant eye of those with land and wealth. Many lubbers did eventually find their way into the yeoman farmer or landed society, but most did not. These people became known as "crackers," especially some time around the end of the French and Indian war.

By the 1760s, "crackers" was in use by the English in the British North American colonies to refer to Scots-Irish settlers in the south. A letter to the Earl of Dartmouth reads:

…I should explain to your Lordship what is meant by Crackers; a name they have got from being great boasters; they are a lawless set of rascalls on the frontiers of Virginia, Maryland, the Carolinas, and Georgia, who often change their places of abode (McWhiney 1988: xiv.)…

A similar usage was that of Charles Darwin in **The Origin of Species**, to refer to "Virginia squatters" (illegal settlers) (p. 35).

Foxhunting with Lord Halifax (Henry Bryan Hall, from Life of George Washington, Irving: 1855-1859).

George Washington, himself, was aware of the problems of these "squatters" pouring into private lands even before the French and Indian war. He was visiting Lord Fairfax for a little fox hunting and the Lord noted:

...His Lordships possessions beyond the blue ridge had never been regularly settled nor surveyed. Lawless intruders - squatters as they were called - were planting themselves along the finest streams and richest valleys and virtually taking possession of the country. It was the anxious desire of Lord Fairfax to have these lands examined, surveyed and portioned out into lots, preparatory to ejecting these interlopers or bringing them to reasonable terms (Irving 1888:62-63)...

The most important factor involved in defining this new group of miscreants was its mobility. Having trespassed, or intruded on Indian land and upon being discovered, these profligates would move on.

According to Mitford Mathews, cracker was the first term to be widely and popularly applied to the poor whites in the western reaches of the British Colonies. Mathews writes: "the term in the sense of a poor white" was first used and defined in a 1766 administrative report to the Earl of Dartmouth. Gavin Cochrane, a colonial officer, wrote to inform the Earl about the behavior of certain British subjects in the Upper Ohio River Valley:

Reported complaints came from the Cherokees that white people came into their hunting grounds and destroyed their beavers, which they said was everything to them....I (sent) orders to have those beaverers made prisoners.... (I) thought it my duty to act in the public good; everything succeeded as I could have wished; the officers at Fort Prince George told the Indians the orders he had received and bid them seize the beaverers and bring them to him without hurting them. They brought three of the lawless people called crackers, who behaved with great insolence and told the officer that they neither valued him nor the Lieutenant Gov(ernor) (Mathews 1959:126).

The earliest explanation of the lifestyle of these "crackers" comes from a Frenchman, Le Clerke Milfort (Paris 1802), who wrote of his travels and experiences in the south after the revolution. In **Memoire ou coup d'oeil rapide sur mes differens voyages et mon sejour dans la Nation Creek,** he described a hard set of ne'er-do-wells who populated the countryside of most of the former colonies.

In 1784, at the time of the American peace, and American independence, there was in the United States a very large number of vagrant and dishonest people, inevitable result of a revolution which gives birth to them and with which they must disappear. Peace taking away from them the means of subsistence that they found in devastation and corrupt practices which are inseparable from war, the result was that the peaceful men and the landlords were easily endangered either in their persons or their property. In order to rid themselves of this scourge, they united and declared a war to the death on all these vagabonds, who could not give up the habit of pillaging. Seeing themselves eagerly pursued, they found themselves compelled to seek another refuge. They withdrew to Georgia, where they have remained in peace; but as they still remember their old habit of stealing, they often go into the hinterland

9

of the two Carolinas and of Virginia and take away from the unfortunate inhabitants all the horses that they can catch.

Chapter 35:
Note on the Americans called Crakeurs or Gaugeurs

I also said in the first part of my memoirs, that while visiting Tougoulou, Franklin, and other places situated in the hinterland of the United States, I had found some Anglo-Americans of a peculiar sort, called Crakeurs or Gaugeurs, who are nearly all one-eyed. I wanted to know the reason for this. The reader will perhaps not be displeased if I give an account at this time of what I learned about this on the spot.

The reader will remember that I said above that the inhabitants of North Carolina harvested a large quantity of potatoes, with which they made a kind of tafia which they call whiskey. These Crakeurs are very fond of this liquor; when they drink some of it, since they are by nature quarrelsome and mean, they quarrel among themselves, and agree to fight on the day they appoint. Their fights are very much like English pugilism or boxing, except that they are more murderous. When the Crakeurs have agreed on the day and the hour when they are supposed to fight, they gather as many spectators as they can; they form them in a circle and stand in the center, and at a signal given by the oldest among the spectators, the fight begins….

These men are very wicked and do not wish to submit to any government; for the most part they live, more often than not, only by hunting. They plant a little tobacco which they carry, during the winter, to seaboard towns, and which they barter for wisky, firearms, and gunpowder. Although I remained only a few days among them, I had the opportunity of being invited to a meal which amused me a great deal by its singularity, although the food was very bad. This is how it was:

One of these men, having recognized me as a stranger, invited me to have dinner at his house with several of his friends; his wife, who had heard that in well-bred company it was proper to serve tea, asked her husband to get some in exchange for tobacco; he brought her half a bushel of it. She put it all in a cooking-pot and added to it a large ham; she boiled the whole lot until the ham was cooked. The guests having arrived, she took the ham out on an earthenware dish, threw away the liquor, and placed the tea leaves on another dish, and served the whole on the table. I saw all the faces light up at the sight of an inviting dish about which they were building up high hopes, and every one was getting ready to have a real treat. I observed, without saying a word, not being in a hurry to be the first one to give an opinion on food that I knew was not fit to eat; and I watched each one chew with all his might the tea leaves which no longer had any agreeable taste, when suddenly the wife flew into a great rage against her husband, at whose head she threw her plate, reproaching him for having brought her inferior tea, and for having used the money, which good tea would have cost, to buy whiskey for himself. This comical scene made me laugh a great deal; but it was not without difficulty that I succeeded in making the woman listen to reason, and in making her understand that it was not the tea leaves which were used, but instead their infusion, mixed with a little sugar.

Since I had not eaten anything, and was very hungry, I decided to taste the ham which I found rather good, and to which the tea had given an excellent flavor. I ate a great deal of it, since it constituted the whole dinner.

These men go around almost naked. They are addicted to idleness and drunkenness to such an extent that it is the women who are obliged to do everything. They are somewhat better dressed than the men. In winter, they spin cotton and flax which they mix together; from this they make a cloth which serves for all their clothes, even for shirts. These women are as hard-working as the men are lazy.

The farther one goes into the hinterlands of the United States, which are nearly all inhabited by the same kind of men, the more dangerous and mean one finds them. They often murder travelers to rob them. Their closest neighbors are scarcely any safer; they go to the homes of those whom they believe to have some wealth; and when they have succeeded in getting into a house they kill all those they find there, lead away the cattle, and carry away all the goods which they sell afterwards in another state. These thieves wear their hair cut very close to their heads, and paint their bodies and faces with different colors in the manner of the savages; so that their appearance is truly frightful.

There is in each state of the United States a governor who, once in office, looks upon himself as an absolute sovereign. He uses all means which are in his power to secure the devotion of the persons under his administration; impunity is one of those which he uses with the greatest success. Thus it is most difficult to obtain restitution of the stolen goods from the thieves of whom I have just spoken, and who are placed under the protection of one of these governors. The request for the restitution of goods is often made without success. (183-191)…

Milfort describes these luckless, landless savages in great detail and provides them with the name which stuck.. Today crackers and their lifestyle are more associated with Georgia and Northern Florida, but they all came from somewhere else before Georgia and Florida were states. One can follow their progress, moving year after year from the tidewater colonies to all those new acres opened up by results of the French and Indian War and the subsequent American Revolution. One can say that crackers moving into the Ohio Valley not only precipitated the French War…but the American Revolution as well as it was the British view that the Ohio Valley belonged to the Indians, while most colonists disagreed with that portion of the Treaty of Paris. From 1763 on the Indians would always choose the British side over the colonists, with few exceptions.

Others described these same people as the frontier expanded. One was Isaac Weld (1800) who travelled through Virginia in the 1790s. He described the same villiany, gambling and fighting Milfort and others witnessed:

Perhaps in no place of the same size in the world is there more gambling going forward than in Richmond. I had scarcely alighted from my horse at the tavern when the landlord came to ask what game I was most partial to…It is chiefly, however, the lower class of people that partake of these amusements at the taverns; in private there is perhaps as little gambling in

Virginia as in any other part of America. The circumstance of having the taverns thus infested by such a set of people renders travelling extremely unpleasant. Many times I have been forced to proceed much farther in the day than I have wished, in order to avoid the scenes of rioting and quarreling that I have met with at the taverns, which is impossible to escape as long as you remain in the same house where they are carried on (142) ...

And:

Of all the uncouth human beings I met within America, these people from the western country were the most so; their curiosity was boundless. Frequently I have been stopped abruptly by one of them in a solitary part of the road, in such a manner, that, had it been another country, I should have imagined it was a highwayman that was going to demand my purse and without any further preface, asked where I came from? If I was acquainted with any news? Where bound to? And finally, my name?

Stop, mister! Why I guess now you be coming from the new state? No sir--Why then I guess you be coming from Kentuc? No sir -- Oh! Why then, pray now where might you be coming from? From the low country-- Why you must have heard all the news then; pray now, mister, what might the price of bacon be in those parts? Upon my word my friend I can't inform you-- Aye aye I see, mister, you be'n't one of us. Pray now, mister, what might your name be (172)?

Weld noted that such encounters were frequent and usually ended after five minutes and a drink at the nearest tavern, then down the road another questioner would appear.

Not all descriptions were as hilarious, adventurous and rowdy. Some were downright appalling, like that mentioned in Dunaway's **Slavery in the American South** (1996).

I cannot omit noticing the many distressed families I passed in the Wilderness (road) Nor can anything be more distressing to a man of feeling to see women and children in the month of December. Traveling a wilderness through ice and snow passing large rivers and creeks without shoe or stocking and barely as many rags as covers their nakedness without money or provision, except what the wilderness affords....to say they are poor is but faintly expressing their situation.....Ask these pilgrims what they expect when they get to Kentucky and the answer is land. Have you any? No, but I expect I can get it. Have you anything to pay for land? No. Did you ever see the country? No, but every body says its good land....and when arrived at this heaven in idea what do they find? A goodly land I will allow but to them forbidden land. Exhausted and worn down with distress and disappointment they are at last obliged to become hewers of wood and drawers of water (69).

Most historians seem to agree that the term cracker arises from a British term for a braggart or loudmouth. The quote from Shakespeare's **King John** indicates the age of the expression, but many other ideas have been put forward to nail down the origin of the term. Evan's **History of Georgia (1908)** includes a list of them:

…The driver of each wagon carried a whip, which he often popped and cracked as he drove along. With the handle in both hands, he would pop his large whip from side to side until it sounded like the rapid fire of a pistol. From this practice the name "Georgia cracker" is said to have originated, the cracker being a man from the country, who, in driving to market, cracked his whip as he went along (191).

From a stereoscope image

A cracker wagon is not like what most wagons were back then; being most often described as like the one I have always personally associated with these landless rogues: It has two rather than four wheels and more often than not pulled by a cow, bull or ox.

Evans also lists several other possible origins for the term "cracker":

1). Because they eat "cracked corn."

2). A group of Georgians in the revolution who were "crack shots" and thus feared by the British.

3). Bill Arp, the writer said they were boasters in the British sense, but also offered that "crack brained" and being "cracked" came from the same source (Evans, 1908: 191)

It is interesting to note that Nelson (2005) in his research on the subject, was able to follow the history of these crackers into the mill towns of the cotton era south, well into the 20th century. He describes the work of a journalist Clare de Graffenreid, who 100 years after Le Clerke, was still describing the cracker community as slothful men with working women:

Edward Windsor Kemble's "Around the Grocery", from deGraffenreid (1891).

Grouped about in a single store of the village, lounging, whittling, and sunning their big lazy frames, sit a score of stalwart masculine figures, while their offspring and womenkind toil in the dusty mill. In these accounts, the work of the women serves only to emphasize what observers saw as the despicable laziness of cracker men. Such condemnations of male idleness were most often misunderstandings of poor white labor practices. Cracker men, in this context, engaged in hunting as a primary labor activity, which was more sporadic work than farming; it was more flexible and created moments of leisure throughout the day, giving the impression of consistent unemployment (121)...

WHY WERE THERE SO MANY POOR PEOPLE IN AMERICA?

Land in America was not divided equally any more than it was given by the Indians. Tax records show that land in the colonies was concentrated in few hands; that there was a yeoman tenant element, but most Americans were without land. After the revolution, land in American began being concentrated into fewer and fewer hands. One of the mere hand full of studies to document this was that by Wilma Dunaway, who found that in many Appalachian states over half the population had no land:

LAND OWNERSHIP IN SOUTHERN APPALACHIA 1790-1810

Appalachian counties of	% of all households	
	Landless	landowning
Kentucky	56.9	43.1
Maryland	42.3	57.7
North Carolina	35.8	64.2
South Carolina	86.0	14.0
Tennessee	55.3	44.7
Virginia	62.9	37.1
West Virginia	62.7	37.3
Region	57.2	42.8

Dunaway 1996: derived from analysis of county tax lists.

Dunaway noted (1996: 56,57,58) that Virginia in 1792 had sold 2,590,059 acres to just 14 speculators and in 1793 had sold its lands so cheaply that most ended up in brokerage houses in Boston and New York. In 1794, the state sold 8 million Appalachian acres which ended up being bought mainly by speculators. In 1783 North Carolina had sold some 4 million acres causing a stampede of speculation.

Absenteeism was another great problem associated with the concentration of wealth in so few hands. Dunaway noted much of the acreage ended up in the hands of Europeans and others who sought to leave the land idle for the time being.

In Tennessee, territorial Governor Blount set out to produce a personal windfall from land sales. His brother ended up with a virtual monopoly of Tennessee and North Carolina land warrants and sold 184,460 acres in the Northeast and Europe. By 1795, the Blounts ended up with large portions of eastern Tennessee (Dunaway 1996: 59)

ABSENTEE ENGROSSMENT OF SOUTHERN APPALACHIAN LANDS 1790-1810

Acres owned

Appalachia Counties of	residents		absentees	
	No. acres	%	No. acres	%
Kentucky	56,855.5	43.8	72,961	56.2
Maryland	169,795.9	67.1	83,410	32.9
North Carolina	237,914.5	57.1	178,676	42.9
South Carolina	48,824.5	48	52,852	52
Tennessee	120,368.3	31.1	266,201	68.9
Virginia	328,994.5	10.7	2,757,465.3	89.3
West Virginia	324,388.5	6.7	4,525,153	93.3
Region	12,526,649.8	24.1	39,451,150.2	75.9

Dunaway 1996: derived from county tax lists.

4 PHASES OF SETTLEMENT IN APPALACHIA

Dunaway notes that settlement of Appalachia proceeded in four steps after the end of the French and Indian War. Once the Ohio River was free for navigation settlers began flat boating downstream to southwestern destinations along the Ohio and Mississippi Rivers. Step off points led into Tennessee, Kentucky, Mississippi and Georgia.

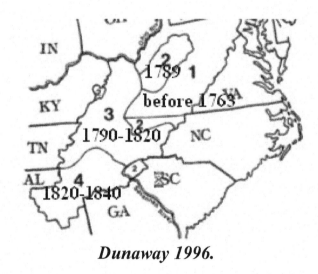

Dunaway 1996.

GEORGIA: WHERE THE CRACKERS ENDED UP

It's obvious all the crackers we have mentioned did not end up in one state, however the moniker "Georgia Cracker" has stuck. It was probably more a situation wherein by the time most State Governments realized there was an underclass of poor whites preying on the settlers, Indians and everyone else in between, they had effectively arrived in the newest state carved out of Indian land: Georgia.

Georgia developed late in terms of the other former colonies, it was the 13th. It was first settled in 1733 by British reformer James Oglethorpe. With a little more than a hundred debtor prison émigrés, the colony was formed as a buffer between the Spanish and Charleston. The fierce Westo had been defeated and chief Tomachichi welcomed the new settlers to the Yamacra Bluffs. That little piece of land east of the Savannah River was all there was of Georgia in the United States through the Revolutionary War.

Tomochichi

James Oglethorpe

Georgia was the only state of all the former colonies settled by land lotteries. It was the only state making land available fairly and disallowing squatters from gaining lots. Though much of the newly acquired lands came into speculation and absenteeism as in the other states, it gave many of the crackers a chance at some land and many took advantage of it. The crackers were still there: they had been there living on Indian land well in advance of the state government, causing problems as these lands were ceded from the Indians to the state.

Anthony Stokes, Chief Justice of the Colony of Georgia, wrote about the influx of crackers into colonial Georgia:

The southern colonies were overrun by a swarm of men from the western parts of Virginia and North Carolina, distinguished by the name of Crackers. Many of these people are descended from convicts that were transported from Great Britain to Virginia at different times, and inherit such profligacy from their ancestors, that they are the most abandoned set of men on earth, few of them having the least sense of religion. When these people are routed from other provinces, they fly to Georgia, where the winters are mild and the man who has a rifle, ammunition and a blanket can subsist in that vagrant way which the Indians pursue; for the quantity of deer, wild turkies and other game their affords subsistence and the country being mostly covered with woods, they have it always in their power to construct temporary huts and procure fuel....during the King's Government these crackers were very troublesome in the settlements, by driving off gangs of horses and cattle to Virginia and committing other enormities: they also occasioned frequent disputes with the Indians, whom they robbed and sometimes murdered: the Indians in return, according to their custom, murdered the first white man they met, by way of retaliation (1783: 165).

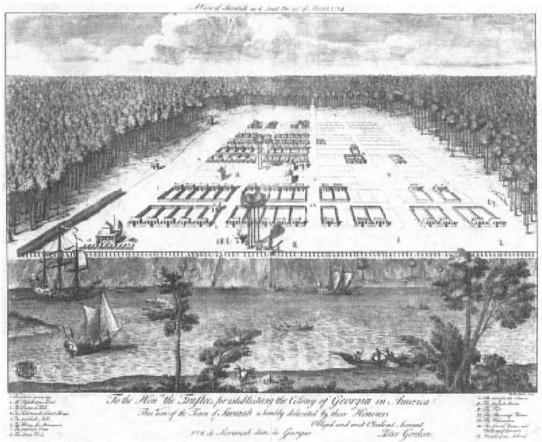

Artist's Rendering of Early Savannah.

Another to voice his concern was Lt. Governor of Georgia, James Habersham, in a letter to James Wright of London dated August 20, 1772:

Savannah:
I enclose a copy of a proclamation I have issued and that you may know my reason for so doing, I will transcribe what I have written on that subject to Lord Hillsborough as follows-- I have lately received advice from Mr. Bernard at Augusta, that several idle people from the Northward, some of whom he are told are great villains, horse thieves and &c and were among the North Carolina Regulators, have settled and built huts on the land proposed to be ceded by the Indians to His Majesty and that more might be expected to join them and if not drove off and they should be suffered to increase, it might hereafter be attended with difficulty to do it, I have therefore by the advice of the Council issued a proclamation commanding these stragglers immediately to remove from those lands (Georgia Historical Society Collections Vol.6 203-204)

Sullivan (2003) also describes the early crackers in Georgia: the familiar lifestyle and the troubles they bring. He emphasizes the nature of crackers: to find uninhabited areas to live in where laws and men will not bother them:

Non slave holding families, which comprised a sizable majority, were typically the small landholding farmers of the poorer class. These "crackers" found in every section of the state, lived generally in the Pine Barrens and swampy regions of southeast Georgia, in the hill and mountain areas of the piedmont and in the sections where the soil was not conducive to productive agriculture. They made their living through subsistence agriculture, lumbering and turpentining. Frances Ann Kimble observed the following in 1839:

...the scattered white population (of coastal Georgia), too poor to possess land or slaves, and having no means of living in the towns, squat on other men's land until ejected. They are hardly protected from the weather by the rude shelters they frame themselves in the midst of these dreary woods. Their clothes hang about them in filthy tatters and the combined squalor and fierceness of their appearance is really frightful (2003:70-71).

Travelers are a wonderful source of information about the early days of the United States. Most are from a better class and perhaps are used to better accommodations as they travel and so they report some overnight destinations in appalling tones. All the trails in this new country were filled with "stands" every few miles…people's houses along the main road known for some level of hospitality allowing one to travel and not be far from a place to stay. How travelers depict those living out in these backwoods is often hilarious by our standards and they are indeed talking about crackers.

One such traveler was Basil Hall who in 1829 described his travels through Georgia:

...the house was not the most agreeable in the world. Our two rooms, put together, would not have made up in size one butler's pantry; there was but one washbasin, as they called it, in the house; only one towel, and everything looked and felt damp and dirty. In the center of the building was a large, public sort of room crowded with other travelers, who talked and moved about the live long night, so that we got little or no sleep and were right glad to be up by peep of day (262).

In 1817, Hugh Montgomery, later an Indian agent for the State of Georgia, was paid 16 dollars for a journey down the Chattahoochee River to what is now Hall, Gwinnett, and Fulton counties. This was freshly ceded Indian land full of white intruders and Montgomery's job was to notify them they had to report to authorities. He mentions seeing persons listed in a deposition concerning intruding, whom he reported to governor William Rabun, saying he had advised them to return to Georgia to face inquiries. He begins:

3rd July 1817
Sir

I have just Returned from the Frontiers & have Down to give you the names of the white persons (heads of Familys) who I find living on the Indian lands adjasent to this County Let it be Remembered that I did not vissit the South west Side of the County, I had no expectation before I set out that any person had Settled over the appalatchee, when I got to the Hog mountain I learnt that the persons named in the Deposition sent to you were all in that Quarter & that they had been all advised to Return before the Depositions were forwarded to you & had Refused. I had a Right to believe that the names of all were sent you, I was also informed that most of them had either moved in or were about to Remove with the exception of a John Camp& a few others.

He then includes a long list of names of white intruders living on Indian lands from Suwanee Old Town, down past Stone Mountain to the Standing Peachtree and perhaps Buzzard's Roost on the river. He has informed some of them that they are subject to inquiries in the State of Georgia and some have indicated they will take care of the problem. Most indicated they will ignore the government.

I then turned up the North west side of the County & the following are the persons I find on the Indian Lands in that Quarter together with the Relative Situations in which they live viz between the Stone Mountain& Chatahoochee River, are Silas McGrady, John Steen, & James Steen Senr.& Clanton Steenin the Settlement Called Raferses Settlement& on both sides of Chatahoochee are James Steen Junr. John Rogers, John Difoor, a man by the name of Bill, two men by the name of Bagwell, John Woodall William Woodall Thomas Woodall, & another Woodall given name not known, & Tabitha Harper a widow Parker Collens, Jonathan Gray, & William Harden above the mouth of Suwanee are William Garner Warren Young John Tidwell, & Austin Dobbs, at & near the mouth of Big Creek are John Mires Thomas Dasset, John Dasset, Obediah Light, James Smith & Robert Smith Junr., at & near the mouth of the Flowery Branch are Bud Mullins, Robert Smith Senr, &

Thomson McGuire at & near the Ferry are John Lessly, Danl May, Caleb Mosely, Benjn Murry, John Gathard, John Wilson & Hugh Wilson, on Flat creek are Simon Strickland, Sion Strickland Irvin Strickland, Lazeras Strickland, Lewis Crow, Sion Crow, & Richard Litteral, and near the Chestetee are Freeman Averbee Danl. Short, Noah Langly, John Martin, & Jese Martin & at and above the Shallowford are William Staker, William Baity, a man by the name Mason, an other by the name of Hainsan other by the name of Hawkins, & John Wagoner, James Abercrombi a Senr James Abercrombi a Junr Benjm Morris, Henry Morris, John Diffy, Henry Barton, Holly Barton, Widow & George Davis. I did not see all of them, but the greater part of those that I did, promised to Come in, Some few will, Say about one in ten, the ballance will not.

Now Montgomery changes the tone of his letter, he begins commenting on the whole idea of white intruders and Indians living together and the morality thereof:

…there are a great many Shifts which those people make to get settling on those Lands Some Rent of Indians or Mixed Bloods others Settle Down on Such place as pleases them & get Some stroling Vagabond Indian to live or Stay with them, they Call themselves his Croppers, he is to hunt & they Cultivate the Ground, they find him a Gun & amunition they have the meat & he the Skins, but it often so turns out that he has two Haggskins for one Dearskin, & this accounts for the Frontier people loosing so many of their Haggs as they do -- others (if possible) More Lax in their Morrels & Still Less Delicate in their taste will Kiss a Squaw for the privallage of their Land & Range, he then becomes a Landlord he has his Croppers, Tenants, & Hirelings &c. thus a whole Settlement Claim under him, and what seems more abominable then all is that others give their Daughters to the Indian fellows for the privallage of Living in their Country themselves, of this Last & and worst Class are John Tidwell & Noah Langly the Former has given four of his Daughters to Indian fellows for Wives & the Latter two thus a Motly Race are propigating fast verry fast on the Chatahoochee & its waters --

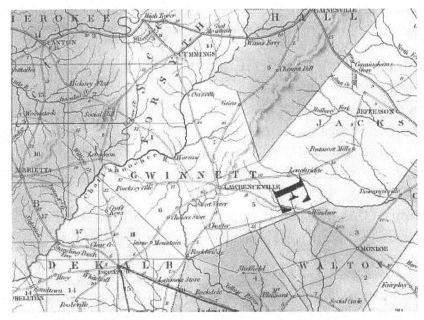

Gwinnett County, Georgia 1839.

I Should like to know how far the Individual Indians have a Right to Rent or Lease Lands, my own impressions are that Indians have not a principle tittle to any Lands, that theirs is a mere occupant claim, that they are tenants at the will of the Government, the Treaty Reserves the Lands to them for their Hunting grounds, it prohibits all Citizens of the U. S, or other persons from Settling on them with out permits from the Agent of Indian affairs, those people have no permits they are not Indians altho Some of them try to look & act like them, & it seems that to get foothold in the Nation by any of their ways which I have Described has all the effect of taking the Indian Black Drink, it makes them inimical to every person who Does not ware a *Long hunting Shirt & mockisins or a Match Coat & Smell like Tainted Dearskins & I think I am warranted in saying that If the Comrs. fail of success in the present Treaty it will be in not intirely to the Clamours of those fellows Seconded by a few of the Mixed Bloods, the spurious product of those Disgracefull & unnatural Matches.*

I am Sir very Respectfully your Obt Humbl Servnt H Montgomery (TCC 453)

The Brutal Side of Crackerdom: Gougers

Foremost among the cracker culture, so to speak, was their unusually brutal version of the "honor code" Dueling seldom occurred with pistols and knives, which is good, but ended up in "gouging' matches. This tidbit from the Gazette of Georgia reminds us of how widespread and common this gruesome practice was in those days:

Jacksonborough has a new C H (court house). It is presumed that this place was named after General James rather than Andrew Jackson: for it must have been in existence many years before Gen. Andrew became distinguished for his prowess in war. This place is 53 miles from Augusta; 72 Savannah. This used to be a "torn down" place, to use our Georgia phrase. It was reported in the mornings after drunken frolics and fights you could see the children picking up eye-balls in tea-saucers! i.e. there was so much gouging going on(Sherwood:1837:180)!

The origins of gouging are not completely known. There is a scene in Shakespeares **King Lear** that resembles a gouging match. It is certain that the British soldiers in the revolution accused American soldiers of gouging out captives eyes, though this was never proven (see for example **History of the American Revolution**: London, 1788: 480). Some even compared eye gouging to taking scalps as a truly American phenomenon.

The best description of this fight first appeared in Milfort's treatise on "crackeurs and "gougers" (Le Clerke, Milfort: 1802):

It is interesting to note that these men are very careful, from their infancy on, never to cut their fingernails which they simply let grow. In order to make them very tough, they smear them with tallow and then hold them in front of the fire; the tallow, as it melts, penetrates the pores of the nail and makes it extremely hard when it has dried. I have seen some which were

22

as hard and as dangerous as the claws of a lion. Not satisfied with this weapon, they even arm their heels with spurs, which they never take off, not even to go to bed, and whose rosette is a very sharp pointed spike. It is with such weapons that they present themselves for the fight; it is easy to imagine how deadly they are.

When the elder among them has given the signal for the fight, by saying: Any thing is allowed, then the two antagonists attack each other with their teeth, spurs and fingernails, which they use very skillfully. When one of the two succumbs, the other makes the most of his advantage, and inhumanly tears him to pieces, and easily succeeds in tearing out one of his eyes. Until then the onlookers watch the fight with the greatest calmness; it is only at this time that they put an end to the fight; and if they do not do it quickly, it happens sometimes that both eyes are torn out. Then the victor climbs up on the stump of a tree, a great number of which are cut approximately three feet above ground; and there, all covered with blood, he crows over his victory; he insults the assembly, challenges all the spectators one after the other, by telling them that there is not among them a man his equal. Anger excites his imagination to such an extent, that when no one presents himself to avenge his insults, he defies the Creator to descend from the heavens to try his strength with him. When he has finished all his provocations, he comes down from the tree stump and every one applauds and proclaims him the victor. Since these fights occur often, it follows that you meet in this nation few men who do not have one eye put out in this manner (Milfort 1802: 183-191).

The sportsmen of the day widely reported this savagery along with pugilism and other sporting endeavors of that time (Apperly 1905: 238) The Sporting appeal was also mentioned recently by Vickers (2002).

Gouging was a sport in itself, usually used to settle gambling disputes over cock fighting or horse racing (although political arguments were sometimes the impetus for engaging in brutal eye gouging, jaw breaking and nose biting match). Not limited to the lower classes, gouging was an unfortunate English custom finely honed by Americans (Holliman, 138). The powerful and educated were just as prone to engage in gouging as the poor and illiterate. Combatants throughout the nation were held in high esteem or their ability to gouge out eyes and bite to the bone….Gouging matches were held much in the same way as wrestling matches (143)…

Other such ghastly scenes are mentioned in: Robert Bollings poem from the 1760s *Neanthe;* Charles Mason's *Burlesque Sermon;* Anita Vickers: 2002 *The New Nation*:143; Charles J. Apperly : 1905: *The life of a Sportsman* : 238; John B. McMaster: 1885: *History of the People of the United States* : 5,5,578; Isaac Weld: 1800: *Travels throught the States of North America..etc* : 143;

Eventually all states would ban gouging as a form of fighting, employing jail terms and even the death penalty to discourage its use. It had a long run in the colonies and in early America's frontier era and had played out about the time of the Civil War:

In 1746, four deaths prompted the Governor of North Carolina to ask for legislation against "the barbarous and inhuman manner of boxing which so much prevails among the lower sort of people." The colonial assembly responded by making it a felony "to cut out the tongue or pull out the eyes of the King's liege people." Five years later the Assembly added slitting, biting and cutting off noses to the list of offenses. Virginia passed similar legislation in 1748 and revised these statutes in 1772 explicitly to discourage men from " gouging, plucking or putting out an eye, biting or kicking or stomping upon" quiet peaceable citizens. By 1786, South Carolina had made premeditated mayhem a capital offense, defining the crime as severing another's bodily parts (Smith: 2001:98).

Gouging seemed to take notice around the end of the French and Indian War, the losers implying that the scalping by Indians was answered by the colonists gouging their victim's eyes out. In the aftermath of the American Revolution, the defeated British cried foul, accusing the Americans of gouging British soldiers' eyes out. One older dictionary mentions this:

Gouge. *To squeeze out an opponent's eye with one's thumb and finger. This brutal practice appears to have been unknown in New England, but to have been practiced considerably by the rougher sort of frontiersmen and in early days along the Mississippi.*

1775 This event may give rise to some malevolent pen to write that many of the killed and wounded at Lexington were not only scalped, but had their eyes forced out of the sockets by the fanatics of New England: not one was so treated, either there or at Concord. -- W. Gordon. **History of the American Revolution** *(1788: I 480).*

1776 A soldier who had been slightly wounded, appeared with his eyes torn out of their sockets, by the barbarous habit of googing, a word and practice peculiar to the Americans. -- **The Rights of Great Britain Asserted,** *(67 of the Philadelphia reprint).*

Gouging was so rife among the new Americans even top officials had become involved. Georgia's Governor from 1798 - 1801, James Jackson, suffered an attempt to gouge his eyes out by Robert Watkins, a backer of the Yazoo Land laws (Cook 2005: 73). It was not unusual to be arrested for gouging in some of the more civilized places of this new country. The punishment on first offense might be flogging while a second offense might result in a death penalty (McMaster 1885: 5) Though the practice was widespread from Maryland through Kentucky and the Deep South, it seems to fill the literature of crackers and of Georgia.

**Washington Surveying
The Great Dismal Swamp**

From Irving: 1855-59, *The Life of Washington.*

1905 Apperley, Charles James, **The Life of a Sportsman,** Kessinger Publishing: Whitefish, Montana.

2002 Baptist, Edward E., **Creating an Old South: Middle Florida's Plantation Frontier Before the Civil War,** Univ. of N. Carolina Press: Greensboro.

1920 **British prisoners sent to America,** The Encyclopedia Americana: A Library of Universal Knowledge, The Encyclopedia Americana Corporation: N.Y.

1909 Darwin, Charles, **The origin of species**, P.F. Collier and Sons Co.: N.Y.

February 1891 de Graffenreid, Mary Clare, **The Georgia Cracker in the Cotton Mills,** *Century Magazine* vol. 41 no. 4.

2005 Dick. Thomas. **The Philosophy of Religion or an Illustration of the Moral Laws of the Universe,** Kessinger publishing: Whitefish, Montana.

1990 Dixon, by Edward H., Mark A. Galan, **The Immigration and Naturalization Service,** Chelsea house publishers: ny

2003 Dunaway, Wilma A., **Slavery in the American Mountain South,** McMillan: N.Y.

2003 Dunaway. Wilma A., **The African-American Family in Slavery and Emancipation,** Cambridge Univ. Press: N.Y.

2008 Dunaway, Wilma A., **Women, Work and Family in the Antebellum Mountain South,** university of NC press

1996 Dunaway, Wilma A., **The First American Frontier: Transition to Capitalism in Southern Apalachia, 1700-1860,** Univ. of N. Carolina Press: Chapel Hill.

1920 The Encyclopedia Americana: A Library of Universal Knowledge, The Encyclopedia Americana Corporation: N.Y.

1908 Evans, Lawton Bryan, **A History of Georgia for Use in Schools,** American Book Co.: N.Y.

1788, Gordon, William, **The History of the Rise, Progress, and Establishment of the Independence of the United States of America : Including an Account of the late War, and of the Thirteen Colonies from their Origin to that Period,** Charles Dilly: London.

1829 Hall, Basil, **Travels in North America in the Years 1827 and 1828,** Cadell and Co.: Edinborough.

2003 Holliman, Jennie, **American Sports, 1785-1835**, Martino publishing: Mansfield Center: Conn.

1887 Irving, Washington, **Washington and His Country: Being Irving's Life of Washington,** Ginn and Co.: Boston.

1866 Lester Charles Edwards**, *The Glory and Shame of England,*** Bartram and Lester publishers: N.Y.

1776 Macpherson, James, **The Rights of Great Britain Asserted Against the Claims of America: Being an answer to the Declaration of the general**

Congress Volume 2, Issue 3 of American Tracts United States, Continental Congress, pre 1801 imprint collection: Library of Congress.

1959 Mathews, Mitford McLeod, **American words: Illustrated by Lorence Bjorklund,** World Publishing Co. : Cleveland

1885 McMaster, John Bach, **A History of the People of the United States: From the Revolution to the Civil War,** D. Appleton: N.Y.

1988 McWhiney, Grady, **Cracker Culture: Celtic ways in the Old South**, Univ. of Alabama Press: Tuscaloosa.

1802 Milfort, Le Clerke, **In Memoire ou coup d'oeil rapide sur mes differens voyages et mon sejour dans la Nation Creek,** Paris.

2005 Nelson, Megan Kate. **Trembling Earth: A Cultural History Of The Okefenokee Swamp,** Univ of Ga. Press: Athens.

1905 **Official Disesteem of the Backwoods Population of Ga. 1772,** *Georgia Historical Society Collections* vol. 6 pages 203-204.

1909 Phillips, Ulrich Bonnell, **Plantation and Frontier Documents: 1649-1863: Illustrative of Industrial History in the Colonial and Antebellum South**, Arthur H.Clark: Cleveland.

1916 Shakespeare, William, Norman Hudson, Ebenezer Charlton Black **King John**, Ginnn and Co. Boston, N.Y.

1837 Sherwood, Adiel, **A Gazetteer of the State of Georgia: Embracing a Particular Description of the Counties, Towns, Villages, Rivers, and & and Whatsoever Is Usual In Geographies and Minute Statistical Works; Together With A New Map of the State,** Printed by P. Force: Washington City, Ga.

2001 Smith, Mark Michael, **The Old South**, Wiley-Blackwell publishers: Malden, Mass.

1956 Stampp, Kenneth Milton, **The Peculiar Institution: Slavery in the Ante-Bellum South,** Alfred E. Knopf: N.Y.

1783 Stokes, Anthony, **A View of the Constitution of the British Colonies in North-America and the West Indies at the Time the Civil War Broke Out on the Continent of America,** B. White: London.

2003 Sullivan, Buddy, **Georgia: A State History,** Georgia Historical Society Arcadia Publishing: Mount Pleasant: S.Carolina.

1912 Thornton, Richard Hopwood, **An American Glossary,** J.B. Lippincot: Philadelphia.

2002 Vickers, Anita, **The New Nation,** Greenwood Publishing : Westport, Conn.

1800 Weld, Isaac, Travels through the states of North America, and the provinces of Upper and **Lower Canada During the Years 1795, 1796 ,1797,** John Stockdale: London.

2001 Woodiwiss, Michael, **Organized Crime and American Power: A History,** Univ of Toronto press: Toronto, Ontario.

2007 Wray, Matt, **Not Quite White: White Trash and the Boundaries of Whiteness,** Duke Univ Press: Chapel Hill.

Typical Cracker Cabin from an old Illustration.

THE INDIANS AND LAND CESSIONS

One thing is for certain in our long twisted history: all of the land here was owned at one time by several tribes of Indians, who lost these lands by manipulation and intimidation. The uneasy peace between the new immigrants and the aboriginals seemed to follow a cycle: discovery, intrusion, warfare and finally cession. Once an area was liberated from the grasp of British, French or Spanish control, as the Ohio Valley after the French and Indian war, intruders would pour in. The Indians would seek redress, either in removal of the intruders or in cash for the cession of the property involved. 26 dollars worth of trinkets for the Island of Manhattan would be repeated numerous times until the last Indian left the east for Oklahoma Indian Territory.

It effectively took about 200 years for Americans to become the population size capable of ousting all the tribes from the Eastern Seaboard and the South. Before this advantage was achieved, there were many depredations on settlers all along the frontiers of America. In the thick of all this strife were the crackers, some of the first to begin trade with the Indian nations. As intruders became traders, they would marry into the tribe and have some reasonable security and stature in the community. Many had both Indian families and White families at the same time. They became known as "factors" and ran "factories," essentially, trading posts where Indians could find guns, ammunition and other western goods in exchange for deer or beaver pelts.

A good example was Dr. Henry Woodward, who in 1685, went on an expedition from Charleston, into the interior of what would become the State of Georgia. He set up a factory at Coweta Falls, just across the Chattahoochee in Alabama, for the specific purpose of drawing the Creek Indians away from the influence of the Spanish in Florida. This was long before General Oglethorpe settled at Yamacraw Bluffs on the Savannah River after the defeat of the Yamassee:

Woodward opened the Creek trade in 1685. He and six other Englishmen entered the Creek towns and, by selling better quality goods more cheaply than the Spaniards, they soon convinced the Creeks to turn their trade to the English (Olexer 2005:108).

The Spanish retaliated by attempting to capture these colonists brave enough to challenge Spanish hegemony over the Creek Indians: Indian Towns were burned and captured goods seized. The Creek decided to move to the Ocmulgee River, where they could be closer to the English traders. Here they could purchase guns from the English, because the Spanish would not sell them to the Creek.

29

Though Woodward was once arrested in South Carolina for trading with Indians by Lord Cardross, he is considered a man of legend there still...he is even said to be the originator of rice cultivation on the East Coast.

The next year the South Carolinians were in Alabama, stirring up the Creeks against the Choctaws and raiding the Spanish Appalachee Indian missions at the confluence of the Flint and Chattahoochee Rivers. The increased pressure on the Spanish caused them to fall back into defense mode, abandoning Georgia completely.

Soon the French were arming the Choctaw and traders were arming the Chickasaw, who were slave raiding the Illinois country. Many of those slaves were sold in the West Indies and the northern colonies. Indian traders began to arrive at all the outposts on the frontier, ready to do a booming business with trade goods or deer skins. Hatley (1993: 42), noted:

...In Georgia alone, by 1740 the traders, packhorsemen, servants townsmen and others depending on that business arriving in the Spring to do business at newly established Augusta, were moderately computed about 600 white men who live by their trade...

It became apparent to Indians very early on that there were different types of people coming into their lands. The French, the British and the Spanish would fight each other as often as the Indians in America. The Indians learned quickly to use these colonial powers against themselves for profit. Some, like Alexander Mcgillavry, would be allied to all three powers and hold rank with each. Son of a scotch trader married into the Creek nation, he would stymie the colonists and the Americans alike for many years, trading with British and up holding Spanish sway over Florida.

But things were moving apace along with a long term trend that had begun in the 1500s. The death of up to 99% of Southeast Indians at the hands of small pox brought by trade goods and the De Soto expedition, had left a great vacuum in the Southeast. Into it poured the Shawnee and Cherokee, from the North and many Souixian groups from the West, like the Saponi and Nansicott. When the settlers began to move West they met fierce tribes like the Tuscarora, Catawba, Yuchi, Westo and the Yamassee.

Small pox outbreaks in the 1690s once again decimated many of the tribes in the East. Yellow fever was also rampant, but the Indians did have something working for them: the rate at which they were intermarrying with whites was diluting their gene pool with new blood capable of withstanding some of the worst diseases. Not only were white traders moving into Indian country, but they were marrying Indian women. In turn their sons and daughters were marrying both white and Indian men and women. A lot can be said about the idea the Indian nation was not pure blood, but this may have saved them from extinction.

Most Indians we remember from history did not have Indian names, they had those of their white kinsmen. In fact some chiefs, like John Ross, were only 1/8 Cherokee, John Rogers was all white. William Proctor on the Cherokee Council was all white. Archulla Smith, the first Cherokee to be executed at Fort Smith Arkansas, was known by the Georgia Governor as Asabel Smith of Lawrenceville, Georgia. There was an undercurrent of trouble waiting to rear its ugly head over the issue of mixed bloods in the Cherokee nation. It would erupt to some extent with the Ross and treaty parties and even later in Oklahoma during the Crazy Snake Revolt.

One thing we have learned from the "cracker" experience is how quickly they realized that they could hide in Indian lands, trade with Indians, marry into the tribes and receive some measure of economic gain from their Indian relationship. Many white intruders became traders. Many had both white and Indian families. Most rose to power within the tribes, espousing the Indian position in later negotiations on removal. Here is a list of the most well known traders in the Indian nations of the East:

James Adair	George Galphin	Payne
Thomas Atkin	Nathaniel Gist (f/o Sequoyah)	Hardy Perry
Timothy Barnard	George Guess, Guest, Gass	Benjamin Perryman
Bean and McBean	Ludovick Grant	Rae
William Blevins	Grierson	Rogers
James Beamer	Greenwood Leflore (Lefleur)	Daniel Ross
Thomas Brown	John Gunter	Robert San(d)ford
Bunch, Bench or Benge	John Jones	Sizemore
Robert Bunning, Bunyan	James Leslie (Leslie & Panton)	Dick Smith
Benjamin Burges	Alexander Long	Robert Steel/Steill
John Caldwell	John Looney	John Stuart
Daniel Clark	George Lowrey	William Holland (Col.
Candy, Cantey, Gundy,	Martin	Will) Thomas
Canada:	John McDonald	George Jacob Troxell

31

Robert Gandey or Gowdy
William Colbert
William and Joseph Cooper
Joseph Cornell
Cornelius Dougherty
John Elliott/Ehlert
Samuel Elsmear
John Forbes
James Francis

James McQueen
John McKee
Alexander McIntosh
Lachlan McGillivray
Abraham Mordecai
William Dixon Moniac (orig. Jacob Monaque)
Thomas Nairne
Richard Pearis/Parris

Joseph Vann
Venn or Benn
Waitie/Waties
John Watts
William Weatherford
Thomas Welch
Dr. Henry Woodward
Eleazar Wiggans

This next list includes traders with white and Cherokee families and their position, economically.

Hightower

Adair, Tom Ben	Well to do
Blackburn, Lewis	Wealthy
Cline, Thomas A	Enrolled for Arkansas
Davis, Daniel	Well to do
Huffaker, Michael	Modest
Humphries, ____	Modest
Hutson, Alfred	Well to do
Jones, Frances	Modest
Landrum, James	Well to do
Phillips, Joseph	Well to do
Reid, William	Well to do
Trott, James J.	Methodist Circuit rider
Whitmore, Stephen	Well to do
Willis, William	Modest
Wist, (West?), Jacob	Well to do
Wright, John	Wealthy

Coosawattee

Bell, John	Well to do
Monroe,____	Modest
Sutton, ____	Modest

Shumate

Bunn, Jesse	Modest
Conner, ____	Modest
Denton, ____	Modest

Oothcalogee

Copeland, ____	Modest
Langley, Ozell	Modest

Crutchfield, Joseph	Well to do
Horn, Jere	Modest
Nicholson, ____	Well to do

Taloney

Chambers, Masfield	Modest
Chisholm, James	Well to do
Lane, Daniel	Modest

Chattahoochee

Colemen, William	Modest
Collins, Parker	Well to do
Freeman, George	Modest
Langley, John	Well to do
Mosley, John	Well to do
Rogers, John	Well to do

Chattahoochee

Vickery, Harry	Wealthy
Wofford, Nathaniel	Enrolled for Arkansas

Chestatee

Daniel, Reuben	Well to do
Hubberd, Uriah	Modest
Ralston, ____	Modest

Stover,____   Modest
Terrell, John
          Well to do

Lookout Mountain
Norris, Henry   Well to do
Scales, Reverend   Well to do

Valley Towns
England, ____   Well to do
William, John   Well to do

Wheeler, John F. Cherokee
Phoenic, Printer

Big Springs
Williams, William   Well to do
New Echota
Gunn, Thomas   Not Known
Rogers, John   Modest

Long Swamp
Harnage, Ambrose Wealthy
Thomason, Franklin
          Well to do
Thomason, James A.
          Well to do

Pine Log

Source: letter, 1806, from John Lowery to Indian agent Meigs.

Pathkiller (1745-1827) and The Ridge (1771-1839) were full bloods; Hicks (1767-1827) was the son of a white father and a Cherokee mother; Ross (1790-1866) was seven-eighths white; John Rogers was a white married to a Cherokee. However…the staunchest support for the new nationalism came from the Valley Towns where there had been comparatively little intermarriage with whites. Nor was there any such thing as a Christian or pagan party; missionary activity had barely started in the nation. The following details indicate the continuity of the new leadership that arose in 1806: Pathlkiller was principal chief from 1811-1827; Hicks was second principal chief from 1819-1827 and succeeded Pathkiller for a short time in 1827; Ross was principal chief from 1828-1866; The Ridge was probably the second most important leader from 1827-1839 (McLaughlin 1984: 88).

The **Creek Indian nation** from the beginning began to show the signs of a large gene pool. From the time of the first Spanish arrival and their relationship with the Appalachee ("ally"), the Creek related tribes began to witness intermarriage. The Moors and other conversos brought much middle-eastern flair to the new continent. Not only did the creek wear the turbans and dress associated with desert lands, but many new African words entered the dialect. Words like cudjoe, which means Monday in Angolan was a surname, while the Kraal, became the crawl, and corall not only in Spanish Florida, but as far north as South Carolina, where the first cowboy crackers developed in the South.

Slaves began running away to the Creek Nation at a very early date and there was considerable black blood at all levels of Creek society. The Spanish, Black and other Middle-eastern influences were met by white intruders from Scotland, mainly, producing a people who favored the Spanish and British at the expense of the Americans.

It became apparent to Indians very early on that there were different types of people coming into their lands. The French, the British and the Spanish would fight each other as often as the Indians in America. The Indians learned quickly to use these colonial powers against themselves for profit. Some, like Creek chief Alexander Mcgillavry, would be allied to all three powers and hold rank with each. Son of a scotch trader married into the Creek nation, he would stymie the colonists and the Americans alike for many years, trading with British and up holding Spanish sway over Florida.

Creeks who married traders

PADDY CARR.--A Coweta Creek leader, interpreter to the Agent at Fort Mitchell. He was the son of Tom Carr an Irish trader among the Indians. Paddy was reared an orphan among the family of Mr. Crowell, the Agent, and served with him to date of the removal of the Indians in 1836.

WILLIAM WEATHERFORD, Indian chief and planter, was born near Coosada in 1765, and died March 4, 1824, on his plantation in Baldwin County; son of Charles and Sehoy (McGillivray) Weatherford, the former a Scotch trader who came from Georgia and established himself on the bank of the Alabama River, built a store and constructed a race-track, and brought blooded horses into the Indian country...

CAPTAIN ALECK, or Captain Elcik, Creek Chief.--The few general facts of the early life of the Lower Creek chief, as given by himself, are that he had lived so long among the white people that he looked upon himself as much a white man as a red man; that the white people had given him the name he bore, Captain Aleck, and that he had always lived in friendship with the English.

TIMPOOCHEE BARNARD -- Mississippi agent of the Lower Creeks in 1793 and 1794 and was one of the interpreters at the treaty of Coleraine in 1796. He died at an advanced age on Flint River, Georgia, the year not known. But little is known of the early life of Timpoochee Barnard. His mother carefully taught him to speak her native Yuchee dialect, while no doubt he learned much English from his father.

WILLIAM COLBERT, Chickasaw Indian chief, was a native Alabamian and Revolutionary soldier, serving under Gen. Arthur St. Clair and leading his tribe against the hostile Indians, who operated with the British. In the War of 1812, he again led his tribe against the Creeks, pursuing them to Apalachicola, Fla...

JOSIAH FRANCIS, or Hillis Hadjo, Creek Chief, born probably about 1770, and in Autauga town, was the son of David Francis a white trader and silversmith, who lived many years in Autauga Town, and made silver ornaments and implements for the Indians. The name of his mother is not known, and apart from his father, the only other fact recorded as to his family relationship is that he was a half-brother of Sam Moniac.

CAPTAIN ISAACS of Tourcoula, Coosada chief, born conjecturally about 1765. He received his English name from an Indian trader, who died at an advanced age in Lincoln county, Tennessee. No facts are preserved of his life

GEORGE LOWERY, A cousin of Sequoyah and second chief of the eastern Cherokees under John Ross, commonly known as Major Lowrey.

ALEXANDER McGILLIVRAY, diplomat and merchant, was born probably at Fort Toulouse, or in the town of Taskigi, one half mile below the fort, and died February 17, 1793, at Pensacola, Fla.; son of Lachlan and Sehoy (Marchand) McGillivray, the former a native of Dunmaglass, Scotland…

PETER McQUEEN, Creek Chief, born probably 1780, and on Line Creek in Montgomery County, Alabama, was the son of James McQueen and a Tallassee woman. James McQueen was a Scotchman, born, it is said in 1683, deserted from a British vessel at St. Ausgustine in 1710…

WILLIAM McINTOSH, Creek chief, born at Coweta, Creek nation, probably about 1775, was the son of Captain William McIntosh, of the British army and a full blood Creek woman.

MENAWA, Creek Chief, born probably at Okfuskee, about 1766, died in the Creek Nation west,--but year of death not known. He was a half-breed, but neither history nor tradition preserved the name of his white father.

OPOTHLEYOHOLO, Creek chief, born probably in Tuckabatchee, year of birth not known, died in Kansas about 1866, was the son of Davy Cornells, who was the son of Joseph Cornells by a Tuckabatchee woman.

The influx of traders and intruders onto Indian lands was not a good thing. Early on it caused the tribes to experience drunkenness and debt and all number of abuses occured. Intruders involved them in the slave trade…mainly slaving of Indians, and the Indian response was to fight back.

The Yamassee War

This war took place in 1715-16, mainly in South Carolina, killing about 100 settlers and an undetermined number of Indians. In Blumer's *Catawba nation* (2007:31) the author explores this conflict:

The Catawba were the key to the Yamassee War in the Carolinas, since they are recorded as being the largest nation, with 570 warriors. By comparison, the Yamassee, who started the conflict only had a little more than 400 warriors on record. With their Catawban speaking allies, the Catawba numbered far more fighting men. All the Catawban speaking groups in both Carolinas joined this effort to expel the Europeans from the Southeast.

No Indian war ever exceeded the Yamassee War in its widespread scope. Geographically, the war spread from Cape Fear in North Carolina to the St. Mary's River in Florida and west to the Alabama. The Indians had numerous grievances against the white settlers. These included abuses of a cruel and obscene nature committed by the white traders who worked among the Indians. Abuses such as murder and rape were common. If needed they would help themselves to the Indian's crops and not pay for this food. In addition the traders fomented Indian wars to foster the Indian slave trade. Other grievances included white settlements that encroached on Indian land. The settlers refused to see their role and sought blame for the tragedy.

South Carolinians blamed the French and the Spanish at St. Augustine, but the fact remained the State of South Carolina was as much the culprit in this matter: *South Carolina's lamentable role was outlined by Dr. Francis Le Jau of Goose Creek, who knew the Yamassee and saw the problem coming. He pointed an educated finger at his State of South Carolina. Some authorities in Charles Town tried to stop the abuses. The Indian Act of 1711 was passed in an effort to make things right, but the abuses were too accepted and too widespread. Part of the problem was the white man deceiving the Indians and getting them drunk to purchase land from them; the Sale of free Indians as slaves and the high handed conduct of the traders who worked in the Indian towns.*

The lessons of the Yamassee War were not lost on the Cherokee: they had been victimized by the slave trade, though they did some slaving themselves. As early as the 1690s the Cherokee had complained about their people being taken into slavery and sold in Charles Town:

Slave raids on the Cherokee became so frequent and so devastating that in 1693 twenty of their chiefs journeyed to Charles Town to seek help in stopping them. The Shawnee and Catawba Confederacy tribes had captured a number of Cherokees, carrying them to the Charles Town slave markets. Governor Thomas promised the chiefs peace, friendship and protection but said he could not return those Cherokee (Olexer 2005: 113).

The Cherokee now saw that the road from Charles Town forked, with one road leading to the Creeks at the Flint and Chattahoochee Rivers and the other to the heart of the Cherokee Nation. It became apparent to them with the Georgia Colony opening up on former Yamassee land that the rival Carolina and Virginia Trading Companies would soon be in Cherokee territory (Hatley 1993:29).

The Cherokee had been moving into Creek country for some time now. Many of the place names in South Carolina indicate they belonged to the Creek Indians, originally. In 1755, one of the great events in Cherokee history occurred, The **Battle of Tali Wa**, which resulted in the tentative southern boundary of the Cherokee Nation and the subject of great political bickering 80 years later. The battle produced perhaps the best known hero of Cherokee women, before or since,

Nancy Ward. She would become a most trusted member of council and a friend, in many cases of Indian and settler alike.

Born Nanyihi, Ward was a niece of the progenitor of the Cherokee nation of the 1700s, Attakullakulla. She married about 1751, Tsu la Kingfisher, born about 1730 at Moss Clay, Tennessee. Both were involved in a fight between the Cherokee and Creek which had begun about 1715, over lands in what is now North Georgia. The story of the battle is retold by Bolgiana:

Beloved women were matriarchs who had distinguished themselves, often in war. This was the case of Nancy Ward. At the age of seventeen, in 1755, Nancy accompanied her husband on a war party against the Creeks. It was her job to chew bullets, which increased their mangling power and to load them into guns. When her husband was killed, she grabbed up his weapon and fought in his place. The Cherokee won and Nancy was acclaimed for her courage. She was said to have been awarded a negro slave as her spoils of war, thereby becoming the first Cherokee slave owner. She also happened to be kin to the wealthiest, most prominent Cherokee leaders. She was therefore chosen at an unusually young age to fill a lifetime office that carried much influence at council meetings. Over the next half century, Nancy Ward became a famous participant in Cherokee negotiations with whites (1998:46).

Nancy Ward and the 500 Cherokee had fought overwhelming Creek forces and won the right to claim that part of Northern Georgia along the Chattahoochee River, where gold would be found years later. She remarried, this time to a white man named Bryant Ward and joined a growing list of Cherokee with two names, one Cherokee and one white. Having her foot in both camps made her as much a hero to settlers as to Indians.

The Indians in the Revolutionary War

After the cessions of the Yamassee War and the founding of the Georgia Colony in 1733, as a buffer between the British and the Spanish, things began to heat up for the colonial powers. In 1739 Britain and Spain fought **The War of Jenkins' Ear**, Jenkins being a British sailor who lost his ear at the hands of the Spanish at St. Augustine. Though fought mostly elsewhere the war did see General Oglethorpe's first attempts to run the Spanish out of Florida (this had been attempted during **Queen Anne's War** [1702-1713] by the governor of South Carolina with little success) and end a long history of raids into Georgia and South Carolina by Spanish, run away slaves and other undesirables. With the Battle of Bloody Marsh on St. Simon's Island, 5,000 Spanish invaders were turned back at some cost by Oglethorpe's Georgia defenders.

Attakullakulla (far right), visits London in 1730, from an engraving in the British Museum..

The French and Indian war had been about the settlement of the Ohio Valley. The proclamation of 1763 was all about Indian rights in the Ohio Valley. Not only did the war prepare the colonists for the revolution, it once and for all put the Indians on the British side and the colonists would be their antagonists from then on.

After the French and Indian War and the treaty of Paris, the Proclamation of 1763 was one of the first documents issued to govern the colonies. This proclamation simply stated that no further settlement beyond the Appalachian Mountains was allowed. To the colonists it was a direct blow to their confidence. The colonists interpreted this proclamation as putting an off limits sign on the Ohio River Valley which the whole war had started over. The proclamations misinterpretation was a big key to the view of the colonials. With some convincing a colonial could be shown that since the French and Indian War the acts, taxes, and proclamations have been directed to repress the colonial growth and extend a firmer grip over North America. The real purpose for the Proclamation of 1763 was to temporarily solve the Indian problem. The Indian's rights and property were being violated and the British government realized this and took action. They had just ended a costly war and couldn't afford small skirmishes and conflicts 3000 miles from home. The effects of the proclamation were small but the connotation of them resonated its way through to the revolution. With Britain's failure to clearly identify its intentions to the colonials it simply began a chain of events that would lead to a revolution (Kravitz 2003: conclusion).

The new attitude of the colonists was that they could raise a large army of volunteers; they weren't going to pay for the French War and the Indians had no

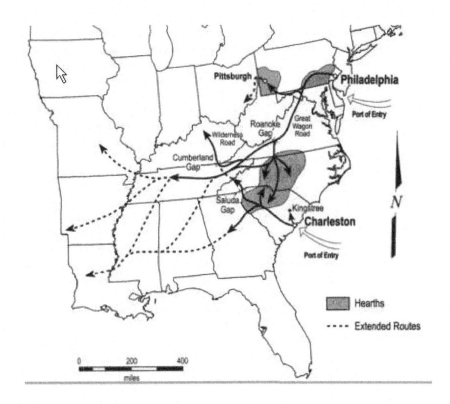

The Way West and South from Philadelphia (see Rehder 2004: 66).

right to the Appalachian land they had taken in war. In the years after the French War relations between the colonists who now called themselves "Whigs" and the British began to strain. As things became polarized, some colonists found themselves on the British side and the target of the Whigs. These "Tories" or "loyalists" were usually government officials, Indian traders or clergymen. The position of the Cherokee in this matter was clear: they would also side with the British:

When the Revolutionary War erupted in 1775, John Stuart, British superintendent of the South, planned to use Indian tribes in conjunction with English troops against the colonists. White encroachers at the Tennessee-North Carolina border along the Watauga, Nolichucky, and Holston Rivers, as well as a delegation of Shawnee and other northern Indians urging the Cherokee to fight against the Americans, inspired their decision to aid the British. The Upper Cherokee planned a three-pronged attack on the intruders along the North Carolina and Virginia frontiers. The Cherokee Middle Towns were to attack North Carolina, while the Lower Towns were to attack South Carolina and Georgia. The Lower and Middle settlements met with limited success. In reaction to these attacks, Gen. Charles Lee, commander of the southern Continental forces, urged a joint punitive expedition, known as the Cherokee Campaign of 1776. Under Col. Andrew Williamson, South Carolina troops moved against the Lower Towns and then traveled northwest to join the North Carolina forces under Gen.

Griffith Rutherford in devastating the Middle and Valley Towns. Virginia troops under Col. William Christian crushed the Overhill Towns in present-day Tennessee. More than 50 Cherokee towns were destroyed in the summer of 1776, and the survivors were left without food or shelter.

These attacks devastated the Cherokee people, who sued for peace, giving up huge parcels of land in the process. The treaties signed after the Cherokee Campaign of 1776 marked the first forced land cessions by the Cherokee, and for the first time the land ceded was not unsettled hunting grounds but the sites of some of the tribe's oldest towns, in which the Cherokee people had lived for centuries. The Cherokee Campaign of 1776 also caused a schism between the old chiefs and young warriors. Many of the latter withdrew to Tennessee and northern Alabama, where they became known as the Chickamauga Cherokee and continued to fight white Americans until 1794.

While the American Revolution brought independence to white North Carolinians, the region's Indians, including the Cherokee, were a conquered people. Nevertheless, the Cherokee managed to maintain a semblance of political independence and cultural integrity despite military defeat. With the Treaty of Holston (1791), the United States initiated a "civilization" program aimed at assimilating the Cherokee people into the mainstream of American society. To a great extent this meant the adoption of sedentary agriculture. Consequently, with Indians living by means of farming, their huge hunting grounds would no longer be needed and whites could easily acquire more Cherokee land. The Tellico Treaty was signed in 1798 as a result of the movement of settlers into Cherokee territory in western North Carolina, west of the 1791 Holston Treaty line. The Tellico Treaty specified that a line, called the Meigs-Freeman Line, was to be drawn from the "Great Iron" or "Smokey" mountain in a southeasterly direction so as to exclude settlers from Cherokee territory. War Department agent Return Jonathan Meigs supervised the running and Thomas Freeman the surveying of the line from July through October 1802. They were assisted by Cherokee leaders and settlers. The line ran from the peak of Mount Collins (located between Clingman's Dome and Newfound Gap) to a point on the North Carolina-South Carolina border near the southwestern corner of Transylvania County (UNC Encyclopedia 2006: 210).

The Cherokee found themselves on the short end of the stick in both Tennessee and Georgia because of their alliance with the British. In 1782, Georgia Gen. Elijah Clarke linked up with South Carolina's Gen. Samuel Pickens for a raid into North Georgia at Tali Wa or Long Swamp, present day Canton, Georgia, to rid the state of British loyalists and their Indian allies.

Many Tories and traders found it to their interest to keep up the hostile attitude of the frontier tribes, with a view to private revenge for losses in the war, or for personal aggrandizement, by monopolizing the trade or lands of the Indians.

A party of these men, just at the conclusion of the revolutionary war, met together, and formed a settlement on the Etowah River, at the mouth of Long Swamp Creek, in Cherokee County, and near to the Indian town of that name.

These person were desperate men, who , having imbrued their hands in Whig blood and glutted themselves with Whig spoil, had fled thither with such property as they could transport, chiefly consisting of negroes and horses and there organized themselves in to a military band, under the command of Thomas Waters. In small parties these Tories, taking with them a few Indians, made incursions into the surrounding settlements, and even extended their forays into South Carolina, daily stealing goods, cattle, horses and negroes, and almost daily murdering those who oppose their course (Stevens 1859: 411).

September 1782 – Andrew Pickens' largest and final Indian campaign: About one-third of his more than 400 men are armed only with the short swords; the goal this time is to capture Colonel Thomas Waters, a loyalist who had been organizing Indian raids along the Georgia frontier. Informed that Waters was encamped at the town of Saiita, Pickens organizes a silent overnight march, attacking from both ends of town at daybreak. Between thirty and forty villagers are killed, and another fifty taken captive; Waters is nowhere to be seen. Valley settlements. Forty villagers are slain, another forty taken prisoner.

October 1782 - Pickens meets with twelve headmen and 200 warriors at Long Swamp, Georgia. The conference ends all Cherokee claims south of the Savannah and west of the Chattahoochee rivers. Except for a few small raids by Loyalist Maj. William "Bloody Bill" Cunningham and other loyalists, this expedition is the Revolution's last in the lower South (Dennis, October 2005:19).

General Andre' Pickens   **General Elijah Clarke**

Cherokee cessions in Georgia actually began before the Revolutionary War, in 1773 and Wilkes, Lincoln and other counties were formed. In 1785 by way of the Treaty of Galphinton, named after that famous South Carolina Indian trader, a large area was opened up of from Creek country on the Ocmulgee River down to the St. Mary. In 1786, at shoulder bone these gains were restated and those who had transgressed from the new boundaries were brought to justice. The Cherokee found themselves suing for peace and at the mercy of the New Americans. However, the Chicamauga Cherokee continued their fight against Americans in general and Tennesseans in particular.

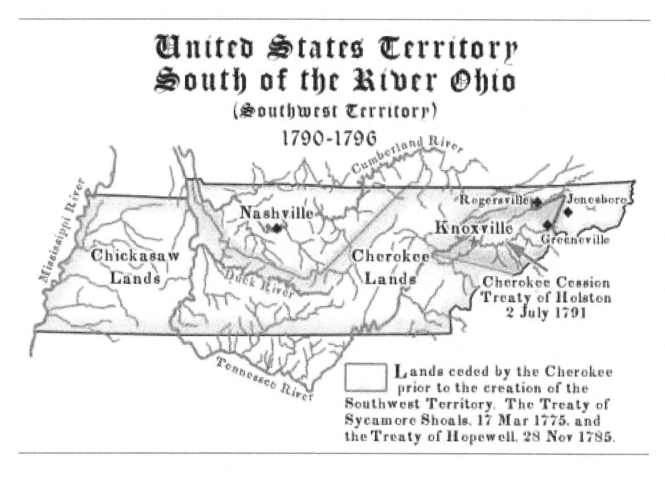

United States Territory South of the River Ohio
(Southwest Territory)
1790-1796

Lands ceded by the Cherokee prior to the creation of the Southwest Territory. The Treaty of Sycamore Shoals, 17 Mar 1775, and the Treaty of Hopewell, 28 Nov 1785.

The most anti-white Cherokees, led by Dragging Canoe, Bloody Fellow, Young Tassel, and Hanging Maw, moved into several abandoned Creek towns, including Citico and Chickamauga along Chickamauga Creek, and began calling themselves Chickamaugas after the "river of death." By this time the Chickamaugas, who had started out as dissatisfied Overhill Cherokees, included many Creeks, Shawnee, French "boatmen," some blacks, and several Scots traders. The Shawnee warrior Cheesekau and his younger brother, Tecumseh, who himself would later lead anti-white uprisings, also lived with them (Ellison, undated).

In September, 1792, Buchanan's Station, near Fort Nashborough (Nashville) in Tennessee was attacked by a combined force of Cherokees, Creeks and Shawnee, with a great loss of Indian life, especially among its leaders. In June, 1793, Cherokees attacked Cavett's Station, near Knoxville, killing everyone in the process. Chief John Watts then continued his attacks on white settlers, spurring John Sevier to come down on the Cherokee Towns and, after a battle at Etowah the Cherokee sued for peace. Though this would result in a peace treaty in 1794, Major James Ore would be called upon to lead yet another campaign against the Towns until peace was finally restored.

The Chickamauga trouble was a priority for President Washington, who desired a treaty to end Cherokee attacks on the settlers at Knoxville. Then provisional Tennessee Governor William Blount also sought to engage the Indians in treaty negotiations. However, Jack "Nolichucky" Sevier, who would become Tennessee's first Governor, opposed the treaty and broke up the negotiations in a small village wherein the delegation took flight and many Indians were killed. Chief John Watts Chicamauga respond by attacking a large portion of Tennessee. Sevier had no problem ammassing a large force to fight the Cherokee and began pushing them out of the Knoxville area into Northwest Georgia.

In **The Battle of Hightower,** Sevier fell on his Cherokee foe with full force:

Sevier follows the largest party down to Hightower a large Chickamaugan village of the day at the site of present-day Rome, Georgia. King Fisher and Doublehead know of the approach of their nemisis, Nolichucky Jack. Taking a secure position on Myrtle Hill, the Cherokee and Creek use the Etowah and Coosa Rivers to protect themselves from the Tennesseans.

In the only written account of the battle, John Sevier describes two attempts to ford the rivers. The successful attempt, about a mile upstream from the confluence of the Oostanaula and Etowah Rivers is met by strong Cherokee resistance. It is during this fighting that the King Fisher is killed.

The death of King Fisher is a crucial blow to the Cherokee. The remaining warriors flee. While the Tennesseeans move west down the Coosa River destroying both Creek and Cherokee villages, the Hightower Cherokee not killed in battle move east along the Etowah to present-day Cartersville, Georgia, where they start a new village, also called Hightower (Golden 2006).

In another account of the battle, By Pickett in his **History of Alabama**, the tenuous position of the Tennesseans is stressed:

... Such was the state of feeling and alarm, that Governor Blount placed General Sevier at the head of six hundred mounted men. Oct. 17 1793: That officer, crossing the Tennessee below the mountains, marched for the Oostanaula, where he made some Cherokee prisoners. Proceeding to the site of the modern Rome, he discovered Indian entrenchments on the opposite bank of the Etowah. Plunging into that stream, the troops gained the southern bank, and, after a fight of an hour, the Indians gave way, bearing off their dead and wounded, but leaving their camp equipage, horses, Spanish guns and ammunition. General Sevier afterwards scoured this whole region, without opposition, and returned to East Tennessee (1900: 436)...

The Chickamauga Towns were not getting the message from the defeat of their British Allies in the Revolutionary War. Raids into Tennessee continued in 1794, after the disastrous Hightower affair:

Sept. 13: The northern frontiers were still disturbed by Indian marauding parties. Major James Ore advanced from Nashville, with five hundred and fifty mounted infantry, to the town of Nickajack, surrounded and attacked it by surprise, and killed many of its inhabitants, while nineteen women and children were made prisoners. On his march from thence up the river, he was attacked at the Narrows by the savages, who, after a few fires, gave way and retreated to Running Water, which was soon taken, and likewise destroyed. Ore re-crossed the Tennessee, before night, and took up the line of march for Nashville, with his prisoners and a large quantity of effects, which had been taken by the Indians from various persons. Andrew Jackson, afterwards President, was a private in this expedition (Pickett 1900: 442).

And:

Some Kentuckians, under Colonel Whitley, had joined the Tennesseeans, who were nominally led by a Major Ore; but various frontier fighters, including Kaspar Mansker, were really as much in
command as was Ore. Over five hundred mounted riflemen, bold of heart and strong of hand, marched toward the Chickamauga towns, which contained some three hundred warriors. When they came to the Tennessee they spent the entire night in ferrying the arms across and swimming the horses; they used bundles of dry cane for rafts, and made four "bull-boats" out of the hides of steers. They passed over unobserved and fell on the towns of Nickajack and Running Water, taking the Indians completely by surprise; they killed fifty-five warriors and captured nineteen squaws and children (Knoxville Gazette, Sept. 26, 1794, in Roosevelt 1917: 395).

The Revolutionary War had been a disaster for the Cherokee and all the British Indian allies. The Creek were able to hold out against the Americans mainly because of two important factors: The Spanish and British were still in Florida and many of the loyalists or Tories congregated in Florida and held Georgia and the rest of the new country at bay. The villainy that had begun as far north as South Carolina was moved south into Florida where it was protected by the British.

2006 Anderson, William L., Ruth Y. Wetmore, Additional research provided by John L. Bell. , *The Revolutionary War, Cherokee Defeat, and Additional Land Cessions,* in Encyclopedia of North Carolina, Univ. of N. Carolina Press: Chapel Hill.

2007 Blumer, Thomas J., **Catawba Nation: Treasures in History**, The History Press: Salem, Mass.

1998 Bolgiano, Chris, **The Appalachian Forest: A Search for Roots and Renewal,** Stackpole: Mechanicsburg, Pa..

1993 Braund, Kathryn E. Holland, **Deerskins and Duffels: Creek Indian Trade With Anglo America, 1685-1815,** Univ. of Nebraska Press: Lincoln.

2007 Cashin, Edward J., **William Bartram and the American Revolution on the Southern Frontier,** Univ of S. Carolina press: Columbia.

October 2005 Dennis, Jeff, **Southern Campaigns Against the Cherokees**, *Heathens, Fairies and Ferries, Southern campaigns of the American Revolution, vol* 2 no. 10.1 @ http://www.southerncampaign.org/newsletter/v2n10.pdf.

2003 Ethridge, Robbie Franklyn, **Creek Country: The Creek Indians and Their World,** Univ. of N. Carolina Press: Greensboro.

Undated Ellison, George, **Dragging Canoe, Cherokee War Chief, @** http://www.marthapeveto.com/sitebuildercontent/sitebuilderfiles/draggingcanoe.ht

2005 **Mountain Passages: Natural and Cultural History of Western North Carolina, was published**. The History Press: Charleston.

2006 **A Blue Ridge Nature Journal: Reflections on the Appalachians in Essays and Art,** The History Press: Charleston.

2006 Golden, Randy, **The Battle of Hightower,** *About North Georgia* @ http://ngeorgia.com.

1994 Gordon, Randy, *The Battle of Hightower*, **About North Georgia**, @http://ngeorgia.com/.

2004 Hahn, Steven C., **The Invention of the Creek Nation, 1670-1763**, Univ of Nebraska Press: Lincoln.

1993 Hatley, Tom, M. Thomas Hatley, **The Dividing Paths: Cherokees and South Carolinians Through the Revolutionary Era,** Oxford Univ. Press: N.Y.

Sept. 26, 1794 *Knoxville Gazette.*

2003 Kravetz, Adam M., **The French and Indian War's Impact on America**, part 4/4, *From Revolution to Reconstruction*, @http://www.let.rug.nl/usa/E/fiwar/french04.html.

2000 Mankiller, Wilma Pearl, Michael Wallis, **Mankiller: A Chief and Her People,** St martins press: N.Y.

1984 McLoughlin, William Gerald, Walter H. Conser, Virginia Duffy McLoughlin, **The Cherokee ghost dance: essays on the Southeastern Indians, 1789-1861,** Mercer Univ. Press: Macon.

2005 Olexer, Barbara J., **The enslavement of the American Indian in colonial times** Joyous Publishing: Milwaukie, Oregon.

1900 Pickett, Albert James, Thomas McAdory Owen, **History of Alabama and incidentally of Georgia and Mississippi, from the Earliest period,** Webb Book Co., Publishers: Birmingham.

1853 Ramsey, James Gettys McGready, Jared Sparks, **The Annals of Tennessee to the End of the Eighteenth Century,** Walker and James: Charleston.

2004 **Rehder, John B. Appalachian Folkways,** John Hopkins Univ. Press: **Baltimore.**

2002 Rolater, Fred S., Chickamauga, **Tennessee Encyclopedia of Culture and History,** @http://tennesseeencyclopedia.net/imagegallery.php?EntryID=C076

1917 Roosevelt, Theodore, **The winning of the West,** vol. 2, G.Putnam and Sons: N.Y.

2007 Rozema, Vicki, **Footsteps of the Cherokees: A Guide to the Eastern Homelands of the Cherokee, J**ohn F. Blair: Winston Salem, N. Carolina.

1999 Saunt, Claudio, **A New Order of Things: Property, Power, and the Transformation of the Creek,** Cambridge Univ Press: N.Y.

2006 Sheppard, Ruth, **Empires Collide: The French and Indian War 1754-63,** Osprey Publishing: Westminster, Maryland.

1920 Snowden, Yates, Harry Gardner Cutler, **History of South Carolina** vol. 1, The Lewis Publishing Co: Chicago and N.Y.

2002 Sokolow, Jayme A., **The Great Encounter: Native Peoples and European Settlers in the Americas,** M E Sharpe publisher, Armonk, N.Y.

1859 Stevens, William Bacon, **A History of Georgia: From Its First Discovery by Europeans to the adoption of the present constitution**, E.H. Butler and Co. Philadelphia.

1890 Thwaites, Reuben Gold, **The Colonies, 1492-1750,** Longman's, Green and Co.: N.Y.

2006 Waselkov, Gregory A., Peter H. Wood, M. Thomas Hatley, **Powhatan's Mantle: Indians in the Colonial Southeast,** Univ of Nebraska press: Lincoln.

Cherokee Delegation to London in 1765 (Engraving British Museum).

SLAVERY

*Slaves begin the arduous journey of runaways through the country to freedom.
(Harpers Weekly, April 9, 1864).*

*The Atlantic slave trade originated as the kidnapping of Africans by Portuguese seamen in the
fifteenth century. But from around 1445 the Portuguese government decided that buying
Rather than stealing slaves was likely to produce more secure profits in the long run, and
initiated a way of doing business with African chiefs and traders that lasted for four centuries
(Woodiwiss 2001:29)...*

Slaves were gotten from Africa the same way they were gotten from Indians in
America. For years one tribe would raid another, capture slaves and sell them to the
colonists. America had relied almost exclusively on indentured servitude to fill
those jobs that a growing country had to fill. Eventually slaves began to replace the
servants who had paid for their passage to the colonies with years of labor. Slaves
did not appear everywhere and all at once, Georgia, for example, outlawed slavery
until 1750.

Almost from the beginning, slaves began to run away into the Indian country. The
permissive nature of the Indians that allowed so many intruders on their land from
very early times also allowed slaves to find sanctuary among the tribes. Foremost
among them were the Creeks, who, by the time of the Seminole Wars, exhibited
much African blood. Florida became a haven of "exiles" as these runaways were
called.

The swamps of Florida gave refuge to thousands of runaways in the years of Spanish rule. In 1738 the Spanish offered freedom to any slave who fled the English colonies and came to St. Augustine. This wasn't out of any anti-slavery sentiment on the part of Spain. They disputed English ownership of Georgia and South Carolina. Inciting slaves to run away was an effective way of disrupting those colonies. The British copied this tactic during the War of Independence (Dunmore's Proclamation), with the same success. Once in Florida the fugitives encountered the refugee remnants of the southeastern Indian tribes who had also fled to the Florida swamps. They also found fugitive communities that had been there since the 17th century. The fugitive communities they established in the Florida swamps became the strongest in the country. Runaway slaves fled to these strongholds throughout the colonial period up to 1819, when the United States took Florida from Spain (Kolhoff, 2001).

The swamps and pine-barrens between Florida and South Carolina began to fill with runaway slaves, half breeds and other mustee, who fled the law or slavery or servitude. They preyed on the Georgians and the South Carolinians alike, raiding settlements like the Indians had only a few years earlier.

In areas such as Southeastern Virginia, the "Low Country" of the Carolinas, and around Galphintown near Savannah, Georgia, communities of Afro-Indians began to arise. The term "mustee" came to distinguish between those who shared African and Native American ancestry from those who were a mixture of European and African. Even after 1720, black and red Carolinians continued to share slave quarters and intimate lives; many wills continued to refer to "all my Slaves, whether Negroes, Indians, Mustees, Or Molattoes (Minges 1999:25)."
And:

Another way blacks tried to obtain freedom was to escape to the wilderness and establish communities there. Formation of these enclaves, or maroons (from the Spanish "cimarron" meaning wild and unruly) had been a long established method of resisting slavery. Slaves would desert their master and go off and eke out a subsistence from the game and food plants of the area, sometimes supplementing this with booty taken by raids on settlements. Maroons existed in Georgia even before the revolution. In 1771, Georgia's acting Governor, James Habersham,...sent militiamen and Indian warriors to wipe out several slave maroons between Savannah and Ebenezer. He said they were marauders, preying on the countryside and he feared the number of maroons would multiply if not properly destroyed. The militia had to be called out the following year for the same purpose (Grant 2001:75).

These problems had been noted earlier in South Carolina where planters and the land owning public were fearful of slaves becoming involved with banditti and Indians. The whole idea of slaves finding allies so close at hand was enough to get the regulators into the back country for the purpose of routing outlaws and runaway slaves:

While Native American involvement in outlaw gangs distressed Euroamericans, their fears were especially heightened when African Americans joined the ranks. Planters were aware that some runaway slaves joined these criminal groups. In mid-July of 1767, for example, a

49

slave named Ben absconded from his master's cowpen on the Carolina frontier. His "being well acquainted with most parts of the backcountry" convinced his owner that he might escape to the interior of South Carolina and then flee the colony. The fugitive, however, did not attempt to obtain freedom elsewhere, as he was spotted two months later near George Galphin's plantation at Silver Bluff. The report indicated that Ben was "in company with Timothy Tyrell, George Black, John Anderson, Anthony Distow, Edward Wells and others, all horse thieves". Ben then led his newfound cohorts back to his master's cowpen and stole three more horses (Bouleware, 2004)...

Other persons of African descent – not just fugitive slaves like Ben – became active members of the outlaw bands. Edward Gibson was a 'mulatto' who broke out of the Charleston jail twice in 1766 and 1767 before he received punishment. Isaac Reeves, a tall man "of a dark complexion" who wore "his own black Hair", appeared at court six times from 1769 to 1774 for various offenses. More notable were the two black outlaws Robert Prine and Winslow Driggers. The court at Savannah found Driggers guilty of cow stealing in June of 1770 and sentenced him to be hanged. A few months later, while under reprieve by order of Governor Wright of Georgia, Driggers broke out of jail along with Prine. The two men crossed into South Carolina and by the fall of 1771, had "collected a Gang of other desperated Villains, in Number near fifty, who committed all Manner of Depredations upon the industrious settled Inhabitants". Settlers near the Cheraws attacked the gang and killed a number of them. One of the unfortunate bandits was their leader, Driggers, whom the vigilantes "tried on the Negro-Act, and hanged"...

Interracial gangs of outlaws, besides the Driggers' band, were also known to have attacked backcountry settlers. A report during the summer of 1768 related that Regulators had assembled near Lynch's Creek because a party of them had been "roughly used by a Gang of Banditti, consisting of Mulattoes, Free Negroes, & notorious Harborers of runaway slaves, at a place called Thompson's Creek" (Bouleware 2004)...

Slaves made quite an impact on the Creek nation and many Creek Miccos had many slaves. When Alexander McGillavry died, he owned 60 slaves. Rollie McIntosh had 52. Robert Grierson, at Hillabee, had forty. McGillavry's sister had 30. Many were bought and paid for and others were booty from the Revolutionary War, when the East Florida Rangers and other banditti stole many slaves from South Carolina and Georgia. The Seminole Wars were a combination of desire for land in Florida and a wish to retrieve those slaves lost during the years to Florida. The British did form a unit of black infantry and cavalry during the revolution under Major Henry Hampton, in 1782, but they did not really understand the down side of using the slave against the Americans:

The problem for British and Loyalist forces was obvious. By using slaves as soldiers with the promise of freedom in payment, they simultaneously threatened the slave system and evoked the specter of insurrection. In so doing, the British could only have alienated people from whose support they might have benefited (Klein 1990:105)...

Sunaffe Tustenukke (Abraham)　　　　　*John Horse, Seminole Scout*

The Cherokee saw little value in slaves until late. They were paid to return slaves they found in their lands and generally had that permissive attitude toward Africans that most Indian tribes had. Indian lands consisted of a hodge-podge of white, red and black individuals living off the bounty of the wilderness and they made the colonists and later all the settled Americans very nervous. By 1800, Cherokee could see that slaves added to their list of assets, like guns and horses, in a system where land ownership was not a factor. From that time the Cherokee would be slave owners like their white counterparts.

...By 1794, there were about 100 blacks living among the Cherokees. Some of them had been captured from whites as booty of raiding parties during the guerilla wars. Some were runaways. Others were freed blacks who preferred to live among a people who did not as yet discriminate (McGloughlin 1986: 31).

1940 Aswell, James R., **Federal Writer's Project - God Bless the Devil**, Univ. of N.Carolina Press: Greensboro.

1998 Berlin, Ira, **Many Thousands Gone: The First Two Centuries of Slavery in North America,** Harvard Univ. Press: Cambridge, Mass.

2002 Brooks, James, **Confounding the Color Line: The Indian – Black experience in North America,** Univ of Nebraska Press: Lincoln.

1980 Brown, Dee Alexander, **Creek Mary's Blood**, Holt, Rinehart and Winston: Austin, Texas.

1855 Edited by Chamerovzow, Louis, A **Slave Life in Georgia: A Narrative of the Life, Sufferings, and Escape of John Brown, A Fugitive Slave, Now In England,** M.W. Watts: London.

2004 Cole, Stephanie, Alice M. Parker, eds., **Beyond Black & White: Race, Ethnicity, and Gender in the U.S. South and Southwest,** Texas A&M Univ. Press:College Station, Texas.

2007 Fields, Uriah J., **Grandpa Benjamin**, Publish America: Frederick, Maryland.

2006 Forret, Jeff, **Race Relations at the Margins: Slaves and Poor Whites in the Antebellum Southern Countryside**, LSU Press: Baton Rouge.

2000 Fradin, Dennis Brindell, **Bound for the North Star: True Stories of Fugitive Slaves,** Clarion Books: N.Y.

2001 Grant, Donald L., **The Way It Was in the South: The Black Experience in Georgia,** Univ of Ga. Press: Athens.

2002 Horton, James Oliver, Lois E. Horton, **Hard Road to Freedom: The Story of African America,** Rutgers Univ. Press: N.J.

1990 Klein, Rachel N**., Unification of a Slave State: The Rise of the Planter Class in the South,** Univ. of N. Carolina Press: Greensboro.

2000 Inscoe, John C., **Appalachians and Race: the Mountain South from Slavery to Segregation,** Univ. press of Kentucky: Lexington.

1892 Julian, George Washington, **The Life of Joshua R. Giddings**, A.C. McLurg and Co.: Chicago.

2001 Kolhoff, Michael, **Fugitive Communities in Colonial America,** *Early American Review,*
@http://www.earlyamerica.com/review/2001_summer_fall/fugative.html

2005 Miles, Tiya, **Ties That Bind: The Story of an Afro-Cherokee Family in Slavery and Freedom,** Univ of California Press: Berkeley.

2003 Minges, Patrick Neal, **Slavery in the Cherokee Nation: The Keetoowah Society and the Defining of a People 1855-1867,** Routledge Taylor and Francis Group: Florence, Ky.

2005 Olexer, Barbara J., **The Enslavement of the American Indian in Colonial Times,** Joyous Publishing: Columbia, Maryland.

2005 Rothman, Adam, Slave Country: **American Expansion and the Origins of the Deep South,** Harvard Univ. Press: Cambridge, Mass.

1854 Stowe, Harriet Beecher, **The Key to Uncle Tom's Cabin**, Jewett: Boston.

2007 Stowe, Harriet Beecher, **Inside View of Slavery ; Or, A Tour Among the Planters,** Kessinger Publishing: Whitefish, Montana.

1922 Talley, Thomas Washington, **Negro Folk Rhymes: Wise and Otherwise,** The Macmillan co.: N.Y.

1994 Wilson, Carol, **Freedom at Risk: The Kidnapping of Free Blacks in America, 1780-1865,** Univ. Press of Kentucky: Lexington.

2002 Wright, William D., **Critical Reflections on Black History**, Greenwood Publishing: Santa Barbara.

The Melungeons

There was another group who helped populate mainly the south during this time after the French and Indian War. They were at first landowners with real standing in their communities married to prominent white families in some cases. They originated as freed Angolans and other African peoples who married Indians and Whites and became known as "Tri-racial Isolates," or more popularly, Melungeons. When the "one drop rule" was finally being enforced by law in the mid 1700s, these groups found themselves being pushed out of white society and into the far regions of the country. Having lost their rights as citizens, most moved into remote regions like Appalachia. When the five civilized tribes were recompensed for removal, many of the Melungeons applied for and received status as Indians.

Some well known people in America are related to these early Melungeon families; Nancy Hanks, mother of Abraham Lincoln and ancestor of Tom Hanks was a Melungeon. Elvis Presley, Heather Locklear and Steve Martin are also related to Melungeons. Benjamin Chavez of the NAACP, Ralph Bunch and Puffy Combs are related to these triracial groups. In **Afeni Shakur**, Jasmine Guy refers to that white man with Indian blood grandma married in the 1920s (2005:12).

These groups began in earnest around the Virginia Colony as early as 1620s and spread throughout the East and South. They are known locally by various names but all are so called tri-racial isolates, with white, black and Indian blood. The Indian blood has been described as Saponic, Tutelo and other Virginia Souian tribes long ago pushed out of Virginia by white settlement. In all cases the Indian blood percentage has diminished considerably over times as Melungians married into either white or black familes.

- *Alabama:* Cajans, Creoles, Melungeons (Ramps)
- *Delaware:* Moors, Nanticoke
- *Florida:* Dominickers
- *Georgia:* Lumbee Indians (Croatans)
- *Kentucky:* Melungeons, Pea Ridge Group (Coe Clan, Black Coes)
- *Louisiana:* Natchitoches Mulattoes, Rapides Indians, Red Bones, Sabines, St. Landry Mulattoes, Zwolle-Ebard People
- *Maryland:* Guineas, Lumbee Indians, Melungeons, Wesorts (Brandywine)
- *Mississippi:* Creoles
- *New Jersey:* Gouldtowners, Ramapo Mountain People (Jackson Whites), Sand Hill Indians
- *New York:* Bushwhackers, Jackson Whites

- *North Carolina:* Haliwa Indians, Lumbee Indians, Person County Indians, Portuguese, Rockingham Surry Group
- *Ohio:* Carmel Indians, Cutler Indians, Darke County Group, Guineas, Vinton County Group
- *Pennsylvania:* Karthus Half-Breeds, Keating Mountain Group, Nigger-Hill People, Pooles
- *South Carolina:* Brass Ankles, Lumbee Indians, Turks
- *Tennessee:* Melungeons
- *Virginia:* Adamstown Indians, Brown People, Chickahominy Indians, Issues, Melungeons, Potomac Indians, Rappahannock Indians, Rockingham Surry Group
- *West Virginia:* Guineas

Price 1953 Fig. 1 (Association of American Geographers Annals Vol. 43 June 1953.)

Tim Hashaw has written extensively on the Melungeons in America as an investigate reporter working from East Texas and has filed stories for CBS, ABC and NBC from network affiliates. Tim has reported for radio, television, and print and has Awards for Best Investigative Reporting from: The Radio and Television

News Directors' Association (RTNDA), Associated Press, United Press International, the National Headliners Club and others. He traces these groups back to a number of Angolans who entered Virginia Colony in 1619, aboard the White Cloud.

The Angolan Founding Fathers of Melungia

The Angolan who became known as John Gowen of Virginia, was born about 1615. Before 1775, his descendants had married into the Angolan and mixed families of Ailstock, Bass, Chavis, Corn, Cumbo, Dungill, Findley, Hill, Jones, Locklear, Lucas, Matthews, Mason, Miner, Mills, Patterson, Pompey, Stewart, Simmons, Singleton, Tyre, Webb and Wilson; most of whom can also be traced to the 17th century.

Thomas CHIVERS/CHAVIS was born in 1630. Before 1775 his Angolan descendants had married into the families of BASS, GOWEN, LOCKLEAR, SINGLETON, STEWART, CUMBO, MATTHEWS, and WILSON along with descendants of John Gowen. In addition the Chivers/Chavis group intermarried with Bird, Blair, Blythe, Brandon, Bunch, Cannady, Carter, Cypress, Drew, Earl, Evans, Francis, Gibson, Gillet, Haithcock, Harris, Hawley, Hull, Kersey, Lowry, Manly, Manning, Mitchell, McLin, Scott, Silvey, Smith, Snelling, Silver, Sweat, Thaxton, Tyner, Thomerson, Taborn, Valentine, Watts and Walden; many of whom were 17th century Africans in the British-American colonies.

The family of Eleanor EVANS, born 1660, shares with the Gowen and Chavis families the following names: BIRD, BRANDON, CHAVIS, DUNGILL, HARRIS, KERSEY, MCLINN, MITCHELL, SNELLING, SCOTT, STEWART, SWEAT, TABORN and WALDEN. In addition the Evans were early related to the families of Anderson, Boyd, Bee, Blundon, Doyal, Green, Hudnall, Hunt, Jeffries, Jones, Lantern, Ledbetter, Penn, Pettiford, Redcross, Richardson, Rowe, Sorrell, Spriddle, Tate, Thomas, Toney and Young.

The GIBSON or GIPSON family descended from Elizabeth Chavis, born in 1672, also shares with 17th century African-Americans Gowen, Chavis, and Evans, the surnames of BASS, BUNCH, CHAVIS, CUMBO, and SWEAT. They add Driggers, Deas, Collins and Ridley.

The family of the Portuguese-Angolan named Emmanuel DRIGGERS, (Roddriggus) born in 1620, also has several families in common with the Gowen, Chavis, Evans and Gibson clans: CARTER, COLLINS, SWEAT, GIBSON and MITCHELL. In addition the Driggers intermarried with Beckett, Beavens, Bingham, Bruinton, Copes, Fernando, Francisco, George, Gussal, Harman, Hodgeskin, Jeffrey, Johnson, King, Kelly Lindsey, Landrum, Liverpool, Moore, Payne, Reed and Sample.

From Margarett CORNISH, born about 1610, comes the Cornish family with ties to GOWEN and SWEAT in addition to Shaw and Thorn. With the CUMBO family dating back to 1644, we have links to GIBSON GOWEN, JEFFRIES, MATTHEWS, NEWSOM, WILSON and YOUNG in addition to Hammond, Maskill, Potter and Skipper.

The BASS family originates in 1638 America and shares several intermarriages from that period with Gowen, Chavis, Evans, Cornish, Driggers, Cumbos and Gibsons which are: ANDERSON, BYRD, BUNCH, CANNADY, CHAVIS, DAY, MITCHELL, GOWEN, PETTIFORD, RICHARDSON, SNELLING, VALENTINE and WALDEN. In addition they have the names of Farmer, Hall, Lovina, Nickens, Perkins, Pone, Price, Roe and Roberts.

If given the space we could find complex scores of intermarriages of Melungeon and other tri-racial surnames beginning in the 17th century of colonial America. These common kinships of cousins show the Melungeon society was becoming cohesive and distinctively apart in colonial America at least one hundred years before the American Revolution. The Melungeon community began before 1700.

For example: The BANKS family originates in 1665 colonial America with related families of Adam, Brown, Day, Howell, Isaacs, Johnson, Lynch, Martin, Walden, Wilson and Valentine and other Melungeon surnames.

The ARCHER family begins in 1647 America with related families; Archie, Bass, Bunch, Heathcock, Manly, Murray, Milton, Newsom, Roberts and Weaver.

The BUNCH clan traces back to 1675 colonial America with kinship to: Bass, Chavis, Chavers, Collins, Gibson, Griffin, Hammons, Pritchard and Summerlin.

The BECKETT family of 1655 ties to Bibbins, Beavens, Collins, Driggers, Drighouse, Liverpool, Mongon, Morris, Moses, Nutt, Stevens and Thompson.

The family of CARTER begins in 1620 America with the related families of: Best, Blizzard, Braveboy, Bush, Cane, Copes, Dove, Driggus, Fernando, Fenner, Godett, George, Harmon, Howard, Jacobs, Jones, Kelly, Lowery, Moore, Norwood, Nicken, Perkins, Rawlinson, and Spellman.

In addition to the above, other mixed families from America in the 1600s are: Artis, Berry, Cane, Causey, Charity, Collins, Cuttilo, Dial/Dale, Hall, Harris, Hammond, Hawley, Hilliard, Holman, Howell, Ivey, Jacobs, Jeffires, Johnson, Jones, Mongom, Payne, Reed, Roberts, Shoecraft, Sisco, Francisco, Stephens, Stewart, Sweat, Tann, Webb, Williams, Wilson and Young. These 17th
century mixed families are each related to a dozen or more later Melungeon surnames with links to almost all mixed communities in America. It might be said convincingly that there are more early 17th century American "blue-bloods" to be found in the shanties of Appalachia than in all of Boston.

Groups like Melungeons, Brass Ankles, Redbones, Lumbees, and many others are all connected by common blood to each other from the first two centuries of English-American colonization. Mixed red, white, and black Melungeons can be found in Virginia and Maryland to within one or two generations of the first Angolan Ndongo appearance in Jamestown in 1619. The general Melungeon community is decisively shown to be more than 350 years old in North America. All of these families descended from 17th century Angolans in Virginia, who began building the Melungeon community long before it appeared in Tennessee in the 19th century.

It should be noted at this point that these surnames represent Melungeons but not everyone with these surnames is Melungeon. Most are well known English or Scotch and Irish surnames. Most have ties to names in the old countries. As such, many whites with the same surnames continued to immigrate to America. These Surnames are shared by White and Black people everywhere in this country who have nothing to do with Melungeons.

One scientist has described the lessening Indian nature of Melungeons in his study using DNA distancing techniques. He found Indian blood to be the discernable trait among modern Melungeons:

Libya (Tripoli*) 0.017

Cyprus (Toodos-Greek) 0.017

Malta* 0.018

Canary Islands (Spanish) 0.019

Italy (Veneto) 0.022

Portugal 0.024

Italy (Trentino) 0.026

Spain (Galacia) 0.027

U. S. Whites (Minnesota) +0.028

Ireland# 0.029

Italy 0.030

Sweden 0.030

Libya (minus Fezzan) 0.030

Germany 0.031

Britain 0.031

Greece 0.032

Netherlands 0.032

Wales 0.033

Corsica 0.034

France 0.035

Spain 0.036

U.S. Whites 0.036

England 0.040

Sicily 0.040

Iceland 0.041

Northern Ireland 0.042

Finland 0.046

Sardinia 0.051

Turkey 0.053

Cyprus 0.058

U.S. Blacks 0.189

Distant Matches:

Gullas (Blacks South Carolina) 0.222

Seminole, Oklahoma 0.241

Cherokee 0.256

Seminole, Florida 0.308

The author has done a number of studies with respect to Melungeon surnames and found it to be almost totally unreliable factor. I studied lists such as census of southern counties early on in history; lists of executions for the Appalachian and Southern states and finally, Indian census rolls. While throughout populations of the late 1700s to mid 1800s, so called Melungeon surnames (using Hashaws list) hover around 30% of all names. In execution lists it slightly increases to 40% because blacks are generally identified in those records and they generally bear the brunt of execution in those states. Only when surnames of the Five Civilized Tribes are studied do Melungeon names appear in any numbers. I found 75% of all of the Indians had Melungeon-related surnames…which, makes plenty of sense, since Melungeons are defined as Indian as well as black and white.

Fig. 1: **English surnames among the 5 Civilized Tribes (2cd no. is how many tribes, *** is Melungeon surname).**

Adams***			Buckner			Colbert	4	
Alberty			Burgess			Cole*		
Alexander	4		Burney			Colly		
Allen	5***		Burton*			Cooper*		
Anderson	4***		Butler	5***		Cox	5***	
Austin	4		Byrd*			Daniels	4	
Bailey			Campbell*			Davis	4	
Baker			Canard			Dean		
Bean			Carolina			Dindy		
Bell*			Carr	4		Dixon		
Berry*			Carson	4		Douglass		
Boyd	4		Carter	5***		Drew		
Brewer			Chambers*			Duncan		
Brown			Charles			Eastman		
5***			Choate			Edwards	4	
Bruce			Clark	5***		Eubanks		
Bruner	5		Clay			Evans	4***	
Bryant*			Cohee			Factor		

Fields*		Jones	4***	Roberts	4***
Fisher*		Kelly		Robinson*	
Flint		Kemp	4	Roe	
Folsom		King	4	Rogers	
Ford*		Lee*			
Foster		Lewis	5***	Rose	
Franklin		Lincoln		Ross	5
Frazier	4	Logan		Russell*	
Freeman*		Little		Samuel	
French*		Love	4	Sango	
Fulsum		Lowe		Scott	5***
Garret		Lowery	4***	Shepherd*	
Gentry		Lynch		Simmons	
Gibson 5***		Mackey		Smith	5***
Givens		Mahardy		Spencer	4
Glover		Martin	4***	Starr	
Graham*		Mccoy		Stewart	4***
Coker		Mcintosh		Mcgee	
Grant		Mckenny		Sutton	
Gray	4	Miles*		Taylor*	
Grayson	5	Miller	5	Thomas	4
Green	4***	Mitchell	4	Thompson	4***
Griffin		Moore	5***	Tucker	
Grimmet		Morgan	4	Turner*	
Hall*		Morris*		Tyner	
Hamilton		Moses		Vaughn	
Hampton		Murray		Wade	4
Harper		Nash*		Walker	5***
Harris	4***	Nero	4	Wallace	
Harrison*		Owens	4	Walton	
Hawkins	4***	Parker		Ward	
Henderson 4		Patterson*		Warrior	
Henry		Payne*		Washington	5
Hill***		Perry	4***	White	5***
Horn		Perryman		Williams	4***
Hughes		Phillips	4	Willis	5***
Jackson	5***	Porter	4	Wilson	5***
James	4***	Powell	4***	Woods	4***
Jefferson		Price***		Wright	5****
Johnson	5***	Reed	5***	Young	4***
		Riley			

Names in 3 tribes
67 of 102 55%

Names in 4 tribes:
4ea 13 of 41 32%

60

Many other explanations have arisen concerning the origins of these people. Some of the Melungeons have described themselves as Portuguese or Turkish... Writing for ***Ancestry.com***, one of the Gowens descendants (Charles Lattimer Gowen, 1992) explained some of those other possible origins:

Mary Sue Going suggests that they were descendants of deserters from a Spanish expedition which explored eastern Tennessee in 1577 under the command of Capt. Juan Pardo. Joseph Judge, an editor of National Geographic wrote an article on this expedition which was published in the March 1988 edition of the magazine.

Authority for his article was a translation of Pardo's report written in April 1569 and deposited in Seville's Archives of the Indies. The archives holds 82,000,000 manuscript pages of well-preserved reports on Spanish efforts in America. The re-port was translated by historian Herbert Ketcham and placed in the North Carolina State Archives.

Pardo arrived early in 1566 with 250 men and established his headquarters on Parris Island. On November 30 he moved in-land as far as an Indian river city called Joara [DeSoto identi-fied the town as Xuala] where he built a fort and left 100 men under the command of Sgt. Hernando Moyano de Morales. Joara is identified as present-day Newport, Tennessee by Mary Sue Going. In the spring of 1567 a letter from Sgt. Moyano addressed to Capt. Pardo's headquarters told of eminent Indian trouble and of swapping insults with an Indian chieftain who "threatened to eat not only Sgt. Moyano. but his dog as well."

Moyano took the initiative, attacking and burning an Indian village. The chieftain retaliated with a force of 3,000 braves. The sergeant withdrew with a remnant of his forces to Chiaha [on Zimmerman's Island. according to archaeologist Polhemus who reports that the city is now submerged under 70 feet of water in Lake Douglas created by a TVA dam.] Capt. Pardo with the help of some friendly Indians rescued Sgt. Moyano and the survivors and brought them back to Parris Island.

The father of Norman Goings used the term "Tuckahoe" to de-scribe the family and told Norman that it was a nickname for people from Turkey. Generally, tuckahoe is defined as a tuber plant similar to the potato that the early Indians of southern states used for baking bread. Locally in Virginia, it became a nickname for the lowlands and for the inhabitants of Lower Virginia, according to "Annals of Augusta County, Virginia," 1902 by Joseph A. Waddell.

At an early date, the people living on the east side of the Blue Ridge Mountains received the sobriquet of "Tuckahoes," and those on the west side were called "Cohees" from their com-mon usage of the Elizabethan term "Quoth he" for "Said he." Wad-dell wrote, "The Tuckahoe carried himself rather pompously and pronounced many words as did his English forefathers in the days of Queen Elizabeth

Another widely quoted description of the Melungeons was that of early explorers Abraham Wood and James Needlum. In 1673, they penetrated into what is now called Melungia. According to Wood's journal:

Eight days jorney down this river lives a white people which have long beardes and whiskers and weares clothing (Alvord, Bidgood 1912: 213).

Samuel Cole Williams, L.L.D, wrote in "Early Travels in the Tennessee Country," 1928:

...There is a tradition among the early Cherokees that they respected a settlement of white men among them (29)...

In **Children of Perdition** *(2006)* ,Hashaw describes how the Melungeons pushed their way into Appalachia after the French and Indian War:

As a matter of record...the occasion that brought melungeons to Appalachia was the French and Indian War of 1754-1763. This conflict pitted Britain and her American colonies against the French for control of lands between Appalachia and the Mississippi, and ended when France and Spain traded territory to Britain (2006: 6).

With the onset of the "one drop" rule and fear of slave revolt, Melungeons found themselves under a microscope in the cities and towns of America. Thus began a movement which resulted in the groups moving into more secluded places like the mountains of Appalachia, swamps of Georgia and Florida and the bayous of Mississippi and Louisiana, but also into locations where acceptance had already been proven. Over time some families split into white and black groups as descendants married exclusively a white or a black group, resulting in the white Goins and the black Goins, for example. Another thing to remember is that Melungeon surnames are not exclusive. There are many, many Goins who are not Melugeon at all: as more and more immigrants arrived in America some had the same surnames as those who married into tri-racial groups earlier in America's history.

1912 Alvord, Clarence W., Lee Bidgood, **First Explorations of the Trans-Allegheny Region by the Virginians, 1650-1674,** Arthur H. Clark Co.: Cleveland, Ohio.

The African Diaspora, Anthropology course taught by Dr. Deidre Crumbley at the University of Florida.

1997 Gallegos, Eloy J., **The Melungeons: the Pioneers of the Interior Southeastern United States,** Villagra Press: London, Ky.

December 1989 Charles L Gowen, *Gowen Research Foundation Newsletter* Volume 1, No 4.
http://freepages.genealogy.rootsweb.ancestry.com/~gowenrf/nl198912.htm

September 1989 **Melungeon "Skeleton Key" Reveals Genetic Ties,** *Gowen Research Foundation Newsletter,* Volume 1, No. 1.
@http://freepages.genealogy.rootsweb.ancestry.com/~gowenrf/melun001.htm

2005 Guy, Jasmine , **Afeni Shakur: Evolution of a Revolutionary**, Simon and Shuster: N.Y.

2006 Hashaw, Tim, **Children of Perdition: Melungeons And the Struggle of Mixed America,** Mercer Univ. Press: Macon.

1997 Heinegg, Paul, **Free African Americans of North Carolina and Virginia: including the family histories of more than 80% of those counted as "all other free persons" in the 1790 and 1800 census**, Genealogical Pub. Co.: Baltimore.

2000 Heinegg, Paul, **Free African Americans of Maryland and Delaware: from the colonial period to 1810**, Clearfield co: Baltimore.

2005 Hirschman, Elizabeth, **Melungeons: The Last Lost Tribe in America,** Mercer Univ. Press: Macon.

1997 Kennedy, N. Brent and Robyn Vaughan Kennedy, **The Melungeons: The Resurrection of a Proud People,** Mercer Univ.Press: Macon.

1994 Nassau, Mike, , Edward Thomas Price, William Harlen Gilbert, Michael Edward McGlothlen, **Melungeons and other Mestee groups,** Michael Nassau Publisher.

Frontier Violence

The New World seemed to be born in violence and reared on mayhem. It is the subject of many scholarly works on early America. It seems that the violence of the old world was merely imported to the new with those hoping for something different. Here are some of the more popular views on the subject.

Much of the point of view Americans had in the 18th and 19th centuries can be found in the literature of the time. It is also represented by some early analysis like that discussed in ***The Fatal Environment*** (Slotkin, 1998) He quotes an early analysis of America by a yeoman farmer:

Crevecoeur sees America as divided into four metaphorical environments, running north to south through all the colonies. Each section has its own geography or natural character, which determines the type of economic, social and political institutions and the sorts of human characters that develop there. The Eastern seacoast is described in terms appropriate to our notions of the Metropolis: it faces Europe, engages in trade and exploitation of marine resources; and it is the realm of merchants, adventurous and commercial in character, sharing both the cultural advances and the 'vices' of Europe—greed and ambition for power in particular.

At the opposite extreme is the world of the Indian: the wilderness, which hunting is the mode of subsistence and savagery the form of social organization. The wilderness dweller too has particular virtues and vices—he has the 'natural' morality and 'nobility' of those who live close to nature and far from cities, yet he is an abysmal barbarian, politically anarchic, violent, capable of great cruelty.

Infringing on Indian territory is the third region, the border, on which adventurous outriders of civilization mingle with the Indians, modifying wilderness in the direction of civilization while themselves acquiring a taste for still wilder freedoms. The borderers are the most dangerous and antisocial characters in the system for even the Indians have a tribal organization, while the borderer is a solitary individualist, recognizing no law but his own will and appetite.

Between the border and coast and graded internally in according to levels of development, Crevecouer locates the realm of the American farmer. It is a utopian district, freed at once of the Indian menace and the corruptions of the city (1998:71)...

These four distinct areas of the New World compare to what we now see as urban and rural. Each has a different density of development and residence. We move as easily from country to city today it seems appalling that anyone could have described one as safe and the other not. If anything cities are now seen as more violent than the countryside, a notion that must have been as alien as Mars to many early settlers in America.

Slotkin also discusses two very distinct themes running through frontier literature. One is the idea of being captured by the Indians, as in Coopers *Last of the Mohicans* and the other is the hunter. Being a *captive* or enslaved by the Indians was an almost universal archetype of terror for women and was reminiscent of traveling to hell and living with Satan himself. It was at once a journey into a savage past away from organized religion and in some way retribution for failure to comport to the doctrine of the time. Great fears are always the subject of great books and the literati picked up on this theme early on and it continued into the western expansion in the story of Quanna Parker.

The myth of the *hunter* is similar to that of the captive in that the Christian is to be asked to overcome the savagery of the wilderness and retain the principles set down in the Ten Commandments despite the demands to the contrary by wild animals, Indians and backwoods miscreants. The message here is simple and tells much of what was going on at the time: Do not go "native"; do not forsake your race, heritage and upbringing to live among godless savages in what Slotkin calls "regression" (1998: 63).

The hunter myth creates many unforgettable characters who eschew the life of the city to further the conquest of the frontier. He is a friend of the Indians and also their master. He opens up the country to pioneers for settlement. Benjamin Church, Daniel Boone, Davy Crocket, Kit Carson and Buffalo Bill come to mind. He is not the yeoman farmer nor the Planter or city merchant. It is clear the hunter is one of those backwoods people always described as hunting deer and as savage as the Indians.

He is the agent of an expansive colonial society, rather than the symbol of a colonial culture adrift in an alien landscape and filled with a sense of peril and anxiety. He is an individualist, bent on establishing himself outside the pale of colonial authority and at times even shares the Indian's antipathy for the colonial authorities—for although the hunter as hero is never a renegade, he speaks for a class of pioneers who were viewed by Metropolitan society as approaching the status of social outcasts, rebels or renegades (1998:64).

There was apparently a very thin line between the Daniel Boones and the squatters on Indian lands so detested by all. Many of our great American heroes came from that group of despised backwoods ruffians who knew the Indians, perhaps lived with them and traded with them, marrying into a tribe and perhaps having another wife and family in the city.

Courtwright (1998) concedes New England may have not been as violent because of the religious groups who settled it were more devout and that Southern and Western Americans faced Indians and slavery and were forced to carry weapons. But that a main factor was gender:

Anyone who looks closely at the underside of American history will find mostly young and single men. They have accounted for far and away the largest share homicides, riots, drug dealing and the like. This pattern is common to all societies. But the American experience with young, single men has been unusually bad because, until recently, the country has had a higher proportion of them in the population than the European, African and Asian nations from which the immigrants came (1998:2).

Aside from the obvious nature of crime and gender were the "codes of honor," especially in the South, which made conflict resolution difficult except through violence. We all know the story of Alexander Hamilton and Aaron Burr and the famous duel, but other famous Americans were involved in "honor" killings. Button Gwinnett, one of the signers of the Constitution was killed by Lachlan McIntosh, in a duel over political issues. Georgia Governor Jackson was known as the "prince of duelists" for the 23 occasions he met opponents "on the field of honor." He had 3 duels with rival Robert Watkins including a "gouging" attempt (Cook 2005: 73).

Courtwright considered other factors in his discussion of the violent society and placed this group of criminals on the frontiers of the nation:

The mixture of demographic, cultural and social characteristics guaranteed that American society would experience unusually high levels of violence and disorder, but not that American society would be uniformly violent and disorderly. These troublesome elements: the surplus of young men, widespread bachelorhood, sensitivity about honor, racial hostility, heavy drinking, religious indifference, group indulgence in vice, ubiquitous armament and inadequate law enforcement---were conscentrated on the frontier (1998:3)...

Whether the idea of young unmarried men can be attributed to all crime for all times is another matter. Courtwright discusses the modern ghetto and places some of the frontier elements there. I would disagree and indicate the city, with its ethnic boundaries is probably a proximal equivalent of a national or ethnic border, rather than a frontier. As such it is possible he does not consider the border factor as much as others do. The whole idea of "sanctuary cities" evokes a Cave in Rock, Ohio, or Hole in the Wall, Kansas image of inner cities. But that is a discussion for another day. Slotkin's *Fatal Environment* (1998) carries this theme further quoting Frederick Law Olmstead and others who refer to the South as 5 times as violent as the North (1998:18). He adds to the mix of gender and honor and
66

restlessness the ethnic Scotch-Irish nature. Historians continue to note the puritan identity of the northeast, the Pennsylvania Dutch and the distinctly Scotch-Irish South; the latter being identified across the board as the most violent prone (1998:24). Slotkin offers the Scotch-Irish up as predestined to violence by nature of their experience vis a vis England:

Like the puritans these immigrants were likely to arrive as family units. Sometimes entire communities emigrated together. Unlike Virginia Cavalier culture, gender ration should not have made these immigrants particularly violent. Instead they brought a culture of violence with them. Two differing theories have been offered to explain this level of violence.

One theory holds that the absence of effective government created a culture in which private violence, both defensive and offensive was the only practical way to survive....Another theory argues that the Scotch-Irish culture of violence was a product of an economy based on herding caused by marginal agricultural lands (1998:27, 28).

The first theory is borne out in the use of "regulators" as mobs to clean up North and South Carolina and relies much on the nasty nature of conditions on the border areas of Scotland and England and Ireland and England, but once again we come up to the reality that's these are border wars and the border is the reason for the conflict. The second theory is perhaps more shaky, though it may have some credence in talking about the cattle days in the old west. In the south horses were nearly the only livestock readily available and horse thievery was probably the most common offense against others in the South. Horses ran free in the back woods and changed hands many times, making it hard to determine whether horses were stolen or ran away. The nature of the Cracker and even the Indian lifestyle made it easy for horses to be taken.

The herding theory also suggests these immigrants were forcibly removed from lands and banished en masse to the New World, which fits in well with the view that Britain was populating America with criminals and undesirables from their border regions. The influx of such ruffians must have caused some discomfiture among the puritans and other religious settlers. Slotkin notes that these new immigrants were used by the older more established colonists as "fencing" to keep the Indians Spanish and French out.

...Their disorderly behavior caused the Quakers in Pennsylvania to encourage these quarrelsome and prideful people to settle the back country, moving them away from polite, ordered Quaker society. More important from the standpoint of later American history, the Scotch-Irish became a highly militant shield between pacifist Quaker Pennsylvania and the Indians.

....Virginia Governor George Gooch gave guarantees to Scotch-Irishmen that they would be allowed to exercise their non-Anglican religion in the Great Valley. By doing so the Scots-Irish became a buffer between settled Virginians and the Indians (1998:30)...

Restlessness

Another factor in the equation is something that remains prevalent even today. Many Americans, some say one third are constantly on the move…changing addresses; changing jobs; changing spouses or just changing their minds. This was also the case in the country's early days. While today we think of the different opportunities available in a new job, or new town or state; in the old days there was a great expanse of land available to those willing to go and conquer it. If things got dicey, or if things just weren't working out, one could pack things in the wagon; hitch the horses and head for Ohio or Mississippi or California. America's frontier expanded because of the willingness of so many to move on. Many times people moved on to lands still owned by the Indians; further exacerbating relations with the tribes of America and inducing Washington to come up with new ways to disenfranchise the owners of these lands.

Alexis de Tocqueville made reference to the new American restlessness:

An American will build a house in which to pass his old age and sell it before the roof is on; he will plant a garden and rent it just as the trees are coming into bearing; he will clear a field and leave others to reap the harvest; he will take up a profession and leave it, settle in one place and go off elsewhere with his changing desires…At first sight there is something astonishing in this spectacle of so many lucky men restless in the midst of abundance(1839: 338).

This is the theme of **Restless Nation** (Jasper 2002), that Americans even today believe there is so much opportunity available they are willing to move at the drop of a hat. The automobile has replaced the conestoga wagon as the means to pull up roots and cavort to new dreams. Jasper sets up the winning combination of a people yearning to be free and a land available once wrested from its original owners:

They are the ones with the stamina, resources, health and the desire to get here despite immense obstacles. Many are escaping social rigidities and political oppression at home, but almost all are pulled by a wondrous image of opportunity awaiting them here (2002:4)...

In many ways the vacuum of space and freedom and wanderlust were at work in America. Jasper notes even in the more settled areas of the country restlessness abounded. In Virginia, in the late 1700s, he notes tax lists for one county showed

68

more than half of those listed moved to another county within 10 years; in more stable colonies like New England, one third were moving each decade and that, for example, turnover rate in Boston in the decades of the mid 1900s approached 50% and does so still today (2002:4).

How people got about in the early days was at walking speed. The roads and technology just were not there to carry millions of people over the mountains and great rivers. But as America emerged from the revolution, infrastructure began to improve. By 1789 the new Federal Government had studied the roads and by 1796 the coastline of the new country. In 1805 a number of road projects began: the Cumberland road from Maryland to Ohio eventually made its way to Illinois. The Federal Road from Charleston to New Orleans was in the works. Infrastructure improved as America gained new lands from Indian cessions after the French and Indian war; the opening of the Ohio valley by that same victory over the French; the Louisiana Purchase of 1803 and the cession of Florida in 1819 after Jacksons victory in the First Seminole War.

America was not just growing it was exploding and immigrants were willing to bet they had a better future for themselves and their families on the other side of the river. Those immigrants moving west carried with them not only restlessness, but a great tendency toward violence.

The first backwoods frontier along the Appalachians, just west of the first areas of colonization, was violent from the start. And not just because of warfare with displaced Indians. Its settlers were primarily Scottish, although some were from Northern Ireland and Northern England.as well as from Scotland itself (2002:110).

These groups had been involved in wars with each other in the United Kingdom and many were involved in thievery, murder and all sorts of acts of barbarity against one another. As we have seen Britain was not only sending criminals here in those days, but also prisoners of war from these countries.

The result of all this was a highly mobile group of immigrants familiar with warfare hardship, prison, criminal activity and being restless. But it did not end in Appalachia or back east. Jasper notes it produced a hardened type capable of organized behavior which answers one of my long time questions about how California was wrested from the Mexicans. Apparently 150 of these ruffians and Fremont were enough to do the job.

2005 Cook, James F., **The Governors of Georgia**, Mercer Univ. Press: Macon.

1998. Courtwright, David T, **Violent Land: Single Men and Social Disorder from the Frontier to the Inner City**, Harvard Univ. Press: Cambridge.

1839 de Tocqueville, Alexis, Henry Reeve, John Canfield Spencer, **Democracy in America,** George Adlard: N.Y.

2002 Jasper, James, **Restless Nation: Starting Over in America,** Univ. of Chicago Press: Chicago.

1998 Slotkin, Richard, **The Fatal Environment: The Myth of the Frontier in the Age of Industrialization, 1800-1890,** Univ. Of Oklahoma Press: Norman.

1995 Tracy, Susan Jean, **In the Master's Eye: Representations of Women, Blacks, and Poor Whites in Antebellum Southern Literature,** Univ of Mass. Press: Amherst.

Conestoga Wagon (1910) from:
http://conestogawagons.wordpress.com/2010/10/08/14/

Settlement After the French and Indian War

The Land beyond Philadelphia (from B.C.Calloway, et al. 1989: 48)

There were three routes available to settlers in Pennsylvania and Virginia for moving into new lands: the Mohawk-Oswego route through the Great Lakes;

Braddock's and Forbes roads, which led to Fort Du Quesne (Pittsburgh) and the Great Warriors Path that went southward across Virginia and ended up at the Cumberland Gap in Kentucky (Calloway, Reese,1989: 47). Dr. Thomas Walker surveyed and named the Cumberland Gap, ridge and river after the Duke of Cumberland son of King George II in 1750.

The new lands opened up by the defeat of the French and their Indian allies began to see settlers from Virginia in great numbers. In 1770 western Pennsylvania and western Virginia experienced an influx of new settlers, Wheeling being established. In the South, eastern Tennessee was breeched for the first time by many families as was "Western Florida," all the way to Mississippi. In 1773, Frankfort and Louisville, Kentucky were laid out and in 1774 more surveyors and hunters arrived (1989: 20).

The legend of Daniel Boone in Kentucky began in 1769, as Hashaw (2006: 7) notes:

…While trading with the Shawnee Indians in present day Kentucky, long hunter John Findley heard of a gap through the rugged Appalachians. He told Daniel Boone of North Carolina about the passage. In 1769, following an ancient buffalo trace known as the hunters trail, Boone, Findley and James Mooney set out to explore the Cumberland Gap and the nearby ridges of the Clinch….

This was the region later known as Melungia (Walden ridge, Powell's Mountain and valley), but in 1769 it was completely empty. Boone's expedition recorded absolutely no one living there at the time—no Indians, no Melungeons. The tameness of the deer convinced them that very few Cherokees even hunted there. In 1769, the Clinch was ghostly silent (2006: 7).

In 1775, Boone laid out the town and fort of Boonesborough and with the stands and fort at Harrods served to foster new immigration into Kentucky. From this point on a series of forts and stands were built as the ridges and valleys filled with new settlers.

The laws of the Virginia Colony were expanded to include the new Kentucky lands in 1776 and the first court held at Harrodsburg after the revolution in 1784, calling for an independent government for the new territory. After years of wrangling Kentucky became a state in 1791. Troubles with the Indians and the allure of trade with the Spaniards down the Mississippi had actually caused some in the new territory to consider becoming a separate country.

The first settlements in Tennessee were made in the vicinity of Fort Loudon, on the Little Tennessee, in what is now Monroe County, East Tennessee, about the year 1758. Fort Loudon

72

and Chissel were built at that time by Colonel Byrd, who marched into the Cherokee country with a regiment from Virginia. The next year war broke out with the Cherokees. In 1760, the Cherokees besieged Fort Loudon, into which the settlers had gathered their families, numbering nearly 300 persons. The latter were obliged to surrender for want of provisions, but agreeably to the terms of capitulation were to retreat unmolested beyond the Blue Ridge. When they had proceeded about 20 miles on their route, the savages fell upon them and massacred all but 9, not even sparing the women and children (Howe 1857:24).

By 1769, permanent settlements were established along the Holstein, French Broad and Watauga rivers.

Colonel Robertson and 40 North Carolina families emigrated to present day Nashville in 1780, building a fort and stands and calling it Robertson's Station. In 1784 it was renamed Nashville after General Frances Nash who died at Brandywine (25). After the Revolution people began pouring into Tennessee from Georgia, North Carolina and Virginia. In 1790 North Carolina ended any claims to what was then called the southwest territory and Knoxville became the seat of territorial government under William Blount. Finally, in 1796, Tennessee was admitted to the union as a state.

In 1790, 1300 men marched out of Cincinnati to quell Indians in the north of the Ohio River. This expedition failed and another organized attempt was decimated in 1791. In 1794, General Wayne of Revolutionary War fame annihilated the Indian opposition. The so called "Northwest" was divided into 5 counties and, by 1802 Indiana was formed; Ohio's constitution drawn up; by 1806 Michigan became a territory by congressional action, as did Illinois in 1809 (25, 26). Indiana became a state in 1816 and Illinois in 1818. A 1795 treaty with Spain gave sole navigation rights to the Americans and the Southwest territories were subdivided, forming the Mississippi Territory.

In 1750, the population of the colonies included 62% English and Welsh, Scotch-Irish 7%, who were

... not Irish but lowland Scots who had first been transplanted to Ireland. Because of severe economic depression in the early 1700s, they pulled up stakes and came to the colonies (Braddock, Reese, 1989: 49, 50)...

Germans made up 6% of the population, while another 5% was made up of highland Scots, Dutch, Irish, Swedes, Hebrews and Huguenots, Another 20% were

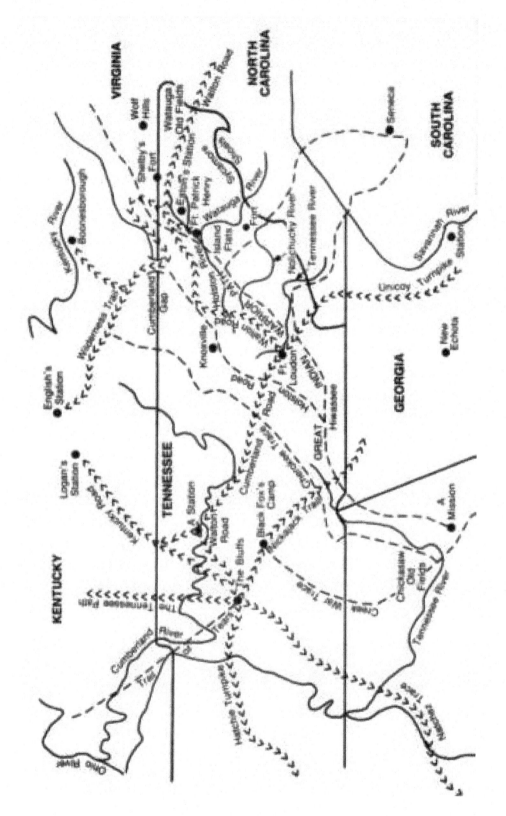

Tennessee Roads and Indian Trails (from B.C. Calloway et al.1989: 19).

African slaves. Ninety percent of these peoples spoke English and 90% lived in a rural setting.

The new settlers of Tennessee were Scotch-Irish from two Scotch-Irish counties in North Carolina and Virginia (Braddock, Reese, 1989: 156). C. D. Kelly reports:

They were nearly all from Virginian and of Scotch-Irish descent, generally poor, and threading the old Indian war path or some narrow trace blazed by hunters, with only a single pack horse, which carried all their worldly possessions (1889:155)...

Pack Mules and Horses carried goods over swamp and mountain from Charleston to Augusta and into Creek and Cherokee territories (from an old magazine on pack horses).

1857 Howe, Henry, **Historical Collections of the Great West**, George F. Tuttle: N.Y.

1989 Calloway, Brenda C. and J. Robert Reese, **America's First Western Frontier, East Tennessee,**: The Overmountain Press.

2006 Hashaw, Tim, **Children of Perdition: Melungeons And the Struggle of Mixed America,** Mercer University Press: Macon, Ga.

1889 Kelly, C.D., **Scotch-Irish in Tennessee,** in **Scotch Irish in America: Proceedings of the Scotch Irish Congress,** Robert Clark and Co.: Cincinnati

Georgia Crackers arrive with their two wheel carts in this early illustration.

Harpes brothers:

The Ohio River from inside Cave in Rock.

In 1759, two brothers immigrated from Scotland to the new colonies, settling in Orange County, North Carolina. John and William Harpe stole a horse and moved on to Virginia, where, during the revolution, they sided with roaming Tory bands bent on raping, pillaging and plundering their Whig enemies. Captain James Wood, an American regular, had previously spoiled a Harpe's attempt at kidnapping, spotted and wounded "little Harpe," John, at the Battle of King's Mountain in 1780. Again Wood saw the Harpes at the battles of Blackstock and Cowpens in 1781. After Cowpens, the two moved across the Appalachians to live with the Cherokee allies of the British; being involved in a battle at Bluff Station, near Nashville, in April, 1781 (Musgrave 1998, Ramsland 2010).

The Harpes moved further into the interior of Cherokee country. Here they killed their first civilian, Moses Doss, and settled into Nickajack Town for the next 13 years. The Chickamauga Cherokee continued to fight American settlers even after the Revolutionary war ended and a great set of banditti arose along the rapids of the Tennessee River. They were seen at the Battle of Blue Licks, in August, 1782 and again in later in Tennessee at Bledsoe's Lick. The Chickamauga Towns were destroyed by John Sevier in 1794, the Harpes brothers, with prior knowledge, escaped and settled near Knoxville where little Harpe married Sarah Rice, a local. From here the Harpes began a murderous spree, resulting in the kidnappings and the deaths of at least 40 people (Musgrave, Ramsland).

In 1795, while living near Beaver Creek, a neighbor accused the Harpes of stealing horses. The Harpes beat the rap and set off to find the person who informed the neighbor:

He may have been the man who enlightened Harpe's' neighbors about the horses' whereabouts. Why him will never be known. The Harpes took and killed him. Some days later

77

a passerby found his body floating in the Holstein River, ripped open and filled with stones —
a trademark of what would become a Harpe victim (Musgrave, 1998).

Filling a body cavity with stones and submerging it in a river became a popular way for highwaymen to dispose of bodies of their victims who seemed to "vanish without a trace!"

The brothers now took to the Wilderness Road leading to the Cumberland Gap. They killed two men from Maryland along the road and a third, from Virginia, whose body was discovered and the suspicion of the Harpes Brother's involvement arose. A posse was formed who caught up with the culprits and imprisoned them at Stanford, Kentucky. The two, leaving their women behind, escaped, killing 3 men in separate incidences. They made their way to Cave-in Rock on the Ohio River, killing three men at a campsite at Pott's Spring before finding the home of river pirate Samuel Mason and the "devils ferryman," James Ford. Here the brothers were involved with piracy of pole boats and flatboats on the Ohio River. The macabre nature of the brothers was too much for the outlaws of Cave in Rock and the Harpes were forced to leave (Musgrave, Ramsland).

In July, 1799, the killing began again: two men near Knoxville, another man near Brassel's Knob; entering Kentucky's Clinton County they killed a man at the beginning of August; A man and his son and two Triswold families and their servants were murdered near modern day Adairsville, Kentucky. The Harpes killed a black boy and a white girl before killing one of their own children near Russelville, Kentucky. Now they turned back to Tennessee with posse pursuing them. They murdered two of the Stegall family on August 20th and a third person near Henderson before a posse caught up with them. Big Harpe was shot escaping camp and tracked down where he was beheaded…his head adorning a pole on the road between Eddyville and Henderson (Musgrave, Ramsland).

Little Harpe escaped and rejoined Samuel Mason's den of thieves at Cave in Rock. Four years later Harpe and another man turned in Mason's severed head for a reward, but were recognized by earlier victims of their piracy. The were chased down and hung, their heads placed on stakes on the Natchez road as a warning to all other highwaymen (Musgrave, Ramsland).

Samuel and Isaac Mason are listed in the ***Dictionary of American Biography,*** the former as a "desperado and river pirate," the latter as a pioneer ironmaster. Samuel (1739-1803) lived in the Buffalo Township from 1779-1784 and was an elected justice and later judge there. He was born in Norfolk, Virginia. He moved to West

Virginia before entering Kentucky in 1784. By 1800, he was in Mississippi and a reward for his capture had been offered by the Governor. Samuel Mason's life is summed up this way:

> 1760s: stole horses in eastern West Virginia
> 1770s: stole supplies at Fort Henry - Wheeling
> 1780s: ran up debts in Washington County
> 1790s: robbed boats on the Ohio River
> 1800s: killed people near Natchez, Mississippi

In 1924, a book by Otto A. Rothert was published in Cleveland: ***The Outlaws of Cave in Rock,*** where both Samuel Mason and the Harpes are chronicled. Samuel Mason operated from Cave-in Rock on the Ohio River, as:

> *The cave on the Illinois side of the Ohio River was near Henderson, Kentucky. When a boat came down the river Mason gave it a warm welcome and invited the people on the boat to eat and sleep there - real hospitality. His men checked over the boat and if it contained anything valuable robbed it the next morning after it went around the bend of the river (Bell 1998).*

The idea of River piracy and later robbery along the Natchez Trace was a crime pattern which became prevalent throughout the frontier areas of America. Pirates operated on the Chattahoochee and Black Warrior rivers of Georgia and Alabama. The Tennessee River around Tescumbia was another focus of menacing pirates. In many cases pirates moved onto land, where they were called "land pirates". Mason left the Ohio River to rob travelers on the Natchez trace at a time when robbery was becoming more organized and the disappearance of travelers was commonplace.

James Ford, the "devil's ferryman" was another pirate on the Ohio River.

> *Following the decline of the pirates, another group of outlaws preyed upon travelers in the general vicinity of the Cave-in-Rock. Known as the Ford's Ferry gang, they took up where the pirates had left. Ford led this group, although from well behind the scenes. For the most part of his life, he acted to be inside the law, when in fact, he actively pursued life outside of it. For the first third of the 1800s, he served as a civic leader in both southeastern Illinois and western Kentucky. At one point he operated a tavern in Illinois, another time one of the saltworks near the Great Salt Springs or the Lower Lick as it would have been known in his time. He also served as a justice of the peace, sheriff and judge across the river. A ferry operator, he built and maintained long stretches of road on either side of his ferry just upstream from Cave-in-Rock. Even today, stretches of it can still be traveled in both states following county road signs that designate it "Ford's Ferry Road (Musgrave 1999)."*

Ford's activities brought him into contact with other well known criminals, including the Wilson gang at Cave in Rock, as well as slave stealers Lewis Kuykendall and John Hart Crenshaw. "Big Jim" was one of Crenshaw's slave stealers in this part of the country, tying him to the most famous slave stealer, John Murrell. In 1834, after years of piracy and robbery, the law caught up with Ford.

One night, in 1834, he was having dinner at the home of a Mrs. Vincent Simpson, the widow of one of Ford's men. He was eating his food at the table and someone brought him a candle and asked that he read a letter aloud for him. Using the candle as a signal, the "Regulators" outside opened fire, aiming between the logs of the cabin. Ford died with 17 bullets in his body!

For years after his death, the slaves told stories about how Jim Ford had died and "landed in Hell head first." At his funeral, attended only by his widow, a few family members, neighbors and some slaves, a terrible thunderstorm came up. Just as Ford's coffin was being lowered into the ground, lightning flashed and a deafening clap of thunder filled the air, causing one of the slaves to loose his grip on the rope holding the coffin. The box dropped into the grave head-first and wedged there at a strange angle. The heavy rain that began to fall made it impossible to move the casket, so it was covered over the way that it had fallen. This left Ford to spend eternity standing on his head (Musgrave 1999).

One of the first successful land pirates on the Natchez Trace, which brought those who had gone down river to New Orleans back up through Mississippi territory into northern Alabama and on to Memphis, was John Thompson Hare. A young dashing, handsome, well-dressed man, he was said to be cursed by the ghost of a wife he had buried alive for being unfaithful:

This is a lad who had found a way to turn his good looks to account: he made a business of marrying young girls and decamping with the dowry. He left a trail of widows up and down the river (Coates 2004: 98)…

He would make note of the size of the merchants' wallets in New Orleans and then follow them on the Natchez Trace, relieving them of their earnings. Hare operated out of a depression anomaly near the Mississippi River called the "devil's punch bowl," with several gang members involved in the same criminal intentions. He was both cruel and successful and surrounded by many ghost stories at the punch bowl and along the trace. He was captured and hanged in 1818.

John Murrell

Perhaps no man in American History achieved more in terms of organized crime before the 20th century than John Murrell. At the time he and his efforts created the most fear in a dozen states; fear of slave revolt and fear of subversive activity on a scale never before achieved by land or river pirates, Indians or any group of marauders in American history. His plans were elaborate and backed by henchmen aplenty to carry them out. For years the trees in the South were filled with men hung for their part in John Murrell's fabulous December 25, 1835 scheme to incite slave revolt and take over of the governments of several states. His life as a murderer and robber in a dozen Southern and Mid Atlantic states is only eclipsed by the size of his organization of crime and mayhem and the scale of his endeavors.

Though much of Murrell's true experience is muddled in legend or even mythology and many to this day claim it so much nonsense, the fact remains he produced a considerable legal and even vigilante reaction in nearly every city in the South in 1836. At a time when abolitionism was beginning to make some headway, but also on the heels of several slave revolts in the West Indies and Virginia, Murrel's plan caused the greatest backlash and fear of slaves to date. In many ways the great fear of Southern planters may have been expressed by secession and fomented by memories of Murrell.

John Anderson Murrell was born in 1804, in either Lunenberg, Virginia or Middle Tennessee, sources differ in opinion, but moved early to Williamson County, Tennessee. His father was an itinerant Presbyterian preacher and his mother, according to sources was a whore who taught John and a brother, William, to steal (Kirk 2002). At age 19, Murrell was fined for "riot" and 2 years later for gambling. In 1826 he was convicted of horse theft twice, receiving a one year sentence in prison.

In his Historic Blue Grass Line, Douglas Anderson tells of Murrell having been tried in Nashville on a change of venue, on May 25, 1825, on the charge of having stolen a horse from a widow in Williamson County. The verdict and judgment was that Murrell should serve twelve months' imprisonment; be given thirty lashes on his bare back at the public whipping post; that he should sit two hours in the pillory on each of three successive days; be branded on the left thumb with the letters H. T. in the presence of the Court, and be rendered infamous.

Mr. Anderson describes the branding from the statement of an eye-witness as follows: At the direction of the sheriff Murrell placed his hand on the railing around the judge's bench. With a piece of rope Horton then bound Murrell's hand to the railing. A negro brought a tinner's stove and placed it beside the sheriff. Horton took from the stove the branding iron, glanced at it, found it red hot, and put it on Murrell's thumb. The skin fried like meat. Horton held the iron on Murrell's hand until the smoke rose two feet. Then the iron was removed. Murrell stood the ordeal without flinching. When his hand was released he calmly tied a handkerchief around it and went back to the jail (Grimstead, 1998: 320-21).

Much of John Murrell's life was exposed in Virgil Stewart's Pamphlet, the highwayman apparently telling the author his life story and the many crimes he was involved in. Much of it is reminiscent of the Harpe Brothers or even Thomas Hair and reads like a modern day crime spree that never seemed to end. One small portion of it represented only a trip to Georgia but left 11 people robbed, dead or both.

I commenced traveling and making acquaintances among the speculators that I could. I went from New Orleans to Cincinnati, and from there I visited Lexington, in Kentucky. I found a speculator about 4 miles from Newport, who furnished me with a fine horse the second night after I arrived at his house. I went from Lexington to Richmond, in Virginia, and from there I visited Charleston, in the state of South Carolina; and from thence to Milledgeville, by way of Savannah and Augusta, in the State of Georgia. I made my way from Milledgeville to Williamson County, the old stomping ground. I robbed eleven men but I preached some fine sermons, and scattered some counterfeit United States paper among my brethren (Howard, 1836: 58, 59).

Perhaps one of the most famous Murrell stories is the robbery of a South Carolinian in the Cumberland area of Kentucky. Here, Murrell was traveling on horseback with his most notable associate in crime, Daniel Crenshaw of Tennessee. They met up with a man from South Carolina and decide to waylay and rob him. The story is recounted by Mark Twain in his *Life on the Mississippi (*chapter 29); Robert Coates' *The Outlaw Years* (1930) and H.R. Howard's *History of Virgil A. Stewart* (1836), which continues the story:

My self and a fellow by the name of Crenshaw gathered four good horses, and started for Georgia. We got in company with a young South Carolinian just before we reached Cumberland Mountain, and Crenshaw soon knew all about his business. He had been to Tennessee to buy a drove of hogs, but when he got there pork was dearer than he had calculated, and he declined purchasing. We concluded he was a prize. Crenshaw winked at me; I understood his idea. Crenshaw had traveled the road before, but I never had; we had traveled several miles on the mountain, when we passed near a great precipice; just before we passed it, Crenshaw asked me for my whip, which had a pound of lead in the butt; I handed it to him, and he rode up by the side of the South Carolinian, and gave him a blow on the side of the head, and tumbled him from his horse; we lit from our horses and fingered his pockets; we got twelve hundred and sixty-two dollars. Crenshaw said he knew of a place to hide him, and gathered him under the arms, and I by his feet, and conveyed him to a deep crevice in the brow of the precipice, and tumbled him into it; he went out of sight. We then tumbled in his saddle, and took his horse with us, which was worth two hundred dollars. We turned our course for South Alabama, and sold our horses for a good price. We frolicked for a week or more, and were the highest larks you ever saw. We commenced sporting and gambling, and lost every cent of our money (64, 65).

MURDER OF WOODS, THE SOUTH CAROLINIAN

From: Life and Adventures of John Murrell, H.R. Howard, 1847.

In yet another story, the nature of Murrell's clan and its association with law enforcement and other higher ups in society is that of the posse ambushed by his men along the Mississippi River:

A most atrocious and diabolical wholesale murder and robbery had been committed on the Arkansas side. The crew of a flatboat had been murdered in cold blood, disemboweled, and thrown in the river, and the boat-stores appropriated among the perpetrators of the foul deed. The Murrell Clan was charged with the inhuman and devilish act. Public meetings were called in different parts of the country to devise means to rid the country and clear the woods of the Clan, and to bring to immediate; punishment the murderers of the flatboat men. In Covington a campaign was formed to that end, under the command of Maj. Hockley and Grandville D. Searcey, and one, also formed in Randolph, under the command of Colonel Orville Shelby. A flatboat, suited to the purpose, was procured, and the expedition consisting of some eighty or an hundred men, well armed, with several day's rations, floated out from Randolph, and down to the landing where wholesale murder had been committed. Their place of destination was Shawnee Village, some six or more miles from the Mississippi. Where the sheriff of the county resided. They were first to require of the sheriff to put the offenders under arrest and turn them over to be dealt with according to law. To the Shawnee Village the expedition moved in single file, along a tortuous trail through the thick cane and jungle, until within a few miles of the village, when a shrill whistle at the head of the column startled the whole line. Answered by the sharp click! click! click! of the cocking of the rifles in the hands of Clansmen. In ambush, to the right flank of the moving file, and within less than a dozen yards.

The chief of the Clan stepped out at the head of the expedition, and in a stentorian voice commanded the expedition to halt, saying:

"We have man for man; move forward another step and a rifle bullet will be sent through every man under your command."

A parley was had, when more than man for man of the Clansmen rose from their hiding places in the thick cane, with their guns at present. The expedition had fallen into a trap; the Clansmen had not been idle in finding out the movements against them across the river. Doubtless many of them had been in attendance at the meetings held for the purpose of their destruction. The movement had been a rash one, and nothing was left to be done but to adopt the axiom that "prudence is the better part of valor." The leaders of the expedition were permitted to communicate with the sheriff, who promised to do what he could in having the offenders brought to justice; but alas for Arkansas and justice! The Sheriff himself was thought to be in sympathy with the Clan. And law was in the hands of the Clansmen. The expedition retraced their steps. Had it not been so formidable and well known by the Clansmen, every member of it would have found his grave in the Arkansas swamp." (Quoted from Kirk, 2002: and Botkin, p. 214)

John's brother William was listed as a druggist, living in Cincinnati, while another brother lived in Sumter, South Carolina. Most of Murrell's life and history were documented and published in 1835 by Virgil Stewart, A Lawrenceville, Georgia man who infiltrated Murrell's gang, as he says, to learn the whereabouts of three slaves stolen from Parson John Henning. Stewart claimed to have taken notes from Murrell's own trailside confessions to murder, horse theft and slave stealing. In 1835 Stewart published **A History of the Detection, Conviction, Life and Designs of John A. Murel, the Great Western Land Pirate** (1835, Cincinnati). Here Stewart outlined a very detailed plan for slave insurrection the burning and taking of towns and the robbery of many by a well-organized "mystic clan" of Murrell followers in a dozen states.

Stewart's Pamphlet, deemed by many as fiction, or even a response to a growing abolitionist movement, was well received in the south and created a great panic among slave owners and the public alike. Fears of a slave revolt had been fueled by the Stono revolt in the West Indies, Nat Turner and a recent affair in Virginia in 1832. Stewart described some of the particulars of the clan and their plan:

The clan are all not of the same grit; there are two classes. The first class keep all their designs and the extent of their plans to themselves. For this reason all who would be willing to join us are not capable of managing our designs and there would be a danger of their making disclosures that would lead to our destruction of our designs before they were perfected. This Class is what we call the Grand Council.

The second class are those whom we trust with nothing except that which they are immediately concerned with. We have them to do what we are not willing to do ourselves. They always stand between us and danger. For a few dollars we can get one of them to run a Negro or a fine horse to some place where we can go and take possession of it without any danger: and there is no danger in this fellow then; for he has become the offender, and of course he is bound to secrecy. This class is what we term the Strikers. We have about 400 of the Grand Council and near six hundred and fifty strikers (116)...

The Grand Council is made up of citizens from a number of states: 61 from Tennessee; 47 from Mississippi; 47 from Arkansas; 25 from Kentucky; 27 from Missouri; 28 from Alabama; 33 from Georgia; 35 South Carolina; 31 from North Carolina; 21 from Virginia; 27 from Maryland; 16 from Florida; 31 from Louisiana and 18 "at large" members. The clan was mixed with members of another group of discounted individuals known as "steam doctors." These quacks had been scamming the American public for years over the cures of disease they associated with using steam. In 1829, the Ohio State Medical Society excommunicated one Dr. Shang and all of his adherents in what they termed the "Thompsonian plan" of healing and the "steam Confederation" that followed it. Two of the first leaders of the Council were Cotton and Saunders of Mississippi, both "steam doctors "and "Thompsonian Empirics":

July 4th, 1835 Confession of Joshua Cotton to authorities in Mississippi:

I acknowledge my guilt and I was one of the principal men in bringing about the conspiracy. I am one of the Murrell clan, a member of what we called the Grand Council. I counseled with them twice, once near Columbus, this Spring and another time on an island in the Mississippi River. Our object in undertaking to excite the Negroes to rebellion, was not for the purpose of liberating them, but for plunder. I was trying to carry into effect the plan of Murrell as laid down in Stewart's pamphlet. Blake's boy Peter had his duty Assigned him, which was, to let such negroes into the secret as he could trust, generally the most daring scoundrels; the Negroes on most all the large plantations knew of it; and from the exposure of our plans in said pamphlet, we expected the citizens would be on their guard at the time mentioned, being the 25th of December next; and we determined to take them by surprise, and try it on the night of the fourth of July, and it would have been tried tonight (and perhaps may yet) but for the detection of our plans (247-48).

One of Murrell's conspirators was already in jail in Mississippi awaiting execution. Alonzo Phelps was a notorious killer and highwayman on the Natchez Trace. Once implicated, Phelps requested the Governor give him time to write his memoirs, also claiming he had planned to break jail and join the insurrection Murrell had planned. Others began confessing, like William Earle, before a Justice of the Peace:

My brother John told me there was going to be a rising of the Negroes; and Boyd said to me about the 12th of June, we can live without work; there was to be a rising of Negroes of Negroes on the fourth of July, and Cotton and Saunders were to be captains; that he was to go to Natchez with his company. Boyd and Saunders told me the same one day, and said that men by the names of Lofton and Donnely were engaging Negroes to enter into the conspiracy (257)...

It was by no means safe for Stewart to make all the accusations covered in his pamphlet. Many of the Council and some of the strikers were powerful men in their states. Many attempts were made on Murrell's life while he was imprisoned and Stewart spent the rest of his life looking over his shoulder for men like Matthew Clanton and Isham Medford who actually wrote a pamphlet opposing Stewart's story. There was considerable fertile ground for discounting the revelation as sensationalism, anti-abolitionist propaganda or complete mythology. Many in the Northeast considered the mass justice which followed as "more lynchings down south" (Natchez C. & J.: 3:3:1837).

There were numerous grounds for the mythology charge, with respect to Murrell's clan. The killing of the South Carolinian can be traced to an actual event involving Bennet Dula, a North Carolinian who killed a South Carolinian on Cumberland Mountain in 1833 (oddly enough the GF of Tom Dula of folk song fame). Another example is that of the ambush mentioned above, of which there were several versions, an indicator of questionable veracity.

Committees were formed in the states involved to deal with the conspirators. Trials were held and both whites and negroes were executed by hanging. Those included:

...The list of white men executed on confession, or negro testimony, or circumstantial evidence, were Joshua Cotton, a steam doctor from Tennessee, who made a confession that he was one of the grand council of Murel's gang, and that the statements of Stewart's book were correct; William Saunders, also of Tennessee, a friend of Cotton's; Albe Dean, a Mississippian of two years' residence from Connecticut, who was hung on the word of Cotton and Saunders; A. L. Donovan, of Maysville KY who was apparently a contraband trader with the negroes, and was accused of being an abolitionist; Ruel Blake, implicated by Cotton; Lee Smith of Hinds County, from Tennessee, implicated by Cotton; William Benson, who had worked for Blake; William Earle, of Warren County, being taken committed suicide; John Earle, who made a confession was turned over to the committee at Vicksburg...(Webb, 1922: 254).

Many Northerners as well as Southerners, moved by the reaction and panic in the wake of Murrell's exposition, recalled the days of "regulators" and speedy justice in the back country of America in the 1700s. *The Jackson Freetrader* of August, 1836 noted:

Another bloody affray, is a sound which often greets our ears. The affair at Vicksburg, the affair at Manchester, the affair at Rodney, other places, and lastly a most horrid affair at Fayette, have followed each other in quick succession, as to make every friend to law and order shudder, lest an entire destruction of rational liberty should be the consequence of these repeated violations of law.

Most Southerners hailed Stewart as a brave defender of America's interests. He was welcomed as a hero by the Mississippi Legislature; the New Orleans City Council republished his pamphlet, noting its truth "cannot now be denied"; The Legislature of South Carolina voted Stewart a reward for his services; and most newspapers in the South gave the whole affair intense and favorable coverage. The Story saturated literature in America for a hundred years, which is remarkable since most Americans today have never heard of John Anderson Murrell.

Murrell, himself was arrested and according to 1841-42 prison records in the Tennessee archives, sentenced to 10 years for slave harboring and reported to jail on August 17, 1834. *The Tennessee Democrat* on November 24, 1844 announced Murrell's release from prison in April, 1844 and his death in November. He was buried at a 45 degree angle from East west according to some sources and was disinterred soon after the ceremony and his head cut off and taken (Kirk, 2002). At this point the mythology of John Murrell began to form. As stated above Northerners believe Murrell's legend was a response to Abolitionism, while Southerners swear to his impact and they responded with many hangings, litigation and vigilante activity.

Murrell's ubiquitous nature is also in question…he is reported to have operated in a dozen states and, after becoming a popular subject, many new places are added to the list:

Even more in debate is the location of his hideout and operations base. Once again, Jackson or Madison County are bandied about, but other places include Natchez, Mississippi in an odd depression on a bluff called Devil's Punch Bowl, Tunica County, Mississippi, the Neutral Ground in Louisiana, and even the tiny Island 37, part of Tipton County, Tennessee. One record, a genealogical note, even places him as far east as Georgia; in fact Atlanta historian Franklin Garrett makes it clear there was a lawless district in that town named for him, "Murrell's Row" in the 1840s. Because Murrell has come to symbolize Natchez Trace lawlessness in the antebellum period, it's understandable that his "hideouts" (whether there were any hideouts or not) have been said to have been located at most of the well-known areas of particular lawlessness along the Natchez Trace (State master Encyclopedia).

An obituary for Virgil Stewart's nephew states "…***One of their hangouts in Georgia was at Jug Tavern, now Winder, county seat of Bartow County,*** (Georgia)…" The history of Forsyth County, Georgia includes a curious section on the comings and goings of the Murrelites to and from the Keyes House. Interestingly, the history states Murrell used the Woolly's Ford hideout and operated under the name **Guy Rivers** "…*An Etowah River cave, utilized for clandestine meetings of the Murrell gang, was known as Guy Rivers' cave*…(Bramblett, 2002: 26)." The property was later developed into a mill complex in 1855 and now lies beneath Lake Lanier, Atlanta's water supply. How Murrell became friends with the Woolys at Keyhole House is not explained.

Grimstead (1998: 149) is another who believes Murrell's life is overexaggerated. He points out Stewarts claim to have taken notes with nothing but a needle and his saddle, or pants or portmanteau to make depressions on is highly unlikely. How he recalled 450 names given him is beyond belief. Furthermore, Stewart did not receive the formal education one would associate with a writer, growing up without means. The pamphlet was published under a pseudonym, Walton, not Stewart and the whole story embellished by such sensationalist media as the Police Gazette. Grimstead 1998: 149) one Mississippian, John H. L. Claiborn had his doubts about all of it, referring to the affairs as **"…*one of the most extraordinary and lamentable hallucinations of our time…*"**

SKELETONS IN A CAVE.

Searcher Found Bones Believed to Have Been Left by Outlaws.

LOUISVILLE, Nov. 3.—A young man named Drane was exploring a cave near Constantine, Breckinridge County, and at a depth of sixty-five feet he found a room ten or twelve feet square, and in it considerable deposits which had fallen from the top. In scratching around with sticks, he found seven human skulls, well preserved, and an eighth one, partly decayed. At least a barrel full of human bones was taken out. No attempt was made to see whether the deposits, which were three or four feet deep, contained any other skeletons. It is believed the bones were those of victims of John A. Murrell's gang.

NY Times, Nov. 4th, 1896

Woodiwiss (2001: 56) mentions Murrells head being displayed at fairs for 10 cents a look. Other myths include the lone pine tree: Murrellites would plant a single pine in the front yard to indicate a safe haven for any gang member (Rascoe, 2004: 50). Finally, John Murrell's capture even has its mythology, Campbell (2002), recounts the tale of the Nevel family who claimed Murrell stopped at their house for breakfast and was captured there at Providence Plantation near Tchula, Mississippi. Why the reward was not taken for the capture isn't mentioned in his sources.

OLD BOLDING HOUSE

Another view showing lantern hole through which signals were flashed by Murrell or members of his gang to another "signal-tower" house on a hill a mile or so away.

Old Bolding House, Hall County, Georgia historical photograph collection, Hall County Library System.

Disregarding the nay sayers, Southerners took Murrell's threat as serious. Even Abraham Lincoln had something to say about the whole affair in a speech at the Young Men's Lyceum of Springfield, Illinois on January 27, 1838:

In the Mississippi case, they first commenced by hanging the regular gamblers: a set of men, certainly not following for a livelihood, a very useful, or very honest occupation; but one which, so far from being forbidden by the laws, was actually licensed by an act of the Legislature, passed but a single year before. Next, negroes, suspected of conspiring to raise an insurrection, were caught up and hanged in all parts of the State: then, white men, supposed to be leagued with the negroes; and finally, strangers, from neighboring States, going thither on business, were, in many instances, subjected to the same fate. Thus went on this process of hanging, from gamblers to negroes, from negroes to white citizens, and from these to strangers; till, dead men were seen literally dangling from the boughs of trees upon every roadside; and in numbers almost sufficient, to rival the native Spanish moss of the country, as a drapery of the forest.

Now books began to appear with Murrell as the main character. In 1847, **Female Land Pirate, the Awful, Mysterious and Horrible Disclosures of Amanda Bannoris** was written by a woman whose husband, Richard Bannoris was a Murrellite. Amanda's criminal history landed her in jail in New Orleans where she committed suicide, leaving the manuscript for later publishing. This helped give rise to a whole series of books with women as highwaymen or land pirates (Cimbala, 2002: 30).

Smith's **River of Dreams** (2007), explains the torrent of books to come on secret societies and **Schemes of Deeper Villainy**:

The three components essential to the emergence of the Mississippi underworld in popular fiction were established in 1835: the Murrell conspiracy and its connection to slavery; the Vicksburg lynchings; the equivocal Mississippi gambler (161)…

When coupled to the already popular European urban mystery genre, the Murrell story was incorporated worldwide. Louis Borges' **The Cruel Redeemer Lazarus Morell** describes the villain in Murrellian terms:

I heard his edifying words and saw the tears come to his eyes. I knew he was a fornicator, a nigger-stealer, and a murderer in the sight of the Lord, but tears came to my eyes too (1998:8)…

The two styles melded appropriately around secret tunnels, hiding places, hidden societies and criminal activity. The deep recesses of the city found their counterparts on steamboats and at cave in rock or any of a dozen places along the Mississippi.

…Such tropes resonated along the panoramic, mazy, sinister Mississippi. River towns produced the most extraordinary antebellum American variations on these established themes. Melville was aware of the genre in **The Confidence Man,** *a novel that shared thematic and tonal qualities with mystery novels. He transformed the* **Fidele** *from a Mississippi steamboat into its own urban mystery (Smith, 2007)…*

90

Whether or not Murrell was mostly hype and fiction or the most notorious highwayman ever, his mark on American History is indelible. He helped create an entire genre of literature in America…the **border romance**. The most famous of these border romance writers was William Gilmore Simms, who turned the Murrell experience into many back country soap operas with characters interacting not only with poor whites; intruders in Indian lands and highwaymen…but Murrell himself. *Guy Rivers* is the lawyer turned bad-man in the wild, wild-west of Northern Georgia. Ralph Colleton is the planter's son who meets up with him on the trail in the back country, escaping his own demise at the hands of a well organized Murrellian gang, the **Pony Club.** Simms follows up with *Richard Hurdis (*1838 and probably derived form the name Buck Hurd, another famous Negro stealer in Georgia's frontier); *Border Beagles* (1840): *Beauchampe* (1842) and *Charlemont* (1842).

Simms' border romance genre comes from a melding of his previous works with the new frontier in the deep-south. His novels deal almost exclusively with the poor white back country class which is always bested by the planter or his stand in hero, the yeoman. It is a natural outgrowth of the Daniel Boone imagery of earlier American novels transported to the rough and tumble Southern frontier where there are still highwaymen, Indians, slaves and wide open back country. Tracy elaborates on this transition from one villain to another:

The poor white is contrasted to the planter and the poor, virtuous and disciplined yeoman farmer, who ' knows his place' in Southern society and serves as a patriot soldier in war and as a solid citizen in peace. In comparison, then, poor whites are life's losers. They have capitulated to vice, corruption and licentiousness early in life and have fallen into a criminal web to which there is no escape….

Throughout this literature, the poor white male is described as a 'dark and swarthy' ruffian who lives in a dilapidated hovel without furniture, curtains or a neat garden plot, thereby reflecting his lack of industriousness and a lack of self esteem (1995: 185)**…**

Born out of the Revolutionary War era, the poor white villain is always cast with the British, as in John Pendleton Kennedy's *Horseshoe Robinson* (1835) and *Swallow Barn* (1832):

…Like Simms, Kennedy is fascinated by the poor white gang; that is bands of poor white men who rob the planter aristocracy and serve as British Mercenaries (Tracy, 1995: 187) …

Simms equates poor whites to criminals, as in his *Forayers* (1855) and *Eutaw* (1856). The Jeff Rhodes gang, which engages in criminal acts in these books, is like those in his other books on Murrell and Slave stealer Buck Hurd and the Pony Club. In fact poor white attacks on the planter class become a subplot in many of the border romances. As Tracy (1995) notes, the civilized nature of the planter class under attack by licentious backwoods whites is a major theme in these post Revolution novels:

(William Alexander) Caruthers, in **Knights of the Golden Horseshoe** *(1842), Kennedy, in* **Horseshoe Robinson** *(1835), and Simms, in* **The partisan** *(1835) and* **Mellichampe** *(1836), created a series of gentleman military commanders and yeoman scouts to answer the egalitarianism of the Northern middle class and to assert the natural superiority of the planter class. At the core of these stereotypical stories lies a conservative vision of masculinity and an argument about what makes the planter class superior to all others (197)…*

By moving the scenery for the Wild West to the southern frontier, Simms is able to take advantage of a new *border area.* He tours Georgia, especially the gold producing areas where the plot not only includes planters versus poor white gangs, but also Indians and runaway slaves. He adapts the Murrell experience in Mississippi to the Chattahoochee River and the real *Guy Rivers* gangs who operate on it: the *Pony Club.*

Murrell Meets Captain Slick, from Frank Triplett (1885).

August 12, 1834, *Banner and Nashville Whig*,

1847 Barclay, Erastus, **The Female Land Pirate: or Awful, Mysterious and Horrible Disclosures of Amanda Bannoris,** E.E. Barclay.

1998 Bell, Raymond, **Raymond Bell Anthology, Geneology in Washington County, Pa.,** @http://www.chartiers.com/raybell/1995-mason.html.

Borges, Jorge Luis, Translated by Andrew Hurley, **Collected Fiction: the Cruel Redeemer, Lazarus Morrell,**Viking Press, NY.

2002 Bramblett, Annette, **Forsyth County: History Stories**, Arcadia Publishing: Mt. Pleasant, South Carolina.

2002 Campbell, Will D., **Providence**, Baylor Univ. Press: Waco.

1845 Caruthers, William Alexander, **The Knights of the Golden Horse-shoe**, Univ. of North Carolina Press: Greensboro.

1998 Chapman, Herb and Muncie Chapman, *Wiregrass Country*, Pineapple Press: Sarasota

2002 Cimbala, Paul Alan and Randall M. Miller, **An Uncommon Time: The Civil War and the Northern Home Front,** Fordham University Press: Bronx, NY

1860 Claiborne, John Francis Hamtramck, **Life and Correspondence of John A. Quitman Claiborn,** Harper Brothers Publishers: N.Y.

1930 Coates, Robert, **The Outlaw Years: The History of Land Pirates of the Natchez Trace,** Kessinger Publishing: Whitefish, Montana.

1877, *April 13, Columbia Herald and Mail,*

1962 Daniels, Jonathon, **The Devil's Backbone**, McGraw Hill: N.Y.

1872 Drake, Francis S**. Dictionary of American Biography 1828-1885,** James R. Osgood and Co.: Boston.

1847 Foote, Henry A., **Casket of Reminiscences**, Chronical Publishing co.: Wash. D.C.

1978, January, *Frontier Times,*

1946 Gallimore, Robert, **The Dowland Papers**, transcribed by*:* Joe Stout,Vicki Shaffer, Mary Carol, for Ancestry.Com.

1998 Grimstead, David, **American Mobbing, 1828-1861 Toward Civil War**, Oxford University Press: Oxford, UK.

2009 Henry, William Edward, **The Great Western Land Pirate, Again An Essay Occasioned by a Diary Entry of Private Tabler,** **@http://www.51illinois.org/page3.html**

1836 Howard, H. R., *History of Virgil A. Stewart*, Harper: N.Y.

August, 1836, *Jackson Freetrader.*

1835 Kennedy, John Pendleton, **Horse-Shoe Robinson**, Carey, Lee and Blanchard: Philadelphia.

1832 Kennedy, John Pendleton, **Swallow Barn**, Carey, Lee and Blanchard: Philadelphia.

2002 Kirk, Lowell**, John A. Murrell**, @http://www.tellicotimes.com/Murrell.html.

1857 Melville, Herman, **The Confidence Man**, Longman, Brown, Green, Longman's and Roberts: London.

July 9, 1999 Musgrave, John, **James Ford: 'Satan's Ferryman' and 'Outlaw of Cave-in-Rock',** American Weekend.@http://www.illinoishistory.com/jamesford.html.

October 23, 1998 Musgrave, John, **Frontier Serial Killers: The Harpes**, *American Weekend, Benton, Evening News, et al.@* http://www.illinoishistory.com/harpes.html

March 3, 1837, *Natchez Courier and Journal,*

1981 Penick, James L., **The Great Western Land Pirate: John Murrell in Legend and History,** Univ. of Missouri Press: Columbia, Mo.

1888 Phelan, James, *History of Tennessee,*: Houghton-Mifflin and Co.: N.Y., Boston.

1847 **The Life and Adventures of John A. Murrell, the Great Western Land Pirate,** *National Police Gazette,* eds., H. Long & Brothers: New York.

1848 **The Pictorial Life and Adventures of John A. Murrel.** *Police Gazette,* Editor T. B. Peterson & Bros.; Philadelphia.

2010 Katherine Ramsland, **America's First Serial Kllers, @** http://www.trutv.com/library/crime/serial_killers/history/harpe_brothers/9.html

2004 Rascoe, Burton, **Belle Starr: The Bandit Queen**, Univ. of Nebraska Press: Lincoln.

1924(2002) Rothert, Otto A., **The Outlaws of Cave-in Rock,** Southern Illinois University Press: Carbondale.

1855 Smith, T. Marshall, **Legends of the War of Independence**, J.F. Brennan, Publisher.

2007 Smith, Thomas Rhys, **River of Dreams: Imagining the Mississippi before Mark Twain,** LSU Press: Baton Rouge.

Simms, William Gilmore:
Guy Rivers *(1834)* Harper and Brothers: N.Y.
The Partisan *(1835)* Belford Clark and Co.: Chicago and N.Y.
Mellichampe *(1836),* Belford Clark and Co.: Chicago and N.Y.
Richard Hurdis *(1838)* Belford Clark and Co.: Chicago and N.Y.
Border Beagles *(1840)* Donohue Henneberry and Co.: Chicago.
Beauchampe *(1842)* S.A. Maxwell and Co.: Chicago.
Charlemont *(1842)* Belford Clarke and Co.: Chicago and N.Y.
The Forayers *(1855)* Redfield: N.Y.
Eutaw *(1856)* Redfield: N.Y.

November 4, 1896, **Skeletons in a Cave,** *NY Times.*

2003-2005 **StateMaster - Encyclopedia: John Murrell (bandit),** @www.statemaster.com/encyclopedia/John-Murrell (bandit).

2009 Stout, Joe, **John Murrell: Notorious Outlaw**, for Ancestry.Com.

1844, November 23, *Tennessee Democrat.*

1995 Tracy, Susan Jean, **In the Master's Eye: Representations of Women, Blacks and Poor Whites in Antebellum Southern Literature,** Univ. of Mass. Press: Amherst.

1885 Triplett, Frank, History, **Romance and Philosophy of Great American Crimes and Criminals, N.D. Thompson Publishing Co.: NY.**

1920 Twain, Mark, **Tom Sawyer**, Harper and Brothers Publishers: N.Y. and London.

1917 Twain, Mark, **Life on the Mississippi,** Harper and Brothers Publishers: N.Y. and London.

1835 Walton, Augustus Q. (Stewart, Virgil A.), **A History of the Detection, Conviction, Life and Designs of John A. Murel: the Great Western Land Pirate,** U.P. James, Publisher.

1922 Webb, George McGruder Batty, **History of Rome and Floyd County,** Webb and Vary: Atlanta.

Friday, Nov. 29, 1844, **West Tennessee Whig**, vol. 3 no. 5, Jackson, Tennessee

2001 Woodiwiss, Michael, **Organized Crime and American Power: A History,** Univ. of Toronto Press: Toronto.

2006 Wray, John, **Canaan's Tongue**, Random House: N.Y.

The Pony Club

While the Harpes and Murrell were busy robbing and killing along the Ohio and Mississippi Rivers, another organized group of criminals arose in Georgia and wreaked havoc for many years on Indians and whites traveling the roads of the peach state. Rather than kill for slave stealing or highway robbery, they set their sights on horses. There are several reasons why horses are easier to steal than slaves. Horses are impersonal and don't think of getting away; they are portable like slaves; everyone wants a horse and of course horses don't shoot back.

Trial of a Horse Thief, Jno. Mulvan; Clay, Cosack & Company lith., Buffalo and Chicago, 1877.

Stealing horses had a long tradition in the colonies and by the early 1800s, had become big business. It had a long history in the frontier for several reasons. Horses represented movable assets for people with no land ownership, Crackers and Indians. To Indians, getting guns had been a priority: the Westos were one of the first tribes to have muskets and they immediately began raiding and enslaving Cherokees. The Cherokee learned and got their own guns and wanted horses. Horses roamed freely in the back country and grazed at will, while the planters and yeomen tended to pen all their livestock. The horse population rose dramatically as most early settlers tended to be single men with pack horses and no wagons or oxen. Horse theft soon became rife especially among the Indians. McLoughlin and
97

Conser (1984), in **Cherokee Ghost Dance,** discuss the evolution of horse thievery among the Cherokee.

...while horse stealing had its roots in tribal warfare, in which booty taken from the enemy was always a sign of prowess and bravery, it also stemmed from the fact that Cherokee owned their land in common. Since no man could buy or sell land as a means of enriching himself, the prime source of frontier enterprise was closed to them...Hence movable or personal property became more important to them than to a white man as a means of investment or growing wealth once they were told to become capitalists (32)...

Land could not be sold; cows moved too slowly and could not be hidden; and slaves could fight back or inform authorities. Another reason Indians became involved in horse theft was the depletion of game. Coming home from a hunting trip without game was nothing to look forward to. Unable to hunt, the adventure and bravado of stealing horses became popular with the younger set of Indians, much to the chagrin of older tribesmen who considered it dishonorable. Furthermore, horse stealing had the inherent dangers of a raiding party with the real expectation of fighting. Indian braves became horse thieves to satisfy a once respected notion of tribal warriors defeating their enemies. Senior tribe members looked on in disgust as more and more braves took up this fake bravery. The braves themselves preferred horse thievery to hoeing a garden day in and day out (McLoughlin and Conser, 1984: 32).

The Indians had a particular system for stealing horses. Horses stolen in the east would be traded in the west and vice versa. McLoughlin and Conser discussed the Indian system:

A detailed study of horse stealing on the frontier would reveal a great deal about its economic development and difficulties. For example, it seems evident in the 1790s the Cherokees stole horses in the West and bartered them for goods in the East where the market was better, while in the early nineteenth century the need for specie on the frontier made it more profitable to steal horses in the East and trade them in the West. "This business is carried on by white people and Indians in combination", wrote (Tennessee Governor) Blount in 1792, "and as soon as a horse is stolen he is conveyed through the Indian nation to North or South Carolina or Georgia and in a short time to the principal towns on the seaboard for sale so as to prevent recovery..." (1984: 33)

Bureau of Indian Affairs chief Meigs is also quoted 15 years later, indicating the horse stealing trade is moving west to east:

...The number of horses carried thro' and into this (Cherokee) country is almost incredible-from Georgia, both the Carolinas and Kentucky (McLoughlin and Conser, 1984: 33).

In either case the Indians found themselves between the eastern and western settlements and used their position to great advantage.

The Cherokee were not the only Indians stealing horses. Menawa of the Creeks' name means "horse stealer." The Creeks found themselves between the French and Spanish and the English and exploited that position not only in terms of politics, but also in terms of selling stolen horses and slaves. Nor was horse stealing mainly an Indian adventure. It was obvious early on the poor whites were involved in the enterprise. In many cases they worked with the Indians to steal horses:

Horse stealing, of course, was not merely a symptom of the breakdown in Indian culture; it was so endemic upon the American frontier, that it obviously represents the breakdown of European culture on its outer fringes. Horse stealing provided one of the few areas of frontier life in which Indians and whites worked harmoniously together sometimes in trying to catch the thieves, sometimes in belonging to the pony clubs constituted to do the stealing (McLoughlin and Conser, 1984: 31).

Cherokee horse theft from white border settlers usually resulted in the Federal Government repaying the victim from the Indians fund for land sales and treaties. In some cases, Cherokees stole from prominent wealthy Indians like James Vann, who sparked the use of "light horse patrols" in the lower towns, but who was undoubtedly killed by those who wished to continue the practice.

Pony Club: a club or set of individuals who deal with horses, but it doesn't mean today what it did in 1827. Like the Murrel Gang, the Pony Club had members in various parts of Georgia who would facilitate the movement of "hot property," mostly stolen horses, from county to county and state to state. These clubs have been called offshoots of the Murrell Gang, Tories, Indians and a number of other things and seem to have taken on lives of their own. They operated exclusively in Georgia Alabama, Tennessee and to some extent South Carolina, from about 1814 until the 1840s and were found mainly in the frontier areas from Hall County to Muscogee County, Georgia, in Indian Country, but also mentioned in Jackson and Bibb Counties as well as along the old Federal Road to New Orleans. Early travelers to the area recorded instances involving these horse thieves. In Freeman's history of Stone Mountain, Georgia, he notes the Goulding party of explorers had a run in with the club:

Goulding's party stopped under a cavern formed by a pile of boulders to escape the heat and eat lunch....At their camp that evening, they had a surprise visit from two members of the "pony club," a gang of horse thieves who specialize in stealing riding stock from unwary travelers. The camp was prepared for such an eventuality, however, and the two rode off with a shot from Scipio's gun (1997: 27).

99

All Pony Clubs seemed to have the same structure and follow the same rules that we saw for the Murrell Gang. Friends and family in different parts of the country handled stolen horses or cattle or whatever for a common cause, the resale of the property. Like slave stealing, property would be passed along and alibis for those suspected provided by a close network of individuals bent on making money the fast easy way. Even as far away as Illinois, groups worked along these same lines. Wildwood (1890:) wrote about an Illinois Lawyer and his run in with a group of horse thieves. A man's wife comes to his office and begs the lawyer to represent her husband who has gotten mixed up with horse thieves:

Ah, sir," said she," a better man at heart than my George never lived, but he liked cards and drink, and 1 am afraid they made him do what he never would have done if he had not drank. I fear it can be proved that he had the horse; he didn't steal it, another stole it and passed it to him.... The gang, of which he was not a member, had persuaded him to take the horse. He knew that it was stolen, and like a fool acknowledged it when he was arrested. Worse still, he had trimmed the horse's tail and mane to alter his appearance, and the opposition could prove it (148-150)…

He was able to get the man off with a light sentence but within a few months saw the woman again at a rest stop on the Shawneetown road. He had picked up fellow travelers along the road and the woman identified them as members of the horse thief gang her husband had gotten in with earlier. He was able to extricate himself from their company and having sabotaged their wagon axles, made it to safety.

There are several theories on the development of the Pony Club in Georgia. That they were related to the Murrell Gang is hard to prove; none of the Council for Murrell in Georgia are listed as members of any Pony Club. There are several instances wherein Murrell is said to have availed himself of hideouts in Barrow, Fulton and Forsythe counties. He is even mentioned in association with the history of Jackson County, at a place called Tallapahoo:

There Britt Langworth, believed to be a member of Murrell's Pony Club dressed in fine broadcloth and sparkling with jewels, was drowned in time of high water...(Wilson and White, 1914: 53).

The Murrell theory doesn't hold up well because the pony club seems to predate his "mystical clan," has an entirely separate set of perpetrators and seems to be germane to Georgia mainly: *If anything, it is more likely the passage of time has telescoped people's memories as it so often does, so that events that are unrelated become mixed together.* Any incident resulting in murder, cattle rustling, slave stealing or horse theft could be attributed to Murrell or the Pony Club or both.

100

One theory, offered by archeologist and ethnohistorian, Larry Meier, of the Greater Atlanta Archeology Society, is that the pony boys began as cut throats in Florida during the Revolutionary War and as a result of actions by the Spanish Governor, were forced up the Chattahoochee River to Sandtown, Georgia, in then Dekalb, now Fulton County. This frontier faced Creek and Cherokee Indian lands at their boundary, Buzzard's Roost Island, a mile north of Sandtown. Meier notes:

...Sandtown had been a base for a gang of marauders called the "Pony Club" or "Pony Boys." The complaints about the raids from these outlaws came from both Creek and Cherokee settlements and from white farmers as far east as the Oconee River in Greene County. They seemed particularly vicious in an age already known for its rough- and- ready resort to violence. They ran off stock killing what they could not take, robbed homesteads of all movables, and were accused of robbing and killing lone travelers.

The depredations under the name "Pony Boys" appear in the records from about 1814 until 1836, when at a time that the enemy of the Georgians was welcome among the Creeks, the gang apparently joined the Upper Creeks along the Talapoosa River where they took up wives and families. Eventually, when the Creek Removal came, the Pony Boys moved westward with their families (Meier,1994).

Meier contends that having removed west, the **Pony Boys** become those fiercesome western outlaws like the Doolins, Daltons Hardens and McQueens that we have become familiar with in books and cinema.

Central to Meier's theory is the commingling of lawbreakers, runaway slaves, British Loyalists and anti American Indians in Spanish Florida. History brings the dregs of the New World to one place and provides the impetus for attacking Georgia and South Carolina, stealing horses and slaves and anything else which isn't tied down, performing depredations in the style of wild Indians in an attempt to undermine the new United States Government. The Yamassee War creates a hot bed of exiled and disenchanted Indians in Florida; slaves join the British or run away to Florida; the Whig governments of the colonies banish all those loyal to the British Crown and the lure of safety for hundreds of thieves and murderers now are directed against the new American government.

Tories, Regulators and The East Florida Rangers

The number of outlaws between the towns of St. John's and St. Mary's is about sixty families. Among them some might be useful to our nation, but the others the sooner we drive them out of the Province the better, as they are men who have neither God nor law.

Garnier to the Governor of Florida, November 10, 1784, (Pennington, October, 1931:63:

Events leading up to the Revolutionary War pressured those who were loyal to the Crown to leave the colonies for Canada or the West Indies. These Tories were tarred and feathered, their property confiscated and their names published on lists of loyalist persona non grata in the New America. Many instead chose to congregate in British owned Eastern Florida where they formed the *East Florida Rangers,* a very effective force for the British fighting the colonists. Among its membership were some of the worst banditti Georgia and South Carolina could produce. Some were members of *the Regulator Movement* in both North and South Carolina.

The leader of the Rangers was one Colonel Thomas Brown, former Georgia mover and shaker who found himself scalped, tarred and feathered and sent out of Georgia on a rail. Others exiled included names like McGillivray, McIntosh, Weatherford and Cornells, all related to powerful Creek Indian chiefs. Still others would remain long time thorns in the underbelly of America, like William Panton of British trade giant *Panton and Leslie* and cut throat killers and robbers like Daniel Mcgirth, John Linder and Benjamin Burgess.

Another aspect of Meier's Pony Club Theory was the South Carolina regulator connection. Coffel, Lee, Mayfield, Burgess and many others involved with the East Florida Rangers were not military at all. Many were simply bandits who had operated in South Carolina and Georgia before the Revolution, and now found it to their advantage to continue from the safety of British Florida. There had been a civil war of sorts going on in the backcountry of South Carolina since at least the 1760s pitting regulators from the landless classes against the planters and yeomen. A regulator movement always arises whenever outlying peoples find themselves with no law nor enforcement. They tend to band into vigilante groups and carry on justice as best they can under dire circumstances. Tyler Bulware, History Professor at West Virginia University, has studied the regulators extensively and noted their importance during the Revolutionary War:

The failure to effectively handle the outlaw threat would have important consequences for South Carolina during the American Revolution. As many scholars have observed, the Revolution in the Carolina interior was more than just a war against the British; it was also a civil war. Neighbour took up arms against neighbour and families were torn apart fighting for either the rebellious whigs or loyalist tories (or by not fighting at all). The two contending parties consisted of many different peoples who held varying visions of the future. Many former Regulators, for instance, became proponents of the whig cause. Rachel Klein stated this was because "It was the whigs rather than loyalists who, in the course of the Revolution, were best able to continue Regulator struggles" by furthering the interests of the planter class. On the other hand, many backcountry outlaws joined the anti-whig forces.

Outlaws were a significant part of those anti-whig forces that fueled the internal struggle for power in the backcountry. David Ramsay, a nineteenth-century historian of South Carolina, stated, "Horse thieves and others whose crimes had exiled them from society attached themselves to the British." Klein agreed with Ramsay that "individual bandits of the 1760s also attached themselves to the British". Others similarly asserted, "most of them joined the tories." Numerous outlaws like James Burgess and one Hutto terrorized back settlers under the loyalist banner. The bandit William Lee, who escaped the gallows for cattle stealing in 1763, rode with William 'Bloody Bill' Cunningham during the Revolution. Cunningham was one of "the most widely feared of backcountry tories." Also of great notoriety was the outlaw and tory leader Daniel McGirt. Klein stated, "by 1779 he had become a bandit leader whose 'corps' resembled the gangs of the 1760s." A newspaper account revealed that atrocities were committed by "a large body of the most infamous banditti and horse thieves that perhaps ever were collected together anywhere, under the direction of McGirt"(Bulware, 2004).

The regulator movement had begun earlier in North Carolina where it had taken a drastic turn in politics. The movement there was squelched with force, many of its adherents fled to other states. In South Carolina it grew up in the back country where law and order was missing and settlers demanded justice. Here runaway slaves, Indians and lawless elements had coalesced to produce formidable banditti since the war with the Cherokee in 1760. Highwaymen were everywhere and settlers banded together and were able to reduce them by 1770. As the revolution approached the regulators opposing the planters found themselves siding with the British.

There were important differences between the Regulator Movements of North and South Carolina and, accordingly, in the forces that determined whether a family supported the Revolutionary movement or remained loyal to the Crown. The South Carolina back-country's leading men of property and local stature launched their Regulator campaign against anarchy and disorder in 1767-68. By 1770, often by excessive means, they had successfully transformed chaos into order. Unlike North Carolina's Regulators, they directed their movement toward consolidation of their own economic and political power, gaining dominance by dispossessing Indians and disciplining or driving off outlaws, thieves, and hunters (Bynum, 2003: 24).

The Cherokee had made a serious mistake by choice of friends in the French and Indian war. They sided with the French and other Indians and fought a long engagement beginning in 1760. They lost and ended up ceding a large portion of their eastern territory, opening up an area which immediately filled with vagrants, runaway slaves, fleeing criminals and those crackers which the Cherokee referred to simply as "Virginians." Backwoods, South Carolina now received the exiled regulators from North Carolina to add to the mix. The incessant robbery and murder disgusted those with a stake in a more stable backwoods economy and they struck back. Bulware's Carolina research has shown just how effective the regulator movement was in controlling the Back Country miscreants:

In the decade before the American Revolution, outlaw gangs wreaked havoc throughout the southern frontier. These bandits were particularly active in the South Carolina back-country, where there was a conspicuous absence of courts, jails, and the effective administration of justice. To counter this threat, back-country inhabitants eventually took it upon themselves to combat the outlaw gangs. Hundreds and thousands of settlers – maybe as many as five thousand – united into large bands of vigilantes and adopted the name Regulators. Eventually sanctioned by the government in Charleston, the Regulators administered their own brand of justice in the back-country. They attacked outlaws and other persons of ill fame who they deemed harborers and abettors of the bandits. By the end of the decade, the outlaw problem was, as the story goes, sufficiently contained (Bulware, 2004: see Monash Univ Studies).

This "dangerous set of horse thieves and vagrants" as they were called in the South Carolina Gazette (Sept 26, 1768), operated in areas with no local government, few magistrates, ineffective militia, no jail facilities...nothing except the desire of the local peoples to respond to the crime wave with harsh punishments, even lynching. Bulware's description of the guilty parties is reminiscent of Milfort's description of "Crackers":

The cultural ambivalence of outlaws was a common concern for the more industrious back-country settlers. Rather than practice settled agriculture, many of the bandits were instead part of a marginalized hunting population. A justice of the peace in 1762, for example, placed an advertisement in the Gazette concerning one Samuel McKay who escaped from him while en route to the Charleston jail. The peace officer called for the recapture of McKay so that he could obtain information about "a gang of Villains who are associated on the borders of this and the North province." It was reported that McKay was near thirty years old and "follows hunting." A petition by back settlers near the North Carolina border also made the connection between hunters and outlaws. They grieved "that there are Numbers of Idle Vagrant Persons, who follow no other employment than hunting and killing of deer…and after the season of hunting is over Steal cattle, Hogs and Horses." Lieutenant Governor William Bull empathized with the petitioners, noting that those whites who lived by "the wandering indolence of hunting" could "endanger the public peace of our Frontier Settlements" by destabilizing Indian-white relations. Governor Tryon of North Carolina warned Bull more specifically that "such lawless settlers on our frontier I apprehend may soon provoke the Cherokees to commence hostilities" (Boulware, 2004).

This was having a dramatic effect on new settlement. The reports of villainy reached Europe and the subject must have been discussed by those thinking of immigrating to the colonies. People were of course wondering if the colonists had indeed lost their civilized nature and the image of the pioneer hunter and Indian fighter was at stake as well.

Another theme running in this discussion was the ever present border between the colonies and the Indians. It represented a haven for criminals, as the Indians felt no compulsion to either be on the lookout for miscreants, or to do anything about them if they were discovered. Banditti regularly slipped into the Indian Country to evade Militia and those chasing them. In some instances the Indians were seen as partners in crime. Indians wanted horse and cattle and hogs, guns, and all sorts of western goods. Thieves were indeed willing to take their stolen property into the Indian Country and barter for deer skins and other goods the Indians had. Many of the thieves were illegal Indian Traders. Furthermore, it was not uncommon to see an Indian raid which included these backwoods vagrants:

Outlaws, then, occupied a sort of cultural 'middle ground' in which it became difficult to distinguish them from other marginal groups on the Carolina frontier. Many reports, for example, observed they were "all painted like Indians," and it was common knowledge that "the Inhabitants [were] wantonly tortured in the Indian Manner for to be made confess where they secreted their effects from Plunder" (Boulware, 2004).

The whole idea of "going native" was not lost on the colonists who were terrified to see Europeans, in war paint, scalping people. They were equally horrified when they realized runaway slaves were also among the banditti. This development sent a chill through all colonists. The idea that runaway slaves could find each other and band together to kill whites was a theme which continued from the first slave revolt, like that at Stono in 1739, less than 20 miles from Charleston (many whites were murdered), through the panic caused by John Murrell, and up to the Civil War. Boulware mentions mulatto banditti like Edward Gibson, Robert Prine and Winslow Driggers all surnames associated with Melungeons, indicating there was a great mixing of blood in the back country which horrified colonists as much as anything else. The tri-racial nature of the banditti can be generalized to the entire population of the back woods.

These stories, along with the Gazette's misinformation, are important because they give testimony to the tri-racial character of the outlaw gangs and to the heightened racial fears found among whites. Reverend Charles Woodmason spoke to this racialisation of the frontier when he wrote of the Flatt creek area, "Here I found a vast Body of People assembled – Such a Medley! Such a mixed Multitude of all Classes and Complexions I never saw." He further added of the backcountry in general that there were "Free Negroes and Mullatoe's [sic], who greatly abound here" and "who have taken Refuge in these Parts." Such observations and fears among whites became more pronounced as they comprehended the threat outlaws posed to the bi-racial plantation system that was edging its way south and west through the Carolina hinterlands... (Bulware, 2004).

One of the worst back country bandits was **Joseph Coffel**, whose Black, Indian and Cracker followers were known as "Scopholites." His career in the Santee to Savannah region of the woods included actions against the regulators and led him to the loyalist cause. He was a constable in the Orange District in 1768-1772, but was recalled for "evil practices" and in 1773 was whipped for cattle rustling and chicken theft (Ward, 1999: 77). He had finagled a commission to round up regulators and instead hired criminal cronies and pillaged the countryside around the Saluda (Edgar, 2003: 72). Of this incident William Bartram mentions the odious nature of the Scoffell name:

…St. Pierre and Whitfield had been observed talking with one Joseph Coffell (sometimes spelled Scophol). Coffell had an unsavory reputation as a leader of the lawless crackers during recent regulator wars when groups of vigilantes had imposed order by shooting some people. The Counsel regretted that Coffell escaped with his life (Cashin, 2007:162).

Stripped of his cloak of credibility, Coffel nevertheless was able to hold the revolutionists at bay in the back-country until the arrival of British regulars.

As the war progressed, "the word Tory was erased from the lips of Carolinians, and replaced by the word, dreaded or beloved, Scoffelite," writes the historian of the back-country "maroons." Whatever the chain of command of the British Regulars, most back-country Loyalists of the deep-south looked to Colonel Scoffell as their leader and inspiration, for he was paramount chief of the Maroons, the predominant Loyalist component. The rebel General William Moultrie referred to "Scopholites" as "some of the tories who were led by one Col. Schophol, Colonel of Militia, an illiterate, stupid, noisy blockhead"(Ward: 77).

The regulator-Scopholite war that had preceded the Revolution became a full fledged civil war by the time British troops arrived. Scoffel and his men began a sweep of the land around 96 District, through Savannah and on to the St. Mary's River in East Florida.

Numbering between five and six hundred, these outlaws marched rapidly for Florida, plundering and destroying everything which came in their way as they passed through Georgia. The sparsely populated districts were incapable of offering resistance. Reaching Florida in safety, these Scopholites joined the enemy and strengthened their purpose for an early and informidable invasion of Georgia (Jones, 1883: 287).

One of the scopholites was William Cunningham, relative to the 3 Tory General Cunninghams. He was recalled in all his villiany as early as 1838, by Judge J.B. O'neil in a Southern literary journal (see Phil Norfleet):

The surprise was complete and overwhelming. Hayes and his men almost without resistance were driven into the house, and Cunningham's pursuit was so close, that John Tinsley struck a full blow with his sword at Col. Hayes as he entered the door. A few guns were fired. One of Cunningham's men was killed in the assault, and one of Hayes' men was killed in the house by a ball shot between the logs. A pole tipped with flax, saturated with tar, was set on fire and thrown upon the house. It was soon in flames. Hayes and his party on a promise of good quarters, (as it has always been said,) surrendered. Cunningham selected Hayes and Maj. Daniel Williams, (a son of Col. Williams who fell at Kings Mountain) as his victims. He was about hanging them on the pole of a fodder stack, when he was accosted by a younger son of Williams, Joseph Williams, a lad of sixteen or seventeen years, who had from infancy known

Cunningham. "Capt. Cunningham, how shall I go home and tell my mother that you have hanged brother Daniel? Cunningham instantly swore that he should not have that melancholy duty to perform. He hung him up with his brother and Hayes. The pole broke with their weight and with his sword he literally hewed them to pieces. While wiping his reeking sword, he observed, that one of his comrades in cutting a captive to pieces had broken his sword, - he gaily handed to him his, observing, that it wouldn't break (O'Neal, 1838: 40-45).

Bloody Bill Cunningham found his way to East Florida and the Rangers there. He was involved with the depredations associated with the rangers until the Spanish reclaimed East Florida in 1784, forcing him to exile in the Bahamas like many of the Tories had. Cunningham's name did reappear briefly in relation to the capture of William Augustus Bowles years later:

The possible exception is William Cunningham, often referred to as Major Cunningham. Within a year or two after his banishment to Providence he must have heard rumors-if he remained in the islands-of the invasion being planned by William Augustus Bowles with the connivance of Lord Dunmore. He must have heard the reports being discussed in the taverns and other places where the outcasts were accustomed to congregate. Here was a fresh opportunity for plunder, particularly if the attack on the Georgians was to be carried out. Cunningham had won for himself the unenviable nick name of "Bloody Bill" by the ferocity of his assaults on the inhabitants of the back country of South Carolina. He too had started out as a Whig, but because of some real or fancied wrong had changed sides. Perhaps he had not yet had enough. Perhaps he did join Bowles. Perhaps he did set foot on Florida soil again. But these are conjectures, not history.

The correspondence relating to the landing in 1788 makes no mention of William Cunningham. Nor is there any trace of him in the papers relating to the intrigues of Bowles during his stay of nearly four years in the Lower Creek towns. At last, early in 1792, an agent of the adventurer was arrested at Apalache. His name was William Cunningham.

The prisoner was taken to New Orleans, where Bowles was already held in custody. Here Cunningham made two statements from which it appears that he was an American Loyalist, and a former officer in the British forces with the rank of major. There the similarity ends. His statements furnish abundant proof of his separate identity. Nor does there appear in the Spanish correspondence relating to him over a period of years the slightest confusion with the man banished from East Florida. That man, we must admit, had been lost to view since he quit the shores of Florida late in 1785 (Lockey, 1945:107-108).

Another "bad Man" from South Carolina was John Linder, especially **John Linder Jr.** The Linders were very wealthy South Carolinians who exiled to East Florida as Tories. They led groups of banditti in raids on Georgia and South Carolina in the style of William Cunningham. After the war, Linder was named by British

Governor Tonyn as one of a group of banditti he sought to exile to the Bahamas. The Linders instead entered the Creek nation, their cattle empire based at Tensaw,

near Mobile Alabama. Spanish authorities in Florida would hear from the Linders on several occasions amidst their troubles with William Bowles:

Little is known of his life in the new home, but apparently he was leading a peaceful existence as a cattle raiser. He was later joined - just when is uncertain but not later than 1786 - by his notorious son, John Linder, Jr. Of him the western trace is less faint, yet the circumstances of his abandonment of his old haunts on the St. Johns are vague in the extreme, as also are the incidents of his westward journey. It is only when he appears with his father at Tensaw that he comes somewhat into focus again (1945:103).

Linder and other former Rangers were queried by the Spanish about the whereabouts and activities of William Augustus Bowles in 1788, who had proceeded with his forces into Georgia. Linder indicated that:

... among other things, that the invaders consisted largely of refugee American Loyalists and that the object was an attack on Georgia in conjunction with the Creeks under the leadership of Bowles (lockey:106).

Another Tory, horse thief from South Carolina was **Benjamin Burgess**. Rachel Klein notes his early involvement with banditry before exiling to East Florida:

That some hunters had become actively involved with bandits gangs suggests that the groups overlapped. Benjamin Burgess, member of a large and violent horse stealing ring, belonged to a hunting and trading community located between the Broad and Saluda Rivers. In 1751, after stealing 331 deerskins from the Cherokees he sought refuge with the Indian trader John Vann. Some years later, Vann appeared in court on a charge of horse stealing...(1992: 60).

Like other Rangers, Burgess disappeared into the Creek Nation.

Yet another bandit found his way into the Tory camp: **William Lee**:

Small bandit gangs of chameleonic loyalty as suited their purpose thrived in war-ravaged South Carolina and Georgia. William Lee was one of the many banditti. He had been sentenced to death for horse and cattle stealing in 1763 but was pardoned on grounds of insanity. Just after the war the South Carolina Legislature offered a reward for his capture, declaring that he was one of the "most noted of the banditti who have so long infested the district of Ninety- Six (Ward, 1999: 78).

Many scholars place the date when the regulators defeated the back woodsmen at around 1770, but as Bulware indicates new troubles were brewing just before the Revolutionary War. It was easy for these gangs to disappear deeper into the back country or even enter Indian Territory where the colonists could not go. As soon as the idea of revolution began spreading, the backwoods people began choosing sides. Scholars on this subject, like Bulware, Klein (1990) and Ramsey (1809) agree a considerable number of the South Carolina Regulators favored the British in the revolution. Names like James Coffield, William Lee, Hutto and James Burgess, veterans of the 1760s banditti, would find their place among Tories like "Bloody Bill" Cunningham, John Linder, Jr. and Daniel McGirth, who cut a swath of death and destruction from South Carolina to East Florida.

Daniel McGirth

Daniel Mcgirth was born in Kershaw County, South Carolina, about 1750. The son of James McGirth, sometimes spelled McGirtt, who was a noted member of the local Militia who had helped suppress the Scopholites around the Wateree below Camden. Like William Cunningham, Daniel McGirth had begun his Revolutionary War experience on the side of the rebels, but an incident involving his horse caused him a great deal of trouble with his commander. The superior wanted to buy McGirtt's horse but was refused...he sought to punish McGirth, who received incarceration and lashes for fighting back. During the expedition of General Baker to St. Augustine, in 1775, Daniel McGirth, and brother James took his and many other horses from his regiment and defected to the British cause. For his actions he was awarded, a Lieutenant Colonel's rank and his brother received a captaincy in the East Florida Rangers, a Loyalist unit made up primarily of Georgia exiles. Daniel McGirth would spend years operating as a bloodthirsty bandit along the Georgia, South Carolina back-country and the St. Mary's River in East Florida.

East Florida British Governor Tonyn, had very early in the war and at the behest of General Prevost of the British Army, formed many regiments from the thousands of Tories who had made their way to Florida from all parts of the 13 colonies. Williams (1976: 473) found: *... records indicate that 2,925 whites and 4,448 blacks emigrated to East Florida during the Georgia, South Carolina evacuation.* The East Florida Rangers main function was to protect the East Florida assets from rebel invasion. As British strength improved the rangers would be used in the invasion and subsequent occupation of Georgia and South Carolina for most of the war. The Charleston *Gazette,* described the ragtag banditti accompanying the Regular troops, during the 1779 campaign of British General Prevost in the lower part of South Carolina,

... a large body of the most infamous banditti and horse thieves that perhaps ever were collected together anywhere, under the direction of McGirtt (dignified with the title of colonel), a corps of Indians, with Negro and white savages disguised like them, and about 1,500 of the most savage disaffected poor people, seduced from the back settlements of this State and North Carolina (July 7, 1779).

Even when the British took Georgia and South Carolina and occupied it the Royal Army began to realize the rangers were merely bandits intent on robbing whomever had anything and regardless of political persuasion. Writing in the **Ga. Historical Quarterly (Volume 58, 1974),** Herald Robinson quotes former Georgia Colonial Governor Wright, who discusses this problem during the occupation:

..., the principal difficulty I have hitherto experienced has been the suppression of plunderers and horse thieves who under the specious pretext of Loyalty, have from time to time daringly assembled in defiance of all law & authority & indiscriminately ravaged the plantations of peaceable inoffensive inhabitants who have received protection as prisoners on parole." Among the more brazen of these brigands was Daniel McGirth, who passed himself off as a Loyalist partisan to disguise his activities as a cattle rustler. Operating with a band of twenty or – more mounted men, he was reported by Governor Wright as having stolen and driven off to East Florida upwards of a thousand head of cattle during the summer of 1780. Another such bandit, who had Whig rather than Tory connections, was James McKay. According to Wright he was the leader of "a party some say of I 2 and others Say twenty, with which he Robs on the Highway between [Savannah] & Augusta & goes Frequently to the Banks of Savannah River and has Stop't, Robbed and Plundered Several Boats." Royal warrants for the arrest of "McGirt and his Gang" went unserved for lack of cavalry, and Wright's repeated pleas to Cornwallis for fifty mounted troops to restore order in the area between Savannah and Augusta were turned down. Capturing robbers, it was said, was a task for local authorities and not the army (429)..

East Florida Rangers: muster roll

John Barclay
Captain
William Bogan Ensign
Thomas Brown
Col.
James Brown
Lt.Daniel Ellis Lt.
Benjamin Douglas
ensign
G.M. Prevost
ensign
Samuel Gray
Lieutenant
William Lucas
Lieutenant
William Peterson
Lt.
James Wright
Major

Wm.Young
Colonel
Staff
John Allen surg.
James C. Brown
Adj.
Thomas Booth
mate
John Clark surg.
James Stewart
chaplain
Gifford Waldren
Qtms
Drummers
Benjamin Burgess
James Brook
John Harrison
William Love
John Mortimer

Conrad Pennybaker
Sergeants
Arch Adams
William Ashley
James Brooks
Thomas Brooks
Hugh Brown
William Bryant
Thomas Eggleton
Charles Fields
Drury Fort
William Jones
John Marshall
Thomas Mitchell
Nethaniel Norrington
David Wilson
John Young
Corporals
Phillip Advison
Roger Boyle

Hawkins
Bryson
Ephraim Clibborn
David Cooke
Phillip Davidson
James Hagan
Bryan Hawkins
Pat Howell
Joseph Hughes
Jonathon Hunt
Moses McKnight
Jones Reed
William Stewart

Privates

Jacob Adams
William Adams
William Allgood
Samuel Andrews
William Baker
Jacob Barclay
Moses Barker
Thomas Barry
Thomas Bates
Peter Batoe
Thomas Bernard
Michael Berry
Thomas Berry
John Billings
William Bishop
Elijah Bishop
Robert Bolton
William Brewer
George Brown
Hawkins Bryant
John Burch
John Burt
Simeon Busby
John Bush
John Cadet
Gilbert Campbell
Jon. Campbell
Simon Cansaller
William Carr
John Carroll
James Clemmons
Robert Cochrane

John Cornish
John Crawford
John Curler
George Damarine
James David
John Davis
Absolom Deane
Peter de Crouse
Aba Deems
Bernard Devent
Hendrick Dicks
William Dixon
John Donnavan
John Dougherty
William Drew
John Dugelere
Jacob Dwyer
Jacob Ebner
James Elmore
William Evans
Frederick
Falconberg
John Ferguson
John Fiddler
Jonathon Finlay
Andrew Fitch
John Francis
Joseph Franks
Robert French
William Fuz
Henry George
Sutherland Gibson
Thomas Goldsby
Phillip Goodbread
James Gormon
John Grizzle
Andrew Gums
William Gunter
Edward Johnston
James Haines
John Haines
Nathaniel Hall
John Handcocke
William Heaton
Gamiel Hayes
Peter Henderson

Richard Henderson
James Hog
Joseph Holman
Barry Holt
Reuben Holt
William Hoope
Patrick Howell
Richard Hudson
John Hugbe
Joseph Hughes
William Hunter
Jacob Huston
Joseph
Hutchinson
Ruf. Hutson
Thomas
Jackson
Richard Jinkins
William
Johnston
John Jones
Thomas Jones
Robert King
Solomon King
Wallace King
Moses
Langford
James
Langham
George Latimer
John Lawrence
Simon Lavine
James Leach
William Long
John Lyman
James Lynch
John Lynn
John Martindale
Reuben Mathews
James Mathiney
Edward McBride
James McBride
William McCay
Joseph McCormack
Thomas McCowan
John McIntire

Thomas McGovern
John
McVayEdward
Middlebrook
James
Middlebrook
Richard Miller
Henry Mills
Jeremiah Mills
Charles Miniham
William Mitchell
William Moon
Hugh Moore
Jares Moore
Henry Mullen
William
Murdocks
John Napier
Thomas Nichols
Thomas North
John O'Niel
Terry Owens
William Niblet
Thomas North
Andrew Parke
John Parker
Parker Pearce
John Pedlar

Hartwel Penticost
Richard Perry
Joseph Ponse
Jesse Prescott
Edward Price
Edward Prichett
John Prichard
Edward Proctor
Philip Proctor
Edward Prue
William Rapids
John Rickman
Het Robert
Henry Robinson
Robert Robinson
Will Roper
William Rudd
Anthony RyaN
Patrick Scanline
John Scott
John Sharp
James Shirley
Martin Shirley
Martin Sisley
Ezekiel Smith
John Smith
George Smyth
Thomas Smyth

William Smyth
John Starnes
Francis Sterling
Charles Stone
Elias Stone
Wlliam Strahan
Jos. Summerlin
John Swords
Moses Symonds
Jeremiah Tate
William Tate
Richard Taylor
Evan Thomas
Jonathon Thompson
John Thoroughgood
Thomas Tomlin
John Vincent
Henry Wall
Joseph Wallis
Jon. Weaver
Benjamin Ward
John Wealt
Samuel Williams
William Williams
Curtis Winfield
John Wyberm
William Zeyner

One American patriot who was involved in fighting McGirth's bandits was William Cone of Bulloch County, Georgia. Serving with Gen. Francis Marion, Cone on several occasions found himself within musket range of those ravaging Georgia and South Carolina. Knight (1913), in **Landmarks of Georgia** tells the story of the Cone-McGirth meeting in the woods of Georgia:

When the notorious Tory, McGirth, and his followers were terrorizing that part of the State, it was learned that one Cargill harbored the Tories and gave them information about the Whigs. Cargill was advised that it meant death if he was again found in company with McGirth. Not long after, when William Cone was hunting deer on the Ogeechee he saw them together in the woods. He shot Cargill, but McGirth escaped, and the next day when they went to bury the dead man it was found that the wolves and almost devoured his body.

At another time the Tories fell on an unsuspecting settlement, stole the settlers' horses, and carried away everything possible. Headed by Captain Cone, the settlers pursued them down into what is now Tatnall County. Finding after a shower of rain that they were close on their heels, they sent forward one of their number to reconnoiter. The approach of this man became known to the Tories through one of the stolen horses, and one of their number, starting out to learn the cause of their confusion, was shot dead by the scout, who was concealed behind a log. This was the signal for an attack, and the patriots rushed forward, drove the Tories into the Ohoopee River and recovered their stolen goods. It is said that this raid broke the power of the Tories in that community (334)

Another story of this now legendary bandit relates to a place on the Wateree, ten miles below Camden where McGirth was once nearly trapped and captured:

One of Daniel McGirtt's acts of daring is commonly believed to have given a name to a locality in this county. With a single companion he once ventured to make a secret reconnaissance in the swamps on the western side of the Wateree. Some patriots of the neighborhood, learning of his presence, determined to entrap him. Suspecting that he would wish to cross a creek with very high banks, on the Bettyneck plantation, ten miles below Camden, they removed the only bridge at that point and concealed themselves on either side of the way. McGirtt and his comrade rode blindly into the ambuscade, but, putting spurs to their horses, passed unscathed by the fire of musketry until they reached the yawning chasm. Retreat was impossible, so both urged their horses to the leap. The distance from bank to bank was quite twenty feet. McGirtt, as by a miracle, passed safely over, but his unfortunate attendant perished in the attempt. The stream has since been known as "Jumping Gully" (Kirkland and Kennedy, 1905: 302).

With so many soldiers away at war, the womenfolk found themselves at the mercy of relentless bands of robbers and cutthroats. In **The Women of the American Revolution**, (Ellet 1849), Eliza Wilkinson describes a visit from the McGirth bandits as they plundered the Savannah River area. Having already suffered the abuse by regular British troops, she found the bandits just as effective in relieving her of her possessions:

This outrage was followed by a visit from McGirth's men, who treated the ladies with more civility; one of them promising to make a report at camp of the usage, they had received. It was little consolation, however, to know that the robbers would probably be punished. The others, who professed so much feeling for the fair, were not content without their share of plunder, though more polite in the manner of taking it. "While the British soldiers were talking to us, some of the silent ones withdrew, and presently laid siege to a bee-hive, which they soon brought to terms. The others perceiving it, cried out, 'Hand the ladies a plate of honey.' This was immediately done with officious' haste, no doubt thinking they were very generous in treating us with our own. There were a few horses feeding in the pasture. They had them driven up. Ladies, do either of you own these horses?' 'No; they partly belong to father and Mr. Smilie! Well, ladies, as they are not your property, we will take them! They asked the distance to the other settlements; and the females begged that forbearance might be-shown to the aged father. He was visited the same day by another body of troops, who abused him and plundered the house. "One came to search mother's pockets, too, but she resolutely threw his hand aside. If you must see what's in my pocket, I'll show you myself;' and she took out a thread-case, which had thread, needles, pins, tape, &c. The mean wretch took it from her. After drinking all the wine, rum, &c. they could find, and inviting the negroes they had with them, who were very insolent, to do the same-they went to their horses, and would shake hands with father and other before their departure. Fine amends, to be sure (228-229)!"

McGirth's military career was short but included some very hot battles. Among them was the 1778 battle of Midway in Liberty County, Ga., in which General Screven was killed. Another was the Battle of Burke's Jail in 1779, in which

McGirth escapes from Rebel Militia (From Harris, Stories of Ga. 1896).

both Col. Brown and Lt. Col. McGirth were forced to retreat from this Burke County battlefield at the insistence of rebel Cols. Few and Twiggs. At the Battle of Kettle Creek, in 1779, Tory General Boyd was defeated in his attempt to link up with McGirth at Little River. Boyd died of his wounds and the British realized they could not hold Georgia and South Carolina. The defeat of the British regulars and Tories sent McGirth and his men into the safety of East Florida. The end of the Revolutionary War did not, however, end the banditry and strife. After several years of plundering Georgia and South Carolina, East Florida began to suffer the treachery of the banditti. As a result of the treaty ending the war, it was learned that the British would have to cede East Florida back to the Spanish. The uncertainty caused by the announcement was a cue for the banditti to rob everyone in sight. Troxler (1981) notes that McGirth and Linder came out of hiding in the swamps and began plundering the estates and farms along the St Mary's River. British Governor Tonyn delegated Col. William Young and a set of militia to stop the robberies. At this time, though, a plot was hatched by some Loyalists to take over East Florida by force. At its forefront was Tory John Cruden, who, when the whole affair seemed to be headed into the hands of the robbers and banditti, changed his mind and worked against the plot.

The conspirators assumed that the British would recognize their fait accompli and rescue them if the Spanish tried to conquer East Florida. Three years later witnesses said that 2,000 refugees and other East Floridians had been "ready to act" in 1783, and that the three provincial corps would have joined them...

At this point the enterprise fell apart. Some of the conspirators wanted to join forces with the robber gangs-perhaps they were the same people- and take over the government of East Florida before the Spanish arrived, This was to be accomplished by about 200 refugees in St. Augustine and more in the St. Johns and St. Mary's regions (Troxler, 1981: 9,10)...

This would not be the end of efforts to take East Florida from Spain.

A list of notorious thieves was put together and given to the incoming Spanish Governor, Zespedes. The list included many Tories who had been trouble before, had looted Georgia and South Carolina during the war, and some who would be trouble even in the future.

Among those mentioned was the brother of Daniel McGirth, James. Lockey notes of him:

James McGirtt, frequently mentioned by Tonyn as one of the "infamous and detestable characters," was a brother of Daniel McGirtt. Sabine, who refers to him briefly, gives Georgia as his place of origin. It is probable however that Georgia was merely a stage on his way to Florida from South Carolina. He too seems to have been a deserter from the revolutionary forces. The British rewarded him, says Sabine, with a commission as captain in Brown's Florida Rangers. It appears that he was never on Tonyn's list of proscribed men; in fact, though Zespedes investigated his connection with the banditti, he found no fault with him. But he had close associations with the outlaws, and, as already indicated, he was among the group attacked by Colonel Young on the night of July 27, 1784. He managed however to evade arrest. Moreover he was not among those who sought voluntary exile. He remained in Florida, and, as far as we know, he was in later years a good citizen (Lockey, 1945: 101)...

James McGirth ended up back in Camden County, Ga. As did many other Loyalists who either snuck back in or took the Oath of Allegiance to the United States.

In January, 1785 some residents of the St; Johns River wrote governor Zespedes, showing their joy over the capture of the bandits who had for some time plundered their homes and estates. Unfortunately, many of the signatories were themselves involved with McGirth either in South Carolina and Georgia or would be part of his gang in the 1795 rebellion against Spain in East Florida:

25 January 1785 - The Inhabitants of the River St. John's to the New Spanish Governor Vicente Manuel de Zespedes:

To: His Excellency Don Vincent Emanuel De Zespedes, Brigadier General, Governor and Commandant General of the Province of East Florida &c &c &ca

> *River St. John, January 25, 1785*
>
> *The Humble Address of the Inhabitants of the River St. John and Part Adjacent*
>
> *May it Please your Excellency*
>
> *We the Underwritten, Inhabitants of the River St John and Part adjacent, under the Protection of His Catholic Majesty, in His Province of East Florida Take this Earliest opportunity to Testify to Your Excellency our Most Sincere Thanks and Hearty Acknowledgements for your Excellency's Providential Care of our Lives and Property, in Having Secured the Persons of Daniel McGirth, William Cunningham, Stephen Mayfield and Others. Who in Defiance of all Law have for these many years past, Disturbed this Province, Plundered many of its Inhabitants and Had our Lives and Property instantly at their mercy, which Rendered our Abode unsafe and Precarious.*
>
> *By having arrested the Leaders of those Robbers and Murderers, we apprehend Ourselves at present perfectly secure under Your Excellency's Government, and we make Bold to assure Your Excellency, that we will exert ourselves in Every Occasion to Procure the Peace and Tranquility to Remain Undisturbed amongst Us, in this Province Offering to Your Excellency all the assistance that may be required at any time to Pursue and Arrest any Person or Persons that should dare to Act contrary to Your Excellency's Orders and Proclamations—And we Promise to Behave in every Respect Becoming the Duty we owe to His Catholic Majesty for His Royal Protection, while He may be pleased to Permit us to Remain in His Dominions.*

We shall continually Pray for Your Excellency's Health and Happiness and Have the Honor to Subscribe ourselves with the Utmost Respect Sir, Your Excellency's most obedient and most Humble Servants.

The signers of the letter, their involvements, their 1783 census information and their desires to leave Spanish Florida:

Solomon King East Florida Rangers 1795 rebellion against Spanish Rule

Frances Starlin EFR **camden co**. Wm Young's Co. 1795 reb Pennsylvania wishes to leave the country; future destination unknown, he lives at the mouth of the Julia Anton (Julinton) Inlet.

Joseph Summerlin EFR Wm Young's Co. 1795 reb

Timothy Hollingswirth 1795 reb

John Burnett 1795 reb

William Bogan EFR Wm Youngs co. Carolina farmer, married, undecided to remain or leave; he has a slave and a horse and lives at the mouth of the Julia Anton (Julinton) Inlet.

Wilson Williams EFR Wm Youngs co. Carolina farmer married and undecided to remain 1 child or leave; he has 2 slaves, 1 horse, 3 cows with calves; lives on the other side of the St. Johns River at the mouth of Doctor's Lagoon. Noted: written above his name "belongs to Young's Company".

Phillip Proctor EFR Wm Young's Co. Ireland farmer married undecided to remain or leave; he has one horse and lives with Joseph MacCormic at the mouth of Julia Anton (Julinton) Inlet.

Samuel Williams EFR Wm Young's Co.

Drury Fort Camden co. Wm Youngs co.

Phillip Goodbread EFR Wm Young's Co.Camden Co.

Robert Bolton EFR camden co Wm Youngs co.

William Bishop EFR WmYoungs Co.

John Scot EFR Wm Young's Co.

William Godfrey EFR (1883 census) Carolina farmer married, wishes to leave the country; his family is away from the province; he has 5,000 acres of land on the St. John's River and 700 acres on the branch of the Nassau River. All land his by purchase. He also has 4 slaves. Does not state where he lives.

William Mitchel EFR S. Carolina farmer wishes to leave the country; has a horse, and lives at the mouth of the Julia Anton (Julinton) Inlet.

William Evans EFR

David Auston at St John's town, mariner, bachelor writes for permission to leave the country; he lives in a house on property he owns at The Bluff.

Joe Wigengs (Wiggins) Carolina Indian Trader, 3 women, undecided on will living with to remain or leave; him and his works for the House, 3 children of Panton and Leslie; has 9 slaves, 8 horses and 12 head of cattle; inhabits a store of Panton's on the St. John's River. Note: He left to live in the vacated estate of Rolles with the permission of the Governor.

Randolph MacDonell Scotland farmer, bachelor, wishes to leave the country; he has 2 negroes, farms and lives on a vacant estate called Forest Oaks on the St. John's River.

A Macdonell (Alexander) Scotland merchant, bachelor, writes for Spanish protection and wishes to leave the country; he has 2 slaves and lives at Public Point on the St. John's River. Noted: On the 18th of October, he presented himself personally declaring himself C.A.R. and desiring to remain.

John Bowdn 1783 petition for land in Nova Scotia

Lewis Fatio stayed in Fla.

Others mentioned

Robbin King	James Chatworth
Joseph Ashworth St John's	Joseph Burcham
William Mangum Natchez	Henry Williams
Alex Ramcy	Alison Stuart
Henry Flicks	John Burnett, Jr.
John C. Ladson	George Brakor
Thos Hall	Joseph Fenner
Charles Hall	Thomas Rennick
John Matlet	Gaspard Barber
Sam Williams	Jesse Hesters
Thos Justin	John Gray
Wm Graystock	Angus Clark

To combat the lawlessness, Tonyn sought to round up McGirth, Cunningham, Mayfield and Linder and their followers. Mayfield, a late bloomer among the banditti, was born about 1730 in Virginia, spent some time in North Carolina and ended up around the Brown's Ccreek settlements of Ninety Six in South Carolina. Like many of his neighbors, he became a Loyalist and fled to East Florida and served in a South Carolina army unit. When Spain took over British East Florida, Mayfield was arrested along with McGirth and Cunningham and sent to Havana, Cuba.

To: Vicente Manuel de Zespedes [Governor of East Florida]

Havana, November 7, 1785

My Dear Sir:

Daniel McGirtt, William Cunningham, and Stephen Mayfield *having been given their liberty by an order of the Conde de Galvez communicated to this captaincy-general with permission to proceed without hindrance to any English colony they might choose, though under no conditions to any of our possessions, this government authorized the said three persons to buy a boat, which they manned with four foreign seamen and one*

118

Negro slave belonging to Cunningham. The corresponding passport having been given them, they set sail for providence on September 31 last...

Bernardo Troncoso

All recieved passports to new Providence in the Bahamas and Mayfield ended up there, while Cunningham and McGirth jumped ship and returned to East Florida. If all this seemed in vain or useless, the reasons for it soon became clear.

To protect the settlers from being despoiled, Tonyn put a troop of light-horse under the command of Lieutenant Colonel William Young and instructed him to bring the marauders to justice. Young arrested McGirtt and one or two others and imprisoned them in the fort in St. Augustine; but as Tonyn desired to end his administration with leniency, he instructed the attorney-general not to bring them to trial. Before further action was taken, the prisoners escaped and were still at large, hiding in swamps and other places of concealment, when the Spanish Governor Vicente Manuel de Zespedes, arrived to take over the province. Forgetting his idea of clemency, Tonyn urged upon Zespedes the necessity of rigorous action against the banditti. To assist in the undertaking, he offered the services of the lighthorse, which, he suggested, might act under the orders of Zespedes in conjunction with such troops as he himself might be able to provide. But Zespedes chose to try a different procedure. He was just as desirous of beginning his administration as Tonyn was of ending his, by acts of clemency (Lockey, 1945: 2)...

McGirth's luck was holding out as the incoming Spanish Governor sought a conciliatory tone towards those who gave the British trouble. The story of Francisco Javier Sanchez is a good indication of the duplicity shown McGirth and other Tory banditti:

Francisco Sanchez always acted in the manner he perceived to be in his best interest; those of his family and the Spanish crown. He endured the winds of change, maintained his loyalty to the Spanish Crown and together with Daniel McGirtt, began to connive against the British.

He openly encouraged the "Banditti" who fought against the British Soldiers and looted unguarded British possessions along the St. Johns River.

In 1783, Francisco Sanchez was accused by the British Governor Patrick Tonyn of committing a long series of trespasses against the British.

Governor Tonyn felt that everything Francisco did was questionable, and was determined to destroy him and his property. Governor Tonyn's major charges were that Francisco supplied the "Banditti" with ammunition, arms and provisions, and gave them shelter at one of his plantations about 18 miles west of Saint Augustine (Mario Hugas, 2002: Los Floridanos Newsletter, see also Lockey).

McGirth was captured again and sent to the Bahamas, and he defied Zespedes and returned to Florida. However, the time for British in East Florida was coming to a close and many returned to the United States or set out for the Bahamas or Nova Scotia. The banditti were breaking up and members going their separate ways. William Cunningham, William Mangum, John Linder, Sr., William Collins, and Bailey Cheney, sought exile in Louisiana, but Cunningham ended up back in

Charleston where he died in 1878; McGirth and other banditti listed as his estate's executors: Thomas Miller, Charles Hall, John Jones, John Linder, Jr., Archibald Sloan, Antonio Garzon, Gerald Byrne, and Henry Snell removed to the Tensaw District of Alabama Territory.

Williams (1976: 478) notes:

On August 10, 1785, Governor Tonyn reported that the evacuation of East Florida was completed. Around 1,000 remained, 3,000 had returned to the American states, and another 4,000 were settling on lands along the Mississippi River. The other loyalists traveled to British territories such as Jamaica, Nova Scotia, the Bahamas, and. England...

The 1795 Florida Rebellion

In the meantime, and amid the machinations of William Augustus Bowles piracies, amphibious assaults and nation- building among the Seminoles and Creeks, currents in East Florida once again were full of intrigue. This time the French appeared with the idea of relieving Spain of all her North American property. French Foreign Minister Genet in Charleston had in mind to send one expedition led by George Rogers Clark from the Ohio area down the Mississippi to take Louisiana and another expedition led by Elijah Clarke to invade and take East and West Florida. For Clarke to achieve his goals he crossed the Oconee River into Indian Territory and set up his "Trans-Oconee Republic," a base of operations for the invasion of Florida. This immediately sent up a red flag to the new Federal Government that something illegal was afoot.

The response of the Federal Government was swift and complete. It derailed Clarke's efforts before they really got off of the ground. Miller (1979: 182) describes the Swift and decisive response of the new Federal Government:

United States troops commanded by Lieutenant Colonel Henry Gaither were sent to St. Marys to assure American neutrality. Gaither, aware of threats to East Florida from within the United States, dispatched a message to Colonel Howard offering, in the interest of peace between the United States and Spain, to notify him of any unauthorized plotting against Florida, particularly by the "Clarkinos." From Augusta, Georgia, Governor George Matthews promised Quesada that he would use the militia against Clarke and his band.

Totally unaware of this development the leader of the rebellion, Richard Lang of Camden County, Georgia, continued his efforts to take East Florida from the Spanish. Lang was one of those seasoned Loyalists from South Carolina who had served as a captain under "Bloody Bill" Cunningham and was very familiar with the former British colony in Florida. Camden County, always a hot bed of banditti who raided Eastern Florida was now an armed camp for the French effort to take La Florida. Others included some just released from Moro Castle prison in Cuba (where Bowles would later die).

John MacIntosh had a plantation, Serro Fuente, on the St. Johns River near the Spanish customs port of San Nicolas. William Jones owned a plantation along the south bank of the St. Johns near the San Nicolas post. John Peter Wagnon, who had entered the province in 1791, had twenty-four slaves, some horses and cattle on his land, and he owned a house in St. Augustine. William Plowden was a trader and owned a large house in St. Augustine. Their relatives and friends lived in East Florida and Georgia and could be relied on for support. It would be impossible to prevent them from returning to the Florida frontier and reinitiating designs against the Spanish government. This time there would be support from Elijah Clarke and his associates (Miller,1979: 175)...

All ended up in the small settlements in Georgia, Coleraine, Temple and Newton, just across the border from their intended target. From the safety of Georgia they wrote threatening letters to the Spanish Government concerning the unjust nature of their incarceration and promises of relieving Florida from the yoke of despotism. On June 1, 1795, Lang and twenty Georgians crossed the border and met with allies inside Florida. Seventy-two strong, they moved down the St. John's River and on the 27th were ready for battle.

On June 27, they approached their first target, Fort Juana, which lay six miles north of the Spanish fort of San Nicolas on the St. Johns River. They captured the commander of the post, Ensign Isaac Wheyler, the garrison, twelve other militia, and a group of prisoners. They also seized 114 head of cattle, several horses, a Negro belonging to Francisco Felipe Fatio, a Spanish subject, and sent guards with the men and animals off to Georgia. They then burned the post and two days later moved out toward the St. Johns River. Their goal was the fort at San Nicolas (Miller, 1979: 177).

When local militia commander, Carlos Howard, learned of the raid, he was approached by several "Clarkinos" who lived on the St, Mary's, who posed as locals wanting to help out the Spanish in setting up the defense of St Augustine. Several of Howard's men were invited to coffee at the house of William Lane. The house was then surrounded and seized by Lang's invaders. Lang and seventy followers burst in as William Lane informed his guests they were now prisoners. The Clarkinos next took the battery at San Nicholas and the gunboat San Simon. Many prisoners were taken and many were forced to sign an oath of allegiance to Lang. This would be a contentious matter in the trial of invaders later on. On July 12th, Howard's soldiers retook San Nicholas, scattering Lang's men in the process and by August 2nd, Amelia Island, which had been taken by French Corsairs earlier, was liberated as well.

Governor Queseda now moved on those captured by Howard. Though Lang and Plowden had made previously moved to Georgia, McIntosh, Wagnon and Jones still lived in Florida. Timothy Hollingsworth, one of those captured by Lang earlier

Translation --

May 18, 1795

My dear Sir:

I have patiently awaited an answer to my letter in which I gave the exact amount of what is owed. But instead of the declared conversation, I find that you have sent a copy of everything to the Governor of that State. I will let you know that I am not yet a citizen of the United States, but a vassal of the King of Spain. Also I want to inform you of the receipt of one without delay on June 10 of the near future. You should remit to me the whole sum which step is the only one which can hinder that I do all that I possibly can so that the yoke of despotism be excluded and the liberty and freedom that God has conceded to all humans be extended. I assure you that as one longs for peace more than I. But the capture which you imposed upon me, and the bad treatment that I received, reducing my large and needy family to bread and water, can't ever pass from my memory. I trust that God will be my protector. If you grant remedy to my solicitude which would wash away the strains, I would infinitely appreciate it. And in that case, I offer you on my word of honor not to bother that government.

I have the honor of being your most obedient and humble servant &c.

Ricardo Lang

His Excellence the Governor in St. Augustine, Florida.

It is a copy of the original filed in my office.

Manuel Rengitte

St. Augustine, Florida
October 8, 1795.

(Folder contained letters No. I, No. 2, and No. 3, and was marked "Letters Govr. of Florida to Gov Matthews 1795. Spanish. Miscellaneous. Foreign Affairs". Original letter in Spanish is in Georgia Department of Archives and History. Translated by Mrs. Cleveland Thompson, of Millen, Ga., 1940. L. F. Hays).

Letter from Lang to the Governor de Zespedes of Spanish Florida

in the battle was now helping the Spanish seize the property of the three leaders and anyone else implicated in the conspiracy. Every day more settlers left families and homes and fled into Georgia to escape prosecution. Queseda kept the wives and families in East Florida as insurance, so another attack would not come. In January, 1796, the trials of the conspirators commenced. Charged and convicted were sixty-nine Georgians and Floridians, half of whom were in absentia.

Many of those convicted were those captured by Lang early on who signed an oath of allegiance. Hollingsworth was one of those who received the death penalty. Many received ten years of hard labor in St Augustine or West Florida. No one was ever put to death or served more than five years, as pardons came not long after the whole ordeal. Many, in fact received land grants having served their time in prison.

Among this last group, which reads like a who's who of Revolutionary War bandits, was our old friend Daniel McGirth. Queseda accused him of being Elijah Clarke's leader in the Florida rebellion of 1795. McGirth was captured:

...General Clarke, who had entered the province, was among those forced to flee. The infamous Daniel McGirtt, distrusted by both Georgians and Spanish, was captured and charged with serving as Clarke's pilot (Miller, 1979: 182)...

He would spend five years in the Castillo De San Marcos at St. Augustine.

Daniel McGirth, his health broken after 5 years of hard labor, returned to South Carolina from whence he came. Hated in both Florida and Georgia, when his wife Mary sought a Headright grant from Camden County; she was refused because she was the wife of Daniel McGirth.

Co-Conspirators in the 1795 Rebellion
Arrested...

Abril, (free black)	Timothy Hollingsworth
George Aarons	John Jones
Uriah Bowden	Solomon King
George Cook	Pierce Lane
John Creighton	William Lane
David Dewees	James William Lee
Nethaniel Eegle	Jim, his slave
John Faulk	Richard Malpas
George Flora	Daniel McGirtt
Robert Gilbert	Manuel Ortega
Francis Goodwin	Cornelius Rain
Cornelius Griffiths	Joseph Rain
Joseph Heguins	William Rain
Daniel Hogans	John Simpson

Joseph Summerlin	Aaron Travers
Henry Sweeny	Edward Turner
Billy Thompson	Jacob Worley

Absent..

James Allen	John Linder
Robert Allen	Jonathon McCullough
William Ashley	John McIntosh
John Burnett	William McKay
Robert Burnett	George Mills
Ephraim Davis	Joseph Mills
William Down	James Nobles
Mills Drury	William Plowden
John Dudley	Robert Rain
George Fillet	John Silcock
Joseph Fillet	Francis Sterling
William Jones	Isaac Sterling
William Jones, Jr.	Tephilo Thomas
George Knolls	John Peter Wagnon
Richard Lang	Nathaniel Wilds
James Leslie	Samuel Wilson
Silas Leslie	

William McGirth had fled East Florida earlier to become an officer in William Augustus Bowles pirate nation. His postion was "Commissary of Marine" and "Judge of the Court of Admiralty" of the Muscogee Nation.

Condemnation of the Schooner Guadaloupe by the Court of Admiralty of the State of Muskogee

Know all Men by these Presents that I William McGirth Judge of the Court of Admiralty of the State aforesaid, upon the application of Captain Richd Power against the Spanish Schooner La Guadaloupe, and her Cargo consisting of Salt & Fish, Prize to the States Cutter Tostonoke, whereof he is at present Master, & upon the Testimony of Francis Hill & other Spaniards proving her to be the property of Subjects of the Crown of Spain, I do therefore adjudge & condemn her the said Schooner La Guadaloupe together with her Cargo of Fish & Salt, Sails, Rigging as good prize to the States Cutter Tostonoke, Captain Richard Power

Given under my hand & Seal of Office this 3d day of Feby 1802

Signed, WM. MCGIRTH

William would end up in the Creek nation and carry on his animosity with the United States as a servant of the Indians. He was one of the husbands of Polly Durant and they had a son, William who married Vicey Cornells and their son, Zachariah would be remembered from the Fort Mims Massacre of the Red Stick War. Other Descendants of the McGirths were removed to Oklahoma Indian Territory, where they were listed in the Dawes Roll:

537	8	4888	McGertt	John	537	20	5548	McGirt	John
537	9	4889	McGertt	Linda	537	21	6057	McGirt	Isaac
537	10	5045	McGirtt	Billy	537	22	6423	McGirt	William
537	11	5046	McGirtt	Dora	537	23	6465	McGirt	Hepsie
537	12	5047	McGirtt	Sophia	537	24	7282	McGirt	Soloman
537	13	5309	McGirt	Jackson	537	25	7283	McGirt	Hattie
537	14	5310	McGirt	Lincoln	537	26	7284	McGirt	Lonnie
537	15	5325	McGirt	Buckner	537	27	7285	McGirt	Jimmie
537	16	5326	McGirt	Linda	537	28	8579	McGirt	Aaron
537	17	5327	McGirt	Robert	537	29	8586	McGirt	Dick
537	18	5328	McGirt	Alex	537	30	8941	McGirt	Jim
537	19	5547	McGirt	Mongy	537	32	6007	McGirth	Houston

James McGirth, who had served with Daniel in his banditti group, moved to Camden County, Georgia where he appears in deed records (as do many former Tories who left East Florida).

E/334) James McGIRTH, late of East Florida, now of Camden County, to his grandson, John Robert McGIRTH, son of Daniel and Susan McGIRTH of Camden County. Gift of slave, dated April 19, 1802.

(F/223) James McGIRT appoints Joseph THOMAS to receive and keep a certain negro boy owned by grantor, and apply one-half of the boy's hire to MCGIRT'D support and one-half to Susannah MCGIRT'S children, and after grantor's death the negro to be sole property of John Robert MCGIRT, son of Susannah. Dated Dec. 6, 1804.

A James McGirth is mentioned several times in Pickett's *History of Alabama* (1851), both as a friend of Alexander McGillivray and as someone who operated a still in Macon County, Alabama.

But even this is not the last time we hear from the McGirths. During the First Seminole War, General Jackson avails himself of one Col. McGirth, of Georgia Militia, probably James, who styles his group as "rangers" in liberating stolen U.S. property, horses and slaves, in Florida (Zedrick and Dilley 1996: 7 and Debates and Proceedings of Congress, 1855).

The theory that the Pony Club was made up of former Tories, halfbreeds and banditti from East Florida does have a modicum of truth to it. Several of the worst outlaws Georgia and South Carolina produced ended up in the Creek Nation. The Weatherfords, Burgesses, McQueens, Linders and McGirths are well represented in Tory and Indian circles, both of whom fought against the United States for years to come.

2002 Baptist, Edward E, **Creating an Old South, Middle Florida's, Plantation Frontier Before the Civil War,** Univ. of N.Carolina Press: Greensboro.

2000 Belleview, Bill, **River of Lakes**: **A Journey on St. John's River**, Univ. of Ga. Press: Athens.

2008 Bethell, A Talbot, **Early Settlers of the Bahamas and Colonists of North America,** Heritage Books: Westminster, Md.

1999 Cashin, Edward J., **The King's Rangers: Thomas Brown and the American Revolution on the Southern Frontier,** Fordham Univ. Press: Bronx, N.Y.

1998 Chapman, Herb and Muncy Chapman, **Wiregrass Country**, Pineapple Press: Sarasota.

1779, July 7, **Charleston Gazette**.

1881 Draper, Lyman C., **King's Mountain and Its Heroes: History of the Battle of King's Mountain, October 7th, 1780, and the Events Which Led to It**, State Historical Society of Wisconsin: Madison.

2003 Edgar, Walter B., **Partisans and Redcoats: The Southern Conflict That Turned the Tide,** Harper Collins Publishers: N.Y.

1819 Ellet, Elizabeth F., **The Women of the American Revolution**, Vol. 1, Baker and Scribner: NY

October, 1931 Pennington, Edgar Legare, **Rivalry in the Creek Country : Part 1: The ascendancy of Alexander McGillivray, 1783-1789,** *The Florida Historical Quarterly* volume 10 issue 2, Florida Historical Society: St. Augustine, p.60-102.

1906 Fuller, Herbert Bruce, **The Purchase of Florida: Its History and Diplomacy,** The Burrows Brothers Co.: Cleveland.

1855 Gibbes, R.W., ed**., Documentary History of the American Revolution, 1764-1776, D. Appleton and Co.: N.Y.**

2001 Hall, Leslie, **Land and Allegiance in Revolutionary Georgia,** Univ of Ga Press: Athens.

2002 Hare, Julianne, **Tallahassee: A Capital City History,** Mt. Pleasants: S. Carolina.

1905 Kirkland, Thomas J., Robert MacMillan Kennedy**, Historic Camden** The State Company: Columbia: S. Carolina.

1990 Klein, Rachel N., **Unification of the Slave State: The Rise of the Planter Class in the South,** Univ, of N. Carolina Press: Greensboro.

1913 Knight, Lucian Lamar, **Georgia Landmarks, Memorials and Legends**, Vol. 1, The Byrd Printing Co.: Atlanta.

2004 McCarthy, Kevin M., **St. John's River Guidebook,** Pineapple press: Sarasota.

1945 Lockey, Joseph B., **The Florida Banditti**, *The Florida Historical Quarterly* volume 24 issue 2, 1783 pgs 88-108.

1984 McLoughlin, William Gerald and Walter H. Conser, **The Cherokee Ghost Dance: Essays on the Southeastern Indians,** Mercer Univ. Press: Macon, Ga.

1978, Miller, Janice **Borton, Rebellion in East Florida 1795** *Florida Historical Quarterly* volume 57 issue 2, pgs 174-187.

2005 Nelson, Megan Kate, Trembling Earth: **A Cultural History of the Okefenokee Swamp,** Univ of Ga Press: Athens.

July 1838, O'Neal, Judge J. B., **Random Recollections of Revolutionary Characters and Incidents,** *Southern Literary Journal and Magazine of Arts*, Vol. 4, No. 1, pages 40-45.

_____ Phil; Norfleet: **Biographical Sketch of Bloody Bill Cunningham** @http://sc_tories.tripod.com/bloody_bill_cunningham.htm).

1851 Pickett, Albert James, **History of Alabama: And Incidentally Georgia and Mississippi…,** Walker and James: Charleston.

1887 Reynolds, Charles Bingham, **Old St. Augustine: A Story of Three Centuries,** Published by E.H. Reynolds: St. Augustine.

1974 Robinson, Herald, **Second British Ocupation of Augusta,***Ga. Historical Quarterly* Volume 58, winter.

1847 Sabine, Lorenzo, **The American Loyalists: Or Biographical Sketch of Adherents to the British Crown in the War of Revolution,** Charles Little and James Brown: Boston.

1929 Seibert, Wilbert Henry, **Loyalists in East Florida, 1774 – 1785** vol. 1, Florida State Historical Society, Members of the Society : Deland, Fla.

1860 Simms, William Gilmore, **Life of Francis Marion**, G.G. Evans, Publisher: Philadelphia.

1905 Suttles, Bernard, **Men of Mark, (as described as a manuscriopt in Clayton County, Ga, Courthouse).**

1981 **Troxler,** Carole Watterson, **Loyalist Refugees and the British Evacuation of East Florida, 1783-1785**, *The Florida Historical Quarterly* volume 60 issue 1 July, **pgs 2-29.**

1999 Ward, Harry M., **The War for Independence and the Transformation of American Society,** Routledge: N.Y.

2002 Ward, Harry M., **Between the Lines: Banditti of the American Revolution,** ABC Clio: Santa Barbara, Calif.

1856 Watson, Elkinah and Winslow Cossoul Watson, **Men and Times of the Revolution: Or Memoirs of Elkinah Watson…,** Dana and Co. Publishers: N.Y.

1890 Wildwood, Warren, **Thrilling Adventures Among the Early Settlers,…,** Keystone Publishing: Philadelphia.

1976 **Williams, Linda K., East Florida as Loyalist Haven**, *The Florida Historical Quarterly*, Volume 54 Issue 4, Florida Historical Society, St. Augustine, Florida, April. pgs 466-479.

1914 Wilson, Gustavus James Nash and William Ellis White, **The Early History of Jackson County, Georgia: …,** published by W.E. White.

2002 Zedric, Lance Q. and Michael F. Dilley, **Elite Warriors: 300 Years of America's Best Gighting Troops,** Pathfinder publishing: Calif.

Nickajack Cave and the Cherokee Banditti

Into this vast cavern, for the purposes of concealment and murder, the banditti of the "narrows" retired with their spoils and their victims. This place now enlivened and enriched by the genius of Fulton and in view of the steamer and locomotive, was then the dismal and gloomy retreat of savage cruelty and barbarian guilt.

James Ramsey, 1853.

The Tories and half-breeds and "moccasin boys" of Camden County, Georgia and East Florida are not the complete story of the precursor of the Pony Clubs. There was another set of banditti, Tories and half-breeds on the move against Wautauga settlements of Tennessee. Ramsey (1853) gives a tremendously poetic description of the Tennessee River where these Back-country miscreants operated:

If the channel of the river presented dangerous physical impediments, its environs held those of another character, not less formidable. Along those foaming rapids and on either side of the river, the shores are wild, elevated and bold, in some places, scarcely leaving room for a path separating the stream from the adjacent mountain, with here and there a cove running back from the river into the heights which surround and frown down upon it, in somber solitude and gloomy silence. In these mountain gorges were fastnesses, dark, forbidding and inaccessible. Their very aspect invited to deeds of violence, murder and crime. No human eye could witness no vigilance detect, no power punish, no force avenge them. A retreat into these dreary seclusions, stimulated to aggression, as they furnished a perfect immunity from pursuit and punishment (184).

The Tennessee River leaves Ross' Landing and Chattanooga and swirls around until it heads into Northern Alabama about Tuscumbia where it widens. Before this happens it passes the "suck," a whirlpool said to have swallowed a fleet of Cherokee Canoe on their way to raid the Shawnee. It brings the river traveler to a cave called Nickajack Cave, with a reputation like Cave in Rock on the Ohio River. Keating, in his History of Memphis (1888: 60), said of the banditti:

…These ruffians made their principal rendezvous at Nickajack Cave, a gloomy cavern, difficult of access and situated in a wild and romantic country…

The dark nature of this Geographic feature began its abysmal history as an almost accidental occurrence which the local Indians adjusted to quite well:

About 1773 or 1774, some families from West Virginia and North Carolina, attracted by glowing accounts of West Florida, sought a settlement in that province. They came to the Holston frontier, built their boats, and following the stream reached Natchez by water. Necessity drove them to employ Indians and Indian Traders, as pilots through the dangerous

129

passes of the Tennessee River. Occasionally a boat was either by accident or design shipwrecked, at some point between the Chickamauga Towns and the lower end of the Muscle Shoals. Its crews became easy victims of savage cruelty—its cargo fell a prey to Indian cupidity. As these voyages increased and the emigrants by water multiplied from year to year, so did the Indian settlements all along the rapids, also extend. The Chickamaugans were the first to settle there and to become depredators upon the lives and property of emigrants. Concious of guilt, unwilling to withhold their warriors from robbery and murder, they failed to attend with the rest of their tribe to treaties of peace (185)...

They formed the five lower towns of the Cherokee and led by warriors like Dragging Canoe, refused to come to peace with the settlers of Tennessee, South Carolina and Georgia. When the revolution became inevitable, some of the Tories fled into the Cherokee Country and found their way to the lower towns. McLoughlin (1986) makes note of the Loyalist nature of those who became leaders of the Cherokee by intermarriage:

...The King's agent, John McDonald, and his son in law, Daniel Ross, lived among them and encouraged them to keep up the war. Scores of adventurous colonists loyal to the King fled from their homes in the colonies to settle in the Chickamauga Towns. Many of these white Loyalists married Cherokees and later played a part in Cherokee history – John Rogers, John Walker, John McLemore, John Fields, John Thompson, John D. Chisolm, John McIntosh, Edward Adair, Edward Gunter, Arthur Coody, Richard Taylor and William Shorey. Once married to Cherokees they were considered full members of the tribe or "Cherokee Countrymen". They assisted Dragging Canoe in his guerrilla warfare against those seeking independence from England and some Loyalists donned buckskins and war paint to participate in the continual raids along the frontier for the next seventeen years (20)...

Ramsey indicates also the treacherous nature of the Lower Towns and the banditti that arose and headquartered in that place on the Tennessee where Indians from time immemorial had crossed the great stream:

...Murderers, thieves, pirates, banditti, not of every Indian tribe only, but depraved white men, rendered desperate by crime, hardened by outlawry and remorseless from conscious guilt, fled hither and confederated with barbarian aborigines in a common assault upon humanity and justice and in defiance of all laws of earth and heaven (186)...

To punish these miscreants an expedition was mounted from Virginia and North Carolina by Col. Evan Shelby and 1000 men from the western settlements and a regiment under Col. John Montgomery. Eleven towns were destroyed and great stores of goods destined for the Indian enemies of the rebellion were captured. Shelby also seized 150 horse, 100 head of cattle and many deerskins, belonging to Indian trader McDonald. The net effect of this victory was to thwart an effort by

British regulars to unite Northern and Southern Indians and supply them with the means of attacking the rebels. This alliance never occurred (Ramsey, 1853: 188).

1888 Keating, John M., **History of the City of Memphis, Tennessee**
D. Masons and Publishers: Syracuse, N.Y.

1986 McLoughlin, William Gerald, **Cherokee Renascence in the New Republic**,
Princeton Univ Press: Princeton: NJ

1853 Ramsey, James Getty's McGready, **The Annals of Tennessee to the End of the Eighteenth Century,** Lippincott Grambo and Co.: Philadelphia

Nickajack Cave from Harpers Weekly, February 6, 1864

William Bowles and the Muskogee Nation

William Augustus Bowles

Sketch made in 1790 by
John Trumbull (1756-1843)

Alexander McGillivray

Perhaps the most memorable Tory of the period was William Augustus Bowles. He was born of Maryland, Tory parents in 1763, joined the British Army at age 13 and went AWOL at age 15 in Pensacola, resulting in his dismissal from the service in the Revolution. Angry, he left to live with the Creek Indians. Bowles had both a Cherokee and a Creek, Hitchitee wife. He spent some time living along the Chattahoochee in Georgia and Alabama and was familiar with the Upper Creek Towns. In 1781, Bowles led a group of Creeks in the defense of British Pensacola when the Spanish reclaimed the city. For this Bowles was back in favor with the British Army. After the Revolutionary War, he exiled to the Bahamas as did many Tories. Here he cemented a relationship with the former Virginia Governor, Lord Dunmore. The prominent Dunmore convinced Bowles to fight the old Panton-Leslie monopoly in Florida under the auspices of the new ***Miller and Donamy*** trading firm. A 1788 failed attempt to capture the Panton-Leslie store on the Indian River earned him the wrath of the Spanish government. The Seminoles were not very motivated to attack the store which provided their shot and powder so Bowles found himself on the run.

In the next few years Bowles sought to form a Muskogee Nation from the various Creek allies in Georgia, Alabama and Florida. He met with Creek leaders at

Coweta in 1791 and received support for his efforts. He would sail to the Bahamas under the Muskogee flag, receiving welcome in many West Indies ports. In 1792, he and a large group of Creeks took the Panton-Leslie store at San Marcos and he began negotiating with the Spanish for his new Creek nation. But the next year the Spanish retook San Marcos and captured and threw him in jail. He escaped and was back in Florida with a boat later that year. He then moved his capital to a place called Mikosuki, near Tallahassee and began his career as a pirate in Apalachicola bay.

Besides an army, Bowles also needed a small navy to prey on Spanish shipping in the gulf. The Muskogee nation's declaration of war on Spain allowed Bowles to issue privateer commissions and to attract sailors interested in earning money fast. In 1802, he commissioned a privateer the Muskogee Micco (the Muskogee Chief) under its owner, a Captain Johnson of New Providence (Bahamas). The privateer or" pirate ship", as the Spanish saw it captured two Spanish ships in the Gulf and took them to the Apalachicola River to rearm them for use in the Muskogee Navy. Bowles commissioned another schooner the Favorite, in the Bahamas, but as it sailed to Apalachicola with cannon, that he planned to put into the prizes he captured, the Spanish seized it and took it to their fort at St. Marks (McCarthy, 1994: 61)

Bowle's navy included several vessels under the command of Tory Richard Powers, whose crews were of English, Spanish, African-American and Indian descent, but were captained by Brits from the Bahamas.

In 1802 he tried to retake San Marcos but failed and the Seminoles signed a separate peace treaty with Spain. Britain and Spain also sought peace with each other and Bowles became unwelcome anywhere. The United States now moved against Bowles, Creek Indian agent Benjamin Hawkins setting a trap for him. Colonel Pickett, in his epic Alabama History describes the downfall of the famous Tory pirate:

A great feast was given by the Indians at the town of Tuskegee, where the old French Fort Toulouse stood, to which Bowles and the Miccasoochy Chiefs were invited. They attended, and during the feast the unsuspecting freebooter was suddenly seized by concealed Indians, who sprang upon him, securely pinioned him and placed him in a canoe full of armed warriors. They then rapidly rowed down the river. Hawkins and John Forbes, of Pensacola, were in the town, but were concealed, until Sam McNac, a half-breed, had caused Bowles to be made a prisoner. Arriving at a point in the present Dallas county, the canoe was tied up, the prisoner conducted upon the bank, and a guard set over him. In the night the guard fell asleep, when Bowles gnawed his ropes apart crept down the bank, got into the canoe, quietly paddled across the river, entered a thick cane swamp, and fled. At the break of day, the astonished Indians arose in great confusion, but fortunately saw the canoe on the opposite side, which Bowles had foolishly neglected to shove off. Swimming over to that point, they got upon his track, and by the middle of the day once more made him a prisoner. He was conveyed to Mobile, and from thence to Havana, where, after a few years, he died in the dungeons of Moro Castle. (1900: 471).

His reign as leader of the Muskogee Nation was brief, but he created a great deal of mischief and as we shall see his men began to roam north into Georgia where there were horses and cattle to be stolen.

Creek Banditti

Beneath all the animosity between the former colonies and the British was an underlying fear of foreign influence over the Indians in the South. The Spanish had long been friends of the "Apalache" or "allies", whose influence spread as far as the mountains that carry their name. The reasoning behind the new Georgia colony was to buffer South Carolina from the vicissitudes of Indian relations. Georgia soon became a springboard for an ongoing war with Spain over the South and the hearts and minds of its inhabitants. This war began even before Georgia was a colony. Dr Henry Woodward, the acknowledged founder of the South Carolina rice industry, in 1674, made a visit to the fierce Westo tribe near present day Savannah to establish trade relations between them and the British and weaken the Mission system the Spanish had established. In 1685, Woodward traveled all the way to Coweta Falls on the Chattahoochee, site of Present day Phenix City, Alabama, for the express purpose of offering the Creeks an alternative to Spanish trade. The Spanish retaliated, burning creek towns and chasing Woodward all over Georgia to no avail. The Spanish response was so vicious all the Indians left Florida and moved to the Ocmulgee to take advantage of the English trade. The Factory or trading post Woodward established at Coweta Falls helped assure the town's preeminence in leadership among the Creeks for years to come.

After the Georgia colony was established, James Oglethorpe made a trip to Coweta Falls to reestablish trade ties with the Creek. Wright, his biographer (1867: 213), makes it clear Oglethorpe had in mind to undermine Spanish influence over the Creek nation:

I have received frequent and confirmed advices that the Spaniards are striving to bribe the Indians, and particularly the Creek nation, to differ with us; and the disorder of the Traders is such as gives but too much room to render the Indians discontented; great numbers of vagrants being gone up without licences either from Carolina or us. Chigilly, and Malachee, the son of the great Brim, who was called Emperor of the Creeks by the Spaniards, insist upon my coming up to put all things in order, and have acquainted me that all the chiefs of the nation will come down to the Coweta town to meet me, and hold the general assembly of the Indian nations; where they will take such measures as will be necessary to hinder the Spaniards from corrupting and raising sedition amongst their people.

134

Oglethorpe saw the opportunity as too great to turn down. Chickasaws, Choctaws and Creeks from towns and villages from 300 miles around were expected to make the journey to Coweta Falls for this talk by Oglethorpe.

So began a relationship with the Royal government which would last well into the 1800s and pit the Creek Indians against the new United States Government. With the end of the French and Indian war, Florida became a British outpost and when trouble started brewing between Americans and the British. In this period, however, **Panton and Leslie** had made tremendous inroads into trade relations with the Creeks. This trading company with headquarters in Pensacola, would influence Alexander McGillivray, leader of the Creek Nation for many years to come. During the revolution John Tait, former British agent for the Creeks spent time in the nation gathering an army to attack Savannah. In all 700 warriors began the expedition to carry out the wishes of the British. William Few, in an autobiography for a family member described the battle as an amazing folly for the enemy. Some Indians faced with battle mutinied, others sought to plunder nearby settlements and go home and another group set out for Savannah. Needless to say Few's men, about half as many as Tait had, made piecemeal work of the creeks with the loss of only one man (Few: unknown date: 13-14).

A long list of Tory thorns, Tonyn, Brown, Bowles, McGirth, Col. Nichols, Woodbine, Arbuthnott and Armbrister would excite the Indians to raid the Americans. In 1783, after the bitter revolution, Georgia Governor Martin sent a talk to Tallesee King about the growing animosity between America and the British influenced Creeks:

I have nothing very particular to mention to you more than what I have already said in the last Talk I sent you up to you by our good friend & Brother the Factor, in which we demanded Our horses, Cattle and Negroes, together with the Torys, Traders and Brown's lying people that are among you making mischief, and Which have been the means of so much blood being Spilled between the Red people and the Virginians, Had it not been for them, their Trifling presents and lies, we should have been at peace long ago -- Therefore these are the people your Vengeance ought to fall upon...

For English are now obliged all of them to leave this great country. Then where will they get goods but from us -- See what the Cherokees are now reduced to, by their folly and pride, had they been wise and dispised the fine cloaths and lying talks of the English that was sent amongst them, they might have been a happy people unto this day. And now they are almost brought to nothing (October 29, 1782)...

George Washington had also given the Creeks a talk about depredations. He reminded them they had not followed the tenets of the Treaty of New York and returned property belonging to the Americans.

Brethren -- you heard yesterday what the great beloved man General Washington told you in the talk the Commissioners delivered that you had not complied with the stipulation you had entered into at New York in all parts that the prisoners and property, such as Negroes, Horses, Cattle &c -- were not restored many of the Chiefs now here were at new York & promised to do this -- You promised to return this property at thrice different treaties before you went to New York -- 1st at Augusta, 2nd at Galphinton and 3rd at the treaty of Shoulderbone, where many of your principal chiefs who now hear us were also (undated)...

Further charges were leveled by Georgia Governor Walton in 1789:

During the two previous years, as appears by a return of depredations, made by Governor Walton to the United States Commissioners, October 4, 1789, the Creeks had murdered eighty-two persons, wounded twenty-nine, taken prisoners one hundred and forty, burnt eighty-nine houses, and carried away horses and cattle and goods to the value of many thousand dollars (Stevens, 1859: 444-45)...

An incident which brought all this to a head was the Trader hill robbery and murders, committed by Galphinton, Burgess and a few other Indians at the Seagrove store in St. Mary's, Georgia. Nearby, Indians had killed 3 settlers and a child, the net result of both instances causing people to leave Camden and Glynn Counties for fear of Indian attack (letter from Ga. Gov. Telfair to Sec. of War Knox, April 3, 1793). Galphinton, Son of the famed Indian trader, was a known bandit and friend of the Loyalists in Florida. In a deposition, he claimed he was not a party to the murders and blamed them on Indians he said were sent to raid Georgia by William Panton of Panton and Leslie in Pensacola. Timothy Barnard, interpreter for the Yuchee, always wary of Spanish and British influences within Creek Power circles, notified Major Henry Gaither that he had reports of Indians with scalps and plunder traveling to settlements near Jack Kinnard's, who are under the influence of Tory Willbanks. He further stated Spanish dons with supply ships nearby had been seen as well (April 17, 1793).

A year earlier, Governor Blount of Tennessee had written Chief Alexander McGillivray a long list of charges: murders, horse stealings and other depredations by the southern Indians, particularly the Creeks and Cherokees. His suspicion that William Augustus Bowles was involved fell on deaf ears as McGillivray suddenly died and was buried in the garden at William Pantons estate in Pensacola. What further evidence did anyone need that the Creek were in the Tories' hip pocket? The British, who had learned to plunder and steal as Prevost and Tarleton did, by example of McGirth and others, now had to find another leader in the Creek nation to continue their undeclared war on the United States.

Meanwhile, the Upper Creek Towns continued their reign of terror on Georgia Settlers, while the Lower Creek Towns sought peace. Fearful of retaliation, some of the friendly Creeks sought just ways to placate the Georgians, but things began to spiral out of their control. Add to this the growing hostility of the Seminoles toward white settlers, especially Americans. In 1795, the new United States had signed the Pinckney Treaty with Spain, which gave America the rights of navigation on the Mississippi River and required that the northern boundary of Florida be set at the 31st parallel. In 1796, Washington chose Andrew Ellicott as head surveyor and by May, 1798, they were near Mobile placing markers for metes and bounds. In 1799, the party approached the Chattahoochee River portion of the survey, where Seminoles began to harass and rob them.

An early indication of Seminole resistance to the advancing tide of white settlers in Florida was furnished by the hostile activities of bands of "bandetti" among the tribe who effectively halted the commission near the confluence of the Flint and Chattahoochee rivers in 1799. The journals, diaries, and correspondence of those connected with the southern frontier at that time clearly indicate the emergence of the Seminoles as a major threat to white settlement (Holmes, 1966: 312).

Elicott found the going very rough: Mosquitoes, rain, heat and humidity were taking its toll. On top of that the depredations of the Seminoles and Eufaulas were jeopardizing the mission:

After arriving at this place, and finding the disposition of the Uphales, and Seminoles, I had serious thoughts of relinquishing a further prosecution of the business on account of the expense which would necessarily be incurred, by the delays owing to so great a number of our horses being stolen by the Indians, and the probability of losing the greater part of the remainder between this, and St. Mary's, which event would effectually put an end to our operations, and reduce us to the necessity of carrying our apparatus and baggage on our backs to some settlement in Georgia (317)...

....The lower towns, and Seminoles, are perhaps a set of the most unprincipled villains in existance, while partaking of hospitality, they will secret and carry off every article of value which they can lay their hands on belonging to their entertainer (318).

Ellicott and his party entered the Apalachicola River from the gulf and proceeded north by boat, hiring canoes to beat the rapid current and began surveying. Each day he would stop at a different Indian Town and avail them of canoes, guides and hospitality.

...Only with difficulty can Your Excellency form an idea of how disagreeable and unfortunate our situation is. We are camped next to an Indian village, and below it is another one. Our camp, our tents, are continually filled with Indians, who are not only not desirable guests, but who are the most skillful and subtle thieves that I have ever seen. Not only have they robbed us of a large number of our horses, but they have also pillaged many articles from the tents. They

take as much as they can carry when they come to see us if we do not watch them carefully. Moreover, we are forced to give daily supplies to a considerable number. Presently we have ninety among us (320)...

William Augustus Bowles and his Creek Nation were barely in the background as these incidents of hostility arose for Endicott. Bowles was fighting the Spanish, the Americans and even wished to supplant the trading house of Panton and Leslie. Creek Agent, Benjamin Hawkins, sought to discuss these matters with William Panton on several occasions, as Bowles was a mutual enemy.

...Just after they had finished their observations there and had fixed the day for their movement to the source of St. Marys they were visited by twenty mischief makers from Talasee, who created a momentary alarm. This banditti aided by some Semanoles stole fourteen horses and plundered a vessel of property of the value of 3 or 400 dollars. I met them on the night of their arrival in the vicinity of our camp with the armed force under command of Capt. Boyer, rebuked them for their improper conduct and ordered them to return home and to conduct themselves agreeable to the voice of their nation. They for a short time seemed obstinately bent on mischief but determined as soon as they discovered we possessed the means and were determined to punish them. . . .

The next day I sent out some chiefs for the stolen horses and they [-----] the hole and brought a message from this Banditti; that they should return home, that what they had done did not [two words torn from mss] with themselves, that they had been out for, that the greatest part of the mischief done was by Indians in our neighborhood and that they had taken but two horses which they returned. I advised Mr. Ellicott with his unwieldy accumulation of baggage to go round by water, and for Major Minor to go through with their escort by land (327, 328)...

Once the boundary was drawn, Ellicott began his journey downstream to the gulf and eventually Pensacola. It was pointed out by many including Timothy Bernard, one of Hawkins deputy agents, that he would probably be accosted and robbed on his way there. Now the party had an Indian escort from the friendlier Creeks, but a group of plunderers were following the group as it headed towards its final Florida destination. When one of Ellicott's horses was stolen within site of the camp he ordered all stock inside the camp, only to realize eight or ten were already missing (334). A schooner ordered by Ellicott had been plundered the night before, the crew's clothes stolen off their backs by marauding Indians.

Ellicott, upon finishing the boundary survey wrote of his experiences, which chronicles the depredations of the Creeks and Seminoles on his party. He concluded:

The Southern Creeks, commonly called Seminoles, with the Tallesees and some individuals in the Upper Towns are certainly hostile towards the U.S. and nothing but the firm language of our Executive will prevent a war with them if encouraged by Mr. Bowles. - But I am far from being certain what part he will act (340).

The Indians followed the party to Pensacola where they kept up the hostilities as the surveyors lay behind the walls of the fort near the Panton store. Ellicott would blame much of this on the Spanish, whose escort, Major Minor, he deemed incompetent. He also pointed out the Indians that the Spanish said were Seminoles were in many cases Tallesee from the Upper Creek Towns. Bowles hold over the Upper Towns and the Seminole would end with his capture in 1804, but the hostility toward America and the Duplicity of the British would make the banditti on the Georgia – Florida border busy as beavers.

One of the concerns of Georgians was horse theft and another was cattle rustling. Creeks had learned to take cattle for their skins and as items to be traded elsewhere, on the other side of their nation. How this worked was similar to how all horse thieves seemed to work in those days. Things stolen in the East were sold or traded in the west. Cattle seemed to be a good thing to steal, and Creeks were learning the ways of ranching. Towns in Florida like Waccahota indicated their use as cattle pens (wacca = Vaca, Spanish for cow). When John Linder left East Florida in 1785, he left with several other of the East Florida banditti and settled in the Tensaw District near Mobile. Linder and later his son as well, got into the cattle business. The Creek seemed to have lots of cattle these days and Linder thought it necessary to trade cattle for ball, powder and clothing.

The only thing we know for certain is that the former bandit was now civil lieutenant of his district and a justice of the peace; and that he was interested in the cattle business. The chosen location was good. The Indians were friendly, markets-Mobile and Pensacola-were near, and the canebrakes along the streams provided excellent pasturage at all seasons of the year. In midsummer of 1788 we find John Linder, Jr. at Pensacola - not on a mission of selling but of buying cattle. With him and at his service were Carlos Hal, a cowhand, and Archibald Sloan, the owner of a small schooner loaded with goods of Linder's ownership. Through the circumstance that these visitors, as well as others from the Indian country, were at this time compelled by Governor Arturo O'Neill to give sworn testimony regarding another matter, we learn something, incidentally, about Linder's cattle business. Sloan's boat, it appears from the testimony, was loaded with shirts, blankets, coarse cloth, rum, and powder and ball. He was to proceed with this cargo along the coast to the town of the Indian "Buly" in the Lower Creek country. There Linder was to barter the goods for cattle. Then, we may infer, he and the cowhands were to drive the cattle overland to Tensaw, while the owner of the schooner was to return to the same destination by water (Lockey, 1945: 103).

Governor O'neill of Pensacola was questioning all visitors about what they knew of Bowles landing in Florida in 1788 and all the former banditti seemed to know plenty. Linder was immediately under suspicion and charged. O'neill rightfully
139

was concerned that Linder and Sloan were arming Creeks at the behest of Bowles for some sort of treachery against Panton and Leslie, the Spanish Government and intrigue with the Americans as well. Linder was apparently trading shot and powder with those Indians who were stealing cattle on the Georgia frontier. The cattle found their way to Tensaw and the Indians received the kinds of goods needed to keep up war against the United States. This sort of relationship between loyalists and Indians went on for years and threatened the peace with the new Government in Washington.

Andrew Ellicott, Surveyor.

Fla. Governor Arturo Oneill.

2007 Cox, Dale, **Two Egg Florida: A Collection of Ghost Stories, Legends, and Unusual Facts,** Lulu Publishing: Toronto.

1905 Chappell, Joseph Harris, **Georgia History Stories**, Houghton-Mifflin Co.: Boston

1966 Holmes, Jack D.L., **The Southern Boundary Commission, the Chattahoochee River, and the Florida Seminoles,** *The Florida Historical Quarterly* Vol. 44 No. 4, Florida Historical Society: St. Augustine.

2002 Kimball, Christopher, **Bowlegs History,** @http://www.kreweofbowlegs.com/bowlegshistory.htm

1945 Lockey, Joseph B., **The Florida Banditti**, *The Florida Historical Quarterly* volume 24 issue 2, 1783 pgs 88-108.

1994 McCarthy, Kevin M. **Twenty Florida Pirates,** Pineapple press: Sarasota.

1859 Stevens, William Bacon, **A History of Georgia: From its First Discovery by Europeans to the Adoption of the Present Constitution Vol. 1** Appleton and Co. in 1847. Vol. 2, E.H. Butler and co: Philadelphia.

1867 Wright, Robert, **A Memoir of General James Oglethorpe: One of the Earliest Reformers of Prison Discipline in England, and the Founder of Georgia, in America,** Chapman and Hall: London.

All Correspondence can be found in the Telemon Cuyler collection at the University of Georgia.

War of 1812

I have my Lord employed them with a Company of Rangers to repel the small plundering Parties of Rebel Banditry from Georgia, and to drive cattle from that Province to this. This my Lord is not a very honourable method of making war, but my Lord it is the only one left for supplying this town and Garrison with fresh provisions, as the Georgians would not allow the Cattle belonging to the Butchers who supply this Market to be drove hence. Besides, my Lord, the love of Plunder, engages many daring Fellows, instead of joining with, to oppose the rebels, and by their means, and a small naval force, I was obliged to engage, I have been able to secure the Settlements on the south of St John River: for my Lord the regular Troops are not well calculated for such moroding services (St. Augustine, 18th October, 1776, Governor Tonyn to Lord Germain).

What began as British Navy officers impressing American citizens into duty aboard their ships, in 1803, escalated into the War of 1812. Meanwhile the frontier was moving west: The Louisiana purchase opened up large areas on the Mississippi River and made navigation the sole jurisdiction of the United States. In both Georgia and Tennessee, new counties formed. In Georgia, settlement was pushed to the Flint River and newly formed Macon, Georgia. Here, along the Federal Road from Savannah to New Orleans, Benjamin Hawkins, the Agent for the Creek Indians, built the Creek Agency and Fort Hawkins. By treaty the Creeks had allowed a Federal Road to be built through their lands and soon overnight inns run by Indians; forts and stands popped up along it. If need be the United States was willing to send militia up and down the road to keep it open, should dire events force them.

Florida was once again filled with intrigue as Aaron Burr attempted to take matters into his own hands in a conspiracy with others to take Florida from Spain.

The plans of the Association called for recruiting 10,000 men from Kentucky, 8 to 10,000 Louisiana militiamen, 3,000 regular troops and 5,000 Negro slaves who were promised freedom. They would meet on the Natchitoches River in February or March. An expedition would be sent by sea to the Rio Grande, under the pretext of quelling existing border troubles. Then the Army would declare its independence from the United States. Some 50,000 American families would be given lands west of the Mississippi (Szaszdi, Jan., 1960: 247).

Burr was arrested and the plot foiled as America sought a wait and see course of action with respect to Spanish territories.

Meanwhile, in 1807, Congress had outlawed the importation of slaves into the U.S. Soon the Spanish had to contend with the "Moccasin Boys" of Camden County, Georgia, again. They now would operate in the Spanish domain for the purpose of smuggling slaves into the United States. British sailors from the West Indies were

142

also involved, this time slaves instead of guns. Blackbirders, slave stealers, were experienced guides for the smuggling operations, seeing the slaves got to markets in Georgia, South Carolina and even Indian Country. The Indians, themselves, had learned the value of slaves; in a culture where land ownership did not exist, horses, guns and slaves were the main assets.

Ft. Hawkins, the Creek Agency in Macon - from an early illustration.

From as early as 1726, the Spanish Government had welcomed runaway slaves from Georgia and South Carolina. These newly freed people had no means of support, so the Spaniards responded by setting up an area north of St. Augustine as a place for them to live and prosper. Its name was Pueblo da Gracia Real de Santa Terese de Mose:

…The Governor undertook to supply the settlement with provisions until its crops should be harvested. These measures were duly approved by the Council of the Indies and sanctioned by the King (Seibert, 1931: 3, 4)…

When the British reclaimed Florida, in 1763, the settlement was renamed "Moosa."

Much of the animosity of Georgians and other southerners toward the British and Spanish had to do with the inability of the British to account for slaves taken during the Revolutionary War and the less than helpful attitude both governments had in regards to the runaway slave issue.

Florida was a center of slave trading activities as early as 1810. To what extent can never fully be known because of the illegal nature of the trade itself and the scarcity of accurate records *for that period. A long and sparsely settled coastline and a close proximity to Cuba made it an ideal location from which to operate. When President Madison noted in 1810, that American citizens were participating in the traffic in African slaves in violation of the laws of humanity and in defiance of those of their own country, he was referring in part to the problem in Florida. The territory was known as a "nursery for slave breeders" and the avenue through which Negroes were regularly smuggled across the boundary into the southern states. Authorities regarded Fernandina and Amelia Island as headquarters for slave smugglers and pirates. <u>A joint resolution of the Senate and House passed on January 15, 1811, empowered the President to order the occupation of the area if necessary to maintain the authority of the United States</u> (emphasis mine, Stafford, 1967:125-126).*

By 1811, other problems were coming to a head for President Madison, primarily the growing hostility of the British and the weakness of the Spanish Government in lands on the United States borders. Suddenly there was another reason to consider occupying Florida, militarily, to keep the British out of an area already festooned with miscreants, pirates, slave stealers and banditti. A strategy presented itself to Madison and congress. For years The Spanish and British had sought to lure more settlers to La Florida. They had been partially successful in populating East Florida with former Georgians and South Carolinians, but they had not really made any inroads into winning their allegiance to a British or even Spanish cause. So here were a lot of "Americans" living in Florida. The President and congress had in mind to induce these "patriots" to overthrow the Spanish authority there and annex themselves to the United States: after all, Napoleon had taken Spain and the Spanish Government could in no way help the Florida colonial administration.

Madison, in 1811, months before the outbreak of the War of 1812, delegated the task of taking East Florida to the former Georgia Governor, General George Mathews, the same George Mathews mentioned in the Richard Lang letter concerning the 1795 rebellion. Col. John McIntosh, a Florida "patriot" became an instrument in this **Patriot War** of 1811-1813. McIntosh and others who had become successful in Florida complained bitterly to the Spanish authorities about the banditti who threatened them constantly with death and privation and into that nest of rattlers stepped Mathews as he prepared to enter Florida:

…It was familiarly termed the "jumping place" of criminals and desperate characters from Georgia and Florida. The Moccasin Boys were even then making their slave and cattle stealing raids into the Indian country. Outlawry was everywhere the dominant influence. The weak Spanish Government could offer no effective protection to the planters in the northeast. Many of the nominal subjects of Spain were disaffected, first among whom was General John McIntosh, an ideal leader for such a revolution as the one contemplated (Fuller, 1906: 192)…

If Mathews seemed unaware of what he was up against, he soon learned the nature of the problem in Florida.

Hastening to St. Mary's, a small place on the American Side of the Line, Mathews encountered a condition of affairs, as he construed his instructions, demanded that immediate possession be taken on the plea of self preservation. The river was alive with British shipping engaged in smuggling goods into the United States in manifest violation of non-importation law. Amelia Island, which was situated at the mouth of the St. Mary's River, just off the coast of Florida, was a notorious resort of smugglers. Fernandina, the Spanish town on the island, was merely an entrepot for their illicit trade. Spanish authority existed there more in fiction than in fact. No law of any kind was in force.

After making diligent Inquiries, Mathews concluded that to obtain quiet possession was impossible. The profits of the illegal traffic were far too alluring to be thus tamely surrendered. Inferring that the country was to be taken at all events, he recommended the employment of force (Fuller, 1906: 191)…

On March 17, 1812, Fernandina was occupied by Mathews' men, and on April 12th Fort Moosa was taken, just a few miles from St. Augustine. From the point of view

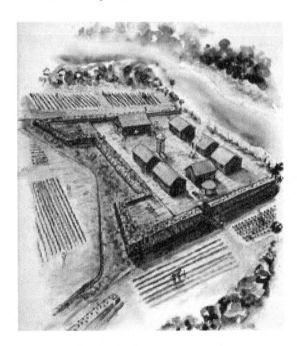

Artist's rendering of Fort Moosa, north of St. Augustine.

of those loyal to Spain or Britain, this was seen as an invasion. The loyalist, O'neill family of Fernandina, recalls the spring of 1812 in dire terms:

Border troubles like the outbreak in which Henry O'Neill lost his life (1791) died down occasionally but they were never wholly extinct. Southern Georgia was overrun by gangs of

145

ne'er-do-wells, troublesome to law-abiding Georgians, hated and feared by Floridians. Moccasin Boys, the name applied to this outlaw element, crossed the St. Mary's River to steal and to destroy. Roaming as far as the St. John's they stole slaves and horses and cattle. They burned buildings. They ruined crops. They stirred up the Indians to a dangerous pitch. In the spring of 1812, the United States Government gave left-handed authorization to the invasion of East Florida and the Moccasin Boys seized upon this authorization as a go-ahead signal to themselves. For more than a year thereafter, only Amelia Island, where United States troops were stationed, and St. Augustine, which held out against the invasion, were safe from their depredations. The St. Mary's area was ravaged (O'neill Family at Rootsweb).

The Spanish retook the fort and burned it, forcing the Americans to build their own fort called Picolata. From here the entire operation began to bog down. Politically, Madison now saw the operation as an embarrassment. The Department of State wrote to General Mathews in March:

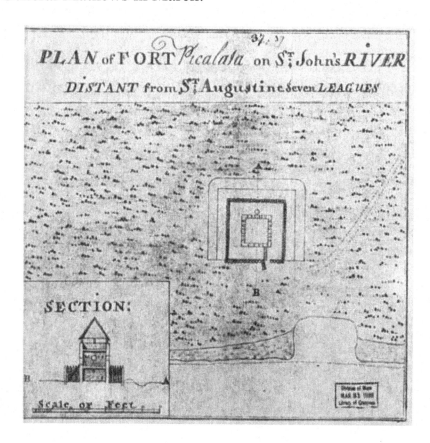

Ft. Picolata storehouse and fort (detail from Roberts Jeffery's Map 1763).

I have had the honor to receive your letter of the 14th of March, and have now to communicate to you the sentiments of the President on the very interesting subject to which it relates. I am sorry to have to state that the measures which you appear to have adopted for obtaining possession of Amelia Island and other parts of East Florida, are not authorized by the law of the United States under which you have acted (April 4th, 1812)…

146

Madison then replaced Mathews with Georgia Governor D.B. Mitchell, who soon found himself surrounded and on his own. He did not have enough men to take the Castillo at St. Augustine and Spanish reinforcements were due in at any time. The Seminoles and Negro banditti were now free to roam through the settlements of the patriots, looting and burning their houses. By September things got even worse. On the 9th Seminoles attacked Ft. Picolata and destroyed the storehouse of provisions. On the 12th, a supply train headed for Georgia was attacked and several men killed by Negroes and Seminoles in ambuscade. The patriots and the Americans were now cut off. Mitchell had fared no better than Mathews, requiring relief in the form of troops from Georgia. Madison responded by relieving Mitchell of duty in East Florida, replacing him with General Pinckney. Of course, by this time, The War of 1812 was in full swing.

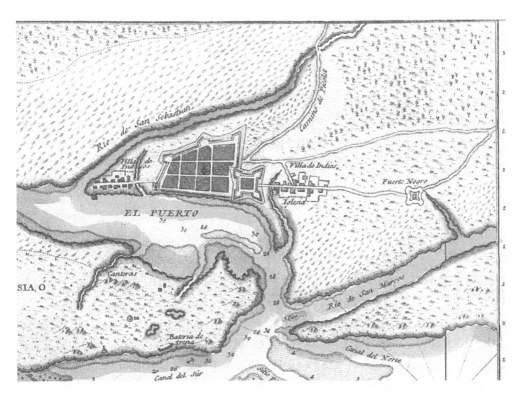

St. Augustine with Fort Moosa on the right, being north on the map
(Tomas Lopez de Vargas Machuca, 1783).

America declared war on Britain and things did not go well at first. Washington was burned and there were many other setbacks. In the South, British Col. Nichols appeared at Pensacola, the Spanish indicating they would not interfere with his war-making. Nichols would begin training Indians and negroes in the streets of Pensacola, for upcoming battles with the Americans.

147

In 1811, the Shawnee Prophet, Tecumseh had given a talk at Tuckabatchee, one of the Upper Creek Towns, eliciting support for making war against the Americans. The Creek nation was divided over this question and the Lower Towns decided to stay neutral and the Upper towns chose "red sticks" indicating they would go to war. They would need plenty of guns and ammunition for this so the Red Sticks headed to Pensacola to be outfitted. At Pensacola, Red Stick Peter McQueen demanded powder and shot from the Spanish governor, who refused on the grounds it would upset Spanish treaties with America. McQueen next went to Panton and Leslie, the Loyalist trading company that had been supplying weapons to the Creeks for many years.

McQueen's insolence was recorded in a letter from John to James Innerary (July 30, 1812), the former a partner in the trading firm:

… McQueen then was about to harangue me, but I interrupted him & told him of what the Governor had informed me, of their threats - & exclaimed against their ingratitude, I told them that they ought to be ashamed of their conduct towards the house & that they were very much mistaken if they thought to get any thing from me by threats & menaces, that I was indeed very much surprised how they could have the assurance to ask any thing from me when I had been from month to month & day to day in the Constant expectation of receiving a large sum from them in Cash in payment of their debts according to their solemn promises to me. Altho' McQueen every now & then interrupted me & tried to change the conversation, yet I continued to talk (West, 1940: 252)…

On the way back to the Upper Towns McQueen and his party were attacked by Americans at Burnt Corn Creek. Scattered at first, the Creeks rallied and drove the Americans from the field. This seemed to set off the Indians to do something of a drastic nature. Within a month McQueen, Jim boy or high head Jim, Weatherford, Prophet Francis and other Red Sticks would descend on Ft Mims, near Mobile and slaughter 350 American men women and children.

America was already at war and General John Floyd was sent by the Georgia Governor to the Chattahoochee to cover the Federal Road from the Creek Agency at Macon to New Orleans. He built Ft. Perry at Mauk, Ga., halfway between Macon and present day Columbus, crossed the river and built Ft. Mitchell on the Alabama side where the Federal Road crossed the river. To supply him, General Thomas Pinckney sought to build a fort at Standing Peachtree, near Cross Keys (Lawrenceville, Ga.) where flatboats would make their way down the Chattahoochee to both Floyd and Gen. Andrew Jackson:

Late in January, 1814, Pinckney conceived an idea to use the Chattahoochee River as a highway for supplying Floyd's and Jackson's armies in the Muscogee country. The Linchpin,
148

in this plan, was a fort to be built at Standing Peachtree, a Cherokee village on the future site of Atlanta, Georgia. Supplies would be floated down the Chattahoochee from that point 150 miles south to Fort Mitchell. In a trial run one boat made the trip successfully (Obrien, 1895: 133)...

Fort Peachtree was built but not used to supply Alabama, but there was indeed flatboat traffic on the upper Chattahoochee.

Protecting the Federal Road from the banditti of Peter McQueen and others was a priority for the Americans and was in an earlier treaty which allowed a federal road from New Orleans to Savannah. Other roads led off to Pensacola and Mobile and all were choked with traffic of new settlers. Built in 1811, by Lt. Lucky and

Ft. Mims Massacre - Keenan engraving, Encyclopedia of American Indian Wars, 1845.

American soldiers, the road went from Fort Stoddert at Mims Ferry on the Alabama River, east to the Chattahoochee River, where Ft. Mitchell was built in 1813. During the war other forts like Hull and Bainbridge were built along the road. At the first sign of trouble, settlers would rush to the safety of a nearby fort. Most efforts at frontier safety in forts succeeded, some exceptions were Fort Loudon and the Fort Mims massacres.

With the massacre at Fort Mims, General Andrew Jackson was pressed into service. He and his Tennesseans went into action at Talladega, Calebee and Holy Ground, routing the Redsticks there. Next the Hillabees felt the wrath of another

149

force of Americans. Meanwhile, Gen. Floyd moved his troops west along the Federal road and defeated the Red Sticks at Atossee, below old Ft. Toulouse. Cherokees under Major Ridge and John Ross joined in the fight as Jackson cornered all the remaining Resticks at Horseshoe Bend on the Talapoosa River. In the fight for the Redsticks were Menawa, the horse thief, and William Weatherford, Red Eagle, the Red Stick leader at the battle of Holy Ground.

Another Red Stick leader who was at Horse Shoe Bend was Savaner Jack, also known as Savannah Jack or Souvanoga Jack. Alabama historian Pickett said of him:

He boasted that he had killed so many women and children, upon the Cumberland and Georgia frontiers, in company with his town's people, that he could swim in their blood if it was collected in one pool (421).

Fort Perry to the crossing at Fort Mitchell. The northern road was built to the covered bridge in Columbus many years later (from an 1839 map).

It was clearly Savaner Jack's banditry among the Tennessee settlements and later Georgia settlements that won him his reputation. He lived near Red Eagles on the Talapoosa River at Souvanoga, a well known Shawnee village in the Upper Creek towns. Shawnee lived all over the Creek and Cherokee nations and were welcomed in both. Savannah, Georgia is named after the word for Shawnee.

Thomas Woodward of Alabama in his **Reminiscences,** recalled discussing Jack's father with William Weatherford and others in years past:

As I have before stated, a number of the Uchees went North-West with the Shawnees, many years ago. And not long after they reached their new homes on the waters of the Ohio, they
150

commenced their depredations on the frontier settlers of Virginia and Pennsylvania. In one of their scouts they captured a white boy on the frontier of Pennsylvania, by the name of John Hague. This boy Hague was raised to manhood among them, and proved to be as great a savage as any of them. He took an Uchee woman for a wife and raised a number of children…

Hague raised an illegitimate son by a white woman named Girthy or Girty, and called his named Simon Girty, after his mother. This boy was brought up about Detroit. It was said that he and a man by the name of Wells contributed much to the defeat of Gen. St. Clair… Hague came South with his Indian family bringing with him some Uchees and Sowanokas, and settled them on Fawn Creek, or what is now known as Line Creek, near its mouth and on the Montgomery side of the Creek. Hague died and was buried on a mound near where there was once a little village, settled by the whites, called Augusta. This I have learned from Doyle, Walton, Sam. Moniac, BillyWeatherford, and many others. And Savannah Jack was his youngest son by the Uchee woman (1858 letter to F.A. Rutherford)…

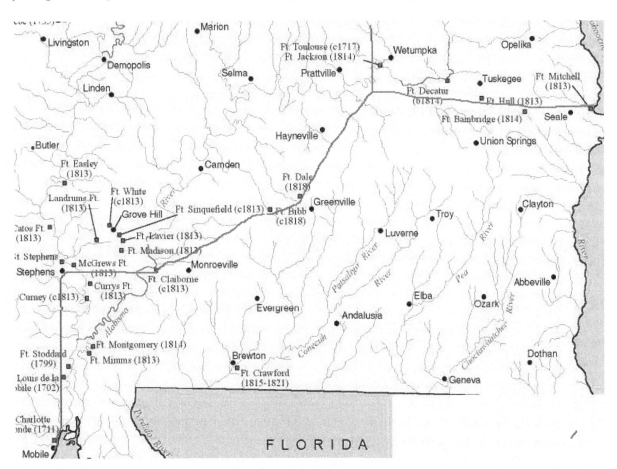

Alabama forts along the Federal Road and the road to Mobile, based on a map at:
http://alabamamaps.ua.edu/contemporarymaps/alabama/historical/index2.html

James Dreisback, noted chronicaler of the Creeks and related to most, called him "..**A man of blood—one-handed Savannah Jack (1885, in *Alabama historical reporter)...*** " Others say he was a Yuchi but it's clear he was light complected and possibly a white man. His history is checkered and surrounded in mystery. Not much is known of his background:

...presumably before the Revolution he had worked at a store in Augusta. By 1789 he was in Pensacola, where Spanish authorities became furious when he killed a local cowkeeper. A decade later, at the head of a party of twelve Shawnees, he was living at Miccosukee, collaborating with Bowles in schemes concocted in the Director General's fertile mind. Savannah Jack served with the Creeks in 1814, survived the bloody defeat at Horse Shoe Bend and subsequently retired to Florida. At some point his ears were cut like an Indian's, indicating that Jack had paid a price for his roving eye (Wright, 1986: 121)...

Jack is best known for two massacres he attended in Alabama. The first occurred along the trade route to Pensacola, in 1788.

The "Pensacola Trade Route" is well known in Alabama history especially on account of the several incidents of a murderous nature which took place along the trail. Murder Creek, a tributary to the Conecuh River, which watershed makes the Escambia in Florida, gets its name from the fact that at a celebrated camping place where the trail crossed a stream northwest of the present site of Brewton, Alabama, Colonel Kirkland and a party of Royalists traveling in the late 1780's from South Carolina to Pensacola and accompanied by General Alexander McGillivray's man servant, were waylaid at this point and all but the servant were murdered. Savannah Jack and a celebrated white man of the Hillibi town, the Cat, two traders, having visited Pensacola and learning that the South Carolinians had a sum of money in their baggage, murdered the party and escaped with the loot. The incident and the scene made the site famous and to this day it is called Murder Creek (Brannon, 1952: 8)...

Pickett, in his **History of Alabama,** recounts the story as well, ascribing the crime to a white intruder:

...This party consisted of a Hillabee Indian, who had murdered so many men, that he was called Istillicha, the Man-slayer—a desperate white man, who had fled from the States for the crime of murder, 1788 and whom, on account of his activity and ferocity, the Indians called the Cat (1859:383)...

Pickett adds a twist to the gruesome nature of the scene, reminding the audience, that the Cat, when captured, was hung upside down on the spot where the murders occurred and shot through with a pistol ball.

The other massacre by the outlaw Savannah Jack was called the Ogley Massacre, which happened along the same road on March 6, 1818. This time the pretext was the First Seminole War and Jack at the time was living in Florida and plundering along the Federal Road. Jack and his warriors attacked the Ogley house, killing Mr. Ogley and 4 of his children and a woman who was visiting. A week later, Jack shot two more settlers dead on the road and accosted and beat another to death
152

(Little, 1885: 26-32). A later pogrom involving the murder of three Hall children and a negro in the vicinity of Fort Dale seemed the work of Jack and his men. He retreated to Florida and safety.

Weatherford appears before Gen. Jackson at Ft. Jackson (From Charles Morris, Pictorial History of the United States 1907).

Jimboy, High head Jim (McKinney-Hall).

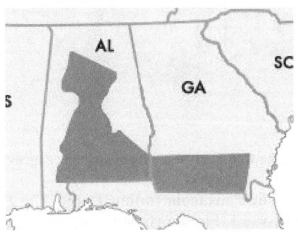

Creek Cessions from the Treaty of Ft. Jackson

After Horseshoe bend, Jack, Peter McQueen, High Head Jim and many Red Stick leaders exiled to Seminole country. Woodward recalls:

…Jack and his people being Uchees and Sowanokas, called a halt on the Sepulga, about there and on the line of West Florida, where he remained until he went West (Woodward, 1859, April 2cd, 1858 to F.A.Rutherford)…

Menawa, the Creek leader at Horse Shoe Bend, wounded, escaped and and hid his people at a place called Cahawba.

The Red Stick War ended with the total defeat of the Creeks at Horse Shoe Bend on the 27th of March, 1814. A peace treaty was drawn up by Gen. Jackson at Ft. Jackson (old French Ft. Toulouse) and the Creek were forced to cede huge tracts of land in South Georgia and Middle Alabama Territory. This only served to infuriate the Creeks to more depredations, and there to help thcm were their old friends the British.

The Canoe Fight during the Red Stick War, from an early engraving.

July 1952 Brannon, Peter A., **The Pensacola Indian Trade,** *The Florida Historical Quarterly* vol. 31 issue 1, Florida Historical Society: St. Augustine. Pages 2-16

1906 Fuller, Herbert Bruce, **The Purchase of Florida: Its History and Diplomacy,** The Burrows Brothers Co.: Cleveland.

1885 Little, John Buckner, **The History of Butler County, Alabama, 1815 to 1885,** Street Printing Co: Cincinnati.

2005 Nelson, Megan Kate, Trembling **Earth: A Cultural History of the Okefenokee Swamp,** Univ. of Ga. Press: Athens

2003 O'Brien, Sean Michael, **In Bitterness and in Tears: Andrew Jackson's Destruction of the Creeks and Seminoles,** Greenwood Publishing Group: Santa Barbara, Calif.

1851 Pickett, Albert James, **History of Alabama: And Incidentally Georgia and Mississippi...,** Walker and James: Charleston.

2008 Schutz, Noel, and Don Green, **Shawnee Heritage,** Vision ePublications: Oregon.

July 1931 Seibert, Wilbur H., **Slavery and White Servitude in East Florida, 1726-1776,** *The Florida Historical Quarterly* volume 10 issue 1 Florida Historical Society: pages 4-24.

October 1967 Stafford, Frances J., **Illegal Importations: Enforcement of the Slave Laws Along the Florida Coast,1810-1828,** *The Florida Historical Quarterly* volume 46 issue 2, Florida Historical Society: pages 125-134.

1922 Swanton, John R., **Early history of the Creek Indians and Their Neighbors**, Smithsonian Institution. Bureau of American Ethnology, Govt. Printing office: wash D.C.

April 1940: West, Elizabeth Howard, **A Prelude to the Creek War of 1813-1814 In a Letter by John Innerarity to James Innerarity,** *The Florida Historical Quarterly* volume 18 issue 4, Florida Historical Society, pages 248-267.

1859 Woodward, Thomas S., **Woodward's Reminiscenses of the Creek, or Muscogee Indians, contained in letters to friends in Georgia and Alabama.** Barrett & Wimbish, Book and General Job Printers: Montgomery, Ala.

1986 Wright, James Leitch, **Creeks and Seminoles**, Univ. of Nebraska Press: Lincoln.

Col. Nicholls stationed himself at Fort Barancas until Jackson appeared.

The End of Tory Dominance

...Peariman had started for pen returned back to his town where their is one of the British offersers and said afte he could send a runner to pencecoler he would cum on -- the British offerser told them if they did not go and spil blood -- he would take from them all his guns again – (letter from Henry Wiggington to Benjamin Hawkins, Dec. 2, 1814)...

The British continued their hostilities even after the end of the War of 1812. The Battle of New Orleans, was actually fought in 1815 after the war had ended but the news had not reached the Southwestern frontier. In May, 1814, British Captain Hugh Pigot had landed **Lt. George Woodbine** at Apalachicola and began arming the local Indians against the Americans. He also had orders to feed and house those Red Sticks fleeing the Creek nation. Pigot assured his superiors he could arm at least 2800 Indians and perhaps take New Orleans in a quick assault (Mahon, April, 1966: 289). He further sought the alliance with Pirate Jean Lafitte and his Baratarian forces in this effort but Lafitte sided with the Americans.

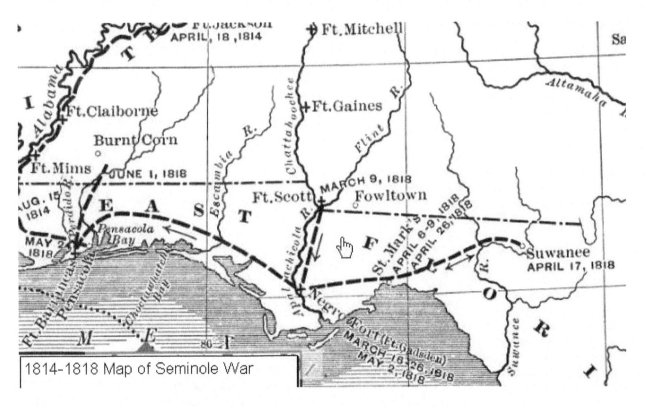

1814-1818 Map of Seminole War

Jackson's Indian and Gulf Campaigns, 1813 -1818. Dixon Ryan Fox, Harper's Atlas of American History (New York, NY: Harper & Brothers, Publishers, 1920).

Meanwhile, Captain Woodbine had worked his way about fifteen miles up the Apalachicola to a place called Prospect Bluff. There, he started what was to become a center of British, Indian, and Negro opposition to the United States for the next two years. He also made an agreement with two chiefs in which they promised to turn all prisoners over to him. One chief, Thomas Perry man, marked the agreement as "King" of the Seminoles, and the other, Cappachamico, as "King" of the Mikasuki. They claimed to represent all the Indians of the region (290)...

Woodbine saw the results of the Red Stick defeat and did what he could to keep them alive and ready to fight the Americans:

...When he first landed, he found the Red Sticks dying of starvation in the swamps around Pensacola, and he saved them with the small quantities of supplies he could spare (293)...

Col. Edward Nicholls, in late 1814, was in Pensacola at Fort San Miguel. The Spanish had looked the other way when he landed to take up operations against the Gulf Coast settlements. Nicholls and his 100 men had several artillery pieces and 1000 stands of rifles and 300 uniforms to give to Indians and runaway slaves. He began drilling them in the streets of Pensacola in the fine points of British warfare. Unfortunately, Gen. Jackson appeared before Pensacola with 3,000 men and 5 cannon and Nicholls fled with all the Indians and Slaves in tow...much to the concern of those owning the slaves. Fort Barrancas and San Miguel were blown up so as not to fall into Jackson's hands and the town was left for the Americans to occupy (302).

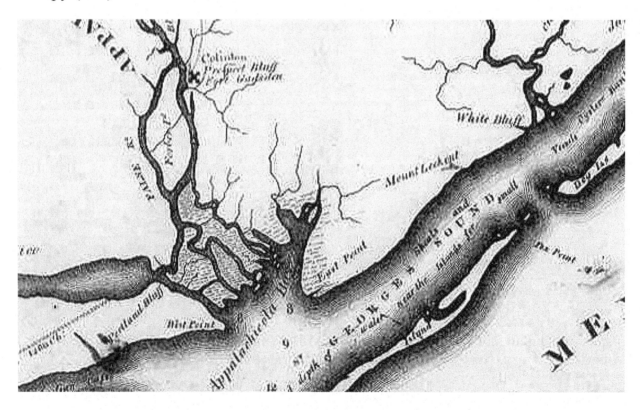

Prospect Bluff and Ft.Gadsden, built over the Negro fort.

Nicholls and his new friends removed to Prospect Bluff to join Woodbine in his activities with the Red Stick survivors of Horse Shoe Bend. Benjamin Hawkins had warned the War Department that the British were intent on rescuing the defeated Indians and setting them against our interests once .

He reported to the Secretary of War on July 13th that he had examined an intelligent runner from the store of John Forbes and Co., east of the Apalachicola, who stated that three British officers had sent him to Coweta and Cussetah to invite the chiefs down to receive arms and ammunition, ostensibly to kill game, and various individual Indians were reported to have already received supplies. He further mentioned that a chief had been sent to invite the surviving hostile Indians from Konocau (Conecuh) to Apalache and had reported they were coming, but so exhausted by famine that many must perish on the way. In a further report dated Aug. 16, Hawkins says that while the British have undoubtedly furnished a considerable supply of ammunition for war, they have deceived the Indians by landing and reembarking men from their armed vessels. They are training the Indians and some negroes for purposes hostile to us (Boyd, October, 1937: 70)...

Nicholls opened a factor or store near the confluence of the Chattahoochee and Flint Rivers to supply the Indians with shot and powder. When the war of 1812 ended, Hawkins was quick to remind Nicholls that British Admirals Cochrane and Cockburn had ordered all British troops out of the Floridas. The troops left but Nicholls stayed. He argued that the Treaty of Ghent ending the war was being misinterpreted and he had every right to arm the Indians (73). Then there was the problem of the 300 slaves Nicholls had taken with him from Pensacola. He had in fact black-birded them against the wishes of their Spanish owners. Panton-Leslie's slaves were involved and complaints were made. The activity of Nicholls and Woodbine at Panton-Leslie had created considerable bad feelings and had the effect of turning the Creek away from the old trading Company. Company manager **Edmund Doyle**, in a letter to John Innerary, in 1815, chronicled the activities of the British at Apalachicola:

Good God, of what substance must the hearts of these inhuman men be made of: figure to yourself a British Colonel and a respectable character a British agent, to sit down coolly at a post belonging to their friends and allies, and meditate the destruction of a poor defenceless set of indians, already ruined by their enemies whom they were sent to protect, and which common humanity would dictate to preserve but hearts hardened with iniquity, such as Nicols and Woodbine are only actuated by private interests ...

...It is well ascertained that hundreds of negroes was carried away from the Nation, that many are left behind, we all know by common report, and every negro I saw says they were seduced from their Masters-we also know that there were only a very few (not more than ten) American Negroes, arrived at the Bluff: Still this villainous affair was so ably managed that it will be difficult to prove that they were seduced from their masters except by the Black people who voluntarily return-all we can say is that the hero Nicolls and Woodbine sat down at the

159

Bluff (except Woodbines trip to St. Augustine) and by help of their agents and black spies, corrupted the negroes of their friends and Spanish allies-(1939: 242)...

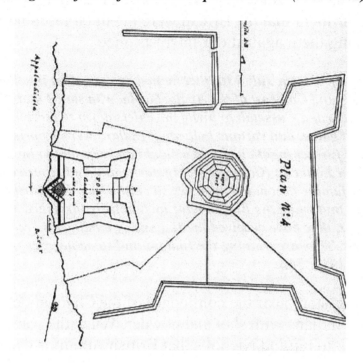

The Negro Fort and Fort Gadsden built over it. (Fla. Historical Qtrly,Vol. 16: 73, July, 1937).

Suddenly, things got worse for Doyle and Panton-Leslie. Nicholls and Woodbine left, putting **Alexander Arbuthnot** in charge of the Nicholls' store. Doyle was forced to work for Arbuthnot, abandoning the interests of Panton-Leslie. The Indians were also looting the assets of Doyle's factor and taking his cattle (FHQ, April, 1933: 192):

*To the Honble. R. C. Spencer Captn. R. [oyal] N. [avy] and Robert Gamble Esqr. * * ***

Pensacola 2d May 1815

The Honourable the Commissioners for Victualling his Majesty's Navy London. Debtors to John Forbes & Co. for the amount of upwards of four hundred Heads of Cattle of different sizes and ages Killed by the Red Stick Indian allies of His Britannic Majesty in the Creek Nation at a time of extreme distress for want of provisions as p. account of same kept in the Books at their Establishment at Prospect Bluff on the River Appalachicola .... $2,668 3 1/2 Deduct

The value of 50 Heads which is reported still exists on the Cattle range .... 400 Dollars 2,268 3 1/2

Arbuthnot opened a second store on the Wakulla River at the location of the old Panton-Leslie store and was soon arming Indians and runaway slaves from that location as well. The Indians began a series of raids on Georgia and on boats coming upriver. In 1816, several U.S. Whaleboats were attacked from the Nicholls fort, now called the "Negro Fort". In response Gen. Jackson sent ground troops under **Gen. Duncan Clinch** and Gunboats under **Jarius Loomis** to destroy the fort. After several days of bombardment a heated ball was sent into the powder magazine of the fort. It exploded, killing mostly women and children. The fort's black commander, Garcia was arrested and shot and Jackson hoped the whole affair was at an end.

The fort was found to possess a surprising armament mounted and ready for use. It included 4 twenty-four-pound cannons, 4 six-pound cannons, beside a field piece and howitzer. In addition there were found 2,500 stands of muskets with accoutrements, 500 carbines and 500 swords. The Americans were informed that it also contained 300 quarter-basks of rifle powder and 162 barrels of cannon powder, besides other stores and clothing; the whole appraised at not less than $200,000 in value. Nicholls' project had not failed for lack of supplies (Boyd, October, 1937: 81,82).

But the plans of Nicholls and Woodbine were still in play. Woodbine sent **Robert Armbrister** into Florida to more aggressively implement what was now a plot to take East Florida from Spain and threaten the Americans. Attacks became more ominous and another war was almost at hand. In November, 1817, Lt. Edward Scott was sent downriver to assist Major Muhlenberg's three supply boats headed for Montgomery and Mobile. Scott and 27 passengers were returning north and when they approached the confluence of the Chattahoochee and Flint Rivers they were attacked by Blacks and Indians under **Homathlemicco.** All were killed save six men who escaped. This incident was soon forgotten by everyone except Gen. Jackson, who was later that year ordered to take Gen. Gaines command at Ft. Scott at the confluence of the two rivers.

Meanwhile, Armbrister's attempts to take East Florida were augmented by **General Gregor McGregor**, formerly associated with Simon Bolivar in South American revolutions, who with a hundred or so men invaded Florida from Georgia.

East Florida had not changed an ounce since Mcgirth and Bloody Bill Cunningham ruled there. In fact, a contemporary letter to President Adams, dated 1818, indicates things might have even gotten worse:

...The people who inhabit the Territory which lays between the two rivers mentioned before are a hardy and desperate set of men who generally possess but little, if any, property except a

161

rifle, a horse, and perhaps a few cattle or hogs - and whom the barrenness, extent and nature of the country have served to assimilate in character to the aborigines of America, or the tribes of wandering Arabs who roam about Africa. These men who had generally been engaged in the Insurrection which took place in the country in the year 1812 absolutely put the Spanish authorities at defiance from that time till sometime in the year 1816. During the time of their complete Independence they established a kind of Government amongst themselves, having found it impossible to live in a complete state of nature - and as but a few of them had any inclination for agriculture, the general poverty of the soil of the country not being adapted indeed to afford any considerable prospect to the honest and laborious husbandman, it being principally that description of land called Pine Barren which this people live on and which is only fit for grazing, they subsisted chiefly by aggression on the property of the people who were well disposed to the Spanish Government and under its authority - negroes and cattle were what pleased the rapacity of this people most as they were able to turn the above description of property to a better and more speedy account than any other kind. The former they generally carried to the back country where people are too anxious to obtain that description of property that they rarely troubled themselves about the title of the seller whether just or unjust - and with the cattle they have helped to supply our markets in these frontier counties with beef - not a single individual's property in that country was safe who was not inimical to the Spanish Government. A number of plantations were indeed entirely broken up and the least connection with the constituted authority was sufficient to provoke aggression on their part (as specially aggressor was so much to their interest) against any individual who was unfortunate enough (I may say) to be any considerable proprietor of negroes and cattle. There has been too for a long time another source for the active exertion of this people and which kind of depredation has been carried to a very great extent by this and another set of unprincipled men belonging to our country; it has been bringing Indian cattle from the Atlotehawa Territory where they were obtained without a purchase.

It is presumed a number of 1000 head of cattle have been taken in this manner which have generally been driven into the U. S. and here disposed of in the same way as the same kind of property belonging to the peaceable inhabitants of the Province has been. This kind of injustice with which the Indians have been treated has no doubt more than any other aggression provoked the vengeance of that misguided people and has been the primitive cause of involving this country in the present war with them. With this horde of men at last the Governor of East Florida was obliged to humiliate himself so far as to enter into a negotiation and make peace with, having found it impossible with his slender forces to reduce them to a state of subjection. The Treaty was principally made in consideration of the deplorable situation of the people belonging to the Province who were disposed to live quietly. The conditions of which were that the Insurgents should consent to be at peace with the rest of the Province for which concession on their part they were invested with the right of trying their own criminals, of making their own laws, and of regulating themselves generally as they pleased, but what those Insurgents principally gained and what was the only cause, I presume, that they were willing to conclude in a treaty (when war on their part was in many respects so much more advantageous) was that the Spanish Government agreed to perfect their different titles to the lands they occupied which they knew in case of a change of Government they held by a somewhat precarious tenure. As to the depredations committed on the Indians by stealing their cattle, they still continued (FHQ, Jan., 1927, 164 -166)....

T. Frederick Davis, Writing about the events following the first "Patriot War", also describes the banditti that made East Florida their home in the absence of real law and order from the Spanish or any other Government:

...Altogether they were a collection of roving frontiersmen who deemed it advisable to make it as uncomfortable for the Dons and the Indians, and everybody else, as possible. As a consequence, there was little attempt to occupy the country for legitimate and peaceable pursuits. The main stamping-ground of this class of people was the territory between the St. Johns and St. Marys rivers, eastward of the King's highway, which led from the cow-ford (now Jacksonville) to the St. Marys River at Colerain, Georgia...

Occasionally Lynch's law, then popular in Georgia, was resorted to with efficacious results. Gradually the people become comparatively quiet. It must be said, however, that their laws did not contemplate the business of smuggling, and the old system of taking cattle from the Indians still continued (July, 1928: 10 -11).

Into all this stepped McGregor, who immediately sold a number of slaves captured on Amelia Island...this served to alarm anyone who owned slaves. At his Headquarters on Amelia Island he outfitted a gunboat and sent it to privateer down the Mosquito way. These pirates and banditti were surprised by regular Spanish troops and 10 were killed plundering a plantation:

...The following are the names of the killed: Capt. Morrisson, Sandford, Robert Wilson, Wm. Wilson, Ledlow, Thomas Williamson, Wellibey, Thomas Osman, Alexandro, and a Frenchman. All were Irishmen, Scotchmen, and citizens of the United States, except the Frenchman (22)...

As McGregor's influence waned in this operation others would appear to take over. One of them was a French Pirate whom McGregor had obviously met in South America, Luis Aury. Aury took over Amelia Island, annexing it to Mexico and used it as a base of operations for his pirates. When he was able to smuggle over 1000 slaves into Georgia in less than two months, locals became interested in his ability to boost the economy and his support among the population rose. At this point the United States Navy stepped in, taking Amelia Island and witnessing the departure of Aury and his thugs.

Woodbine rescued McGregor and brought him to New Providence, the Bahamas to encourage him to continue the quest for East Florida. In the meantime, Armbrister landed at Tampa to build a settlement that would be the springboard of his Florida empire. He ransacked the Arbuthnot store, commandeered Woodbine's schooner and sailed to the Suwanee River to collect Woodbines Indian allies (Davis, July 1928: 656, 657) But Gen. Jackson was also on the move. Prophet Francis and

Homathlemicco made the mistake of boarding a schooner they thought was British and were caught by Jackson's men. After Jackson took Fort St. Marks, the two were brought before him and hanged. Arbuthnot was captured at the fort and Armbrister was later caught at Old Town. Both were court martialed at St. Marks and executed by Jackson. That ended the First Seminole War.

Prophet Francis and Homathlemicco are delivered to St. Marks. (Fla. Archives).

"The trial of Ambrister during the Seminole War: Florida" (illus. from 1848)

October, 1937 Boyd, Mark F., **Events at Prospect Bluff on the Apalachicola River, 1808-1818:** *The Florida Historical Quarterly* volume 16 issue 2, Florida Historical Society pages 56-97.

Oct 1926 Cubberly, Frederick, **John Quincy Adams and Florida,** *The Florida Historical Quarterly* volume 5 issue 2, Florida Historical Society, pages 89-94.

2000 De Wire, Elinor, **Guide to Florida Lighthouses**, Pineapple Press: Sarasota

July 1928 Davis, T. Frederick, **MacGregor's Invasion of Florida,** *The Florida Historical Quarterly* volume 7 issue 1, Florida Historical Society, pages 4-72.

July 1944 Davis, T. Frederick, **Pioneer Florida,** *The Florida Historical Quarterly* volume 23 issue 1 Florida Historical Society, pages 40-45.

July 1933 **Letters of John Innerarity and A. H.,** *The Florida Historical Quarterly* volume 12 issue 1, Gordon Florida Historical Society, Pages 38-42.

July 1926 **Letters Relating to MacGregor's Attempted Conquest of East Florida, 1817,** *The Florida Historical Quarterly* volume 5 Issue 1, Florida Historical Society, pages 55-58.

July, 1966 Lowe, Richard G., **American Seizure of Amelia Island**, *The Florida Historical Quarterly* volume 45 Issue 1, Florida Historical Society, pages 19-31.

April 1966. Mahon, John K., **British Strategy and Southern Indians: War of 1812,** *The Florida Historical Quarterly* volume 44 issue 4 Florida Historical Society, pages 286-303.

Jan 1939 **The Panton, Leslie Papers: Letters of Edmund Doyle, 1815,** *The Florida Historical Quarterly* volume 17 issue 3 Florida Historical Society pages 238-243.

April 1939 **The Panton, Leslie Papers: Two letters of Edmund Doyle, Trader, 1817,** *The Florida Historical Quarterly* volume 17 issue 4, Florida Historical Society, pages 313-319.

July 1939 **The Panton, Leslie Papers: A letter of Edmund Doyle, Trader, 1817,** *The Florida Historical Quarterly* volume 18 issue 1, Florida Historical Society, pages 62-64.

Jan 1927 **The Patriot War-A Contemporaneous Letter,** *The Florida Historical Quarterly* volume 5 issue 3, Florida Historical Society pages 163-168

July 1952 Rutherford, Robert E. (ed.), **Settlers from Connecticut in Spanish Florida, 1808-1816,** *The Florida Historical Quarterly* volume 31 issue 1, Florida Historical Society, pages 34-51.

Jan 1960 Szaszdi, Adam, **Governor Folch and the Burr Conspiracy**, *The Florida Historical Quarterly* volume 38 issue 3, Florida Historical Society, pages 240-252

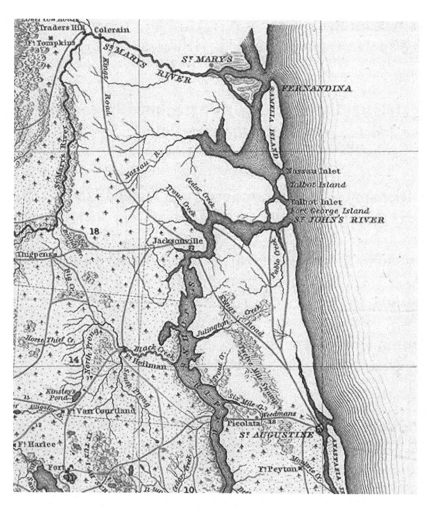

St. Augustine, 1839 War Dept. Map.

NEENOSKUSKEE

Gen. Jackson became the American Caretaker of the Floridas. There was an uproar in Washington from his critics who said he had violated the sovereignty of La Florida by entering the country, but this fait accompli was just what was needed and the Spanish were soon convinced to part with these lands. After years of wrangling, Florida had become U.S. territory in 1821 and a state in 1845. The vagrant, Tory, Indian, runaway slave, banditti nest along the St. Marys River was now under American control.

Were these banditti forced up the Chattahoochee where they began robbing and murdering as a **Pony Club**? There is proof some of that banditti moved into the Creek Nation, but the Creek had their own set of banditti: people like Peter McQueen, Savaner Jack and Menawa all of whom had their own bloody reputations. Some McGirths ended up with Bowles and in the Creek nation and many went to Oklahoma. Those names familiar with the banditti based in either Camden County, Georgia or East Florida are gone and a new set of names ascribed to the Pony Club in various Georgia counties appears. There is no evidence that the former has anything in common with Professor Meier's Pony Club.

To discuss how Pony Club came to be in a place like Carroll County, Georgia, we must digress and talk about a group of people who had absolutely no love for the Indians nor the authority of the states of Georgia, Tennessee or Alabama. Leslie Hall, in **Land and Allegiance in Revolutionary Georgia,** talks about a group of malcontents who moved into Georgia as soon as it opened up:

Outlaws had come into Georgia as soon as it began to be settled. James Oglepthorpe complained of outlaws from Carolina coming into Georgia during the 1730s, and Johann Bornemann note the arrival of thieves from the neighboring provinces in the middle 1750s. By the mid 1760s the South Carolina backcountry, with approximately 35,000 settlers had become overrun by bandits as a result of inadequate civil authority (2001: 10).

Hall notes that as early as 1767, 20 horse thieves were operating in the Savannah area **with the help of local residents** (emphasis added: 11). Outlaws like these were pouring in from Virginia and the Carolinas, taking horses and cattle from settlers and Indians and selling them in Virginia. Many simply lived on Indian land to escape colonial law.

…The Creeks viewed these squatters as troublesome and wished the royal government would stop them from trespassing on their land. When the "crackers", or "Virginians", as the Creeks referred to them, ignored the boundary between Georgia and Indian territory, that had

167

resulted from the 1763 Treaty of Augusta, they threatened the peace. The squatters despised the Indian and British policy of upholding Indian treaty rights (11).

This was echoed by Creek Agency head Benjamin Hawkins, who in 1796, visited many of the towns in the Creek nation. He admitted to many chiefs that organized theft by white intruders was becoming systematized:

What would most likely the soonest disturb this friendly disposition of the Indians? Intrusion on the hunting grounds and horse stealing….The latter was encouraged entirely by the whites in the nation, many of whom were more depraved than the savages, had all their vices without one of their virtues. The whites have reduced the stealing of horses to a system, their connections are extensive. Some in Cumberland, Georgia, Tennessee, and among the neighbouring tribes. This evil being now so deep-rooted that it would require much exertion and some severity to put an end to it (Hemperly, 1969: 210-211)...

As soon as new lands were opened in Georgia, squatters arrived to trespass on them. The Back-country was filling up with poor, landless drifters, like the ones described living along the Great Dismal Swamp in Virginia or the Ninety-Six in South Carolina. Another important thing is that these crackers would not join local militia units and couldn't be counted on to defend settlements. Hall points this out, placing the number of possible Indian enemies of Georgia, in 1773, at 10,050 and the state's potential Milita at only 2,828 (2001:13).

In describing early Talladega, Alabama, Vandiver (1954: 40), explains a distinction between the early whites in Creek country and the later squatters.

Many white men were here in 1800, adventurers, "Indian countrymen," who had married Indian women, and were mostly traders, speaking the language, wearing the dress and accepting the customs of the Indians...

But the squatters were not the kind of people who would later become famous Indian Traders or interpreters. Unlike the McGirths, Linders and Burgesses, these bandits were not welcome in the Creek or Cherokee Nations and showed no compliance with British or American authority. They had no leaders and no compunction about trespassing on land owned by Indians or planters. They were Milfort's "crackers"; the sum of nearly 200 years of emptying Europe's prisons and a set of people with generations of disrespect for any type of authority. They were most responsible for the removal of the Indians, because they simply refused to stay out of Indian lands. In fact they hosted the runaway slaves and the criminals hiding from the law, making Indian country a complete nuisance for the yeoman farmer and the planter.

The fuel for this engine that was eating up the frontier was the Law of Pre-emption, which, by 1807, allowed squatters to stay on government land (not Indian land as was usually the case) until it was sold, at which time they had to leave. The **cycle of forcing Indian land into American hands** worked thusly: As soon as land was snatched up by local planters and rented to the yeoman farmer, the landless were encouraged to move onto Indian lands where they would serve as a buffer between the landed and the Indians. Lawlessness would reign, causing regulators to arise, who would put it down in a most bloody way, overstepping their bounds and creating the type of society which now feared its own government. Government would finally step in and the Indian land would be annexed. The cycle was repeated everywhere on the frontier and would continue to be for another 100 years in the West. It all started with vagrants trespassing on land that belonged to someone else.

In 1791, Caleb Swan traveled through the Creek Nation and described the people and culture to Secretary of War Henry Knox. Swan's report indicated the cycle of cultural destruction was already underway there:

…the whites living among the Indians, with very few exceptions, are the most abandoned wretches that can be found perhaps this side of Botany Bay; traders; hirelings; pack-horse men; licenses; purchasers; but the Indians don't suffer them to cultivate much land (May 2, 1791)…

One way to control intruders was to require a pass from the State Government, or a license from the Indians. Thousands who passed through Georgia and Tennessee on their way to Alabama, Mississippi and Louisiana are listed in books kept by the State Governors. This did not solve the problem, because the vagrants and squatters almost never had permission from anyone to do what they were doing. In many cases Militia would find a group of licensed hands of local Indians side by side living with these unwanted intruders. This list from 1809, in Tennessee, indicates the problem: Some intruders were in Cherokee Country at the behest of Indians while others were squatting, and separating the two was not always easy.

Sequchee Valley on Indian Land, 22 April 1809

Intruder	Indian who hired him
* Reuben Rogers	Cropper for Settler Terrapin
* Harris K. Wylly	Cropper for Jno Rogers Senr

* James Haney	hired by Jno Rogers
* Jeremiah Rogers Senr	Hirelings for Tarrepin
* Jno Hamilton	Cropper for 8 Killer
* Jacob Hamelton	Hireling for ditto
* Jeremiah Alexander	Cropper for Salaisger(?) Junr
* Wm. Burke	D° for Jno Watts
* John Carrson	Do for Jno Jolley
* John Livingston	D° for Charles Rogers
* Wm. Farmer	Do for Richard Benge
* Andrew Farmer hireling	for D°
* Adam Stinson	Cropper for James Rogers
* Wm. Steward	Do for Ezekiel Harlan
* Thomas Johnson	D°. Tolantuskee
* Robert O Niel hierling for	D°

* with permits

Without Permits

Andrew McWilliams,	James Hogan,
Joel Wheeler,	Mr. Bassam,
Robert Walker,	Mr. Bassam,
Hercules Jones,	Mr. Bell,
Davis Griffith,	Thurmon Shelton,
Hines Griffith,	James Robbinson,
Thomas Woodcock,	Mr. Ellis,
Robert McGrew,	Randal McCaniel

In North Georgia was the Wofford Settlement and in Tennessee were settlers over the new territory line by mistake. It caused Indian agent Return Meigs and later Benjamin Hawkins much grief to try to reduce these illegal settlements. The settlers refused and eventually lines had to be rerun to accommodate them.

The intruder problem annoyed the Creeks as well. In 1805, A Clark County, Georgia Militia Col. sent this "return", presumably, to the Governor Listing trespassers against the 1802 Treaty of Fort Wilkinson:

A return of the Tresprs on the South Side of the appalacha on the Lands purch at A treaty of Forte Wilkonso in the 1802 and on the Lands beteen the Line astablisht by that Treaty and the okmulgay River --

[Signed] Joseph Childers1	*[Signed] Grifen Morgin-21*
[Signed] Richmon Shearly2	*[Signed] William Morgin-22*
[Signed] Michel Childers-3	*[Signed] William Lambard23*
[Signed] Nathanuel Ward-4	*[Signed] William Lafton-24*
[Signed] William Crane-5	*[Signed] John Studars-25*
[Signed] Isaac Bankston-6	*[Signed] Finest Watley-26*
[Signed] John Stagner-7	*[Signed] John Eads-27*
[Signed] John Dudleay-8	*[Signed] Henry Jones-28 -*
[Signed] Thomas Townsin-9	*[Signed] James Fant South State*
[Signed] William Maxwell10	*[Signed] John Wooten-30 -*
[Signed] Abslam Still-11	*[Signed] John Dunn-31 -*
[Signed] Isaac Han South 12 State	*[Signed] Charles Dunn32*
[Signed] Joseph Han South 13	*[Signed] Eligay Lambard Se 33*
[Signed] Francis Walls-14	*[Signed] William Lambard Jun*
[Signed] John Walls-15	*[Signed] Bengamon Briges 35*
[Signed] Ely Hulcay-16	*[Signed] William Ellis 36*
[Signed] Joseph Philips-17	*[Signed] Bengamon Conner-37*
[Signed] John Magee-18	*[Signed] Francis Person-38*
[Signed] Lewis Brantly-19	*[Signed] Wm [illegible] -39*
[Signed] Edwin Lambard20	

We Do sartify the above Return is a true Statement us this 5th march 1805
[Signed] Sam Braswell
[Signed] A Braswell

[Signed] Edwd Moore Colo of Clark County Redgiment] June 27th 1805.

Between October 16, 1811 and March 16, 1812, 3,700 Whites traveled down the Federal Road to Mississippi (Ethridge, 2003: 220). Anyone could see the inevitability of Indian lands becoming overwhealmed by emigrants. The central portion of Alabama had become U.S. territory after 1814, and in a short time much of the land was inundated with intruders.

The white settlers in the county (Chambers) at that time were located mostly in the northern and eastern portions of the county, in such neighborhoods as where there were but few Indians. The

171

white inhabitants were mostly from the State of Georgia, and were intruders on Indian territory (Richards, 1942: 418).

Before the land sales Huntsville was a straggling village of squatters, living on government land and in the rude log cabins (Taylor, 1930: 308)...

One James White reportedly settled at the location (Cahaba) in 1816 and for a time it was called "White's Bluff." The second white settler in the vicinity is said to have been Lorenzo Roberts. Both were probably squatters (Hobbs, 1969: 156, quoting Edgefield in Dallas Gazette, February 24, 1854)...

During the years 1810, 1811 and 1812, General Hampton gave the squatters, through this county (Limestone), on Indian lands, much trouble and loss, by sending squads of Soldiers through the country to burn and destroy their patches of corn, vegetables, fences, etc.; in some instances burning their huts and cabins. The squatters, in turn, gave him much trouble, in various ways; to-wit: in secreting the stock, horses, cows, and other property, run out of Madison county, into this, then Indian sections, to evade impressment, the paying of debts etc., etc (Malone, 1867: 2)...

The Idea that Indian land would be used by squatters as a place to hide booty from robberies and land pirating was not confined to Alabama. Col. Return Meigs, responsible for running squatters out of Limestone County, Alabama Territory, also had problems in Tennessee. Citizens of that state pleaded with him to remove intruders from Cherokee lands who were plundering the countryside:

We the citizenry of Franklin County beg leave to represent that lately a band of Thieves has been discovered who when at their respective places of residence are found to be Interspers'd among the People of Franklin, Warran & Madison Counties and a considerable proportion of Them Residing on the Indian Land who have founded places of Deposit for Stolen goods. It has been clearly discovered by the confession of some of the parties and by a great Quantity of Stolen goods being found on the Indian Land that theft & There only they make their places of Deposite. By means of which their business is Very much facilitated. There has been found of the Stolen goods 12 Horse Loads. the number of thieves is Said to Exceed one hundred all Connected by the Usual ties that bind such Characters -- as our Country Is Very much Infested and Our property Very Unsafe by Reason of these Nefarious Characters We beg that you will Interfere and Use Such means or procure Such force as you may think necessary to Remove all persons who Contrary to Law has Settled on the Cherokee Land which we believe will be one of the most Effective means to remove those pests by which our Country is Infested (May 7, 1814: Wallis Estile et al. to Col. Meigs)...

This was also happening in South Georgia where large groups of men were trespassing onto Creek lands:

Tatnall Decr. [December] 28th 1816

Sir; His Excellency D. B. Mitchell

I take leave to inform your Excellency that this Frontier is ogmenting fast, with vagrants, their is many new Settlements made on the Indian land Since the 1st of November, and the evil Continues the settlers have no visible means to subsist. the alternative of Course must be theft It intirely escapd me; when with you last to ask for the appointment of State agent that I might have removed those Vagrant Intruders; I now Request that appointment for I am well convinced that if Something decisive is not done the Frontier Setlers will Suffer more than they wou'd from a Hord of Savages that negro thief Williams is who made his escape from the Sheriff of this county Sum time past is now in Tatnall Jail, what Course will be pursued as Regards his detention. I am at a loss to Conjecture he Williams, denies the Jurisdiction of our Courts, to try him as the theft was Committed in Florida it is a pity that the United States and the Spanish Government Cou'd not make Sum arrangement, to punish those offenders against the laws. think that if their is not Sum measure adopted that Considerable bloodshed will be the final Result; as Vagrants from all parts of the Union are flocking to Floriday, or the Indian Land. I submit the ways to your Excellency, the means you are in possession off.

I pray your Excellency to accept the Homage of my Consideration

 M. Hardin

The Treaty of Indian Springs, February 12, 1825 from an 1825 illustration.

However, The State of Georgia was winning the battle against intruders on Creek Indian lands. After the 1st Seminole war, Governor Troup sought to negotiate the

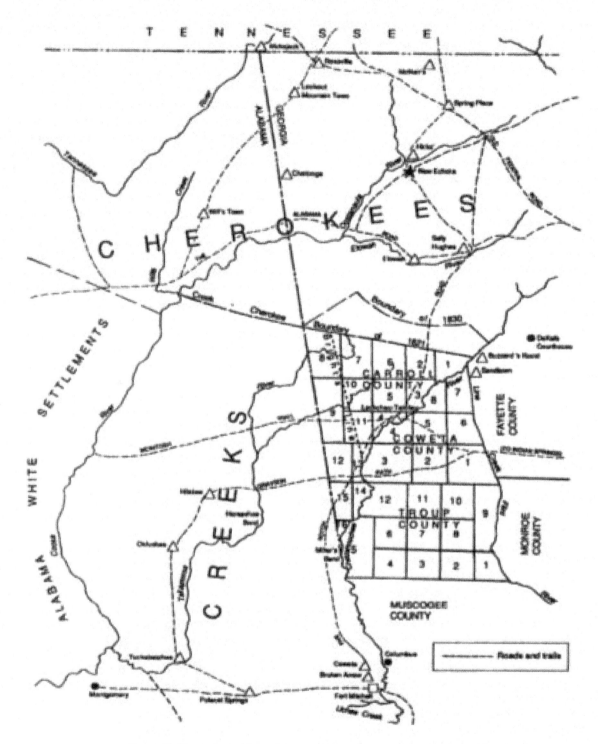

Carroll County and environs, 1827, from Bonner 1971: 258.

removal of the Creek Indians altogether. From 1816-1821 more land was ceded and counties like Gwinnet and Dekalb as well as many others were formed, leaving only a strip on the western border of the State in Creek Indian hands. William McIntosh and several minor chiefs signed away that strip in 1824 at the Treaty of Indian Springs and were immediately murdered by Menawa and other Creeks. The Creek were paid some $400,000 to emigrate west of the Mississippi and counties like Carroll and Muscogee sprung up in 1827. The Creeks were no longer in Georgia.

With the Creeks gone, Intruders in Georgia concentrated on the Cherokee lands in the northwest section of the state. In an old Hillabee village, peopled by exiles from the Red Stick War and called Oktahasasi or Sandtown, located on the Chattahoochee River in Dekalb County a new set of horse thieves settled. They would steal horses in newly formed Carrollton and sell them in Cross Keys (Lawrenceville) or, later, Marthasville (Atlanta). They were reported as far north as Stone Mountain and as far south as Macon and along the Federal Road. Reports of their activities would later come in from Alabama, west of Carroll County. As Dekalb developed, these miscreants crossed the river and settled in Carroll County, which at that time extended all the way to Creek lands on the Alabama-Georgia border. Immediately situated above Carroll County was the Cherokee nation, another border to be plundered and intruded upon.

Most of what is known of the Pony Club is in relation to the problem of intruders on Cherokee lands, illegally mining for gold. The Georgia government had described them as trespassers and in response formed the **Georgia Guard** or rangers in 1830, to run intruders off Indian land. The Cherokee reacted in a less than lukewarm fashion, extolling the shortcomings of a mere 60 men with the responsibility of covering the Cherokee Nation in Georgia. It wasn't long before the Guard was accused of helping the Pony Club.

The Roll Book of the Georgia Guard-1831

Col. John William Augustine Sanford, Commander
Headquarters of the Guard Agency at Scudder's, Cherokee Frontier

Whereas, by an Act of the General Assembly of the State of Georgia, passed the 22d December, 1830, his Excellency the Governor is authorized and empowered to raise and organize a guard for the protection of the gold mines in the Cherokee Nation, and for divers other purposes, and Whereas, His Excellency the Governor has appointed Col. J.W.A. Sanford, Commander, and Col. Charles H. Nelson, Sub-Commander of said guard,

NOW Know all men that we whose names are hereunto subscribed have enrolled ourselves members of said guard under the above mentioned officers, and, hereby, obligate ourselves

to perform all the duties of good, faithful and trusty Soldiers for 12 months from the date annexed to our respective names, unless sooner discharged by the Commander - in - Chief.

Enrollee's name	Enlisted	Residence
Jacob R. Brooks, 1st Sarg't.	8 Jan. 1831	DeKalb
Caleb Sappington, 2nd Sarg't.	3 Jan. 1831	Wilkes
Elias Henderson, Sarg't.	8 Jan. 1831	Jackson
Thomas J. Rogers	6 Jan. 1831	Jackson
William C. Perry	8 Jan. 1831	DeKalb
---nt T. Henderson	13 Jan. 1831	Hall
---vid Booker	6 Jan. 1831	Jackson
--- Sample	10 Jan. 1831	Hall
--- R. Brown	12 Jan. 1831	Hall
--- Barnes	15 Jan. 1831	Gwinnett
--- PettyJohn	7 Jan. 1831	Jackson
--- Whetchel	11 Jan. 1831	Hall
--- Miller	5 Jan. 1831	Jackson
--- M. Cantrell	10 Jan. 1831	Hall
--- Yancy	12 Jan. 1831	Hall
--- Haines	14 Jan. 1831	Hall

We whose names are hereunto subscribed consent to the foregoing obligation:

James M. Reed	13 Jan. 1831	Hall
John T. Cox	13 Jan. 1831	Hall
John C. Pope	3 Jan. 1831	Wilkes
Jacob Butman	12 Jan. 1831	Hall
John W. Hay	2 Jan. 1831	Wilkes
William Word	7 Jan. 1831	DeKalb
Green W. Durham	1 Jan. 1831	Baldwin
David Roundsavell	8 Jan. 1831	Clarke
Nathaniel G. Henderson	8 Jan. 1831	Jackson
Charles Haynes	14 Jan. 1831	Hall
Bechel Bradley	14 Jan. 1831	Hall
R.T. Fowler	14 Jan. 1831	Clarke
John Daniel	14 Jan. 1831	Hall
Nathaniel B. Harben	14 Jan. 1831	Hall
Redding Pinson	4 Jan. 1831	Hall
Jesse Townsend	6 Jan. 1831	DeKalb
John Ballard	3 Jan. 1831	Wilkes
John M. Jay	8 Jan. 1831	Clarke
Joseph W. McSherry	6 Jan. 1831	Jackson
William Tippen	14 Jan. 1831	Hall
Thomas F. Booker	3 Jan. 1831	Wilkes
Samuel Hall	1 Jan. 1831	Baldwin

Battle of Leather's Ford

The Georgia guard had been created by the Georgia government for the express purpose of policing the Cherokee nation as part of the program to enforce jurisdiction over it from the 5 adjacent counties. The Guard was to arrest those illegally gold mining, whether they be white or Cherokee and to keep the peace between the Cherokee and whites in the nation. On January 16, 1831, the Guard found itself in quite a predicament as it sought to bring some intruders to justice. Writing to Governor George Gilmer, Col. J.W.A. Sanford, commander of the Guard chronicled the difficulties faced by Col. Charles Nelson as he attempted to carry out his orders in the Cherokee Nation:

Received Thursday, February 10, 1831, letter from Col. JWA Sanford, to Gov. George R. Gilmer:

"Agency, at Scudder's, January 22, 1831

Sir,
In my letter of the 15th inst. to your Excellency, I mentioned that Col. Nelson was charged with an expedition to the Upper Mines. On Monday the 17th inst. he returned to Head quarters, having successfully accomplished the object of his march. I regret, however, to add, that in the performance of that duty, he has had to encounter difficulties of the most serious and embarrassing nature. I regret it the more, inasmuch, as I may have induced the belief that the law in relation to this territory would be readily submitted to, and would itself, thus become a sufficient safe-guard of the interest it was designed to protect. I must confess, however, that I have been mistaken - not, indeed, in the character of those from whom the position has arisen, but from the DARING and OUTRAGEOUS manner of their resistance. Col. Nelson, in his enterprise upon Daniels' (Upper Mines) having succeeded in arresting several persons, guilty of working the mines since the 1st, their friends and former associates became apprised by some means of their capture, and from their subsequent conduct, no doubt, resolved upon their release.

For this purpose, they assembled in force (between 50 and 60) early in the morning of the 16th at Leather's Ford, having ascertained that the command with the prisoners, would cross the Chestatee at that place. The first act of their hostility was indicated by their having caused a number of obstructions in the passage of the river, with the view of harassing the detachment and otherwise perplexing and retarding its movements. These were, however, avoided without any great difficulty and the opposite shore having been reached in safety, the van escorting the prisoners resumed its line of march. It had proceeded but a short distance, when the sergeant commanding the rear brought intelligence of its being attacked to Col. Nelson. Having secured the prisoners (11 in number) with a sufficient guard, he hastened immediately to the scene of engagement. Upon his approach, the assailants desisted from their attack, with the exception of three, who continued the assault with great fury until checked by the bayonet. One of these, the vilest of the vile, received a couple of severe wounds, believed at the time to have been mortal; but upon examination, it was found that he was not likely to experience the fate so richly merited by his infamous life, and still more infamous conduct in this affray. Previously to the encounter, he had, I learn, professed the utmost contempt of Georgia, her laws, her officers, denied her jurisdiction over this territory, and encouraged those who were inclined to violate her recent enactments in relation thereto, with the protection of his chivalrous arm. In the practical demonstration of his prowess, he has learned a lesson, which may hereafter be servicable to himself and a hint to rights or infringe our laws. Its good effects have already been experienced, for I understood, that no less than 70 of those desperate and abandoned wretches have suddenly disappeared from their former haunts in the settlements. Even before the occurrence of the affair at the Ford, individual members of the guard, when alone, had been insulted and menaced in a manner that evidenced the most inveterate and rancorous feeling. Aware of their hostility, from what he too had seen, Col. Nelson advised his men to a cautious and circumspect deportment whilst passing them, and to refrain from any expressions or observations. In obedience to this order, the command were proceeding quietly and peaceably, when the outrageous abuse of this horde elicited a reply from one of his men. In an instant, as if by pre-concert, the whole clan commenced gathering stones, billets of wood, and every species of missile, discharging them at the guard. It was with the utmost difficulty that they were restrained from returning this unexpected salutation with a volley of musketry. Again and again were their pieces leveled whilst the often repeated, order 'reserve your fire' alone prevented their discharge. Your Excellency will discover in this attack, a plan previously arranged and directed (?) with considerable military tact. They calculated that by engaging with the rear, that the front having charge of the prisoners, would be necessarily called to its relief, and that an opportunity would thus be presented of effecting their escape in the confusion which would ensue. The precaution of the commanding officer prevented the accomplishment of this design. Having failed in their attempt, they next sought his arrest by legal process, and accordingly a warrant was obtained, demanding the surrender of himself and command. Seeing the very improper purpose for which this writ was issued, he (col. Nelson) doing his duty, and accordingly marched to Gainesville with his prisoners, where eight of them were committed for trial at the next (Superior) court. Having thus gotten rid of his charge, he declared that it was neither his wish nor intention whilst apprehending others for violating the law, to oppose any resistance to it himself; that the course he had pursued was founded in a sense of duty; if in its discharge he had done wrong, he was willing to submit himself to any tribunal having cognizance of his offence. The hue and cry against the Guard for its conduct in this transaction has spread far and wide through the country. Falsehoods, accusing them of crimes of the most atrocious and aggravated character, are daily fabricated and circulated for the purpose of rendering them odious to the public. The motive for this is too palpable to be mistaken for a single moment. The mines under the protection given them are no longer a source of profit and employment - - Misrepresentation and calumny have busied themselves in exciting clamour; and clamour it is thought will effect the removal of the troops. The mines will then be left defenseless, and an opportunity again afforded them of renewing their depredations, whilst impunity is secured them by their number. These are the calculations of the idle and dissolute. These are their avowed objects, and really, Sir, they have set at work systematically for their accomplishment. In my former letter, I said something about this class of people. I cannot now dismiss them without expressing to your Excellency my conviction that there does not exist on earth elsewhere, beings so vicious and so depraved. To me they seem to be predestinated and incorrigible, and that the punishment of this world are inadequate to their crimes Yet even with *these miscreants, when compelled to an intercourse, I have uniformly inculcated a respectful deportment, and I hope your Excellency will believe that nothing has been done which the good of the country did not IMPERIOUSLY demand.*

This has been my constant aim, and every thing will be done having a tendency in the least degree towards its promotion. The Guard, notwithstanding their exposure, retain fine health. Twenty of them, under command of Col. Nelson, left this (place) on the 19th for the Lower Mines, Sixes, Alatoona, etc. Daniels' will be again visited upon his return (Cherokee Phoenix, March 12, 1831, page 4, col. 1-4).

JWA Sanford

Col. Nelson had written a friend in Gainesville, Ga., Hall County, who in turn sent the letter to the **Cherokee Phoenix** on the 18th of January where it was reprinted.

Gainesville, January 18, 1831.

Dear sir,
In haste I inform you that on yesterday we had warm work at Leather's Ford. A detachment (of the State Guard), under my command was conducting eleven prisoners, when we were attacked by about sixty men who used everything but guns. We charged on them and dispersed every one of them without damage to my men. One of the assailants received severe bayonet wounds from which his recovery is considered doubtful (page 2 col. 2-4).

Col Nelson

Almost immediately, several private citizens sent in letters to the **Phoenix** indicating the gallant battle had not taken place at all and that the resident white miners had been abused by the Georgia Guard. H. Small, Robert Ligon, U.H. Snow, R. Hall and P. Kroft all signed documents indicating Nelson was lying about the events at Leather's Ford on the 16th of January. They were quick to point out things had gotten out of hand a day earlier when Sergeant Sappington of the guard knocked one man named Cron unconscious with his gun. The man had refused to open a gate for the guard. Next another man, Ligon had asked about the prisoners taken on the 16th and was threatened by the guard, with a musket. Col. Nelson then advanced on the crowd with Ligon with fixed bayonets, one man, Mr. Taylor being severely stabbed. The **Phoenix** (March 12, 1831) was convinced the whole affair was another incident wherein the Georgia Guard had overstepped its bounds in the treatment of people in the Cherokee Nation:

I notice Col. N. supposes the number in the battle array on the occasion to be 60. I am credibly informed there were not more than 15 or 20 and but two of those participated in the conflict and with them it was a matter of necessity, that is in self defense. Taylor has not recovered, Ligon by the timely aid of his friends escaped uninjured. Thus ended the brilliant achievement of the 16th, ult. and had it been me, sooner than have blazened it to the world, I should have let it sleep, and numbered it among the little unfortunate deeds of my life (page 4 col. 4).

Gold was discovered throughout north Georgia about 1829, though it was rumored to have been discovered in Indian Territory as early as 1818. Dahlonega, in northeast Georgia filled up with miners, as did Carroll County where, at Pine Mountain settlement, near Villa Rica, the precious metal appeared.

Villa Rica attracted considerable attention in 1830 with the discovery of gold on a nearby 200 foot rise called Pine Mountain in Douglas County (then Carroll). Within a short time Villa Rica was a bustling town of two thousand people, several hundred of whom were regularly employed at the mines around Pine Mountain (Williams, 1995: 64)…

Gold mining attracted not only the adventurous fortune seekers, but the claim jumpers and thieves as well. The worst sort of people arrived in North Georgia, and with them was Edward Isham, a man famous merely for being chronicled by his lawyer as the type of person found in gold-rush Georgia. **The Confessions of Edward Isham: A Poor White Life of the Old South (1998)** was written by Charles C. Bolton and Scot Culclasure from notes kept by Isham's attorney, Charles Schenk, later a noted North Carolina judge. Isham had killed a man in North Carolina named James Cornelius and was executed for it, his story kept in notes by his attorney. Of more interest are the notes on his time in Georgia, which chronicle the life of a "cracker' who has no respect for laws, is constantly moving to avoid prosecution, has little or no loyalty to family or women, but is attracted to the gold mining boom town. His story exhibits all the qualities associated with many who formed the Pony Club in North Georgia.

The authors note:

A pattern of life familiar to many white southerners developed in the Isham household. With an upbringing dominated by a father who taught his son to live by his fists and by a mother who is only a shadow in the narrative, even though she continued to live with her son long after the father abandoned them, Edward Isham grew up an aggressive boy. Added to the inculcation of violence was the uprooting of migration (51)…

Isham moved to Alabama to live with with his sister in law, causing a fight with his brother which forced him back to Carroll County…

When he next visited Ringgold, Isham cohabited with Caroline Brown, the sister of Mary's (in Alabama) cousin. Finally, when Caroline "became pregnant" Isham "quit her and married

Rachel Webb". Not only did Edward Isham freely consort with a large number of women; the women he knew-along with their other lovers-often knew each other as well (56)...

Only once did Edward indicate any remorse for his actions in life, while recovering from a fight in Chattanooga... but he had warrants against him and he had to move on (page 56). Isham's entire life story is a story of those vagrants and drifters, who indicate no love of any authority and therefore move on to the frontier. The have to move as land becomes more settled and controlled by law enforcement. As the authors indicate:

...Antebellum society likely viewed Isham as a threat because of his personal failure to subdue the violent passions that other southerners had overcome (50).

Gold mining activity required trespassing on Indian land most of the time. It required a complete lack of civility and disregard of the rights of others. It was a get rich quick scheme that bordered on outright robbery and so it was popular with those landless ne'er-do-wells that Virginia and other states pushed to the frontier to serve as cannon fodder against the Indians. The worst elements seemed attracted to Sandtown on the Chattahoochee River opposite the future site of Carroll County, Georgia. Early Dekalb County is described by Price (1997).

**Gold-Mining in Georgia. Harper's New Monthly Magazine,
June to November 1879: 519.**

The Etowah Trail continued westward to Sandtown on the Chattahoochee River, which at the time was considerably larger than the "settlement" at Decatur. Sandtown was as rough a town as the notorious "wild west" places like Dodge City. Gold had been discovered just across the Chattahoochee in Villa Rica, and fortune-hunters came in droves.

"Contemporary "youth gangs" had nothing on the "Pony Boys" who headquartered at Sandtown. The Pony Boys spent their time "rustling cattle, pillaging and harassing the Indians who lived across the Chattahoochee River. The Indians complained to authorities, and claimed the Pony Boys came from DeKalb County. Catching the perpetrators proved difficult, since it was easy for them to escape by crossing the river, where the white man's government had no jurisdiction."

A few Creek Indians continued to live at Sandtown even after the cession of 1825. Much of what is known about the settlement comes from testimony in the 1828 redrawing of the Coffee line, the boundary between the Creek and Cherokee from an 1821 agreement.

William McIntosh from McKinney-Hall.

Chili Mcintosh Picture from Indian Springs signing, he escaped assassination attrempt by Menawa and others.

Apothleyoholo came from Tuckabatchee to murder McIntosh (Mckinney-Hall).

Menawa from Okfuskee killed McIntosh (Mckinney-Hall).

1916 Betts, Edward Chambers, **Early History of Huntsville, Alabama 1804 to 1870,** Brown Printing: Montgomery

2007-05 **BlackSheep-L Archives,**
http://listsearches.rootsweb.com/th/read/BlackSheep//117

1942 Brewer, Rev. George E., **History of Coosa County part 1**, *The Alabama Historical Quarterly,* vol. 4 no 1, Spring, Walker Printing Co.: Montgomery, pages 9-151.

1959 Bryan, Mary Givens, Georgia Governor, **Passports Issued by Georgia Governors, 1785-1809,** National Geneological Society.

1991 Cadle, Farris W, **Georgia land surveying history and law**, Univ of Ga Press: Athens.

February 12, 1831 **The Gold Diggers, *Cherokee Phoenix***, page 2 col. 2-4.

March 12, 1831 **From the Ga. Journal, *Cherokee Phoenix***, page 4, col. 1-4).

1921 Eaton, RachelCaroline, **John Ross and the Cherokee Indians**, Univ of Chicago libraries: Chicago

2003 Ethridge, Robbie Franklyn, **Creek Country: The Creek Indians and Their World,** Univ. of N. Carolina Press: Greensboro.

2001 Hall, Leslie, **Land and Allegiance in Revolutionary Georgia,** Univ. of Georgia Press: Athens.

1953 **Historic Sites in Alabama,** *Alabama Historical Quarterly* vol. 15, no 1, spring, pages 25-56.

1969, Hobbs, Sam Earle, **History of Early Cahaba: Alabama's First State Capital,** *Alabama Historical Quarterly* vol. 31 no. 3 and 4, fall and winter, pages 155-182.

1998, Isham, Edward, Charles C. Bolton and Scott B. Culclasure, **The Confessions of Edward Isham: A Poor White Life of the Old South,** Univ. Of Georgia Press: Athens.

1870 Longstreet, Augustus Baldwin, **Georgia Scenes, Characters, Incidents,Etc in the First Half Century of the Republic,** Harper and Bros Publishers: N.Y.

1907 Lumpkin, Wilson Wymberley Jones De Renne **The removal of the Cherokee Indians from Georgia,** Dodd Meade and Co.: N.Y.

1964 Martin, John M, **The Senatorial Career of Gabriel Moor,** *Alabama Historical Quarterly* vol. 26 no 2, summer, pages 249-281

March 7, 1867 Malone, Thomas Smith, **Relating to the early history of Limestone County. Number Two,** *Athens Post*, Page 2, Column 3.

March 21, 1867 Malone, Thomas Smith, **Relating to the early history of Limestone County. Number Three,** *Athens Post*, Thursday, Page 2, Column 2.

March 28, 1867, Malone, Thomas Smith, **Relating to the Early History of Limestone County Number Four,** *Athens Post*, Thursday, Page 2, Column 2,

April 4, 1867 Malone, Thomas Smith, **Relating to the Early History of Limestone County. Number Five,** *Athens Post*, Thursday, Page 2, Column 2.

1988 McWhiney, Grady, **Cracker Culture: Celtic ways in the Old South,** Univ of Alabama press: Tuscaloosa.

1903 Michie Thomas Johnson, **Georgia Superior Courts**, **Georgia Reports,** The Michie Co. Law Publishers Charlottesville: Virginia.

1997 Peyer, Bernd, **The Tutored Mind: Indian Missionary-Writers in Antebellum America,** Univ. Of Mass. Press: Amherst.

1997 Price, Vivian **The History of DeKalb County, Ga. 1822-1900** DeKalb Historical Society: Decatur.

May 2, 1791 **A Report to Secretery of War Henry Knox on Travels Through the Creek Country in 1791,** @http://wardepartmentpapers.org/document.php?id=5135

1942 Richards, E. G., **Reminiscences of the Early Days in Chambers County 1,** *Alabama Historical Quarterly* vol. 4 no 3, fall, pages 415-445.

1989 Southerland Jr., Henry De Leon, and Jerry Elijah Brown. **The Federal Road Through Georgia, the Creek Nation, and Alabama, 1806-1836,** University of Alabama Press: Tuscaloosa.

1930 Taylor, Thomas Jones., **Early History of Madison County And Incidentally of North Alabama,** *Alabama Historical Quarterly* vol. 1 no. 3, fall, pages 308-317.

Spring 1954 Vandiver, Wellington, **Pioneer Talladega, Its Minutes and Memories** *The Alabama Historical Quarterly* vol. 16 no. 1, pages 9-155

1995 Williams, David, **The Georgia Gold Rush: Twenty-Niners, Cherokees, and Gold Fever,** Univ. of South Carolina Press: Columbia.

1987 Warren, Mary Bondurant and Eve B. Weeks, **Whites Among the Cherokees**, Heritage Papers.

Pony Club is formed

New mining towns sprang up in Carroll and other counties. Pine Mountain was a community of several hundred and Gainesville, in newly formed Hall County became a gold producing town. Clarksville in Habersham County and two towns in what would be Lumpkin County were formed. Dahlonega became the county seat, beating out Auraria, named after the Cherokee word for gold.

1864 War Dept. map indicating Leather's Ford, Auraria, Dahlonega and the US Mint.

As soon as Carroll County, Georgia was formed, the Pony Club moved in. Now that their border was gone, they could either operate as bandits against the Creeks if they moved west, or they could operate against the Cherokee from Carroll County. Eventually they would operate from several locations near Indian Country:

The Indians particulary suffered from the predations of an organized gang of thieves known as "The Pony Club" (Neenoskuskee in Cherokee), based in Carroll County, GA (especially Clean Town, Sand Town, Leather's Ford, and Buzzard's Point{roost} (Clark, 2004, Johnson, 2007).

In this setting, Richard, James, and Reuban Philpot and Allen, Josiah and Thomas York arrived as a group from Tennessee. They were related by marriage and had lived in several counties in Tennessee including McMinn, Rhea and Roane. Other relatives, the Ramseys, Johnsons, Uptons, Shipleys, Majors and Mahaffeys came with them. All indications from descendants are that they moved to Carroll County for the expressed purpose of being part of a criminal empire. All families were guilty of different kinds of thefts, mainly from the Cherokee, but most later became noted citizens and served in the Confederacy during the Civil War. Some had served in the Revolution, the War of 1812 and even the Seminole and Creek wars, they were not the shiftless vagrants who formed the entire Southern frontier.

William Philpot was married to Elizabeth York, daughter of Capt. William York... I don't know all that much about Reuben. He came to Carroll County, GA in 1826 with his father, siblings, other family members and members of the York clan. He was a member of the Pony Club, of which "old man Philpot" (probably his father, Richard) was identified as the leader (Lester: personal Communication).

A descendant of the York family also indicates the reason for the two families moving to Carroll County was for criminal purposes:

It was only a few years after Josiah's marriage, most of William's family, along with sons-in-law James and William Philpot, their father, Richard, and Sarah's brother, Thomas, migrated to Carroll County, Georgia, Indian land surveyed in 1826. The reasons why this area was chosen is a mystery since Josiah's father, William, was not awarded land in this lottery, however the choice of area was possibly dictated by their affiliation with the notorious Pony Club. Carroll County, which shared a border with Alabama, made an ideal field of operation for this notorious gang of thieves, slave traders, and claim jumpers, although it is not very likely that the York men were involved in most of these pursuits (D. Sanfilippo. June 20, 2007)...

Other members of the pony club, as listed in **Whites Among the Cherokee** in Carroll included:

Joel Leathers   Alexander Ramsey
James Johnson   William Shipley
Asa Upton   John Goodwin
Nathan Upton   Jack West

John West
Tom Hogan
Jesse Humphrey
Joshua Smith
JohnWelch
Mark Welch

Pinckney Welch
Edward Tatum
John Tatum
Hugh Tatum
Thomas Tatum

Other members listed in Newspaper articles *Columbus Enquirer, Macon Telegraph, Milledgeville Southern Recorder* and *Georgia Journal*, include:

Calloway Burke
James Cartwright
James Upton
Garret Langford
John Gilly
Willis Gilly
John Sappington
Allen G. Fambrough
William Wright
Thomas Blake

John A. Jones
Rabun Burke
Francis Adams
Nelson Allman
John Goodwin
Richard Blackstock
Thurmond
Gay
James Cannon
Roberts

Other people not mentioned as members of the Pony Club stole stock and belongings from the Cherokee Indians. Among them were:

Bart Bailey
John Price
Bethel Quillian
John Wright
Wiliam Wright
John Stancel
John Stancel, Jr.
Oliver Stricklin
William McKinney
Berry Atkison
James Wilson
William Lay
William Baker
Daniel Bird
Samuel Jones
Solomon Ratley

John Reaves
Moses Hendrix
George McDuffie
_____ Winn
_____ Huftutter
_____ Plum
_____ Bolen

Joel Leathers was mentioned specifically by the Cherokee as a thief and cattle rustler and leader of the intruders.

Leathers had a place located at Leather's Ford on the Chestatee River near Dahlonega, GA where the "Gold Digger's Road" crossed the river. He had another store on Salaquoya Creek in the Cherokee Nation. The Cherokee towns of Sixes and Dahlonega were in the area where gold was discovered in 1828, resulting in America's first full-blown gold rush. This event became the main reason for Cherokee removal According to Cherokee claims, Leather's stores frequently served as storage areas for many horses, cattle, and hogs stolen from the Indians (Johnson 2007, Clark, 2004).

The Pony Club's success can be tied directly to its position of power in Carroll and later Paulding and Polk Counties. Beginning in 1827, Members of this gang served on the Grand Jury and though not everyone on the jury was a member of the club, there were enough to assure members would not be indicted. They continued to appear on the Grand Jury and Petit Juries until 1832 when the "slicks" defeated them at the polls.

CARROLL COUNTY GEORGIA
INFERIOR COURT - AUGUST TERM 1827

A list of Grand Jurors drawed to serve at December 1827

JOHN MURKERSON	JAMES HARRIS
LITTLEBERRY WATTS	WILLIAM J. ARINGEN
JAMES DICKIN	JOHN GILBERT
HARREL FELTON	**JAMES UPTON**
THOMAS YORK	WILLIAM WATSON
JOHN P/ GILLISPIE	JOHN H. ROOKER
ROBERT COOPER	**SEABORN WATTS**
CHESLEY BURKES	FELIX H. WALKER
WILLIAM BRICE	**SAMUEL LEATHERS**
GEORGE MARLER	**WRIGHT MAJORS**
THOMAS BONNER	GEORGE W. NELSON
STEPHEN JAMES	**THOMAS HOGAN**

WILLIAM RIGHT
JOHN LONG

JAMES A. GARRISON
JOHN GADEN

A List of Petit Jurors selected for December term 1827:

SYRUS YORK
ALLEN YORK
JOHN WESENHUNT
HENRY WESENHUNT
GEORGE WESENHUNT
PHILLIP WESENHUNT
PETER WESENHUNT
JOHN MAREDITH
JOHN STEWART
BENJAMIN FREW
JAMES BRUMLEY
RUBEN PHILPOT
WILLIAM PHILPOT
JAMES PHILPOT
JOHN WRIGHT
CRAWFORD WRIGHT
EMSLEY HOGAN
CALAWAY BURK
LAWSON HOLMES
JAMES HOLMES
RICHARD CARNES
MARLIN JONES
ALEXANDER HOGAN
JOHN RIGSBY
JOHN LEATHERS
JONATHAN BOX
JOSEPH RISCHER
JACOB ELDERS
JOHN J. TAYLOR
JOHN CANIDA
JOHN WEBB
JOHN LUNA?
JESSE WRIGHT

WILLIAM URSERY
ALEXANDER TIDWELL
JOSHUA SMITH
EDWARD TATUM
WESLEY TATUM
ALLEN MCDOWELL
JOHN DURKIN
FREDRICK ADDERHOLT
JOHN E. GILON
SAMUEL HAR--?
CEARNEY YOUNG
STEPHEN E. FAIRLEY
ROBERT ROPELY/ROSSLEY?
BENJAMIN BURNS
JOHN SHEARER

JAMES LOLLAR
JAMES CURBOW
POWEL WARD
WILLIS DEAN
SHEROD PORCH
HENRY DEAN
RUBEN H. POGUE
JOE/IRE? WARD
JAMES WAGNON
JAMES M. SMITH
WILLIARD HITCHCOCK
WILLIAM DOBBS
JOHN BOWERS
SAMUEL QUINTON
JAMES R. CHECK

List of Petit Jurors drawn to serve 1827.

WILLIAM HENRY?
JOHN E. GITON?
ANDERSON TIDWELL
JAMES HOLMES
DANIEL D. HARRISON

ROBERT PRESSLEY
BENJAMIN BURNS
JAMES SMITH
JOHN BOWEN
JAMES WAGNON

JAMES CURBOW
HENRY DEAN
JOHN RIPLEY
WILLIAM DOBBS
CRAWFORD WRIGHT
SAMUEL QUINTON
JOHN STEWART
WILLIAM HITCHCOCK
WILLIARD H. POGUE
CARNEY YOUNG
JESSE (w)RIGHT
ALLEN MCDOWELL
STEPHEN E. FAIRLEY

FREDERICK ADDERHOLT
ALLEN YORK
JOHN J. TAYLOR
JAMES CHECK
WILLIS DEAN
PETER WESENHUNT
WILLIAM PHILPOT
JOHN LEATHERS
JOHN CANEDA
IRE WARD
POWEL/ROWEL WARD
JONATHAN B--?

Inferior Court for Carroll County met agreeable to appointment July Term 1828
The court then proceeded to draw Petit Jurors for January Term of the Inferior Court

A List of Jurors to serve at Jany. Term 1829

JAMES SELLARS
ELIAS NEILL
THOS. YORK
JAS. HILL
PHILLIPS
WILSON CARTWRIGHT
FREDERICK CORDAMAN
ANDERSON TIDWELL
MARTIN JOINS
LARKIN TURNER

FRANCES RICHARDS
THOS. BLAKE
DANIEL HARRISON
LUKE BLIVINS
MICAJAH DEASON
JAMES PHILPOT
JOHN WESIENHUNT
WILLIAM B. BOX

The court then proceeded agreeable on order of the Judge of the Superior Court to draw Grand and Petit Jury for said Superior Court at September Term 1828. The following is a list of Grand Jurors drawn:

LEVI BENSON
WRIGHT MAJORS
CLAMEY YOUNG
HODGE RABUN
JAMES S. ROOKER
CHARLES ARRINGTON
ALLEN M. MCWHORTER
JOHN P. GILLASPY
THOS. GODDARD
WILLIAM WALKER
JOHN GAYDEN

JOHN ROBINSON
RANDSOM THOMPSON
JAMES WAGNON
FORD F. ALLEY
JAMES DICKIN
WALLIS WARREN
RICHARD PHILPOT
BARTLETT BUSSEY
SAMUEL LEATHERS
HIRAM SHARP
JOHN WARD SR.

JOHN BARTON/BOSTON?
JONATHAN SANDERS
JAMES HARRIS
JOHN B. PENDLETON
EMANUEL MARTIN

WM. R. (w)RIGHT
JAMES WEST
CARINGTON KNIGHT

The following is a list of Petit Jurors drawn:

PETER WESENHUNT
JAMES WALKER
RICHD. CARNES
JONATHAN W. DAVIS
THOMAS KENNON
MILES JENNINGS
JNO. BURDINE
REUBEN PHILPOT
ELBERT HARRIS

CRAWFORD WRIGHT
JOHN RICHARDS
DRURY STRICKLAND
ARBIN MOORE
WILLIS GILLERY
EBINEZAR FRASIER
JOHN B. ROBINSON
WM. SHIPLEY
SIMON CARDELL

Jury No. 2

DANIEL POSEY
DORMAND
J. WESLEY TATUM
JOHN LAWSON
WM. USERY
JA-TURNER
JAMES HARROW
ANSON REYNOLDS
MARLIN MAHAFFEY

JAMES WEATHERLY
WM. WORSHAM
JOHN WISTER
WILLIAM MAY
ALEXANDER HOGAN
JOHN BURNS
WM. R. BOON
JOHN MITCHELL
FREDERICK ADERHOLT

Josiah York became a magistrate in Paulding County and was involved in the removal of the Cherokee in 1838. He also served as Justice of the Peace and Postmaster at Yorkville, named after the family.

It didn't take long for news of the Pony Club and its operation to get out. As early as 1828, Alabamians had heard of this new scourge.

Pony Club-In Carroll County, Georgia, we are informed by a gentleman who has recently passed thro' that place , of indubitable credibility, that there is a club, who makes profession of stealing horses as well from their own citizens as from strangers-There plans, from their contiguity and intercourse with the Cherokees have been so judiciously executed as to elude detection. They do not, we understand, profess to take the life of a traveler, but only his horse, in order, it may be presumed that in cases of conviction their punctilious clemency may establish a contested principal in penal law, that there is a distinct and tangible difference in value between property and life. This policy reminds of the reply of Judge Barnes, to the horse
192

stealer, upon being asked what he had to say, why judgement of death should not be passed upon him and answering "that it was Hard to hang a man for only Stealing a horse," was told by the judge, 'man thou art not only to be hanged for stealing a horse, but that horses may not be stolen'. That punishment should be proportioned to offenses is just and politic we admit, but there is a lamentable deficiency in the justice and morality of this new county overlooking the alieni appetens which is so manifestly a nuisance to their neighbors and strangers is equally notorious (Ga Journal, Sept 29,1828, page 3).

{Huntsville Advocate.

The ***Cherokee Phoenix*** added a little note to the same story which ran on September 24, 1828 (Vol. 1, No. 30, page 2):

We have frequently heard of this pony club.- It is said by a Traveller who passed this place some time since directly from Carroll, that this stealing association has become so dexterious (sic) in its profession, that if the devil had been in the shape of a pony, he would ere this have fallen a prey to its agility. "Pony club" is but a limited name and will by no means give a correct idea of this neighboring combination- "cow club," "hog club," &c. may properly be added.

Governor Gilmer asked the Federal Government to step in and patrol the Cherokee country, which they did with groups of 12 men per area. This did not stop the Club and intruders and the Indians began to mine as well. In 1830 Gilmer made it illegal to mine on Cherokee lands, for whites and Cherokees, but enforcing it would be no easy matter. The issue of gold mining in Cherokee Territory was frought with land mines and it cost Governor Gilmer his job, when his ideas lost to those of Wilson Lumpkin, the new governor: rather than mine the gold on behalf of the state of Ga., for the benefit of all, Lumpkin would instead have a land lottery and give the land to Georgia citizens. There were about 85,000 people competing for 18,309 160-acre lots, and about 133,000 competing for 35,000 40-acre lots. Widows and orphans of veterans and veterans themselves had first choice. To qualify one must have been living in Georgia for 3 years and could not be a member of "the Pony Club". Those pony Club members, like the Yorks and Philpots had been in the Militia in the War of 1812 or the Seminole War and were able to receive lottery lands.

1971 Bonner, James Calvin, **Georgia's Last Frontier: The Development of Carroll County,** Univ. of Ga. Press: Athens.

2/13/2002 Clark, Jerry L, **Richard, Reuben, & James Philpot**
http://genforum.genealogy.com/philpot/messages/673.html.

September 24, 1828 *Cherokee Phoenix* Vol. 1, No. 30, page 2.

Congressional Serial Set: 197, 21st Congress, 1st Session, House Document, GPO: Washington D.C.

1883 Fielder, Herbert, **A Sketch in the Life and Times and Speeches of Joseph E. Brown,** Press of Springfield Printing Co.: Springfield, Mass.

1939 Federal Writer's Project, **Tennessee: A Guide to the State**, Viking Press: N. Y.

1935 . Green, Fletcher M**., Georgia's Forgotten Industry***: Gold Mining, The Georgia Historical Quarterly* XIX: 108-111.

May 20, 2007 Johnson, Don, **Joel Daniel Leathers & The Pony Club,** @<http://genforum.genealogy.com/leathers/messages/729.html>

1902 Martin, Thomas H., **Atlanta and its builders: a comprehensive history of the Gate city of the South,** Century memorial publishing co.: Atlanta.

2000 Prucha, Francis Paul, **Documents of United States Indian Policy,** Univ. of Nebraska: Lincoln.

1971 Prucha, Francis Paul, William Thomas Hagan, Alvin M. Josephy, Americasn Indian Policy by indians of North America, Indiana Historical Society: Indianapolis.

1962 Prucha, Francis Paul, **American Indian Policy in the Formative Years**, Harvard University Press:

2003 Rozema, Vicki, **Voices from the Trail of Tears**, John F. Blair, Publisher: Winston Salem.

20 Jun 2007 Sanfilippo, Diane Stark,**Josiah Cowan York, Sr. and His Family, Updated**, @http://files.usgwarchives.net/ga/paulding/bios/york929gbs.txt.

2002 Satz, Ronald N., **American Indian Policy**, Univ of Oklahoma Press: Norman

1986 Schoenleber, Charles Herbert, **The Rise of the New West,** Univ of Wisconsin: Madison.

Josiah Cowan and Sarah Blake York. Josiah was a member of the Pony Club in Carroll and Paulding Counties, having come to the Sandtown area of Dekalb County in 1826, according to Indian records. This is the only known picture of a club member (courtesy of Diane Sanphilippo).

The Cherokee strike back

The Cherokee had been forced to come up with a response to intruders and horse thieves operating in their territory in the 1820s. The Light Horse was a police force of sorts with the mission of dealing with a growing problem associated with both white and Indian criminals. Its main purposes:

A. The police force grew out of Light Horse Brigade that had been formed to recapture stolen horses.

B. Membership in the group was temporary, task oriented, voluntary and it acted on behalf of individuals NOT on behalf of the group.

C. Until 1820, the groups attach themselves to town councils but they extended the group's powers to capture the horse thieves and "other rogues" on behalf of the entire nation.

The idea that Indians might be working with the Pony Club and other whites to steal horses and other things were not new to the Cherokee. The April 3, 1828 *Cherokee Phoenix* reported just such a situation:

...If the officers of this district are not more vigilant than they are at present, we should not be much surprised if the old game should be played over—the existence of a league between white and Cherokee thieves. This is the worst of all confederacies, for as soon as the stole property passes the boundary line the owner need not flatter himself to see it. It is incumbent on the civil officers of this nation to secure those vagabonds who carry with them wherever they go, the deep stain of the guilt of stealing; and now is the time to arrest this practice by inflicting an exemplary punishment on those, who are now acknowledged by all to be really guilty. Yet nothing is done with them—they are permitted to go at large, running stolen horses to Sandtown and other places on the frontiers of Georgia, where there are not wanting men whose professed business is to receive stolen property.

The *Macon Telegraph*, October 16, 1830 compared the Pony Club to the Cherokee nation, claiming the latter were protecting several hundred "headmen and warriors" of the Club. Perhaps the activities of the Club energized some Indians, who relished the raiding aspect of horse theft. McLoughlin (1986), saw it as indians stealing horses to get back at whites who were stealing land.

...Horse stealing was a group enterprise and the gangs that engaged in it regularly were called "pony clubs". They had their own chiefs, their own rules, their own professional code and secrets. Out of the chaos of their old system, these men created a different sort of organization and discipline. Success in these activities brought back a sense of self respect or perhaps even won the respect of other angry Cherokees (55).

Thus, early on, Cherokee horse thieves were reported stealing in Carroll County. The *Cherokee Phoenix,* May 21, 1828 noted:

> *At the last Circuit Court held in Hightower, three persons were convicted for stealing horses out of Carrol [sic] Co. & were sentenced to receive fifty lashes each. These persons, we are told, stole upon the principle of rendering evil for evil. How backward some of our neighboring whites may be to do justice to the Indians, we confess we feel a pleasure in noticing this instance of the impartiality of our courts. It would be well if the authorities of Carrol [sic] County (Gov. Forsythe's [sic] Ministers) will look about and punish their offending citizens. It would be a sweeping work if they were to begin. So much "for the success of the new Constitution."*

John C. Bird appealed his conviction to the Cherokee Supreme Court where he lost and received 100 lashes instead.

In December, 1829 a white horse thief was caught in Indian Territory and faced Cherokee justice. The incident would serve to show the limitations on Indian justice against the white man before the removal in 1838. Involved was a man named John Stancel, or Stansel. The Stancels are listed in Habersham County records, and both John Senior and Junior appear in an earlier Cherokee Claim, set forth in 1842, for losses incurred before the removal. Jacob Harnage, made claim (no.125) for two horses worth $120:

> *...He lived at Frog Town on Chestatee (river), where he had two horses stolen by young John and old John Stansel {also Stancil} they owned to the claimant that they took his horses, but it was out of his power to get redress from them as they were white men of Habersham County, Georgia (Shadburn, 1993: 652).*

Bryant Ward, an Indian, attested to the theft, which occured in 1822, saying he had heard the two thieves acknowledge their deed.

A letter to the editor of the *Cherokee Phoenix*, dated December 5, 1829 by Cherokee George Saunders described the capture of John Stancel:

> *Sir—I wish to insert in the Phoenix a few lines concerning a white man that was whipped at Elijay for horse stealing. Myself being foreman of the jury, sentenced him to receive fifty stripes on the bare back, which is fifty less than what is common in our country for such offence (see Cherokee Phoenix, Nov. 5, 1828, John (L)Bird and May 28, 1828, Three whipped from Carroll County). The thief, since he was whipped, has made oath that he was arrested and whipped with large hickory switches. We acted agreeably to the laws of our country in punishing the man. Since his making oath in the state of Georgia, the officers of that state sent armed men to take all the Indians that were concerned in whipping him. I understood*

that they were on their way and went to Long Swamp to meet them. They met me there. I gave them my bond and security for my appearance at court at Gainesville in Hall County...

There was another company with this horse thief, and his father among them, that came by way of Amakiloley. When they came to the village they lay out until dark, and then went into the fields and stole potatoes and pumpkins. They also stole six or seven horses and then returned home. Since that fifteen in number, with the said thief, well armed came by way of Stamp Creek Village, and there made pretence they were buying hogs. They bought none, however, but made free to kill and barbecue one, without leave. They also made free to go into houses, and take such things as they stood in need of to eat and said that they had orders from the Governor and that he would pay for the things that they took. Your Friend.

George Saunders.

Jesse Stancel filed with Judge Henry Clayton in Habersham County an affadavit that he had been arrested by: George and John Sanders, Harry Downing, Riddle Cricr, Old Hog, Overseer, John Love, Martin Smith, Pretty Woman, Young Duck, John Potatoe, Partridge and Dick Carey and had been held against his will for 30 hours and whipped with hickory rods fifty times.

On December 16, the *Cherokee Phoenix* reported open hostilities between whites and Indians in 3 separate events. In one of these 8 armed white men entered a home at Hightower Town and took 3 negroes, two of whom were free, and returned to Georgia. In another incident 7 armed men from Habersham County killed a hog and stole some items from Indians and lost a gun in a scuffle and then fled back into Georgia. The 3rd incident was a direct result of the Stancel affair, a group of white men appearing to arrest the 13 Indians involved in the whipping of the horse thief.

In February, 1830, the Cherokee were on the offensive again, in a raid involving 17 families of intruders living in the Creek Path area of the Cherokee Nation. Major Ridge and David Vann of the tribe responded with a raid on the intruders. In mid-winter they turned out a number of white families with women and children forcing them into the elements. One Cherokee prepared an affidavit which was attached to a letter by Col. Hugh Montgomery, Indian Agent to the *Cherokee Phoenix (May 8, 1830, page 2 col. 5):*

Certificate of Abraham Birdwell
Alabama, Jackson County,
February 9, 1830

I Abrahan (sic) Birdwell, of said State and county do hereby certify, having been into the State of Georgia, and on my return home through the Cherokee nation, and on and within the
198

territory claimed by Georgia as Creek land; and on Thursday, the 4th present instant, had my attention attracted by the burning of houses, and by a company of Cherokees, under the command of Major Ridge, a Cherokee Chief; an inquiry of Ridge, thro' Mr. David Vann, another leading character of the nation, I was informed that Major Ridge was authorized by John Ross, principal Chief of the Cherokee nation, to the burning and otherwise destroying the houses, &c. occupied by the intruders, saying that they were a parcel of scoundrels and rogues, and that the Government would not injure them for thus treating them. These acts were committed on Cedar Creek and Beaver Dam settlement. The property thus wantonly destroyed, was, as I was informed, valued by the assessors, and paid for by the Government of the United States. After leaving Vann's on the 5th, I saw about four miles on the route home, a woman on a cart, who I was informed had had a child only four days before. Coming on three miles further, I saw another, who had a midwife with her, and in a critical condition. The Cherokees were all armed with guns, pistols, and Ridge himself was clothed in all the garb of Indian warfare,viz; His headdress was a buffalo's forehead & horns, &c., there were sixty Indians; the Indians exalted highly, particularly David Vann; the Indians around the fire, with expressions of Indian joy, yelling, shouting; &c. &c. I met some men on express to the settlements for aid.

> *ABRAHAM BIRDWELL.*
>
> *Test.*
> *H. Pearson.*
> *We certify that Mr. Abraham Birdwell is a man every way entitled to confidence and belief, as a gentlemen of veracity.*
>
> *WILLIAM WELBORN,*
> *J. H. PEARSON*

The actions of chief John Ross and John Ridge precipitated a backlash from elected officials in Carroll County. Sheriff Henry Curtis and about 25 members of the Pony Club set out to arrest the two Cherokee headmen. Unable to do so they arrested four members of the party that burnt out the intruders. In the process one of the Indians was killed. In a letter to agent Montgomery one of his deputies described the activities which led to the death of **Chuwooyee.** The **Phoenix** was quick to note the Georgians had escalated difficulties first:

FIRST BLOOD SHED BY THE GEORGIANS!!

Since writing the above, we have been told by a gentleman who passed this place as an express to the agent, from the principal chief, that a Cherokee has, at last, been killed by the intruders, and three more taken bound into Georgia (Feb. 10, 1830, page 2 col 4-5)..!

Elias Boudinout, editor of the Phoenix, recounted the Cherokee side in the escalating events of that day:

Mr. Elias Boudinott.

199

Editor of the Cherokee Phoenix.

Sir-...

...The intruders living on the public road leading to Alabama and at Saunders' old place were turned out of doors with all their effects. The company were fully persuaded that if the houses were not destroyed the intruders would not go away; they therefore determined on the expediency of setting fire to them. There were eighteen families of intruders thus removed, and having executed this duty with the utmost lenity towards them, and not having injured any of their property, the Cherokees felt no uneasiness, or alarm from any quarter, and returned home in small detached parties. Unfortunately, four of them became intoxicated and remained at Samuel Rowe's house where there was whiskey. In the course of the night of the 5th inst. a party of intruders, upwards of twenty men, armed with guns, came and arrested them; that is, The Waggon, Daniel Mills, Rattling Gourd, and Chuwoyee. The first named was found in strings by the intruders, the Indians having tied him to prevent him from doing injury, and the second was beaten with a gun and stampled [sic] by the intruders, and the third was not hurt, but the fourth, who was unable to walk (being very drunk) was tied and put upon a horse, but not being able to sit on, and falling off once or twice, he was most barbarously beaten with guns &c. in the head, face, breast and arms, and was then thrown across the pummel of a saddle on a horse, and carried by the rider in that situation about one mile and then thrown off. The poor unfortunate man died the next morning and his corpse was left on the ground without any person to take care of it. The other three were sent into Carroll County, Georgia, under a guard.

As soon as I received intelligence of this unhappy affair, and understanding that the lawless intruders had threatened to kill Major Ridge and myself, and to burn our dwellings, I despatched an express to the Agent with all possible speed, demanding the arrest and punishment of the murderers, and the restoration of the prisoners, and also requesting the immediate interposition of his authority in preserving peace and harmony on the frontier. On the 7th I despatched a small waggon [sic] after the corpse of the murdered man, and on the 8th he was decently buried at his own house by the side of the graves of his father and mother. The corpse was shockingly mangled.... In the meantime, The Waggon & Daniel Mills, two of the prisoners who were taken into Carrol County, returned, having made their escape from the guard, when within a few miles of Carrolton. The Wagon received a severe stab in the breast with a butcher knife, and a cut across his left wrist, from the hands of the notorious Old Philpot....

I have since been informed that the Sheriff of Carroll County was at the head of the band who fired on Mr. West, and that when Mr. West returned the fire, they made a sudden halt and turned back to the Turnpike gate.- ... It is also stated that the number of armed men who escorted the Sheriff was about 25. The most of them were intruders upon Cherokee lands and of debased character, and that some of them were also accessary to the murder of Chuwoyee.

Your ob't Serv't
JNO. ROSS.

The murder of a Cherokee resounded all the way to Washington D.C.

CALHOUN, 4th March, 1830

To Col. HUGH MONTGOMERY,
  Agent for the Cherokees
  East of the Mississippi.

...I have the honor to report that immediately on the receipt of your order I set out for Mr. Ross' and reached there on the Wednesday following. On my arrival at Mr. Ross', I learned from him that, in consequence of his having had some intruders of notorious characters removed who had taken possession of the improvements abandoned by the Emigrating Cherokees- that the Intruders had assembled together to the number of twenty five or thirty, and on the 5th February commenced pursuit of Major Ridge who commanded the party ordered out by Mr. Ross. The Ridge having fulfilled his orders on this day discharged his men at Cedar Town, and they had all returned to their respective homes, with the exception of Daniel Mills, Waggon, Rattling Goard [sic], and Chuwoyee, who remained. On the night of the same day the company of intruders came to the house where these four Cherokees were and finding them all in a state of intoxication, they seized upon and tied them. Chuwooyee, the last mentioned one, not understanding the cause of this confinement, and almost unable to stand from the effects of whiskey, refused to go, altho he was tied, upon this one of the whites struck him with his gun on the back part of the head, & three or four others commenced on him with Clubs &c. &c.

After this barbarous treatment and finding that he was unable to walk, they threw him across a horse before one of their company and Marched off about a mile where they encamped for the night. After reaching the camp ground the man who had charge of him threw him from the horse upon the ground; and he was suffered to lie there exposed to the inclemency of a cold wet sleeting night without the least vestige of anything to protect him from the severity of the weather, but the few clothes he had on when taken prisoner. Early on the next morning he expired. The company started immediately afterwards with the other three for Carrolton in Carrol County, Georgia-on their way to Carrolton the two first mentioned, Mills and Waggon, effected their escape, though The Waggon in getting off received a severe wound in the breast with a butcher knife from the hands of Old Richard Philpot. ....

The Rattling Goard [sic] they succeeded in putting in Jail.

After getting all the information that was in my power to obtain relative to the murder of Chuwoyee, which is above stated- I repaired to Carrolton for the purpose of trying to release the Rattling Goard [sic], from his confinement- On my arrival at the Court House, I was informed that he had employed four counsellors- I waited on three of them- They informed me that if it could be made to appear to the satisfaction of the Judges of the inferior Court that the prisoner was not an officer of the company ordered out by Mr. Ross, but was only acting under the orders of the commanding officers, there would be no difficulty in having him discharged. To obtain the proof required agreeably to the opinion of his Lawyers, I had to return to the Nation, a distance of fifty miles from the Court House. While in the Nation for the purpose of getting the necessary proof I procured from Mr. John Ross, the volume of the Laws of the United States containing the law of 1802, commonly called the "Intercourse Law"- On my return the second time to Carrolton, I called upon John Roberson Esq. formally of Tennessee, and requested him to inform me of some Attorney that stood high at the Bar.- Mr. Roberson recommended Mr. John Ray. I employed Mr. Ray, and I have no doubt that it was owing to his argument and the laws of 1802 that the Court released the Rattling Goard [sic].

I herewith enclose you Mr. Ray's direction relative to the course to be pursued against those concerned with the murder of Chuwoyee, together with a list of the names of a part of the company charged with it,- also his account against the Government for his fee in the case of the Rattling Goard [sic].

After the Rattling Goard [sic] was discharged by the Hon. Court, I had an interview with Col. Fambrough, the Attorney for the prosecution who agreed to suspend all further proceedings against the Ridge and his company for the present-of this I informed Mr. Ross and Ridge.

For the want of funds I was unable to make any attempt towards arresting the party charged with the murder of Chuwoyee-Having been furnished with only fifteen dollars when I set out from the office.

All the information that I was able to get relative to this unfortunate affair was derived from Mr. John Ross, and others, citizens of the Nation.- And I have no doubt, Sir, that it is a plain unvarnished statement of facts.

While engaged in the above business, I hired Mr. William Jones to accompany me, for which I agreed to pay him one dollar per day for himself and horse, and to bear his expenses. Mr. Jones was with me fourteen days,-all of which is respectfully submitted.

I have the honor to be
Very respectfully,
Your Ob't Ser't
JAS. G. WILLIAMS

The third party involved in the struggle between the Cherokee and the State of Georgia, the Federal Government, chose to head off the looming war between the other two by assuring both sides troops were on the way. Secretary of War J.H. Eaton thus ordered:

As soon as the information was received, orders were despatched to the commanding Officer at Fort Mitchell to move with such disposable force as could be spared, to the point of disturbance and adopt measures for preserving the peace and quiet of the frontiers. He will speedily as possible arrive, and until then you are directed to instruct both whites and Indians

202

to forbear further acts of aggressions, or otherwise exemplary punishment will be inflicted for breach of the laws.

Things got off to a good start, according to the Cherokee, who reported 9 intruders had been siezed at the mines and sent to Savannah for trial (Cherokee Phoenix, June 26, 1830, page 3 Col. 2). However it wasn't long before the troops took on a more sinister presence and were seen as an adjunct to enforcing the laws of the State of Georgia. Writing in the ***Cherokee Phoenix*** for June 24, 1830, Elias Boudinot lamented the treatment many received at the hands of U.S. troops. Though many intruders were dealt with, the troops had come together with a local sheriff and had arrested many of the Cherokee, made them walk many miles and in general treated them badly. The troops halted all Cherokee mining, destroyed the machinery and in one case made a poor Cherokee's metal milk jug the subject of target practice (July 3, page 2, col. 5).

Walter Adair, a Cherokee, added to this in the January 1, 1831 ***Cherokee Phoenix***, that some white miners and some Cherokee miners were arrested for breaking Georgia law against mining in Indian Territory. He stated the Indians were badly treated by Major Wager and his troops; their gold stolen; soldiers going through their pants pockets looking for anything of value and several buildings burned.

…They also destroyed Mr. Samuel Gray's groceries (a citizen of this nation) and stopped his wagon and team on the road, when he was on his way home from the mines the soldiers were also suffered to plunder his wagon and broke open his trunks. A quantity of goods and wearing clothes were taken and a pocket book with money in it (col. 3-4)...

After a short tenure, the federal troops returned to Fort Mitchell, Alabama, and things began to turn for the worst. The future of the Cherokee Nation was being discussed. While agents roamed the nation signing up Cherokees for early removal to Oklahoma Indian Territory, the State of Georgia began renting their improvements, paid for by the government, to citizens of Georgia. The issue of intruders was to be settled by a new Governor as George Gilmer was defeated for reelection by Wilson Lumpkin
.

An Attempt on Ross' Life

The year 1831 ended with a plot to kill Chief Ross hatched by the Pony Club. Two men, one directly related to Richard Philpot planned to catch Ross crossing the local ferry and then gun him down from a nearby hill. The escalation of violence and the hatred of the Cherokee by Pony Club members led to a confrontation in Indian Territory on November 30, 1831. Writing about it in the ***Cherokee Phoenix***,

January 21, 1832, John Ross outlined a plot by the Club to kill Ross, the chief of the Cherokee nation. It begins when John and Andrew Ross, brother of the chief were visiting Major Ridge at his house in Georgia. Suddenly a gaunt looking white man appears at the door, interrupting the conversation of the 3 Indians: "is John Ross here?"

…he inquired if I knew of anyone crossing my ferry in the course of the past night; I answered him in the negative. He then stated that a horse was stolen from him that night, which he had tracked within a few hundred yards of my ferry landing and there lost the sign…

He introduced himself as a Mr. Harris and said he was from North Carolina. He then went to Lavender's store nearby to hire an Indian to guide him through the country and later reappeared on horseback as Ross and his brother started home. Accompanied by Oonehutty, a local Indian, Harris again asked if he were John Ross. Chief Ross assented and they all boarded the ferry and headed across the river. The ferryman indicated to Harris he had seen a lone horseman on a hill above the ferry as if waiting for someone.

After watching Mr. Harris and his guide gallop to the top of the hill the chief's curiosity got the best of him and he and his brother rode to the far side of the hill. Here they saw that Harris and Oonehutty had captured the other man.

…the other man proved to be the one who was discovered on top of the hill—he was a chubbed, grim looking fellow, with a pair of large reddish moustaches which curled at the corner of his mouth and several of his foreteeth out, his eyes , mouth and the general features of his countenance uninteresting…

The Indian guide took the man's gun and Harris indicated to Ross that this was the horse he was looking for. Ross asked who the man was and though Harris wasn't willing to say, Ross got out of the man that his name was Looney and he was from Rhea County, Tennessee. They all began the trek back to the ferry landing when Looney said:

…"Harris I am now gonna tell the truth about this whole business". Said I the truth alone was what I desired to know—said he, "I have not stolen this horse". How came you to be riding this horse when Harris claims him? Whose horse is he? "myown"—do you know Harris? "No". At this moment my brother then told me to take care that Harris was going to shoot me. I looked around and saw Harris dismounted, at the same time I heard him say, "I have been for a long time wanting to kill you and I'll be damned if I don't now do it". As he presented the gun I wheeled my horse and galloped off; looking back I saw my brother setting on his horse at the same place. Harris then got behind a tree to shoot him—he then rode off and we returned home, late in the evening…

Concern now turned to Oonehutty, left behind with the Pony Club outlaws. Ross the next day made his way to the store and at once saw Oonehutty's horse tied up outside. Ross discovered him sitting inside, his right cheek severely bruised. The Indian related to Ross his life and death struggle with Harris over the gun after the chief and his brother had escaped. Oonehutty received a bruised cheek but he had stabbed Harris with his own knife.

Having defied the assassin, Ross later learned who the assasin was:

...Looney is the brother in law of James Philpot and that he had accompanied Harris from Philpot's house to the place where he was stationed on the hill—that the poney on which Harris rode, belonged to said Philpot. Upon Reuben Philpot representing the rifle gun for the property of Saul Ratley and that it had been left in his care, taken without his knowledge and in his absence from home and that he would be held responsible for it. Oonehutty surrendered it up to him, saying that he had no claim to It further than wrestling it from the hands of an assassin who had attempted to rob him and take his life with It (col. 3-5).

Ross complained bitterly that Governor Gilmer had let things get to these extremes, citing the statements that no intruders lived in the Indian Territory while it was evident to all Indians the Pony Club covered the land and the woods "were alive with them." Of the 300 white men in Cherokee lands, who had taken the oath to Georgia as required by law, Ross noted, few if any were actually part of the tribe by marriage or any other affinity (page 3 col 1).

John Ross

Andrew Ross at the signing of the New Echota Treaty.

April 3, 1828 **New Echota,** *Cherokee Phoenix,* page2 col. 5, page 3 col. 1.

May 28, 1828 **Three Whipped,** *Cherokee Phoenix,* page 2 col. 5.

May 21, 1828 **A Trial in Hightower,** *Cherokee Phoenix,,* page 2 col. 5.

November 5, 1828 **John Lird,** *Cherokee Phoenix,* page 1 col. 5.

December 3, 1829 **Charleston Observer,** *The Cherokee Phoenix ,* page 2 col.4.

December 10, 1829 **Letter to the Editor,** *Cherokee Phoenix,* Page 2 col. 2.

December 16, 1829 **Savage Hostilities,** *Cherokee Phoenix,* page 3 col. 2.

May 8, 1830, John Ross lettcr, *Cherokee Phoenix,* page 2 col. 5.

May 22, 1830, **New Echota,** *Cherokee Phoenix,* page 2 col. 1.

May 29, 1830, **New Echota,** *Cherokee Phoenix,* page 3 col. 1.

June 12, 1830, **Creek Path,** *Cherokee Phoenix,* page 3 Col. 2.

June 26, 1830, *Cherokee Phoenix,* page 3, Col. 2.

July 30, 1830, **Gold Mines,** *Cherokee Phoenix,* page 2, col. 5.

October 16, 1830 **New Dynasty,** *Macon Telegraph,* page 3 col. 2.

January 1, 1831 **Walter Adair, Cherokee Phoenix.** Page 1 col. 3,4.

January 21, 1832 **John Ross,** *Cherokee Phoenix,* Page 2 col. 3-5, page 3 col. 1.

1907 Lumpkin, Wilson, **The removal of the Cherokee Indians from Georgia** Dodd Meade and Co.: NY

1986 McLoughlin, William Gerald, **Cherokee Renascence in the New Republic,** Princeton Univ press:

1998 Sargent, Gordon D., **Polk County, Georgia,** Arcadia Publishing: Mt. Pleasant, SC

206

1993 Shadburn, Don L., **Unhallowed Intrusion: A History of Cherokee Families in Forsythe County, Georgia,** W.H. Wolfe associates: Alpharetta.

1995 Williams, David, **The Georgia Gold Rush: Twenty-Niners, Cherokees, and Gold Fever,** Univ. of South Carolina Press: Columbia.

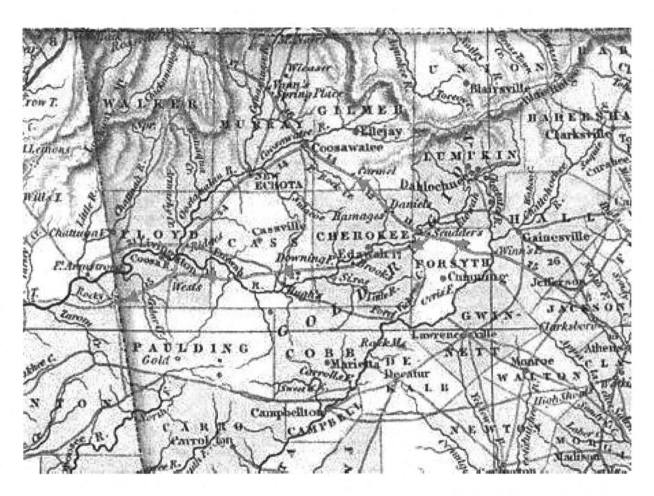

From near Carmel Station on the Federal Road all the way down the Alabama Road, the Cherokee burned Pony Club and intruder houses and sent them scurrying back to Carroll County (1834 Ga. Map).

Activities in Alabama

The Pony Club also traveled into Eastern Alabama in search of plunder from the Cherokee Indians living there. Several events were recorded involving the Carroll County criminals, the citizens of Alabama, Indian Territory and the Indians living nearby. On May 29, 1830, Boudinout, editor of the **Cherokee Phoenix,** wrote about the Pony Club assault on The Hog in Terrapin Creek, Alabama Indian Territory:

In the neighborhood of Terrapin Creek, there lives a Creek man by the name of Hog, who, by his industrious habits has been enabled to accumulate some property, consisting chiefly of large stocks of horses and cattle. Living as he does near his white brothers who are clamorous for the removal of the Indians, that they not be harassed by savage neighbors, his best horses became the object of desire by some of them. By the precaution of the Hog and the constant watch he kept about the stables and lots, he was able to preserve these horses. Finding they could not steal them, we understand another expedient was resorted to lately by these members of the "Poney Club." Four white men came to the Indian's house, two of whom were armed with rifles. Finding the Hog alone with his wife, one of the two men who was armed, proposed to buy his horse, and offered his gun for compensation. The Creek Indian refused to sell for such a trifle. The white man then proposed to exchange with the Indian. The offer was again rejected, the Indian's horse being greatly superior in value to the other. At this the white man observed he would have the horse and proceeded toward the lot with a bridle. Hog's wife, discovering the intentions of these men, followed, and in attempting to prevent them from catching the horse, was knocked down by the other armed man with a gun. She fell senseless to the ground. Hog ran into the lot, and by driving off the horses and giving the alarm, prevented these robbers from accomplishing their design. The woman lay for some time apparently dead, but finally came to herself. We understand she is better and likely to recover.

On one occasion where the Pony Club ventured into the Terrapin Creek area, the citizens fought back. Club Members Calloway Burke and James Upton (Philpot in-law) had just stolen cattle from John Goodin and several Creek Indians. They were pursued by the Alabamians into Carroll County, Georgia where they stopped at the Home of a Mr. Almon, where the cattle were retrieved in his cane brake and driven back to Alabama by the Indians.

Through fear of the Pony Club, Almon would not let them stay all night but loaned them a gun, and they started for Hixtown, now Villa Rica. After near where Hart afterward had settled, they met Burke and others, all armed. Goodin's party was on the alert and each party soon detected the character of the other. Burke leveled his gun and Goodin shot him dead (G.A.S., letter to editor, Carroll Times, June 8, 1883)

This incident represents one of the few deaths of a Pony Club member in all the years they operated in the South. Calloway Burke was once employed by Carroll County to build the new jail in the new courthouse: *...in May, 1830, the justices*
208

employed Calloway Burke to remove "the gaol from the old court house" to the new county site (county records 1830) ...

James Upton, who accompanied Burke in this expedition, was related by marriage to the Philpots and had been involved with the family when they were living in Rhea County Tennessee, before moving to Georgia.

Little is known of Carroll Countian Hawkins Phillips, but John Goodwin (Goodin) was a well known legislator from Northern Alabama in the 1850s. He was described by Guinn (1942, page 394) in his **History of Randolph County, Alabama**   (The Alabama Historical Quarterly, Vol.04, No. 03*)*

John Goodin was a whig, farmer, land speculator and negro trader. He was 47 years of age when elected. He had no education, could neither read nor write, except his name, yet his callidity seemed boundless. With ready wit, tireless tongue and an inexhaustable fund of anecdotes, which he told in a fluent flexible and humorous style, without and vapidness; he higgled them out by the wholesale on all public occasions.

Goodin had dark skin, black hair and eyes, and was one of the first pioneers of the county, being here before and at the time of the Creek treaty in March, 1832.

Goodin was residing in Creek lands and listed along with Isaac Goodin as whites among the Creek in Chiawha Town along the emigration road. He shared the name with another John Goodwin, who lived near the gold mines in northwest Georgia and was mixed up with the Pony Club. This caused him some trouble at home in Alabama. One day he was stopped by local Indians and confronted on the rumor he was in league with the miscreants of Carroll County:

...One day as Goodin was riding along two Indians met him in the road, and one of them recognized him as one of the Pony Club, who had recently whipped one of their clan, and they said to him, "Light, you are one of the Pony Club that whipped one of our clan and we are a-going to whip you." Goodin protested his innocence and denied being in any way connected or sympathizing with the Club. "But," said the Indian, "A itsee hatkee", (all white men whip Indians). Goodin realizing that a charge so broad as to embrace "all white men" left him only one plea that could touch the sympathy of an Indian's heart. He thought quick and fast. It was his only alternative. It seemed feasible and he took courage and said: "K'ok shi (good) dakoe (friends or comrades) ma (why) luk i a (this) te-k win-te (is unexpected) horn (to me) yat-ton-ne (today). Horn (my) tsita (mother) ton (is thy) an (own) shi-i-nan (flesh) kiah-kwin (and blood). Ha (I) tanka (am) hatkee tsau na (the little man or son of) seme-hechee (hid it away) waukau warrior) harno-o-na-wi-la-po-na (holder of the paths) ton (of thy) na dowe si (enemy) wompi (white) hatkee (man) "U-u-g-h", said the Indian, and at the same time run his hand down Goodin's back and, pulling it out, said, "No Indian here—Negro, by G-d.

This was a stunner and Goodin felt it keenly, but he was the last man to succumb or be driven from his ambituous desire to go to the legislature (395).

There were many other characters involved in the Calloway Burke affair and in a way the reporting of the incident seemed to have a life of its own, spreading suspicion to many others. The **Columbus Enquirer** reported on the 20th of June, 1832, how the incident began.

The circumstances that led to the death of the poney club man, are these: A respectable old gentleman of Alabama had his horses, one after another, stolen from him until his saddle horse, a valuable animal, only remained—he could not run a plough. The saddle horse and 30 head of cattle one morning soon after disappeared—the quarter whence the marauders came being notorious, he crossed into Carroll, and, though unsuccessful at identifying the thieves, ascertained the person in whose possession the horse and cattle had been transferred (1832: col. 4).

The **Macon Telegraph**, having heaped accolades on Goodin for his "Alabama" courage in facing the Pony Clubs which had made life terrible in North Georgia, elaborated on the incident, stating that Goodin spent the night, after shooting Burke, in a local gold mining settlement. It wasn't long before the Pony Club showed up with a Constable to arrest him. Shouldering his gun, the Alabamian was able to keep them at bay and at once indicated to the Constable that his services would be needed soon as he had summoned the county sheriff...this news served to put the Club on notice and they fled rather than face the sheriff (June 14, 1832, col. 1)

The **Columbus Enquirer** fed the drama, naming more Pony club members involved in the raid on Alabama.

About the last week of April, a party of men from Terrapin Creek, Alabama, broke over the State line, and being joined by some of the white citizens and a few Cherokee Indians, settlers and residents of Cherokee County, formed themselves into an association under the denomination of regulators, proceeded to take up and whip (without warrant), in the course of one or two days five persons, namely, John and Edward Watts, John Sappington, John Gilly, William Wright and Thomas Blake. About this time or shortly after, they took up and held in confinement William Shipley and Allen York, the last they whipped, and as he says took from him 60 odd dollars, the first they let off without punishment A day or two after they took Calloway Burke from his home and after detaining him several days...Burke was then released (col.2).

This done, some of the club sought redress from Gen. Coffee and even the governor. Many of the regulators were brought up on charges. This all came to a head, according to the **Columbus Enquirer** version, when Goodin and Burke met

210

many days later on the streets of Carrollton. Burke sought to assault a man named Adams, with the regulators but Goodin interfered and the incident escalated:

The party, Burke, Cartwright, Goodwin, Adams and Allman agreed to go to the house of a justice about two miles off to have Adams bound over. Goodwin, by consent of the party sent Worsham to the mines to apprise some friends he had there of the situation of affairs. After the party arrived at Raubun's (the Justice) Burke...a party of from fifteen to twenty five arrived there, one had Burke's horse and one stated that Burke had gotten away—that if they had caught him they would have given him hell...

Goodin then with his party and attorney set out down the road when they met Burke and his attorney coming up the road, they passed each other and as they did Burke turned round and leveled his gun at Goodin who, seeing this, shot Burke, who died some 12 days later (col. 2).

The writer in this instance, a citizen of Carroll County then lists the members of the Pony Club whipped by these regulators:

On the day Wright was whipped, Cartwright was whipped and on the next day Gilly was whipped. Wright was one of the State's tenants and had been run from home—Cartwright and Gilly are citizens of Carroll. In Cherokee County, Gay, Cannon, Philpot and Roberts, and another whose name is now not recollected were whipped. Gay, Cannon and Roberts lived all of them within ten miles of one of (Gen.) Coffee's stations (col. 2)...

Thousands of dollars were raised to benefit those regulators held by Carroll officials and the recriminations resulting from the incident seemed to reverberate to the halls of the Georgia State Legislature and beyond. In December, 1832, the Grand Jury in Carroll County began its long battle to eject the Pony Club from its midst.

Writing in the *Federal Union,* Grand Jury head William G. Springer, who would later be an Indian Agent for Georgia, filled the paper with charges against lawyer **Jack A. Jones** and State legislator **Allen Fambrough**. Both were implicated as representatives of the Pony Club in their legal defense and representation in Milledgeville, the State Capital. Springer referred to Jack A. Jones as "Poney Club Jones," who was involved in the defense of members Garret Lankford and Willis Gilly. Jones was vilified for expanding on the desires of Gilly to seek redress against 6 individuals, by naming 50 persons as victimizers, including the State Representative from the county that Jones was currently running against.

In these two cases Jack was evidently incited by a desire to become popular with the Poney Club, and at the same time to avenge himself of such citizens as could not consent to confer public honors on a petty conspirator or stoop to amicable association with a blackguard and nuisance (Dec. 13, 1832: cols. 3-5)...

TO THE PUBLIC.
The Grand Jury of Carroll County.
WILLIAM G. SPRINGER, Foreman.

E. B. Martin,	Caleb Garrison,
James F. Garrison,	Jonathan Walker,
David Barnwell,	Riley W. Walker,
A. M. McWhorter,	Henry Reid,
Robert Shaw,	George M. Monk,
Aaron Miller,	Thomas P. Wilkins,
Thomas Blake,	James Greyham,
James L. Adair,	Hiram Sharp,
Stephen Ingram,	William Adams.
Solomon Wynn,	

Southern Recorder, Nov. 15, 1832

Springer also notes that Jones has been mentioned as a fence for stolen Pony Club plunder, citing the witness of Gen. Thomas Woodward of Alabama who published the last words of one of the club members, one of the Watts boys killed by a Creek Indian:

...General Woodward of Alabama heard Watts, while dying, declare, that he had been assured by the Poney Club, the best thing he could do with any stolen property he might have, was to take it to Jack, who would instantly give for it half its real value, as he kept a ready market for their plunder (col. 4)

The Grand Jury was serving notice on Jack Jones and Allen Fambrough that it would seek to "sleek" this "feed counsel," as they called the legal arm of the Pony Club. The jury no doubt was aware of Jones' ties to many Pony Club members, as was shown in a letter to Governor Gilmer, May 31, 1831 concerning holding upcoming elections in Indian Territory. He has the following advice for the Governor:

...The election for the 4th Section (western Cherokee territory) will be convenient to the mass of the residents in the section if held at James Hemphill's and Alexander Ramsay, James

Hemphill and Thomas Hogan have the requisite Qualifications and character to conduct it properly (see Warren and Weeks, 1987: 75)...

In the July 5, 1832 issue of the **Georgia Journal,** Jones replied that he and Fambrough had indeed answered the call of William Shipley and Allen York after they had been whipped by the regulators or "slicks" under Goodin et al. Jones also indicated he had asked Gen. Coffee and the Georgia Guard to intercede on behalf of the "tenants of Cherokee County," but no such interference appeared. Next was a litany of fears he and Fambrough shared concerning the actions of the "slicks."

On Thursday the 31st of May, I left Milledgeville for home, on Saturday the 2nd of June, I arrived in Campbellton, late in the evening, and was informed by several friends that the slicks or regulators were so highly incensed at Col. Fambrough and myself, for affording legal assistance and advice to the persons who they had abused, that they threatened us with unmerciful whipping or death; that Burke had been shot, that Col. Fambrough, to quiet the alarms of his family who feared he would be assassinated, had been forced to quit his home; that an attempt to reach home would endanger my life, and finally they begged me not to make the effort (Col. 4)...

Jones later had notified Governor Lumpkin of this "insurrection" but could not understand the inaction by Gen. Coffee and the Georgia Guard. Nor was he happy when the Grand Jury made its presentments. Instead of summoning a bill for the incarceration of the regulators the jury rebuffed Jones on every count. Fambrough fared no better in his attempt to stay out of the Pony Club suspicion cast on many.

Columbus Enquirer, Aug. 18, 1832 -- page 3

For the Enquirer:

I understand that a scurrilous production has lately made its appearance in that dirty polluted lieing paper, called the Macon Telegraph, in which my character is feebly attempted to be assailed, and an effort made by innuendoes, such as calling me an ex-aide-de-camp to the ex-Governor, &c. and afterwards connecting my name with the Pony Club, in order to injure me personally, as well as to throw contempt upon that party, in state politics, in whose ranks, I am proud to be found. I have not defiled my hands by taking hold of the paper, neither will I ever disgrace myself to read it. I know not, nor care not whether the piece is editorial or communicated. But I dare the FLAGACIOUS LIAR AND POLTROON to attack me in any manner in his proper name; though I expect he has long rendered it so contemptible, that he dislikes to own it.

ALLEN G. FAMBROUGH

The actions of Jones and Fambrough, however indicate the Georgia Government was very soft in its enforcement of crimes against the Indians and turned its head

213

whenever citizens of the state were involved. Perhaps the attitude is best described in a letter from Governor Gilmer, early on, to Militia personnel in counties near Indian Territory. In **Whites Among the Cherokee**, Warren describes the letter as a call to arms against the Cherokee.

On January 26, 1831, Governor Gilmer wrote William Ezzard and Major Hines Holt of Dekalb County, Col. Nathan S. Hutchins of Gwinnett County, Col. Allen Fambrough, Col. IWA Petit, and Col. Andrew Moore of the need to "organize volunteer companies in every frontier county near the Cherokees, for the special object of compelling the Indians to submit to the authority of the laws, and of removing vicious and refractory white men residing among them, whose influence has been directed to excite them (the Cherokees) to disobedience"(70).

The Burke affair underscored the need for law and order in backwoods Georgia and Alabama and respresents the kind of thing that was responsible for the rise of vigilantism in the frontier.

TWO HORSE THIEVES PUBLICLY WHIPPED.

In Georgia and most southern states, hickory rods did the whipping. Here Omaha justice prevails, from Sorenson (1889).

214

1971 Bonner, James Calvin, **Georgia's last frontier: The Development of Carroll County,** Univ. of Georgia Press: Athens.

.... Boudinot, Elias and Theda Perdue, Cherokee editor: **The Writings of Elias Boudinot**, Univ of Ga Press: Athens.

1883 Fielder, Herbert, **A Sketch of the Life and Times and Speeches of Joseph E. Brown,**

January 14, 1897, Folsom, Montgomery M., **Old Abraham**, *Macon Telegraph*, page 2, col. 1,2.

1942 Guinn, J. M. K., **History of Randolph County,** *The Alabama Historical Quarterly,* Vol. 04, No. 03, Fall Issue pages 291-414.

2002 Hutton, Frankie and Barbara Straus Reed, **Outsiders in 19th-Century Press History: Multicultural Perspectives**, Univ. of Wisconsin Press: Racine.

1902 Martin, Thomas H., **Atlanta and Its Builders: A Comprehensive History of the Gate City of the South,**

1986 Schoenleber, Charles Herbert, **The Rise of the New West: Frontier Political Pressure, State-Federal ...** Univ of Wisconsin: Madison

1889 Sorenson, Alfred Rasmus, History of Omaha from the Pioneer Days to the Present Time, Gibson, Miller, Richardson printers: Omaha

June 16, 1827 Walter, Ellwood, **Art, The Ariel,** Vol. 1, no. 4, Philadelphia

April, 1832, **A String for the Poney,** *Columbus Enquirer*, col. 4.

June 1832, **Civil War in Georgia,** *Columbus Enquirer*, col. 4.

August 4, 1832, **A Citizen of Carroll,** *Columbus Enquirer*, col. 2,3.

August 18, 1832, **Allen G. Fambrough,** *Columbus Enquirer*, page 3, col 5.

July 5, 1832, **John A. Jones,** *Georgia Journal*, col. 3,4.

December 13, 1832, **William G. Springer,** *Federal Union*, page 3, col 3-5.
215

October 3, 1835, **Miner's Recorder,** *Federal Union*, page 2, col. 3.

October 16, 1830, **A Dynasty,** *Macon Telegraph*, col. 1.

June 14, 1832, **War in Georgia,** *Macon Telegraph*, ...col. 1.

June 27, 1832 **Civil War in Georgia,** *Macon Telegraph*, page 1, col. 2.

December 11, 1830, **Georgia Legislature,** *Southern Recorder*, col. 2.

November 15, 1832, **John A. Jones,** *Southern Recorder*, page 1, col. 3, 4.

The Calloway Burke affair ignited a series of events which in 1832 resulted in the deaths of several pony club members at the hands of the slicks (an early viglante illustration).

Captain Slick and the Pony Club

Shortly after the Red Stick War of 1813-1814, and the cession of the middle portion of Alabama Territory to the United States, white intruders began pouring into these new lands by the thousands. Until counties were set up with governments and land was sold legally, it was every man for himself. On several occasions Return Meigs, the Indian Agent, was forced to send U.S. troops into Alabama to burn the squatters towns and destroy their crops in order to make them leave. It was, indeed, against the law to squat on federal land, but intruders, as we have seen, were banking on the "law of preeminence" to assure them land no one wanted at a fraction of the cost. Amid all this anarchy, depredations on settlers and Indians were rife. As settlers had done in North Carolina and in South Carolina, they formed into groups of regulators to punish the worst offenders in the territory. In every state the regulators were different and Alabama was unique in producing the legend of *Captain Slick.*

All indications are that Captain Slick never existed, that he was a term used to describe what would happen to horse thieves and claim jumpers...they would be "slicked" or "sleeked," that is whipped and run out of the territory.

...A man of that name lived a few miles from us across the Georgia line. ... who was ever ready to "slick" the "pony club." (AHQ, 1946: 319)...

The term caught on and was also used in Georgia, Mississippi and even Missouri. In the final fight with the Pony Club in Carroll, Paulding and Polk Counties in Georgia, the Slicks would emerge triumphant, having pushed the club out of contention for local power.

Slick punishment for stealing horses was usually thirty-nine or more lashes with hickory branches. All children brought up in the South remember the ordeal of the hickory switch, the worst part of it was having to choose the branch of your own demise. Rather than hang horse thieves, it was common to give lashes for a simple reason, everyone had done it or was doing it. It also reflected Indian thinking of the jurisprudence assigned to borrowing livestock, a severe whipping. The Indians, who ushered in the idea of stealing wandering horses from one area and selling them in another, originated the laws of whipping horse thieves and until their removal and when laws were strengthened the practice never stopped.

A similar fate awaited other criminals who were so numerous in the frontier areas.

...Some groups, such as the followers of Captain Slick in Northern Alabama during the 1830s utilized corporal punishment. Frequently vigilantes held an ad hoc court and tried the "suspect" before sentencing. On April 24, 1831, about twenty Alabama slicks rode up to William Hall's house, took him to a swamp, went through the motions of a trial for counterfeiting, and then gave him fifty lashes on the back (Gilje, 1996: 81).

Writing on the history of Lauderdale County, Alabama, William B. Wood documented the early history and how things were tended to in those days:

John Edie was an early merchant about whom I have very little recollection. I remember, however, of a great excitement produced by the robbery of his money drawer by one of his clerks. The unfortunate young man hid the money under the steps which lead to the galley in the Presbyterian church. There was at that time a company of Regulators, composed of some of the best citizens of the town, who often took the violaters of the law into their hands without waiting for the "due course of justice," which was too dilatory; they called themselves "Captain Slick's company." This company took the young clerk in hand, and after putting him through what they called an examination, he confessed his guilt, and returned the money. They then bestowed on him their benedictions and gave him a coat of tar and feathers, and sent him out into the world to seek his fortune (as it appeared in Florence Gazette, July to September, 1876: 4).

The laws at this time were somewhat uniform and covered everyone, making no distinction for male or female. The following excerpt from Mississippi law shows not only the uniformity throughout the South, but the fate of the receivers of stolen property:

...if any person do feloniously take or steal any horse, mare or gelding, foal or filly, ass or mule, the person so offending shall restore the property so stolen or pay the value thereof, which shall be adjudged by the jury trying such offender, to the owner or owners thereof, and be fined at the discretion of the jury in a sum not exceeding five hundred dollars, and shall moreover receive thirty-nine lashes on his or her bare back, well laid on, and be branded on the face, or in the right hand, as the court shall think fit, with the letter "T," and be imprisoned for a term not exceeding twelve months." Anyone knowingly purchasing such stolen property was similarly punished (Statutes of Mississippi Territory, Edition 1816, page 98, as quoted in Betts, 1916: 15-16)...

Activities of "Slicks" had been reported in many areas of the south over the years. They were involved in that whole sordid affair with John Murrell, as Virgil Stewart noted in his exposition of the notorious slave stealer:

After they found that they could do nothing with him at law, they formed a company, which they called Captain Slick's company, and advertised for all honest men to meet at a certain school-house in the neighbourhood on a certain day. They met and bound themselves in certain matters; made rules and laws for the government of the company; and in this company he had some strong friends, who would inform him of their movements in the shortest time (Howard, 1836: 20)...

In 1835, In Livingston, Mississippi, two men recieved 150 lashes each, by a company of slicks, when two negroes let on that they were John Murrel's men and planned a slave insurgency. Other conspirators in the Murrell plot were hung or ran from the County, as reported in the **Southern Recorder** (Oct. 27, 1835). In Macon, Georgia, the **Macon Telegraph,** noted:

Good citizens must unite and frown down that class of persons, the pirates of society, who occasion the necessity for such prosecutions. The law is a dead letter, and Grand Jury presentments a mere nullity, while public opinion upholds and tolerates the perpetration and perpetrators of crime. Lynch law, in years back, did what the civil law could not effect, in ridding society of useless vermin, and the "Slicks" have done more than all the courts in the world in relieving the frontiers from the terrors of the Pony Club (quoted in Butler 1879:110)..

In **The History of Huntsville,** Betts (1916), notes the presence of the slicks in this Northern Alabama town at an early date:

Before the laws were extended over the county, Judge Taylor, in his article tells us, there had been no organized law enforcement, but this settlement was not unlike other pioneer settlements of that day and this neighborhood, and had its band of men, known as "Captain Slick's Company, the origin of which name, neither Judge Taylor nor the author has been able to trace (16)...

Taylor (1830: 159), reports the same for Madison County Alabama:

For the enforcement of law there was in every community an organization known as "Captain Slicks" company (I have been unable to ascertain where the name originated) who were the conservators of the peace. Whenever a man became notorious as a counterfeiter or a horse thief he received a notice signed by "Captain Slick" to leave the country in a certain number of days...

For Chambers County, Alabama, Richards (1942):

Most of the present inhabitants of Chambers county have heard that as early as the years 1835 and 1836 there was a company formed composed of many of our best citizens, which was known and called the Slick Company, who took the law into their own hands and administered punishment upon whom they thought deserved it. But not many of them knew the cause which led to the formation of said company. That I will relate. In the years 1835 and 1836 so many negroes ran away from their owners who could not be heard of afterwards, induced the belief that they were decoyed off by thieves and sold in other States. This belief was strengthened by the discovery of several caves in the upper part of Chambers and the Southeastern part of Randolph County. These were not natural caves but caves dug in very secluded places, not near any public road, some of them large enough to hold several persons, and which showed signs of having been but recently occupied for some purpose. This caused a number of our best citizens, men of property and respectability, to form themselves into a vigilant company to ferret out and detect and punish the thieves if discovered (434-437)...

Anthony (1946), in **Cherokee County, Alabama: Remeniscences, etc.**, also mentions companies of slicks used to fight itinerant thieves who stole everything that wasn't nailed down.

On our arrival in "the nation" we found no law in existence among the whites, except what was known as the "Slick Law." This law was enacted by an organized company of men scattered over an area of country which extended from the Tennessee river on the north to the line of the Creek nation on the south, and reaching east far back into the State of Georgia, and how far west I could never learn (334)...

In Montgomery, Alabama in the 1820s, the slickers took the name "The Regulating Horn," more familiarly known as "Jake Odum's Boys" or the "Rail Society."

Men blew horns to summon the rest of the group. They gave suspects a hearing on the spot. If they found a man guilty, they tarred and feathered him and rode him out of town on a rail. Violence can be an addictive habit; success sometimes breeds excess. The community that nurtured them began to turn against the Regulating Horn. At that point they were doomed to fail (Friedman, 2005: 214).

Friedman and Schieber (1988), writing on the subject of vigilantism in America lists several periods of citizen movements to quell lawlessness:

The first wave was from 1830-1835 and it took place in the lower southern states of Alabama and Mississippi where Captain Slick's bands operated against horse thieves and counterfeiters and vigilantes attacked gamblers and the alleged Murrell conspiracy. The second wave took place in the early 1840s and included the Bellevue Vigilante War in Iowa; the East Texas Regulator-Moderator conflict, the Northern and Southern Illinois Regulators and the Slicker War of the Missouri Ozarks (179)...

The Turk-Jones feud in Polk and Benton Counties in Arkansas more resembled that of the Hatfields and McCoys, rather than a slick movement against an organized criminal element.

Like any good idea, vigilantism had its time and place. It outlived its usefulness or was corrupted in a hurry. It can be said and several have so stated, that the Pony Club itself started out as movement of Slicks. Even Joel Leathers of the Carroll County, Georgia Pony Club complained about all those vagrants and miscreants filling up the lands newly taken from the Creek Indians. One of Joel Leathers first acts when he moved to Carroll County was to write Col. Montgomery of Indian Affairs in Georgia about intruders on Indian lands:

In 1829 Joel Leathers of Carroll County, GA wrote to Col. Hugh Montgomery, US agent to the Cherokees, that he was "frightened" of 400 families of intruders who had settled in Carroll County (recently ceded by the Creek Indians). Leathers warned that these intruders were a lawless and unruly bunch of land grabbers (Clarke, 2004).

In his detailing of the Slicks in Cherokee County, Alabama, the Rev. J.D. Anthony describes the leader of the Slicks as someone almost macabre in nature:

...Many a poor Indian lost his pony, his cows, and hogs, by the base villians, who screened themselves behind the specious show of "slick law." Any new comer among the whites, who chose not to cast his lot with these ruffians, was sure to bring down their ire upon his unfortunate head. Prominent among "the slicks," as an old man of small dimensions, in every sense of the term, except, it might be truthfully said, that he far excelled all mankind in indescribable ugliness. He always impressed me as being the personification of the connecting link between the ape and the noble animal designated by the term man, the former element largely predominating—This sui generis was known and recognized, afortiori, as "Captain Whips." He lived alone in a little cabin on the south bank of Coosa about one mile below the mouth of Mud Creek. He rode a fine black horse, and always carried when riding on horseback a medium sized wagon whip in his hand, which I suppose was the insignia of the exalted position he held as "Captain of a company of Slicks" (1946: 333)...

Shortly after our arrival these sticklers for law and order "slicked" an old man by the name of Hendricks, i.e. they gave him about two hundred lashes on his naked back. They then determined to -"slick" his son Joab, who lived near where Porterville, where DeKalb County now stands. They took both the Hendricks across the Georgia line to "slick" them. The work was done near the residence of a Mr. Dempsey. Whether Dempsey or Whips did the "slicking," or whether they divided the job between them, I never knew (334)...

In Chambers County, Alabama, things also got out of hand for the Slicks operating there. Richards describes an incident involving taking a man from a hotel which caused an uproar and many slicks were sued. The result ended the vigilantes enterprise once and for all.

That the Slicks rendered the country valuable service for awhile by running a set of thieves out of the country much sooner than it could have been done by process of law, no one can deny, but not stopping at the proper time, got themselves involved in a troublesome lawsuit and having to pay heavy damages for the violence of others, which some of them were, at the whipping of Herring, trying to prevent, but belonging to the Company were made liable (1946: 437).

The slicks movement once numbered about 600 in Alabama, according to Grimstead (1998: 311) and an undetermined number in other states. It would play a major role in removing the Pony Club from Georgia in the 1830s. What eventually was the undoing for vigilante movements in the south, such as regulators and slicks was the continuing inmigration of more stable peoples, who demanded law and order and overpowered both Slicks and vagrants alike. New laws in those days included acts to punish vagrancy and idleness, the two mainstays of border living.

*Another punishment for horse theft was tarrin and feathering,
as in this illustration from Twain's Huckleberry Finn.*

Fall, 1946, Anthony, Rev. J. D., **Cherokee County, Alabama Remeniscences of its Early Settlement,** *Alabama Historical Quarterly* vol 8 no 3, Pages 319-342.

2005 Banks, Cindi, **Punishment in America: A Reference Handbook**. ABC- CLIO: Santa Barbara, Calif.

1916 Betts, Edward Chambers, **Early History of Huntsville, Alabama 1804 to 1870,** Brown Printing: Montgomery

April, 1958 Bragg, James W., **Captain Slick, Arbiter of Early Alabama Morals** *The Alabama Review* Volume XI - - Number 2.

1879 Butler, John Campbell, **Historical Record of Macon and Central Georgia,** J.W. Burke Printers and Binders: Macon.

1988 Friedman, Lawrence Meir and Harry N. Scheiber, **American Law and the Constitutional Order,** Harvard Univ. Press: N.Y.

1994 Friedman, Lawrence Meir, **Crime and Punishment in American History.** Basic Books: Jackson, Tenn.

2005 Friedman, Lawrence Meir, **A History of American Law, 3rd Edition**. Simon and Schuster: Riverside, N.J.

1996 Gilje, Paul A., **Rioting in America,** Indiana University Press:

1998 Grimsted, David, **American Mobbing, 1828-1861,** Oxford University Press: U.K.

2001 Hall, Leslie, **Land & Allegiance in Revolutionary Georgia**, Univ. of Georgia Press: Athens.

Spring and Summer 1965 Powell, George A., **Description and History of Blount County, The Alabama Historical Quarterly**, Vol. 27, Nos. 01 & 02, pages 95-132.

Fall, 1942 Richards, Hon. E. G., **Reminiscenes of the Early Days in Chambers County,** *Alabama Historical Quarterly*, Vol 4, No. 3, pages 433-451.

July to September 1876, Wood, William B., **Historical Address of Hon. Wm. B. Wood, July 4, 1876**, *Florence Gazette,* page 4.

Summer, 1930 Taylor, Thomas Jones, **Early History of Madison County and, Incidentally of North Alabama,** *Alabama Historical Quarterly* vol. 1 no 2: 159, pages 149-168.

Oct. 27, 1835 **Transactions in Mississippi,** *Southern Recorder*, -- page 2 col. 2.

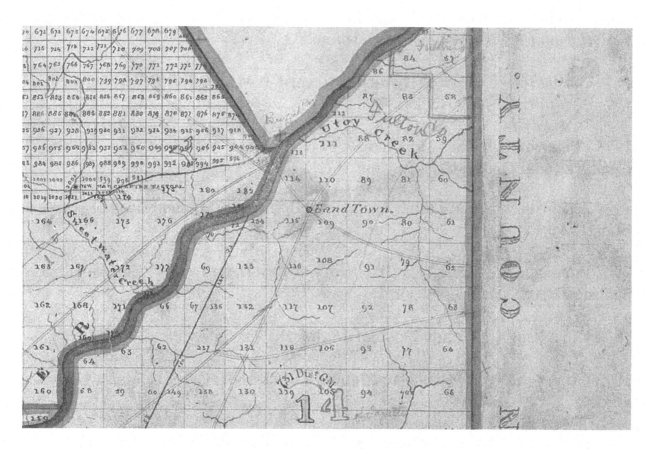

From the original plat survey of the Fayette County 14th district, Sandtown and environs.

GEORGIAN PROMOTION.

What has become of the *Pony Club?* asked a Georgian the other evening, "I believe," replied a gentleman living in the nation, "some of them have been elected Judges of the Inferior Courts in these new counties; one was whipped just before his election."

The Cherokee Phoenix, July 20, 1833, page 3 col. 5.

The idea of having a place in Indian territory where the regulators or slicks and local militia could not operate was not a new concept. In 1739, the Colonial government went after a German doctor, living with the Cherokee and enciting them against British causes. Dr. Christian Pryber was described in the *South Carolina Gazette* as:

…Scheming to set up 'a town at the foot of the mountains among the Cherokee which was to be a city of refuge for all criminals, debtors and slaves who would fly thither from justice or their masters.(Crane 1919:48).

This person Pryber had written a book on how all this was to be achieved, how the town would be laid out; the rules and regulations… a sort of early communist doctrinaire treatise…with whimsical privileges and extraordinary inherent rights.

It is easy to see Pryber was considered a dangerous sort in terms of the rallying not only the Cherokee, but also the French, Spanish, runaway slaves and criminals to a cause against the crown. Trader Ludovick Grant, writing to Governor Glen of South Carolina described the German doctor, of some notable education as "going native":

Ludovick Grant -
One Pryber who called himself a German but was certainly an agent for the French. He went up from Amelia Township to the Cherokee Nation, and lived in the Town of Telliquo, and being a great Scholar he soon made himself master of their Tongue, and by his insinuating manner Indeavoured to gain their hearts, he trimmed his hair in the Indian manner & painted as they did, going generally, almost naked, except a shirt & Flap, he told these people that they had been strangely deluded, that they had been tricked out of a great part of their Land by the

225

English, That for the future they should make no concessions to them of any kind but should profess an equal regard for bothe the French and the English, and should trade with both upon the same footing, which would be their greatest security for they would then be courted & carressed & receive presents from both.

I sometime after went up into the Townhouse with a Resolution to try what could be done, but I found that he was well apprized of my design and laughed at me, desiring me to try it, in so insolent a manner that I could hardly bear with it, and I told him although I knew the Indians would not permit me to Carry him down to be hanged, Yet they would not find fault I hoped if I should throw him into the Fire, which I certainly would do if he gave me any further Provocation. (Grant, in Trivette, Appalachian Summit).

Pryber was dealt with by colonial militia, but the backwoods was becoming a meeting place for all the bad elements of the new country and was the springboard for generations of lawlessness and organized crime to come.

New Hanover, in colonial Georgia, was a haven for the lawless and runaway slaves.

After Edmund Grey was driven from Brandon, in the northern part of the state, he and his followers settled on the Saltilla River, not far from the present village of Bailey's Mills. The settlement was named New Hanover. Here outlaws, fugitives from justice, etc., always found a welcome and in time the surrounding territory was peopled with that class of inhabitants. Another settlement was on Cumberland Island, (q. v.) These desperadoes had no valid title to the lands and acknowledged allegiance to no civilized government. The people of Georgia and South Carolina entertained fears that this lawless element might foment trouble with the Spaniards of Florida or the Creek Indians and petitioned the crown for their removal. Commissioners from the two colonies were appointed by order of Mr. Pitt; these commissioners succeeded in inducing the outlaws to remove from the territory and New Hanover ceased to exist (Knight 1913: 360).

Sandtown

At the very edge of the Georgia frontier, located between the Creeks and the Cherokee and bounded by the mighty Chattahoochee River was the village of Sandtown. During the Red Sticks War of the War of 1812, Many Creek and even Cherokee moved to get out of the war zone. The Nickajack left the Chickamauga region because of its affiliation with the British Tories and settled in Cobb County where Nickajack Creek still bears their name. The Hillabees of Alabama removed from the battle area to a Creek village below the Buzzards Roost Island, where it was rumored the French had a trading post around 1650 and later, Dr. Henry Woodward, himself had set up a factor in 1685. The Hillabees called their village in exile Octasahasi or as it was called in Alabama, Octahazauza; some called it

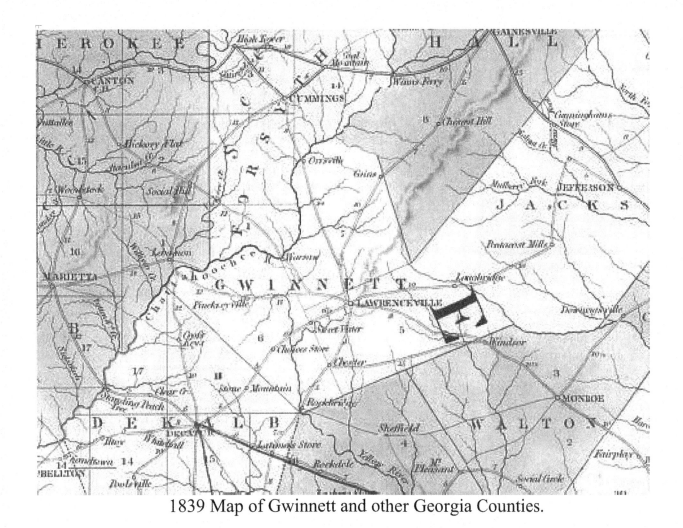

1839 Map of Gwinnett and other Georgia Counties.

Octahatalofa, but it meant sand town. The Indians stayed until about 1818 and then returned to Alabama. On the abandoned village a new frontier town sprang up. Peopled of the sort associated with intruders, runaway slaves, fugitives from the law and perhaps even some of the remnants of the "Moccasin Boys," Sandtown soon became synonymous with outlawry and the home town of the Pony Club.

In 1818, the nearest courthouse was in Jackson County, miles away. Georgia had just received a Cherokee and Creek cession opening up the land from Northeast Georgia all the way to the Buzzard's Roost. Hall, Gwinnett and Habersham Counties were formed in 1818 from the **Treaty of the Cherokee Agency,** July 1817 and the **Treaty of the Creek Agency,** January 1818. Originally surveyed as part of Fayette County, district 14, Sandtown became part of Dekalb County, which was formed in 1822 from portions of Gwinnett and other surrounding counties.

Sandtown was left to its own machinations and criminal activity began to be the rule of law. The town continued to be a center for miscreants throughout the early history of Dekalb and later Fulton County. These bad men gravitated toward Marthasville, later Atlanta in the Whitehall district, inhabiting Snake Nation, Murrell's Row and Slabtown (see Price 1997: 273-301).

The Sandtown trail was a much traveled east-west path linking The "Rock Mountain" and Decatur area west to the Chattahoochee River. From there trails to Marietta and west to Alabama proceed. No doubt this trail saw Alexander McGillavray on his trek to Rock Mountain, as it was called back then, and to the signing of the Treaty of New York in 1790. It was to become a major road for intruders and gold miners seeking their fortunes in the illegal lands of Carroll County and points North and West. Thirty years later Sandtown would serve as the center of the Federal line against Atlanta; two pontoons bridges being erected as the army of the Ohio crossed and moved on to destroy the railheads below Atlanta, sealing its fate. A comment in a diary or a regimental history mentioning the place is about all we have.

Little is known about the history of Sandtown other than its proximity to the original **Cherokee Purchase Line**, or, as it appears in Campbell and Douglas County records **The Dry Line**, because liquor was not to be traded beyond that point. It is certain, however, that early reports began coming in of depredations against the Indians in the vicinity of Sandtown:

Fayette County. Fort Troup.
July 11th. 1825.
To His Excellency,
Sir,

I have received information, (which I conceive my duty to communicate to you) that the Citizens of---- are intruding and trespassing on the Indians, by taking and conveying off the corn and other property of Genl. William McIntosh, together with other Friendly Indians. From a letter I this day received from Coln. Wagnow of DeKalb County, and from the information of other persons of respectability, I am informed that the Whites citizens of this State are commiting depredations, and in fact stealing and taking off the property of the Indians on the head of Talapousa. From my situation I have thought it the most adviseable to communicate the above facts to your Excellency and elicit your opinion as to the most adviseable plan for me to pursue against these intruders, as in my opinion I do deem it necessary that something ought to be done to put a stop to these plundering whites divested of every principle of right and Justice. I have sent on this by a friend of mine Mr Jones, who was going to Milledgeville, and who will hand you this, and permit me to solicit your Excellency, to send me an answer by the bearer.

With Sentiments of Esteem your Excellencys Obt. Servt.

Alexander Ware

In 1828 Col. Samuel Wales was given the task by Governor Forsythe of redrawing the Cherokee-Creek boundary which was derived from their 1821 treaty. In testimony both Buzzards Roost Island and Sandtown would come up and some information on it given. Most Indian witnesses questioned indicated there were but a few Creek Indians still living in Sandtown in 1821 (***Cherokee Phoenix***, May 29, 1830 page 4 col 1-3), Chulowee Indicating:

There were seven Creek Men of them who had Married his relations; he says there were no other Creek families living at Sandtown at the time he lived there (Cherokee Phoenix, 6-5-30, 1/5).

Sandtown was the first Post Office in this area, even before Campbellton or Atlanta. A popular crossing, the approaches to the ferry can still be seen on both sides of the river. On the Fulton County side the trenches and rifle pits of the Militia and Mississippi Cavalry are still visible on the bluff overlooking the river.

The Pony Club consisted mainly of one extended family from McMinn and some other counties in Tennessee. Why they chose to move out of Tennessee is not clear though descendants suspect they had to move. They arrived somewhere on the frontier in Georgia in 1826, more than likely Sandtown. This is indicated by two claims made against the Yorks, indicating crimes committed near Sandtown and Buzzard's Roost in 1826.

Josiah York of Sand Town took cattle & hogs (worth $144) belonging to Nelly (a Cherokee), near Sally Hughes' Ferry on the Etowah [or Hightower] River

1826 Allen York, Alexander Ramsey, members of the Welch family, and Philpot clan stole cattle of Archy Rowe (Cher.) on the Tallapoosa River. The cattle were traced to Buzzard's Roost

This is born out by the descendants who note births indicate the family moved from Tennessee in 1826:

…Carroll County was surveyed in 1826 - and I know that the York family, with the Philpot family, and others was in the county by 1827 when Frances York was b. 22 Nov 1827. The next oldest sister, Delilah was b. between 1826 to early 1827 in McMinn County, Tennessee (Sanfilippo, personal communication 10-20-2009)…

And:

...We are pretty sure that 1826 (or late 1825) was the year that the Philpot and York families left McMinn County, TN and moved to Carroll county. The original Philpot, James, the fellow who immigrated from Ireland died in 1825 or 1826 and after his death in McMinn county, we figure they all left for west Georgia (Lester, personal communication 10-20-2009)...

Though Pony Club members Cannon, Goodwin, Fambrough and Jones received land from the 1827 land lottery for Carroll County, none of the extended family of Philpot and York did. But as soon as Carrol County was formed they were all there, serving on the grand jury. It is not clear whether the Pony Club had the complete support of the Carroll County Sheriff and Militia but there was the incident involving the death of Chuowee and others and another incident in late 1830 which cast a dark shadow on the Carroll officials.

In a letter to the **Cherokee Phoenix,** February 12, 1831, Chief John Ross discussed an incident concerning the arrest of Joseph Beanstick the previous December and the involvement of the sheriff and the head of the Militia in Carroll County. Deputy Sheriff Henry Curtis and Militia Major Jiles G. Bogges, were in the company of Thomas York, a known Pony Club man and all three were looking to levy on two horses reportedly stolen and perhaps purchased by Indians. The Cherokee in that Etowah District having been given written permission by Federal Lt. Fowler to arrest any intruding whites, acted against the three from Carroll County. They were taken to a nearby residence where two were identified as Carroll County officials and released.

...The deputy sheriff stated that he had an execution order in favor of Major Bogus (sic) against a certain white man who had sold two horses a year or two, previously, to the Cherokees, and these horses were subject to said execution, and that they had come to levy upon the horses and had brought York along as a witness by whom to prove the horses (page 2 col.3)...

Next the Indians and the three whites removed to join Lt. Fowler of the Federal troops at Sixes to clear all this up. Fowler ordered the three and the horses to be sent to troop headquarters at Camp Eaton. Here the commandant freed Bogges and Curtis, who took the two mounts from the Cherokee Indians and rode off. Ross lamented:

York was ordered under guard by the commanding officer and there kept a number of days. The two Cherokees who were thus dismounted had to walk home (col. 3)...

Joseph Beanstick spent time in the Carroll jail, according to Ross, 4 weeks in the coldest time of winter with hardly the clothes on his back.. He suffered frostbite of one foot which had swollen to the knee. Finally Cherokee David Vann was able to prove the bailiff not in authority and the youth was released. The whole affair was just another indication the Officials of the surrounding counties were acting as or on behalf of the Pony Club.

Militia Major Bogges also brought in Old Field, Sam Roe, Bill Walking Stick, Crow, Lee and Spirit as members of the group who imprisoned him and Henry Curtis. They were charged with damages in the extent of $ 10,000 and lodged in the Carroll County jail. Lawyer for the Indians, Thomas Lothaw was able to get them released and the damages placed at $ 1500 (Bonner 1971: 31, 32).

A similar incident had taken place in December, 1830, when two white men went through the nation to levy on a horse. Wilson Cartwright, a prosecutor from Carroll County accompanied a Mr.Mahaffey to the house of widow Lee to speak to an Indian named Scott about the $20 levy. Scott refused to cooperate so the horse tied up out front was taken. Widow Lee indicated it was her horse but the men took it anyways. The *Phoenix* described the outcome:

…Mahaffey told Cartwright to levy upon him, he did so; yet when attempting to take him away the widow Lee caught the bridle and George Lee coming to her assistance took the horse from Cartright, supposing him to be one of the Poney Club. Cartright returned to Georgia and obtained two warrants one for George and one for Johnson Lee (page 2 col. 4)…

Georgia in the 1830s was experiencing growing pains which included local governments and officials who would not pass muster just a few years later. Many counties had incidents involving the Indians and local government which by any account was deemed despicable under the light of a few years passing. Sheriff Dukes of Coweta County is a good example. The July 27, 1833 edition of the **Cherokee Phoenix** carried a story of a rape attempt by the Coweta Sheriff. Dukes was in the country to locate his lottery winnings and stopped at the house of Mrs. Oosunely and Mrs. Foster. His attack on Oosunely was thwarted by Mrs. Foster, but both were horse whipped. Upon reporting the incident the magistrate failed to respond as Georgia law prohibited the Cherokee from witnessing against a white man.

Dukes calumny did not stop in Indian Country. He left Newnan under seedy circumstances as well:

There seemed to have been some problem with the honesty of public officials even in those years. In 1833, Sheriff David Dukes absconded, owing many debts and leaving his bondsman to make the money good (Newnan/Coweta Historical Society 1988: 9)...

Likewise, there seemed to be a problem in Habersham County with the Sheriff there.

...I do not know that Henton A. Hill former Sheriff of Habersham County was ever known or suspected to be engaged in this business. He absconded from this state on account of his inability to meet the rules which he knew would be taken against him at an approaching Sup. [Superior] Court. He is an unprincipled man & I think it more than probable that he may have cautiously passed counterfeit money (TCC 524:March 8, 1831, letter from Sol. Gen. Trippe of Habersham County to S. Carolina Governor Hamilton)...

After the Land Lottery of 1832, many of those tormenting the Cherokee became part of the local governments in the newly formed counties. Some examples are those who formed the new Cherokee County; Oliver Strickland, who Indian Margaret Baumgartner (nee Vickery) claimed took her property and lands for another, was Clerk of Superior Court of Cherokee County. Lizzy Sanders of Going Snake District, Oklahoma in her 1842 Spoliation Claim cited two Justices of the Inferior court, William Lay and William Baker as having stolen her money and a rifle in two separate incidents in 1830 (Shadburn 1993: 646, 649). Another Inferior Court Justice, John Witcher, whose Militia was charged with drunkenness during the removal, will be discussed later.

With the help of people like John A. Jones and State Senator Allen Fambrough of Carroll County, local officials and the stacked Grand Jury were able to keep the Pony Club from being prosecuted. This resulted in backlashes like that involving John Goodwin of Alabama and Hawkins Phillips in 1832 and the capture and whipping of Moses Hendrix in 1835 by Andrew Cunningham and Soloman Mays and a regulating company (Shadburn 1993: 655). The tide was turning against the Club in Carroll County and the William Springer Grand Jury was not going to allow the thieves to continue operating.

James C.Bonner, 1971, in **Georgia's last Frontier,** described the life and downfall of the Pony Club in Carroll County.

...The principal rendezvous for this gang was on Hominy Creek (below Hickory Level on lot 22) near where it flows into the Little Talapoosa, on a farm later owned by John D. Morgan. This was an area of swamps and dense thickets. Barnes Williams once reported seeing "twenty five or thirty" of these renegades sitting on a fence in the sunshine. Upon discovering the visitor "they dropped like turtles off a log" and retreated to their lairs in the swamp (32, 33).

Bonner recounted the last days of the Club in Carroll County:

Honest citizens, known as "slicks" and who bore no aliases, could be spotted easily. Soloman Wynn and George S. Sharp each headed a group of vigilantes who caught many horse thieves, whipped them and then ordered them to leave the county. The Pony Club did not relinquish political control of the county without a struggle. In an election of 1832 gang members engaged in a desperate street fight with citizens on the public square at Carrollton. The representatives of law and order, led by Jiles Bogges, who was then sheriff, were victorious. At the next session of the Grand Jury some members of the defeated ring charged Bogges and his associates with assault and intent to murder. Instead of bringing in true bills, however, the jury expressed gratitude to Bogges for his efforts to banish crime in the community. In their presentments they cited lawyers John A. Jones and Allen G. Fambrough as being in league with the Pony Club. The youthful Judge Walter T. Colquitt attempted to have these references to the two lawyers stricken from the record, claiming that as member of the court they could not be intimidated in this manner. The foreman of the jury, William G. Springer, is said to have jumped to his feet and openly defied the judge whereupon Colquitt then consented...

In the 1833 presentments, more was done to discourage the Club.

In the same presentments the Grand Jury indicted **Thomas Mederis** *for keeping a drunken and disorderly company about his house, allowing "fiddling and dancing" and for making whiskey on the Sabbath and for "menacing voters" in the 682cd District.* **Thomas Hogan** *was also indicted "for assaulting and violently beating Absalom Adams on election day in the 649th District," and also "for threatening to beat...Thomas Wynn and having pistols and rocks to annoy the good people of the said 649th District (Bonner 1971: 33, 34)"...*

Mary Talley Anderson, in **The History of Villa Rica** (1976), also retells the story of the great fight on the courthouse square. She indicates guns and knives were not employed but that fist fights produced a victory for the slicks.

A check-up revealed that no slick was seriously hurt during this period and only one member of the Pony Club was killed. The latter met his death while attempting to escape with a horse near where Hickory Level Post Office was located (14).

Defeated in Carroll County, in 1832 and 1833, the Pony Club moved into Indian Territory, into the new counties opened up by the Georgia Land Lottery of 1832.

1976 Anderson, Mary Talley, **The History of Villa Rica**, Georgia Bicentennial Committee: Carrollton.

1971 Bonner, James C., **Georgia's Last Frontier: the Development of Carroll County,** University of Ga. Press: Athens.

May 29, 1830 **Cherokee Boundary**, *Cherokee Phoenix*, page 4 col 1-3.

June 5, 1830 **Cherokee Boundary,** *Cherokee Phoenix*, page 1 col. 5.

January 1, 1831 **Hightower: Cherokee Nation,** *Cherokee Phoenix*, Page 2 col. 4.

February 12, 1831 **Head of Coosa,** *Cherokee Phoenix,* Page 2 col. 3.

July 20, 1833 **Georgia Promotion,** *Cherokee Phoenix*, page 3 col. 5.

July 27, 1833 **Sufferings of Cherokee Ladies,** *Cherokee Phoenix* Page 3 col. 2.

1919 Crane, Verner W., **A Lost Utopia of the First American Frontier**, The Johns Hopkins University Press: Baltimore.

1999 **Huxford Genealogical Society Magazine**, Volume 26 The Society: University of Wisconsin, Madison.

1913 Knight, Lucian Lamar, **Georgia's Landmarks, Memorials, and Legends**, Vol. 1. Byrd Printing Company: Atlanta.

1988 Newnan/Coweta Historical Society, **History of Coweta County, Georgia**, W.H. Wolf and Assoc.: Roswell, Ga.

1997 Price, Vivian, **The History of Dekalb County, Georgia, 1822-1900**, Wolfe Publishing: Fernandina Beach, Fla.

1993 Shadburn, Don L., **Unhallowed Intrusion**, W.H. Wolfe and Assoc.: Alpharetta, Ga.

March 8, 1831 **TCC 524**, letter from Sol. Gen. Trippe of Habersham County to S. Carolina Governor Hamilton. Georgia Digital Archives.

2001-2009 Trivette, Jerry, **Ludovic Grant, Historical Relation of Facts Delivered by Grant,** @ http://appalachiansummit.tripod.com/

On the Move

January 14th 1831
Dear Sir

There is some fifteen or twenty improvd places within the slipe of Country claimd under the Indian Spring treaty, that would in all probability rent for from one to two thousand dollars. These places are most entirely occupied by men of bad character. If it is not intended that these places should be rented by the Legislature. It is to be hopd that your Ecclency will have it done. There is a plenty of Honest good men that would rent those places & would pay for them, while the present Occupants use them as Harbers for stolen property &c chiefly.

I am inducd to write you this from a belief that the Legislature alluded to the emigrated places only. & thinking it possible you are not apprisd of their extent and value If I am correct in my view of that matter it is important how soon they could be rented their being many persons waiting to know what disposition will be made of them.

You will excuse me for writing your Excelency in this pressing manner I am at this time living on the Chattehoochy opposite these fellows and am disappointed every morning in finding all my Horses &c within my enclosure,

Your Obednt Servant &c
Alston H Greene

NB. Should you want an agent for the above business myself or Martin Kolb will either or both attend to it without any compensation, in order to get rid of the Pony Club & others of suspicious character Free.

His Excelency G.R. Gilmer
Milledgeville, Geo.

Things began to change for the Pony Club and for the Indians in 1831 and 1832. Governor Gilmer's idea of seizing the mines for the state of Georgia lost out to that of Wilson Lumpkin, who wanted another land lottery to give lots to deserving Georgians. The new Governor was a well known friend of Senator Allen Fambrough and they were working on a solution to the Cherokee question. The Senator suggested early on that lands abandoned by Indians leaving for the West voluntarily should be rented to whites. Lumpkin picked up this idea and soon the Indian Country was to teem with renters. This meant the end of the question of white intruders on Indian land; it could not be stopped. Special Agent for Cherokee Immigration Benjamin Curry had the task of enrolling Cherokee who chose to leave Georgia early, and agents like William Hardin and William Cleghorn would sign up whites and collect rents.

Gov. George Gilmer

Gov. Wilson Lumpkin

The Cherokee had broken under the pressure and a faction led by **John Ridge** and **Elias Boudinot** favored signing a treaty on the best terms while Chief John Ross chose to fight removal to Oklahoma in the U.S. courts. The factions began to murder each other's members and things began moving downhill fast. Lumpkins solution was to have the Cherokee lands in Georgia surveyed and sold to state citizens in a lottery. In 1831 the survey began and in late 1832 the lottery was held. Now there were whites living among the Cherokee as renters, land owners and outlaws.

The land lottery was just in the nick of time for the Pony Club in Carroll County. Many of the family had served in the War of 1812, so the provisor that no member of the Pony Club or the intruding miners could draw a lot was null and void and many won new lands in Indian Country. Now the Club could operate next door to their victims. The following members won lots (district-section- LL):

RICHARD PHILPOT	8-2-249	Gilmer County
	21-2-1215	Cass County
	12-1-7	Lumpkin County
JAMES PHILPOT	8-3-106	Murray County
WM YORK	26-2-190	Murray County
ALEXANDER HOGAN	7-1-142	Union County
JAMES UPTON	18-3-741	Paulding County
THOMAS WELCH	3-27-2	Gilmer County
ABRAHAM LEATHERS	5-2-81	Gilmer County
JOEL LEATHERS	3-2-405	Cherokee County

236

Pony Club in Paulding County

The Pony Club, rather than dying out in Carroll County, merely moved to newly formed Paulding County. The activities of the Pony Club here were mainly in the vicinity of CleanTown and Van Wert, the county seat. In 1851, while Carroll County was divided to add Haralson County to Georgia, Polk County was formed from Paulding and because Van Wert was in Polk County, Dallas became the new county seat of a smaller Paulding. Most of what went on in Paulding County before 1851 is mentioned in Polk County History.

Listed in the original 1837 census of Paulding were the following members of the Pony Club:

Richard Philpot	Allen York
James Philpot	Thomas Hogan
Reuben Philpot	John Wright
Jesse Philpot	William Shipley
William Philpot	James Johnson
J.C. York	

Much of the activity of the Pony Club in Paulding County is written with the history of Polk County. In 1897, Dr. Charles K. Henderson (1875) wrote a history of Polk County which delved deep into the workings of the Pony Club after it left Carroll County.

The Pony Club, a famous organization, figured conspicuously in the early history of Polk County and very largely, if into wholly, controlled the politics of the county. Van Wert was the headquarters of the club, while the hindquarters of the club were in the saddle.

About the time of the removal of the court house, Mr. Shipley was Sheriff, and Cols. Jack Jones and Thomas Sparks were elected to the Legislature. At that time, Gov. Lumpkin, the father of our townsman Mr. John Lumpkin, visited Polk County, and was entertained by a leading Pony Club man at old Van Wert. It was the finesse of Gov. Lumpkin that made his stay at Van Wert a success (June 5, 1875).

Writing for the Cedartown **Record,** Henderson recalled:

Cedartown and Clean-town were the two rival cities in the county. Cedartown was the name given to it by the Indians, from the great quantity of cedar that grew around it and in the valley, and was noted as a general council ground, green corn dance and ball play.

Cleantown was also named by the Indians, in the language the most stinking and filthy name they could think of, in order, as they said, to suit the class and character of the people who lived around it. The white people, though, modestly called it Cleantown.

Cedar Valley, during the summer and fall of 1832, was settled by a few scattering white families, generally respectable and honest, and a great number of poor, degraded Indians, reduced to poverty, they said, by the "Pony Club," who had stolen all their horses, cows, hogs and money, and they would frequently track up their horses and cows, and be afraid to claim them, as the Pony Club were cruel to persons hunting stolen property, and would frequently lynch an Indian for no other crime than claiming his own property (June 5, 1875).

This view is borne out by Gordon Sargent, in **Polk County, Georgia**, who noted:

More of a threat to life and property than the Cherokee Indians was the company of thieves located in Cleantown and known as the Pony Club. Their horse stealing raids were often accompanied by burning and murder. Some farmers grew discouraged and simply pulled up stakes to move again to safer areas. Others banded together as the Slick Club and after a few years were successful in ridding the county of the Pony Club (1998: 6).

Henderson continues with this fascinating account of the workings of the Club.

A large majority of the settlers of Cleantown, or Euharley valley at that time, were members of the Pony Club, with some good, honest, respectable citizens among them. But this class was generally forced to keep dark, or say nothing as to the acts or doings of the Club. In fact it was dangerous for a citizen of Cedar Valley to come out and openly oppose the Club. They were a set of men who had fled from justice from the States, and had banded themselves together for the express purpose of thieving, with a regular set of by-laws, said to be similar to those of Murrell. They had the Indians perfectly submissive, but the better class of the whites, as they would move in, were disposed to resist their conduct. The good people were finally forced to form what was known as the "Slick Company," for the protection of persons and property (missing sentence or sentences) them for stealing a horse or anything else on a certain day, he would frequently get two or three witness from Alabama or some other place, to come over and swear that he was in Alabama or Tennessee on the same day the horse was stolen, and the result was, a bill of costs to pay and the thief set free; hence the necessity for the Slick Company.

When a citizen of Cedar Valley lost a horse, he would summon his Slick Company and track up his horse, and when overtaken, they would take both thief and horse over into Floyd county or Alabama, and give him from thirty-nine to sixty-six lashes on his bare back, and he would frequently confess or reveal the fact of all the horses and cattle that had been stolen for months previous, where traded and by whom stolen…

238

...Nearly every week during the winters of 1832 and 1833 scouts would come from Cleantown to Cedartown, with the threat that every man in Cedar valley who was a member of the Slick Company who did not leave the county in three days, would be either hung, shot or whipped. I had forgotten to mention that a great many low, degraded Indians were engaged with the Pony Club, more as guides or "lackey boys," to do their low work. The pure, full blood Indians, unadulterated by the whites, were honest, and denounced stealing or anything dishonest (Henderson: June 5th, 1875).

Henderson's writings for the Cedartown **Record** are perhaps the most comprehensive effort to save the history of the Club. It represents what the early history of Sandtown and Carroll County must have been like. Although there is much room for interpretation in this subject; what with the Indians claiming everyone was a member and the Georgia Government, to this day hiding its complicity, it's easy to see how many could be accused, or omitted from accusations over the years. In many cases some of those rumored to be members actually put disclaimers in local newspapers, decrying their innocence. The laws against the Cherokee, in Georgia, were so bad that anyone enforcing them might be construed as a Pony Club member. In this milieu, Henderson records the activities in Paulding, later Polk County.

The accuracy of Henderson's memory seems good as he recalls when Andrew Cunningham, Soloman Mays and some Alabama regulators appear after the elections in Cedartown:

They had counted out a sufficient number of votes to ascertain who was elected, and a very prominent candidate of the Cleantown persuasion, for Judge of the Inferior Court was decided to be elected. He and his friends were rejoicing in a big way when suddenly all was sad -- Slicks are coming. Men commenced running, hiding, and dashing in every direction and in a short time, Captain Cunningham and Lieutenant May had charged over the yard fence horseback, with sixty Alabama Slicks, and formed in line before the door of the house in which the election was held, and Captain Cunningham called aloud for this prominent Cleantown candidate to come out of his house. At this time about a hundred guns were cocked and presented. Slicks and all others were in madness. Officers were hollowing "I command the peace, don't shoot." Captain Cunningham continued calling for him to come out. Someone told him he was just elected Judge. The Captain replied that he had come over to ___ him, at the same time took a large __ rope from his saddle, and ordered the Judge to cross his lands. The Judge drew his pistol and said the first man who laid hands on him he would shoot a ball through. The Captain followed him up, rope in hand, the Judge backing, until he got in the corner of the fence, and said if he had taken any man's property he had the money to pay for it. One of the Alabama Slicks said that was what they came for, you or your money, and further said, "when I track my cows and horse to your house, you threatened to shoot me if I didn't leave, and now, sir, nothing will satisfy me but you or the money." The matter was finally compromised, the Judge paying fifty dollars, all the money he had, and gave his note and security for the balance.

239

E. R. Forsyth was elected Clerk Superior Court, Elisha Brooks Clerk Inferior Court; Isaiah (Josiah) C. York and Wm. S. Houge Sheriffs, Woodson Hubbard, J. G. Deritt, James Cleghorn, John Lawrence and James Johnson were elected Judges Inferior Court. Cedar Valley got many of the offices, and several prominent men were candidates. This valley at that time possessed more wealth and intelligence than any other portion of the county (Henderson, June 12, 1875)

After the March election, the Pony Club became more desperate, and at the same time were jubilant. They were certain the held the balance of power, and could turn the election upon whom they pleased. They would go to the Democrats and say, "you stand up to us, we can elect you -- we have a special use for you -- we intend to rule the country; no man shall have an office unless we say so." They would go to the Whigs and tell them the same thing. They said "this country must be purged -- Cedar Valley shall never have an office; the Slicks and all their friends shall leave the country; we will place the county cite (Van Wert) at Cleantown and we will mob every Slick that comes to the polls; it is our town." And they did mob several persons.

Cedar valley at length got bad off for a town -- it was to be mobbed if they went to Van Wert, and in the spring of 1834 they sent a petition to the Governor, setting forth the facts, and he promptly responded and sent up a company of United States troops and they made a dash on Cleantown, and oh Jerusalem ! what squandering and hiding with the men, and yelling and squalling among the women. "The wicked fleeth when no man pursueth." and every man that felt that he had been connected with the Pony club fled to the mountain, sold their lands and other valuables, signed up deeds while in the mountains and left, went where the "woodbine twineth." The result of their leaving was a Democratic victory in 1834 and Wilson Lumpkin, who was then Governor and a Democrat, was charged by the Whigs of using his office for political ends (Henderson, June 19, 1875)

For the second time in as little as two years the Pony Club had been run out of a county by slicks and those opposed to their lawlessness. As in the case of Carroll County, many stayed in Paulding and Polk. Josiah York, who served as a Sheriff for the Pony Club also served as magistrate from 1838 on. Yorkville in Polk County is named after him. Many of the Club members remained and joined the local militia to fight the Creek War of 1836, also called the Second Seminole War, and joined the Confederate Army to fight in the Civil War. Though the Club never had the power to run a County Government again they did not disappear completely. The thefts from the Indians continued unabated until they removed in 1838.

27 June 1884 **Early Settlers,** *Paulding New Era.*

June 5, 1875 Henderson, Dr. Charles K., **Early History of Polk County***, Cedartown Record.*

June 12, 1875 Henderson, Dr. Charles K., **Early History of Polk County***, Cedartown Record.*

June 19, 1875 Henderson, Dr. Charles K., **Early History of Polk County***, Cedartown Record.*

June 26, 1875 Henderson, Dr. Charles K., **Early History of Polk County***, Cedartown Record.*

July 24, 1875 Henderson, Dr. Charles K., **Early History of Polk County***, Cedartown Record.*

August 21, 1875 Dr. Charles K., **Early History of Polk County***, Cedartown Record.*

This series of articles, transcribed by **Debra Tumlin** can be found on line at: http://www.rootsweb.ancestry.com/~gapolk/cs19jun1875t.htm

1998 Sargent, Gordon D., **Polk County, Georgia**, Arcadia Publishing: Mt. Pleasant, S. Carolina.

1986 Schoenleber, Charles Herbert, **The Rise of the New West: Frontier Political Pressure, State-Federal Conflict, and the Removal of the Choctaws, Chickasaws, Creeks, and Cherokees, 1815-1837**, University of Wisconsin: Madison.

1838 Smith, James F., **The Cherokee Land Lottery, Containing a Numerical List of the Names of the Fortunate Drawers in said Lottery, With an Engraved Map of Each District,** Harper & Brothers: N.Y.

Jan. 14, 1831 **TCC522,** Letter, [to] G[eorge] R. Gilmer, [Governor of Georgia], Milledgeville, Georgia, Alston H. Greene.

Beginning of the End.

1833 witnessed the beginning of the end for the Cherokee and the Pony Club. There were so many white people in Cherokee Territory, as winners of land lots; renters from the State of Georgia; renters of Indian lands; hired whites and intruders there to rob them all. Captain Gardner of the United States and troops were summoned in Tennessee to rout some families of intruders there. The result was reported in the *Cherokee Poenix*:

In the latter part of April and early in May, this officer with a company of soldiers made an excursion on the Tennessee line to remove intruders from Cherokee land. But few families were found on this line, perhaps 40 or 50. Some of these families fled over the Georgia and Alabama lines of the Cherokee lands for refuge; to take the benefit of the nullification doctrine. The effect of this process is making bad worse, removing intruders from Tennessee to intrude on the Cherokee there already too much oppressed and made unhappy by such people. The remainder of these scums of society penetrated the mammoth cave at Necojack, and have since made it their habitations.

Capt. Gardner applied the torch to their houses and wigwams, amounting to about 180 and then returned to their encampment at the gold mines on Croker Creek (July 20, 1833: 3/2).

Meanwhile in Columbus, Georgia things were getting worse for the Creek Indians as well. An 1832 treaty sealed their fate, ceding all their lands east of the Mississippi, giving them a reserve for five years at which time it must be sold, requiring them to be removed to Oklahoma. The resulting chaos included intruders, theft of Indian lands and seedy land speculators. Problems had begun earlier, laws against Creeks hunting for food and other measures were creating starvation among the Indians. Add to this the problems associated with thieves and speculators and things had become very serious in Alabama. Eneah Micco, Chief of the Lower Creek Towns wrote to **John Crowell** the Indian Agent at Fort Mitchell. Foreman (1985) discussed the content of the letter:

…1500 whites, including horse thieves and other criminals had squatted in the Creek country and a large number of them were actively engaged in marking "out the situations they design occupying, by blazing and cutting their initials on the trees" around the homes of the Indians. "We expect to be driven from our homes" …Yesterday, in your hearing, we were notified by a white man from Georgia that he had located himself in our country, and, should any of his be misplaced or interfered with, he should prosecute us under the law of Alabama (109, 110)…

In fact intruders had invaded Indian country, run the inhabitants out and built homes of logs in place of the lodges. To route them Secretery of War Cass had sent Marshall Austill, of the **Canoe Fight** fame in the war of 1812, to Fort Mitchell. He found there were 3000 Intruders on Indian land involved in the worst crimes. Replacing agent Crowell was **Tarrant Crawford,** who noted:

…Among the intruders were some of the most lawless uncouth men I have ever seen; some of them refugees from the State of Georgia for whom rewards are offered (Foreman 1985: 117)…

One such place was the Eufala Town below Columbus on the Alabama side of the river. Intruders had built a town there and had the State Legislature recognize its new name, Irwinton. The Federal Government now began to act on the Creek's behalf. Irwinton was seized and burned to the ground, the intruders sent packing. As with any time the United States Government got involved in local affairs, things soon turned terribly wrong. When Governor Gilmer ordered Cherokee lands in Georgia surveyed, he had to replace one of the surveyors, Benjamin Sturges, who, instead of doing his duties was stumping for a candidate in an election. Gilmer replaced him with another surveyor named **Hardeman Owens** (Cadle 1991: 273, 274).

Lt. Col. Hardeman Owens, Columbus Enquirer, April 28, 1832.

In the July 27, 1881 edition of the Columbus Enquirer-Sun there was an article which retold the story of Hardeman Owens and how his death caused so much trouble in Alabama in 1833.

During the year 1833 there lived in Russel County, on the road leading from Columbus to Uchee Post Office and about twenty four miles from the former place, one Hardeman Owens, who kept an Inn and a store. He traded extensively with the Indians and, after a while he became quite obnoxious to them, when he was reported to the authorities and was ordered to

243

leave the county. Owens declined going, whereupon a detachment of U.S. troops were sent to move him. Owens heard they were coming and prepared a room for their reception, under which he placed a keg of powder with a fuse running to a convenient point, by which he could touch them off. The soldiers arrived and were kindly received by Owens, who invited them into the room prepared for them, After a while he managed to set fire to the fuse, which, being poorly gotten up, burned too slow—too slow for poor Owens—for ere the fire reached the keg the trap was discovered And Owens made an attempt to escape by running, when he was shot and killed by James Emmerson, a United States soldier (page 1 col. 4).

The State of Alabama reacted swiftly, and a true bill of murder came out of the fall, 1833 Russel County grand jury, accusing the Federal soldier of killing Owens. The **Phoenix** (October 5, 1833, 2/5), tongue in cheek, reported the death at the hands of U.S. troops as well. Here was a state in conflict with the Federal Government over intruders and policy with the Indians. The implications here weren't new, though, in 1824 U.S. troops under Col. Archibald Turk's Company had killed an intruder in Georgia named James Dickson and it had created a great public uproar. This time the Secretery of War sent the lawyer **Francis Scott Key** to Columbus, Georgia to try and straighten the mess out in Alabama. Key was able to get the charges dropped in exchange for allowing the "least obnoxious" intruders to stay on Indian lands (Foreman 1985: 124).

As things deteriorated in Alabama, some Creeks began to flee to Cherokee lands for sanctuary. This did not go unnoticed, however by the new settlers in Northwest Georgia. In a letter to Governor Lumpkin, several Paulding County residents indicated with trepidation the Creek movement into Cherokee lands.

Cedartown, Paulding Co., Ga.,
May 27, 1834.

Dear Sir:—We hasten to inform your Excellency that recently a large number of Creek Indians who have disposed of their reservations in the State of Alabama have moved to and settled in this county, near the line of Alabama, and continue to come in daily.

We have held a friendly talk with them on the subject of their removal here. They say the Creeks have sold their lands to the white people, and that they are not willing to go to Arkansas, and that they have come to reside permanently among the Cherokees, who are willing and wish them to do so. Since their arrival here the Cherokees have become much more impudent and hostile than they were before, and say the Creeks are willing to aid them in killing up the white people, and taking their lands back again. They have been continually robbing and plundering our citizens ever since they came here, and we do assure your Excellency that, unless the Creek Indians are speedily removed from this country, our honest white citizens must either remove from the country or submit to savage ambition and violence.

We then hope that your Excellency will adopt some speedy measure to have them removed from our country (Lumpkin 1907:289).

With the highest esteem, we remain, your Excellency's obedient servants,
M. S. EDMUNDSON,
S. F. BURGES,
JOHN KIRBY,
WADDY THOMPSON,
TURMAN WALTHALL,
HIRAM WRIGHT,
HENRY PEEK,
LACY WITCHER,
JESSE STEPP,
JOHN WITCHER.

Only a week earlier, Gen. Henry M. Terrell had ordered local companies to begin confiscating weapons from the more hostile Cherokee in Georgia:

Col. S. D. Crane, Col. Wm. N. Bishop, Gen'l Jas. Hemphill, Col. Hargrove.
Cherokee County, May 17, 1834.

Dear Sir:—From the general excitement, caused by the frequent depredations committed on our good citizens of this County, I have ordered out a guard of twelve or fifteen men, under the command of Captain Robert Johnson, for their protection, not having arms to defend themselves.

He is ordered to take peaceably from the Indians their guns, town by town, from all the hostiles (sixes) of this County; or from such other hostile town of the Indians as may be known and proven to be unfriendly to the whites. This was the most efficient plan that suggested itself to my view. The arms will be taken good care of, and returned to the Indians when ordered by your Excellency, and we trust not before a regular guard of at least thirty men, either of the United States or State troops, are known to the Indians to be stationed with us. This step will promote emigration. The lives and property of the citizens demand a guard. With much respect,
Yr. obt. servt., (Lumpkin1907:289)

HENRY M. TERRELL

Lumpkin acted swiftly to the news of Creek movement into Cherokee lands. He asked Gen. R.M. Echols to gather the troops and supplies that would be needed to put down a Cherokee uprising. Not ordering a military operation, he feared a massacre of settlers, but was cautious about the whole affair:

...Nothing yet, however, has occurred which would, in my opinion, justify military operations. So long as the civil authority can be enforced, it ought not to be superseded by the military (293)...

To calm the waters in Paulding County, the Governor sent a delegation to the Cherokee to discuss the matter. Utilizing Charles Vann as an interpreter the position of the Cherokee was explained:

...they had come amongst the Cherokees in conformity to a usage which had long existed between the Creeks and Cherokees, that they were ignorant of having violated the rights of Georgia, and expressly disavowed any hostile intent (296)...

Further, Vann indicated the Cherokee intended to stay "aloof" from the problem between the Georgians and the Creek. Foreman (1985) notes the somber facts and figures and the outcome of Creek intrusion into Cherokee lands:

Many of the Creeks sold all their provisions, corn and cattle, so they would be ready for removal; numbers had become destitute having sold their land and dissipated the proceeds; or having been evicted by fraudulent purchasers, they became wanderers, wretched and miserable and a menace to the whites. Finding no refuge among the latter, they began drifting into the Cherokee country in Alabama and Gerogia u ntil in February, 1836, 2,400 destitute and hungry Creeks of the Sakapatayi, Kan tcati, Tallase-hatchee, and Talladega towns found shelter among their red brothers who were themselves soon to be evicted.

A company of Georgia Militia attacked and fired on fifty of these Creeks who were encamped on the Georgia side of the Coosa River, killing and injuring a number of the Indians. The Georgians afterwards killed some defenseless old Indians who were picking cotton along the Chattahoochee River. Because the Indians attempted to defend themselves the Georgia General of Militia ordered 1000 men to assemble for the purpose of crossing the river and attacking the Indians of Alabama (141, 142)...

The situation with the Creeks began to spiral out of control as more and more white depredations, which included finagling land out of the Indians using Chilly McIntosh and Tyger as real Estate agents, to the point where hostilities finally broke out in May, 1836. 50 or 60 Indians attacked the stagecoach from Columbus, Georgia to Tuskeegee, Alabama, and several passengers were killed. Roaming bands of landless Indians began attacking whites and destroying their property. A great panic ensued in Columbus as hundreds of new Alabama settlers scrambled for safety within the city limits. Governor Clay of Alabama ordered Militia Gen Shearer to act, but the press and many others including the general believed the whole incident was a set up by whites to take the pressure of scrutiny off of their fraudulent attempts to take Indian land (Foreman 1985: 146). Finally, activities of the Seminoles reached tipping point to create a second Seminole War, commonly called the Creek War.

One of the main characters of this war had a storied background, according to Montgomery Folsom (1897) of the Macon Telegraph, who wrote about Old Abraham.

In the old days of John A. Murrell and his gang there was an organization known as **The Pony Club,** *extending from the borders of Kentucky down through Tennessee and Georgia and into Florida. The latter state had but recently been purchased from Spain and a few Americans inhabiting East Florida were the roughest element, the outcasts of civilization. What is now Lake City was then called Alligator and was the Southern headquarters of the Pony Club.*

Murrell was a daring desperado, and he and his men would steal horses and negroes from the wealthy planters and spirit them away through the aid of the Pony Club and then sell them again. Many a Kentucky thoroughbred was passed from hand to hand along the line until safe within the limits of Florida, where the laws were laughed at even when the thief was detected. Negroes were stolen and passed through the country in the same way, their captors traveling along unfrequented ways by night and lying concealed at the residence of some member of the club during the day until safe from pursuit (Page 2 col. 1).

Folsom tells the story of one of Murrell's men, McDuffie, who was taking some stolen slaves to Pensacola. One rebellious surly slave, Abraham, and a compatriot waited until their captors were asleep, then cut their throats and escaped. They swam the mighty Appalachicola and were given safe haven by the Seminoles. Abraham met up with Osceola, who later married the runaway slave's sister. Abrahamtown sprung up in South Florida and became a center of runaway slaves. From their base in the swamps, Abraham's band of cutthroats would plunder the new settlers of Florida.

…The deeds of Abraham and his band would form a thrilling tale if they could be collected, but they have been preserved only in tradition, and the cracker mothers frightened their children with threats of Old Abraham long years after Gen. Jesup had driven the remnants of the Seminoles into the depths of the Big Cypress and the desolate wilds of the Everglades (page 2, col. 1)…

One of the former slave's greatest fetes was stealing his sister from her Alabama master. Not too long after Abraham had escaped, he chose some allies and ventured back to his former home in Alabama where he surreptitiously induced his sister and some other slaves to run away to Florida. Osceola upon seeing Abraham's sister, Maggie, fell in love and married her.

247

Osceola and Abraham and their constant raiding of the settlers spurred a reaction by the State of Florida. Major Francis Dade and 100 men made their way along the road from Tampa across the Ouithlacoochee River to Lake Panasoffkee. Here they were ambushed and massacred by Abraham's men and the Creek War was on. The Second Seminole war ended as badly for the Seminole as the first had. Osceola was captured and imprisoned at Fort Moultrie where he died soon thereafter.

Abraham, Sounafe Tustenugge

Wildcat caught and under guard (Eastman 1841).

Micanopy (Mckinney-Hall).

Osceoloa (Catlin1838).

Abraham, Cornplanter and Tustenugge were removed west, while Micanopy and Billy Bowlegs escaped into the swamps to fight yet another day. Folsom's account is the only evidence this author has ever seen indicating a connection between the Pony Club, Murrell and the Mocassin Boys of East Florida. I suspect as many of the readers may, that someone has rolled three separate stories into one. Time has a way of collapsing categories and telescopingevents into one event. We saw this in county histories in Georgia, when they speak of "Guy Rivers" cave or Murrell's row.

Map of the Second Seminole War.

Many of the Pony Club members fought in the Creek War. It was the most costly U.S. war in history until the Civil War and ended the chances for any Creeks fighting removal. In many cases Indians fearing retribution fled to Fort Mitchell for U.S. protection only to be marched to Gunter's Landing on the Tennessee and sent by steamboat to Indian Territory in Oklahoma.

1991 Cadle, Farris W., **Georgia Land Surveying History and Law,** Univ. of Ga. Press: Athens.

July 20, 1833 **The Way to Execute Treaties,** *Cherokee Phoenix*, page 3 col. 2.

October 5, 1833, **Indian Affairs,** *Cherokee Phoenix*, page 2 col. 5.

April 28, 1832 **Regimental Appointments, Columbus Enquirer,** page 2 col. 4.

July 27, 1881 **Old Times in Russel County,** *Columbus Enquirer-Sun,* page 1 col. 4.

1985 Foreman, Grant, **Indian Removal: The Emigration of the Five Civilized Tribes of Indians**, Univ of Oklahoma Press: Norman.

1907 Lumpkin, Wilson, **The Removal of the Cherokee Indians from Georgia,** Dodd Meade and Co.: N.Y.

January 24, 1897 Folsom, Montgomery M., **Old Abraham,** *The Macon Telegraph.*

Murrell steals a slave, from Howard's History of Virgil Stewart.

Blackbirding.

Reminiscent of the activities of John A. Murrell, some of the Pony Club had been accused of stealing slaves as well as stock. Charges of slave stealing go way back and involve all sorts of Banditti and ne'er-do-wells. The Cherokee claims for spoliation, made at differing times, reflect their loss of slaves. During the Redstick war, Margaret Vann, David Vann's mother, found herself at the mercy of raiding Creek Indians who burned her house down and stole a negro boy. Her husband was on duty with U.S. troops fighting the Creeks at the time, so she made a claim in 1836, but it is uncertain it was ever paid (Shadburn: 656, 657). In another incident, in 1829, slaves were taken to satisfy a judgement.

...A party of white men, eight in number, well armed with guns, in the dead of the night, a few days since, came into Hightower and forcibly entering a house, kidnapped three negroes, two of whom were free and made their escape into Georgia (Dec. 18, 1829 Cherokee Phoenix, page 3 col. 2.)...

As Marshall of the Cherokee Nation, Joseph M. Lynch (on behalf of William Richardson) had taken property to satisfy a judgement as was reported in the Phoenix (Oct 8, 1830 3/5). Agent Hugh Montgomery was quick to react, ordering the slaves to be returned to the owner, John Harnage, immediately.

Cherokee Agency 5 March 1833
Mr John Miller
Sir

I understand that Mrs Joseph Lynch and James Foreman have Taken away from ther camp four Negroes - Left in my care by John Harnage a woman and her three Children. You will please go and demand of Mrs Lynch & Foreman their said Negroes be Fourth with Dellivered to you or returned to the Camp from whince they were Taken.

H. Montgomery

N.B. If they have any process agains the negroes Endeavour to get a Certifyed Copy of it from Mr Foreman & of the Oath and which it was Issued.

H. M.

Mr. Miller} Mr Harnes informs me that Mr Foreman has Taken two more of his Negroes a boy Will & a girl Polly you will also make a formal demand of them and of a mare also which he states was Taken with the two Last negroes. Report the result.

James Foreman, Cherokee, would later be charged with murder and held at Athens Courthouse, Tennessee in 1834 (Austin deposition, 1836).

As was mentioned in an earlier chapter, slaves had been running away and hiding in Indian Territory for many years. Fort Moosa, near St. Augustine was an early settlement. Near Columbus, Ga., in 1793 was a town called **Chiaja,** made up entirely of runaways, and led by legendary black Creek leaders like **Ninnywageechee** and **Philatouche** (Wilson 1994:122). One of the great causes of strife between the Colonies and Britain and Florida after the Revolution centered on the return of runaway and stolen slaves. Southerners did not feel enough was being done by the British or the Spanish to return these slaves. As such many raids into Creek lands and Florida were made to sieze any blacks found there. After the Redstick War, General Thomas Woodward and hero of the fight against Dan McGirth, Captain William Cone went on slave catching expeditions to Florida. Woodward mentions this in his Reminiscences (1859):

I returned to Georgia, and in November Gen. Clark and some other gentlemen employed me to go to St. Augustine after some negroes that had left them. I went to Camden County, and got a Captain Wm. Cone to go with me into Florida. I failed to get the negroes, but I saw Peter McQueen and Josiah Francis for the first time I had seen them for years, for it was before the war that I had seen them last…

Some time in January, 1817, I took a trip to North Carolina. I returned to Georgia in March, and was again prevailed upon to go to Florida for runaway negroes. I got a half-breed, named Laufauka — better known to the whites as John Blount — and an old Cusseta Indian named Tobler, who spoke fine English for an Indian — we put out and reached Bowlegs' Town. Arburthnot had a store close by, and he informed me that he believed the negroes, or a part of them, were in the neighborhood, but that I would hazard too much in attempting to arrest them. I quit the place, and saw nothing more of it for over a year, at which time I helped to burn up the place (letter to J.J. Hooper, Dec. 13, 1858).

During this period of the waning years of Spanish control of Florida, weak local government allowed bands of Americans to infiltrate and steal free blacks and those belonging legally to Indians and settlers. Claims from these incursions continued until the 1860s (Williams 1949: 101). In many respects, the First and Second Seminole Wars were mainly about stealing slaves. The headquarters for this operation seemed to be in Columbus, Georgia after the first war.

It was easy enough, therefore, to credit the tale, it was only one of twenty similar cases of which I had heard. The acts of Colonel Gad Humphreys, the Indian agent—of Major Phagan, another Indian agent —of Dexter, the notorious negro-stealer—of Floyd— of Douglass—of

252

Robinson and Millburn, are all historic —all telling of outrages committed upon the suffering Seminole. A volume might be filled detailing such swindles as that of Grubbs and Ringgold. In the mutual relations between white man and red man, it requires no skilful advocate to shew on which side must lie the wrongs unrepaired and unavenged. Beyond all doubt, the Indian has ever been the victim….

One remarkable fact discloses itself in these episodes of Floridian life. It is well known that slaves thus stolen from the Indians always returned to their owners whenever they could! To secure them from finding their way back, the Dexters and Douglasses were under the necessity of taking them to some distant market, to the far 'coasts' of the Mississippi—to Natchez or New Orleans (Chambers 1858: 91).

Continuing into the 1840s, slave stealing from Columbus became a big business. One man named Douglass, who is mentioned over and over with regard to slave stealing, had his own dogs and would enter Indian Territory hunting any blacks said to belong to Creek Indians. After the Redstick War many hostile chiefs had left their slaves in Alabama and moved to Florida. Douglass and others made full time work of finding them and reselling them in New Orleans. Abolitionist Joshua Giddings recalled Douglass' slave stealing activites in his **History of the Rebellion** and his biographer, G.W. Julian (1892: 94), recalled Gidding's actions on the subject before congress:

He then read reports of the Indian agent to show that persons residing with the Seminoles, though born free, had been seized and enslaved by desperate men from Columbus, Georgia; that a number of men, headed by one Douglass, who kept a pack of bloodhounds, had invaded the Indian plantation, seized whole families of free colored persons, carried them to Georgia, and sold them as slaves. In reference to this he said, —

"Our army was put in motion to capture negroes and slaves. Our officers and soldiers became slave-catchers, companions of the most degraded class of human beings who disgrace that slave-cursed region. With the assistance of bloodhounds they tracked the flying bondman over hill and dale, through swamp and everglade, until his weary limbs could sustain him no longer. Then they seized him, and for the bounty of twenty dollars he was usually delivered over to the first white man who claimed him. Our troops became expert in this business of hunting and enslaving mankind. I doubt whether the Spanish pirates, engaged in the same employment on the African coast, are more perfect masters of their vocation. Nor was our army alone engaged in this war upon human rights. They merely followed the example of a class of land-pirates who are ever ready to rob or murder when they can do so with impunity."

In another incident, Giddings recalls the commentary of a Seminole Chief, in his **Exiles of Florida**:

Another chief named Walker, also residing on a reservation, with some slaves and Exiles, discovered that a notorious slave-catcher from Georgia, named Douglass, and some associates, were hanging around his plantation, with the apparent intention of capturing and enslaving the colored people. Warned by the outrage committed upon E-con-chattimico and his people, both Indians and negroes collected together, armed themselves, and determined to resist any violence that should be offered them.

When the piratical Georgians approached, they fired upon them. Finding the people armed and determined to resist, the man stealers retreated and disappeared. Feeling they were in danger, Walker wrote the Agent of the Seminoles, calling for protection, according to the stipulations of the treaty of Camp Moultrie. In his letter he says, "Are the free negroes (Exiles), and negroes " belonging to this town (slaves), to be stolen away publicly in" the face of law and justice—carried off and sold to fill the pockets "of those worse than land pirates? (1858:91)."

These affairs were nothing to sneeze at. Men fought and died to steal slaves from the Indians. Many times it was the stealer who was waylaid and not the slave or slave owner. In his chronicle of slave times, Fields, in **Grandpa Benjamin,** recalls some of the bloody action:

A few weeks after they arrived in Florida a posse numbering twenty white slave catchers from Georgia and Alabama came to Florida with the intention of capturing runaway slaves there and returning them to their slave masters or selling them to other slave owners. Isabella and the other runaway slaves with her resisted the slave catchers as they put up a "hellava" fight. Isabella's Indian Lover Hitchitaw overpowered one of the slave catchers, took his gun and killed him, one other slave catcher and a horse before he was killed. During that bloody confrontation four other slaves and three slave catchers were killed (2007:21, 22)...

In many cases Creek Indians friendly to the Georgians were employed in fighting the Second Seminole or Creek War. They caught many slaves as did other Militia Battalions. A letter from Gen. Thomas S. Jesup to a Capt. Searle includes a list of Indians who had captured slaves. Jesup instructs the Capt. To pay twenty dollars each for captured slaves so that the Indians will not kill them.

No	Negros Names	Age Yrs	Sex	By Whom Captured	date of Capture	at what place	Owners name	Remarks
1	George Measles	40	Male	Tustun nugga Emathl a	A Jany 20th 1837	Anuttelli ga	Jehu Measles	Taken Feby 5th 35 by Hostiles
2	Tricy	40	5 1 Fe male	Billy Hadjo	Ը "	"	"	" from Orange LakeAla

									chua Co
3	Charles	13		Male	Otulga Yohola	A "	"	Mr. De Piester	28th Decr 35 from Musquito
4	Dick	55	5 8 "		Spoak oak Hadjo	E " 10th "	Pau ah Sofe Kee	Col Humphries	
5	Jack	45	5 4 "		Johnny Chopce	" "	"	Mr. Helpenstine	" Spring 35 from
6	Katy	25	5 4	Female	Talloa Hadjo	K "	"	Col Humphries	a defect in right Eye Cousin to Murray
7	Fanny	2	"	"	"	" "	"	"	Child of Katy
8	Katy	25	5 6 "		Euehar Fixico	L "	"	"	
9	Primus			Male	Charlo Hadjo	E "	"	Mr. Rogers	former Interpreter for Genl Clinch
10	Murray			"	Spoak oak Hadjo	C 24th "	Cabbage Hammock	Col Crowell	
11	Primus	20	5 6 "		"	" "	"	Genl. Clinch	Taken in May 36 from Fort Drane
12	Jeffrey	20 10 54	5 1 " 0		Columa Hadjo	E "	"	Mr. Sanches	" from Alachua Co.
13	Margaret Wauton	5 4 3	5 4	Female	Hathlo Hadjo	B "	"	Ed Wauton	"

No.	Name	Age	Ht	Sex			Place	Owner	Remarks
14	Joe	21	5 4	Male	2d Battn	27th	Great Cypress Swamp	Maj. Woodruff	28th Decr. 35 from S. Garden
15	Guniea Tom	40	5 8	"	"	"	"	Col Reece	"
16	Tilla Reece	37	4 11	Female	"	"	"	"	wife of G. Tom
17	Ben Forrester	67	5 8	Male	"	"	"	Mr. Forrester	Taken with the above
18	Peggy"	27	5 4	Female	Assune Hadjo	K "	"	A. Forrester	Mother of Sandy
19	Sandy Forrester	1		Male	"	" "	"	"	Child of Peggy
20	Mary"	22	5 3	Female	2d Battn	"	"		Taken 28th Decr 35 from S. Garden
21	Delpha"	38	5 7	Male	"	"	"	"	"
22	Lucy Woodruff	23	5 1	Female	"	"	"	Maj Woodruff	wife of William " "
23	Wm	25	5 3	Male	"	"	"	"	Husband of Lucy
24	Silla	2	6	Female	"	"	"	"	Child of Wm & Lucy
25	Hester"	5		"	"	"	"	"	Niece to Lucy Taken 31st Decr 35 from Musquito
26	Maria"	26	5 6	"	"	"	"	Jos Woodruff	Child of Maria
27	Jane"	2	6	"	"	"	"		

256

No.	Name	Age		Sex	Band		Captor	Owner
28	Hercules De Piester	26	5	Male	Hillabee Hadjo	F 24th "	Coopers	Wm De Piester
29	Sabina"	25	5 4	Female	"	" "	"	"
30	Wm	1	6	Male	"	" "	"	"
31	Bella"	4		Female	2d Battn	"	"	"
32	Margaret"	4		"	"	"	"	"
33	Nancy"	40	5 5	"	"	"	"	"
34	Dolly"			"	Hillis Yohola	A 9th "	Pau ah Sofe Ree	Col. Humphries
35		50	5 1 1	Male	Cow Tom	27th "	Great Cypress	"

Th. S. Jesup
Major Genl. Comd .

To prevent the Indians from Killing the Negros of Citizens in the Indian Country a reward was offered for all who should be taken alive. The owners to whom the Negros have been delivered have paid nothing but the promise to the Indians must be fulfilled. Captain Searle will pay to the Chiefs to be distributed among the Captors Twenty Dollars for each Negro on the Enclosed list for which their receipts will be taken

Th. S. Jesup Major Genl. Cmd.
Duplicate

1st Battalion 12 × 20 = $ 240`

2   23 × 20 = $ 460

*   35 × 20 = $ 700*

All of this, of course, is reminiscent of the activities of John A. Murrell. One would think stealing slaves from Indians would be easier and less likely to cause a big response from settlers or their law enforcement people. The ***Cherokee Phoenix*** never complains about John Murrell, they complain about the Pony Club. As stated before, none of Murrell's men ever appear in lists of Pony Club members or in those of the East Florida Rangers and the 3 groups of banditti appear to be totally unrelated. Though historians and others consistently mix these groups up in the records and attribute all sorts of things to them separately or even together (one cave is actually named after Guy Rivers, a known fictional character from a book) they never appear to overlap. There is one shady character mentioned in Indian claims and also with respect to Murrell and slave stealing. He is a legendary figure in Dekalb County, Georgia history.

William G. "Buck" Heard was a name feared by slaves and their owners He was also known by the Indians and is listed as having stolen things from Cherokee Charles Moore, which was witnessed by Noo Tan Hilla of Hightower, according to records of claims made to Governor Lumpkin in 1836 and 1837 (220). He also stole from both George Still and another Cherokee named Soap. He is mentioned several times in connection with John A. Murrell, but is not on his list of primary compatriots assembled by Virgil Stewart. He is not on any list of identifying members of the Pony Club.

In slave literature he is well known. In his **Slave Life in Georgia,** John Brown details his encounter with the mysterious Buck Hurd:

I do not know what made Stevens so cruel-hearted to us poor slaves. We all led a dreadful life; I did, I know; and this made me more and more anxious to get away. In this I was encouraged by one Buck Hurd, who was what is called a nigger-stealer. He belonged to a club, the head of which was a man of the name of Murrell, in Tenessee. This club was a company of "nigger and pony-stealers," and was composed of a great many persons. They had stations in various parts of the country, at convenient distances, and when a member of the club succeeded in stealing away a negro or a pony, he would pass him on as quickly as he could to the nearest stations, from which point he would be forwarded to another, and so on, till the negro or the horse was quite safely disposed of. By this system of stations they would run off a "nigger or a pony," three hundred miles sometimes, without stopping. The partners, or agents, belonging to this club, were always on the lookout for negroes and horses, and Buck Hurd used frequently to come round to our quarters of a night, and try to entice some of us away. I heard him say, more than once, that Murrell had got slaves to run from one master, and after selling them to another, would induce them to run from him, and then sell them to a third; and that he had been known to sell the same "nigger" three or four times over. One of them, whom he had so sold, he was like to get into trouble about. The masters heard about it, and Murrell became alarmed. He did not know what to do with the stolen man--though he kept him closely concealed--fearing that the various masters should claim their property, and the facts come out. So he got the poor fellow to go down to the spring, in the woods, after some water, and there shot him.

But although I heard all these things, I was so hard used, that I gave in, and consented to run off with Buck. We started one night, walking on as fast as we could, until daylight, when we took to the woods and lay down to rest. I cannot say how far we went, for I was ignorant of that part of the country. I know it was a long way, for we were out some days, walking at night, and hiding in the woods and swamps by day. At last, however, we reached the station Buck Hurd had been making for, and there we heard that Murrell had been found out and was then in the States' prison. This frightened Buck, who said I must go back. I agreed to do

258

so if he would get my master to promise not to flog me. To this he consented, and we made our way for home. On the road, however, Buck called at his own house, and took a gun and a dog, to make it appear as though he had been out nigger hunting and caught me. At any rate he told Stevens so when we got to the house, and Stevens believed him and paid him thirty dollars for catching and bringing me home.

Before he gave me up, he made me promise I would not run away any more. This I did, telling a downright lie, for I meant running off if ever I got the chance. However, I did not get flogged that time, and thought I had been very lucky. I may here state that negro stealing is quite a trade in the States, and that it is carried on to a great extent (1972: 49-51)…

John Brown

In **Bound For the North Star (2000),** Fradin recounts the same story as he chronicles the life of a slave named Fed:

…Around the age of twenty, Fed ran off with Buck Hurd, a member of Murrell's gang. They hadn't gone far when Hurd learned that Murrell had been captured and sentenced to prison (18, 19)…

He is also mentioned by the Baughman ancestors in **The Chain Rejoined** (2005) and has made his way into fiction in Chappel's **Brighten the Corner Where You Are** (1990). It is obvious this person has achieved the status of legend, his many crimes mentioned in slave lore and Indian records, but he has also been noted in many theses on the subject of slave stealing. Most notably, Wilma Dunaway, in several

of her books, describes the blackbirding scheme and the crimes of Buck Hurd:

At Lexington, Virginia, An eight year old boy "was taken from the lower end of town by kidnappers," and carried off in a row boat. In West Virginia blackbirders kidnapped slaves who had been hired out to the salt works, then sold them at Wheeling or Richmond. Promising their captives a march to freedom, Floyd County, Kentucky, "slave rustlers" stole blacks at night and "hid them in Campbell's cave." When their trail had cooled the kidnappers exported the black laborers to Clarksville, Tennessee, where they would "sell them again on Mr. Dunk

Moore's slave market." Similarly, Lewis Robards, a Lexington slave dealer, used the services of slave stealers in rural Easter Kentucky. Some blackbirders formed regional networks for their illicit traffic. In Rutherford County, North Carolina, for example, William Robbins colluded with poor whites to rustle slaves. In one instance, Robbins even convinced a free black that, by "stealing slaves" he could "make money much faster than he was doing" as a blacksmith. In Surry County, North Carolina, "a number of colored people" were "illegally held in bondage" after they were kidnapped and sold by a group of blackbirders. One company of slave and horse rustlers was made up of several men scattered through a four-county area along the Eastern Tennessee Northwest Georgia border.

They had stations at various parts of the country, at convenient distances, and when a member of the club succeeded in stealing away a negro or pony, he would pass him on as quickly as he could to the nearest station, from which point he would be forwarded to another, and so on, till the negro or horse was quite safely disposed of.

By promising them freedom, another gang was able to attract slaves to leave with them voluntarily. In North Georgia, Buck Hurd "used frequently to come around to (the) quarters of a night" to "try to entice' slaves away. The kidnapper bragged in his community that he "had got slaves to run from one master and after selling them to another, would induce them to run from him, and then sell him to a third." In that way "he had been known to sell the same (slave) three or four times over (2003: 33)."

William Cone once fought McGirth.

Gen. Thomas Woodward, from his book cover.

The blackbirding and constant theft of property from the Indians, both Creek and Cherokee, had caused great hostility among the Indians and in Columbus and along the Federal Road, warfare broke out in 1836. The hostiles made there way to Florida killing and plundering and soon the Seminoles also joined in the battle. The result for the Creeks and Seminoles was dire, as many groups captured or who surrendered, were taken to waiting boats and sent to Oklahoma by way of New Orleans. Without a treaty many were shipped off or left on their own. The Cherokee, who had signed the New Echota Treaty in 1835, were faced with removal as well, by a date stipulated to in the document. Their time in Georgia was running out and the dominance of North Georgia by the Pony Club was running out with it.

2005 Baughman, J. Ross, **The chain rejoined: or, the bonds of science and mystery amongst family, including many attempts to recover ties across the Atlantic Ocean to ancestors and cousins of Baughmans and Bachmans,** Shenandoah History Publishers: Edinburg, Va.

1972 Brown, John, **Slave Life in Georgia: A Narrative of the Life, Sufferings, and Escape of John Brown, A Fugitive Slave,** Beehive Press: Bronx, N.Y.

1990 Chappell, Fred, **Brighten the Corner Where You Are**, St. Martin's Griffin: N.Y.

1858 Chambers, William and Robert Chambers, *Chambers's Journal of Popular Literature, Science and Arts,* W. & R. Chambers: London.

Dec. 18, 1829 **Savage Hostilities, *Cherokee Phoenix*, page 3 col. 2.**

Oct 8, 1830 **George, *Cherokee Phoenix*, page 3 col. 5.**

1837 **CIM007** Letter From Gen. Jesup to ?, Creek Indian Manuscripts, Hargrett Rare Book and Manuscript Library, The University of Georgia Libraries: Athens.

Winter 2002 Davis, Jr., Robert S., **Some Cherokee Indian Spoliations 1836-1837**, *Georgia Geneoligical Society Quarterly*, Vol. 38 no.4.

2003 Dunaway, Wilma A. **The African-American Family in Slavery and Emancipation,** Cambridge Univ Press: Cambridge, U.K.

2007 Fields, Uriah J., **Grandpa Benjamin**, Publish America: Frederick, Maryland.

2000 Fradin, Dennis B. **Bound for the North Star: True Stories of Fugitive Slaves,** Clarion books: NY

1858 Giddings, Joshua Reed, **The Exiles of Florida, Or, The Crimes Committed by Our Government,** Follet Foster and Co.: Columbus, Ohio.

1864 Giddings, Joshua Reed, **History of the Rebellion: Its Authors and Causes**, Follet Foster and Co.:N.Y.

March 5, 1833 **Hugh Montgomery** to Agent John Miller, **http://idserver.utk.edu/?id=200800000003056**.

Dec. 16, 1836 **John Austin** Deposition to John Camp, Justice of the Peace, McMinn County, Tenn., **http://idserver.utk.edu/?id=200800000003104**.

1892 Julian, George Washington, **The Life of Joshua R. Gidding**, AC McClurg and Co: Chicago.

Oct. 8, 1835 **Murder, *Georgia Telegraph***, page 2 col. 2.

1993 Shadburn, Don L., **Unhallowed Intrusion: A History of Cherokee Families in Forsythe County, Georgia**, W.H. Wolfe associates: Alpharetta.

1848 Sprague, John Titcomb, **The Origin, Progress, and Conclusions of the Florida War:** D.Appleton and Co.: N.Y.

October, 1949 Williams, Jr., Edwin L., **Negro Slavery in Florida, *The Florida Historical Quarterly*** volume 28 issue 2, Florida Historical Society: St. Augustine.

1994 Wilson, Carol, Freedom at Risk: **The Kidnapping of Free Blacks in America, 1780-1865**, Univ. Press of Ky.: Lexington.

1859 Woodward, Thomas S., **Woodward's Reminiscenses of the Creek, or Muscogee Indians, Contained in Letters to Friends in Georgia and Alabama,** Barrett & Wimbish, Book and General Job Printers: Montgomery, Ala.

Removal

In 1802, when all the controversy over the Yazoo Land Fraud was in the air, Thomas Jefferson convinced Georgians to sell all their western lands to the federal government. This included the future states of Alabama and Mississippi. As part of the compensation, Jefferson promised to remove all the Indians from the state as soon as possible. Then it became a political issue in the Northeastern States. Several presidents later, Georgia was screaming about federal betrayal. From this perspective one might say the problem of Indians and the removal atrocities were the fault of the Federal Government and they would be partly right. The state had done nothing to impede removal, had fought for it in Washington D.C.; had weathered the slings and arrows of Northern animosity on the subject and, with Andrew Jackson in charge, had finally won: the president would have the Cherokee removed no matter what the Supreme Court said. In 1832, Creeks had agreed to move west and in 1835 the Treaty or Ridge Party of the Cherokee had signed a treaty for removal by 1838.

Since the early 1830s some Indians had opted for removal and signed up to go west, being appraised and their property paid for by funds earmarked by the Federal Government for such purposes. These abandoned properties were claimed by intruders until the state government began renting them to whites from neighboring counties. The Land Lottery of 1832 was then employed to assign abandoned property to settlers en masse. For 6 years whites and Indians lived side by side in the Cherokee lands, not without friction and not without wholesale theft of Indian property. Finally the time arrived for the Cherokee to leave.

To prepare for removal the Federal Government built a series of forts in Georgia, Alabama, Tennessee and North Carolina, not for the purpose of incarcerating Indians but to warehouse supplies and soldiers given the task of enforcing the removal. Many "forts" were merely encampments and had no walls or buildings associated. Sarah Hill, in her treatise on the removal (2005), listed the following forts in Georgia:

Fort Wool
Fort Buffington (Canton, Cherokee County)
Sixes (Cherokee County)
Fort Floyd (Dahlonega, Lumpkin County)
Fort Hetzel (Ellijay, Gilmer County)
Fort Gilmer (Rock Springs, Murray County)
Fort Newnan (Blaine, Pickens County)
Encampment at Chastain's (Blue Ridge, Union County)
Fort Hoskins (Springplace, Murray County)
Fort Campbell (Blaine, Forsythe County)
Fort Cumming (Lafayette, Walker County)
Fort Means (Kingston, Floyd County)
Cedar Town (Polk County)
Camp Scott (Rome, Floyd County)
Perkins, Dade County

Artist's rendering of Fort Wool.

Fort Wool was named after Gen. John E. Wool, A New York soldier who was a hero of the War of 1812. Wool had been picked to lead the removal efforts of the U.S. Army, but was soon replaced by Gen. Winfield Scott. Wool had second thoughts about the justice in removing the Cherokee and was sympathetic to their plight in Georgia.

If I could I would remove every Indian tomorrow, beyond the reach of the white men who, like vultures, are watching, ready to pounce on their prey and strip them of everything they had (Eisenhower 1999: 189).

264

Gen. Scott was also busy with the Creek or Second Seminole War, an action designed to remove all the Creeks and Seminoles from Alabama and Florida. In many cases captured Seminoles or Creeks were summarily marched onto boats and sent packing to New Orleans for shipment to Oklahoma. The Cherokee were next.

An 1835 census of Georgia recorded 8,936 Cherokees — plus 776 Cherokee-owned black slaves and 68 intermarried whites — living in North Georgia, most of them in small towns and log-house farmsteads. Their property included 6,000 dwellings and outbuildings, 80,000 head of livestock, and 63,000 peach trees (Hill 2006).

By the summer of 1838 no Cherokees were left in Georgia, Alabama or Tennessee. It had taken only 20 days to remove them in what can only be described as a mass round up. Contrary to popular belief all the Cherokee were not involved in the trail of tears. In fact many Cherokees had gone West in 1817, creating what was called the Western Band of Cherokees. Between then and March, 1838, many others had gone to Oklahoma. In fact those on the *trail of Tears* were the holdouts from the Ross party, the Ridge Party having already removed to Oklahoma Indian Territory. By fighting removal to the last minute, that remaining group subjected themselves to the massive roundup, incarceration and removal, sometimes on foot, down the *trail of tears* in the midst of a cruel winter.

Late removal parties:
Here are some parties leaving under their own supervision, the difference in numbers also reflects desertions and births.

DETACHMENT	DEPARTED	ARRIVED	DEPART	ARRIVE	DEATHS
Hair Conrad	Aug 23, 1838	Jan 17, 1839	729	654	57
Elijah Hicks	Sep 1, 1838	Jan 4, 1839	858	744	54
Jesse Bushyhead	Sep 3, 1838	Feb 27, 1839	950	898	38
John Benge	Sep 28, 1838	Jan 17, 1839	1200	1132	33
Situwakee	Sep 7, 1838	Feb 2, 1839	1250	1033	71
Old Field	Sep 24, 1838	Feb 23, 1839	983	921	57
Moses Daniel	Sep 30, 1838	Mar 2, 1839	1035	924	48
Choowalooka	Sep 14, 1838	Mar , 1839	1150	970	NA
James Brown	Sep 10, 1838	Mar 5, 1839	850	717	34
George Hicks	Sep 7, 1838	Mar 14, 1839	1118	1039	NA
Richard Taylor	Sep 20, 1838	Mar 24, 1839	1029	942	55
Peter Hildebrand	Oct 23, 1838	Mar 24, 1839	1766	1311	NA
John Drew	Dec 5, 1838	Mar 18, 1839	231	219	NA

Source: New American State Papers, Vol. 2 pages 58, 59.

Oloocha, the Widow of Sweetwater, for whom Sweet Water Creek in Douglas County, Georgia is named, described her round up from the Etowah District near Carroll County, Georgia, in her 1842 claim:

The soldiers came and took us from home, they first surrounded our house and they took the mare while we were at work in the fields and they drove us out of doors and did not permit us to take anything with us not even a second change of clothes, only the clothes we had on, and they shut the doors after they turned us out. They would not permit any of us to enter the house to get any clothing but drove us off to a fort that was built at New Echota. They kept us in the fort about three days and then marched us to Ross's Landing. And still on foot, even our little children, and they kept us about three days at Ross's Landing and sent us off on a boat to this country (Skin Bayou Claim 258).

The descriptions of what happened to most of those rounded up are appalling. Though Gen. Scott ordered humane treatment and the officious round up of Indian property, reports of beatings and looting prevail to this day. In one set of accounts, by Anthropologist James Mooney, who lived with the Cherokee, soldiers removed Indians at bayonet point, accompanied by beatings and houses burning in the background:

…Under the orders of Gen. Winfield Scott, troops were stationed at various points throughout the Cherokee country, where stockade forts were erected for the purpose of coralling the Indians preparatory to removal. From these forts large squads of troops were sent out to search with rifle and bayonet every small cabin hidden away in the coves of the mountains and to make prisoners of all the occupants, however and wherever they might be found. Families at dinner were startled by the sudden gleam of bayonets in the doorway and rose up to be driven with blows and oaths along the weary miles of travel leading to the stockades. Men were seized in the fields all along the roads. Women were taken from their wheels, and children from their play. In many cases, as they turned for one last look as they crossed the ridge, they saw their homes in flames, fired by the lawless rabble that followed on the heels of the soldiers to loot and to pillage. So keen were these outlaws on the scent that in some instances they were driving off the cattle and other stock of the Indians almost before the soldiers had started their owners in the other direction. Systematic hunts were made by the same men for Indian graves to rob them of the silver pendants and other valuables deposited with the dead. One of the Georgia volunteers, afterwards a colonel in the Confederate service, said: 'I fought through the Civil War. It has been my experience to see men shot to pieces and slaughtered by thousands. But the Cherokees' removal was the cruelest work I ever saw.'(Mooney 1975: 124)…

The Reverend William J. Cotter took issue with Mooney and others, reminiscing when he was a 14 year old boy; his father working to supply one of the removal forts:

Gen. John E. Wool

Gen. Winfield Scott

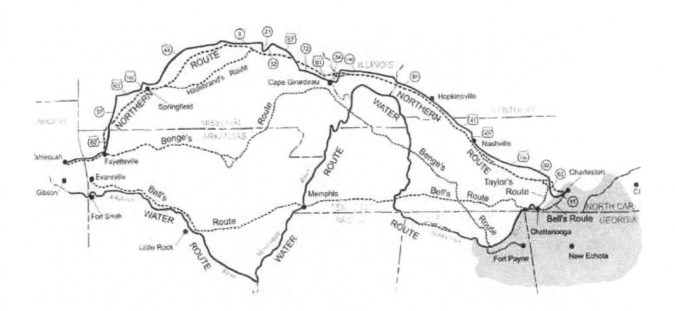

Routes of the Trail of Tears (Hill 2006).

I feel justified in saying that there were neither blows nor oaths on the way to the fort. Men were not seized anywhere, nor were their houses in flames. Not one hoof of cattle was driven away, not one Indian grave disturbed, and there was no lawless rabble. I have never seen on any page of history such a malignant, unmitigated, slanderous absurdity. On reading it my blood boiled. This is a slander upon General Scott and every man in that command, and now it reaches to the second and third generations of those noble men. (1917: 47, 48)…

267

Not only did Cotter and his father supply the troops and Indians with supplies, but they were detailed to pick up the belongings of the Indians who had been rounded up:

In hauling the stuff from the cabins a file of six or more men went with me as a guard. They forced open the doors and put the poor, meager household effects into the wagons, sometimes the stuff of two or three families at one load. After following me a mile or two the guards galloped away, leaving me in worse danger than any one else; for if there had been an Indian hiding out, I would have been the one to suffer.

But few of the Indians ever went back to their homes. We turned the cows and calves together, as they had been apart a day or two. Chickens, cats, and dogs all ran away when they saw us. Ponies under the shade trees fighting the flies with the noise of their bells; the cows and calves lowing to each other; the poor dogs howling for their owners; the open doors of the cabins as we left them — to have seen it all would have melted to tenderness a heart of stone. And in contrast there was a beautiful growing crop of corn and beans (1917: 39).

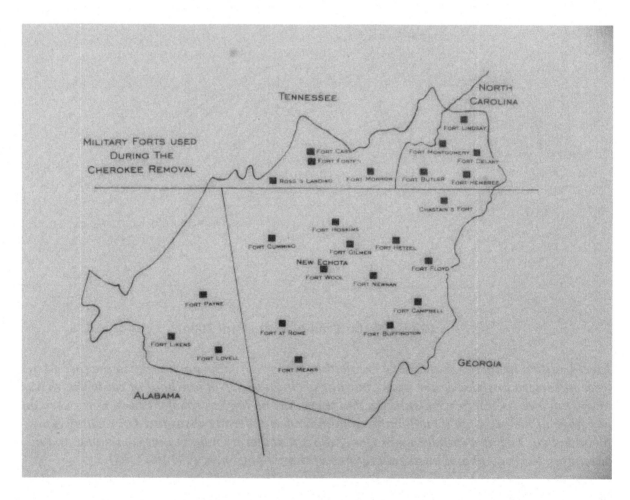

Cherokee removal forts in the South.

But Cotter was only in one location, serving one fort out of many. In other locations things were not going as well. As would be expected, Gen. Scott called on the Georgia Militia to help not only with the Creek War, but the removal as well. Many served in both endeavors and some until 1842 when the War was ended. Most militia units merely did their job and then went home, but some left their mark on the whole affair. The activity of the Paulding County Militia was a black mark on the entire operation.

John Witcher of Paulding County was also a justice of the Inferior Court of Cherokee County by the election of 1832. He had served in both the War of 1812, commanding troops and the 1835 Creek War, commanding local militia. With the looming removal, Witcher sought to become involved from his former home of Paulding County. He was aided in this by W.H. Adair, who wrote Governor Gilmer asking for armed men at Cedartown.

Milledgeville Dec. 15th 1837

To His Excellency George R. Gilmore

Sir in answer to your letter under date of the 22nd ult. I take this oppertunity of saying in relation to the Indians in Paulding County that there are any Considerable settlement of Indians. This Town is the nearest Cherokee vilage to the Creek country and besides have intermarried with the Creek Indians and consequently have many of the renegade Creek Indians lurking about this Town. In addition to this the whole of the Cedar Town Indians belong to the Ross party and oppose emmigration. From this state of things my belief is that a small force should be stationed at Cedar Town as a rallying point say 25 or 30 men. What makes this more important is, that the distance from Cedar Town to New Echota where the principle force is stationed is considerable and in case of any difficulty the necessary assistance would be too distant. If a few of the regular troops were stationed in Cedar Town they would answer every purpose.

With Sentements of esteem your Excellency obt. servt.

W. H. Adair

Hill (2006) picks up the story:

…Soon after, Witcher urged the governor to call into service his mounted company of 43 men, and by April 1838, he had received his munitions from Capt. Buffington in Canton.

Although the federal command under Maj. Payne was assigning troops to specific locations, Witcher apparently enjoyed the support of some local citizenry. In mid-May, Gen. Scott declined a request from a group of prominent white Cedar Town residents to muster in Witcher's company. Nonetheless, Witcher continued to act as leader of the Cedar Town militia. Agent Lacy Witcher (relationship unknown) complained to the governor that John Witcher and his company were often intoxicated, unfit for service, and antagonistic toward the Indians, who had remained friendly and peaceful. After John Witcher's company camped near Cedar Town and shot at passing Indians, many had moved away. Gilmer acknowledged that Witcher was serving in defiance of the state, but took no immediate action.

When Floyd learned of the Cedar Town controversy, he promptly dispatched a staff officer to investigate and arrest Witcher if necessary. On June 18, Floyd accepted Witcher's "explanation," which has not been located, and Gilmer cautioned against punishing him if the Indians had been removed "as the object of punishment will have passed." Such was the political power of the local citizens during the removal crisis.

The story of Witcher's company is instructive as an indicator of the governor's lack of control over the local militia, the local popularity of rogue groups in the removal process, and the choices Cherokees were forced to make between flight, accommodation, and resistance. Witcher's behavior as organizer of an armed and unauthorized mob beyond the reach of discipline represents the worst expression of Georgia's callous behavior regarding the removal of Indians (Hill 2006).

Captain John Witcher's Company Mounted Volunteers, Paulding County:

Officers:

John Witcher	Capt.	John Stocks	3rd Sgt.
John Ledbetter	1st Lt.	**Castello Wright**	4th Sgt
Joel W. Butts	2nd Lt.	Thomas Stocks	1st Cpl.
John Hackney	1st Sgt.	B.W. Witcher	2cd Cpl.
R.W. Pollard	1st Sgt.	Joseph Walthal	3rd Cpl.
John W. Barton	2nd Sgt.	E.D. Chisolm	4th Cpl.

Privates:

Austin Ayers	B. Gravely
Eli Bailey	Robert Hackney
Joshua Bailey	Orren Henson
Allen Brooks	James H. Hobbs
Milborn Cambron	J. Jerdon
Thomas Carter	Jesse R. Johnson
George Cargle	William T. Jones
Milton Durough	**Joseph Looney**
James Finley	William Phillips
William Finley	**William Philpot**
Charles Fuller	William Powell
Henry Fuller	Dudley Rowell

Fletcher Sanders	B.H. Walthall
Stephen Sanders	G.H. Whatley
Richard Sappington	John Wilson
Mansel Tidwell	James Wither

Some of Witcher's men were known Pony Club members and there can be little doubt some of the many men who were said to accompanied his militia were members as well. No other militia unit in the removal raised more suspicion nor created more chain of command action than that of Witcher's unit.

Much has been written of the rabble that followed the troops in the Indian round up, burning houses and stealing everything in sight. Mooney's version is born out by some of the soldiers involved. Ed Noland's eyewitness account in Whitmire (1990) is a good example:

The people do far as my observation went are poor and lazy, dirty and slothful, particularly in Georgia. Their only aim is to dispossess the Indians of their lands. Tricks and dishonesty in all its distorted forms is resorted to effect their purpose.

The government is bound to protect these poor people, yet, alas with shame I confess it, it is aiding and abetting these vultures in human form, to draw the last drop of blood in the veins of these unfortunate people (1990: 13, 14).

Another Militia trooper, From Forsyth County, Ga., Capt. James Word wrote Lt. John McKay with certainty that Cherokee property would fall into the hands of the white rabble.

…And while upon this subject, I will inquire, what shall be done with the Indians' property? Shall it be left a prey to waiting white men who are now ready to seize all and hold it as their own? (Cashin 1994: 138). . .

Word's premonition came to pass as Indian property was seized by groups of roaming whites. As Indians awaited steamboats or wagons for the removal, days turned into weeks. To alleviate problems with supplies, some Indians were allowed to try and retrieve their property left behind;

Treaty Party members had prepared for removal and therefore saved much of their property, but those caught in the roundup often had no more than the clothes they wore when captured. In the stockades, the soldiers had built almost no shelters inside the 16-foot-high walls, and thus most Cherokees slept exposed to the elements. Also, because they had no implements with which to cook, the Cherokees often ate their daily ration of salt pork raw. Eventually, Scott ordered his officers to allow a few women outside the walls to hunt for fruit and edible plants.

271

A few men also received permission to return to their homes to retrieve property, but usually they found the abodes had been stripped bare by roving hordes of whites who followed the soldiers as they collected the Cherokees (Logan undated: 42)...

The Treaty Party and most of its followers had proceeded to Oklahoma in a timely fashion and did not have the troubles the late parties experienced. John Ridge was quick to blame the deaths during the trail of tears and the atrocities committed by Georgia's white rabble on John Ross:

But there was justice in the General's claim that a great deal of the Cherokee's trouble was their own fault for having placed too much faith in John Ross. Many of their hardships might have been avoided if they had put their affairs in order and prepared themselves for the exodus. "If Ross had told them the truth in time", John Ridge complained bitterly, "they would have sold off their furniture, their horses, their cattle, hogs, sheep and their growing corn." The soldiers had no time to let the Cherokees do what they should have done beforehand. It was for that reason that so much of their stock and personal property was lost (Wilkins 1989: 322).

The white rabble and the Pony Club would have a field day stealing from the Indians, taking horses, cows, hogs, personal effects and even whole crops ripening in the fields. The state of Georgia allowed it and the Federal Government allowed it because it was their policy to have the Indians removed at all costs. Gen. Wool was replaced for not sticking to this policy:

Wool's orders were to "apply force only if hostilities are initiated by the Cherokees," a mandate he found farcical considering the wretched state of the Indians. Although Wool staunchly believed in removal -- he warned John Ross that resisting the treaty would do the Cherokees "much evil" -- the general nonetheless sympathized with the plight of the Cherokees. He ordered his troops to protect both whites and Cherokees, allowing "no encroachments on either side" and suppressing the sale of whiskey. Wool's loose interpretation of his orders angered Jackson, who believed the acute stress of living day after day with scurrilous whites would break down the resistance to the Treaty of New Echota by John Ross and his followers (Logan: undated: 35)...

Now that there were no more Indians in Georgia, all there could celebrate the new lands created, the property taken and the victory of those who hated the Cherokee so much. History has a way of condemning those responsible for heinous acts against a weak and poorly equipped foe. In the Case of Georgia, there is the accusing finger left in indelible ink, by 4,000 claims cached in hidden places, almost unknown to most Americans. These claims, made mostly in 1842 by the Cherokee in their new homes in Oklahoma, not only are a litany of stolen property but a list of the culprits involved in thefts of all kinds.

272

1994 Cashin Ed, ed., **A Wilderness Still The Cradle of Nature: Frontier Georgia** Beehive Press: Savannah.

1917 Cotter, William Jasper, **Charles O. Jones, My Autobiography**, Publishing House Methodist Episcopal Church, South:

1999 Eisenhower, John S. D., **Agent of Destiny: the Life and Times of General Winfield Scott**, Univ. of Okla Press: Norman.

2004 Featherstonhaugh, **George W. Canoe Voyage Up the Minnay Sotor 2, Volume 2,** Minn. Historical Society Press: St. Paul.

1985 Foreman, Grant, **Indian Removal: The Emigration of the Five Civilized Tribes of Indians**. University of Oklahoma Press: Norman.

2006 Hill, Sarah, **Cherokee Removal: Forts Along the Georgia Trail of Tears,** The National Park Service/The Georgia Department of Natural Resources, Historic Preservation Division: Atlanta.

May 21, 2006 Hill Sarah H., **Sarah Hill: Historian Documents Georgia's Role in Trail of Tears,** The Atlanta Journal Constitution.

Undated Logan, Charles Russell, The **Promised Land: The Cherokees, Arkansas, and Removal, 1794-1839**, the Arkansas Historic Preservation Program: Little Rock.

1999 Marks, Paula Mitchell, **In a Barren Land: American Indian Dispossession and Survival**, Harper Collins Publishers: N.Y.

1900 Mooney, James, **Myths of the Cherokee**, *19th Annual Report of the Bureau of American Ethnology, 1897-1898, part 1*: page 3-576, GPO: Washington, D.C.

1975 Mooney, James, **Historical Sketch of the Cherokee,** Aldine: Chicago.

Undated **The New American State Papers 1789-1861: Indian Affairs VOL 11**: Gales and Seaton: Washington D.C.

2003 Rozema, Vicki, **Voices from the Trail of Tears,** John F. Blair: Winston-Salem.
273

1990 Whitmire, Mildred E., Ed., **Noland's Cherokee Diary: A U.S. Soldier's Story from Inside the Cherokee Nation**, The Reprint Co., Publishers: Spartanburg.

1989 Wilkins, Thurman, **Cherokee Tragedy: The Ridge Family and the Decimation of a People,** Univ. of Oklahoma Press: Norman.

The things lost by the Cherokee: Grist Mill owned by Cherokee George Welch appears in Bramblett's Forsyth County: History Stories (2002: 48).

Claims of Spoliation

In an 1828 Georgia law the Cherokee were stripped of their rights in their own lands. Carroll, Dekalb, Gwinnett, Hall and Habersham Counties were given jurisdiction over the Cherokee lands. Every time Indians fought back, the Pony Club and their allies would use Georgia law to defeat their efforts. Finally, after the Cherokee were removed, they got their day in court. They filed claims with the Federal Government for everything taken from them by the Pony Club and others. These were filed in the courthouses of the various districts in Oklahoma, Indian Territory in 1842. What resulted was a litany of charges against named members not only of the Pony Club, but also the **Georgia Guard**, the **Removal Militia**, various **Sheriffs** and **elected officials** in several **counties** adjoining the former Cherokee Nation and **State Government.** Most of what we know of the Pony Club and its crimes is a result of these Indian Claims.

The state of Georgia had done evaluations before; for the emigration of 1817 and in 1828 when many were forced to move because the boundary line was redrawn. As has been stated before, Indians had been receiving recompense for earlier treaties and land buys. These annuities were for previous assets, so when some were forced to move they were repaid from an evaluation made by an agent. In 1824, a letter was sent to some agents to outline what should be listed on an Indian claim:

Hartville
October 2nd, 1824

Instructions for Alexander McCoy & Nathaniel Hicks as commissioners for taking the numbers of the Cherokee families who have claimed on the United States for compensation for their improvements which they have left on the ceded lands, coming under the provisions of the Treaty of the 27th February 1819, lying in North Carolina Tennessee Georgia & Alabama, 1st upon which you are to act with care and enquire whether they had removed from the ceded lands before or after the cession was made to the United States, as some of the Cherokee families may have moved before the land was cede, who might be Impressed with a belief they were equally entitled to compensations for their Improvements, with those families who had removed Since the cession of the lands to the Government. (2cd) The best manner in which you can adopt for Collecting the numbers & names of the Heads of Each families that moved from the ceded lands, will be to go the head man who moved with them, & to notify him the objects of your visit and let as many claiments gather there as are convenient, and proceed to make enquiries of their names and the Town of vilage they belonged to, the numbers of Cabbins they had left, the number by paces of length [added: and width] of their fields, the number of fruit trees, if any on their improvements when they left and to enter Each of the above items in Separate Columns, by numerical numbers before their names, & what losses they Sustained from the Whites in their Stocks & corn & make such remarks opposite to Each

275

name as may have sustained the loss & to Enquire from others Such losses as they may represent (3) You will be particular to Enquire of Each Head of families, whether they had taken certificates of Restoration for Land, And if taken the Reason they had in leaving their reservations, as several of which were returned to me, & forwarded them to Colo. Meigs which had been taken for them by their relatives not being present themselves, & you will observe also to enter all the Heads of families who have been drove off Frog Town by the Whites but not as claiments for their Improvements, but only with the object of ascertaining the losses they may have Sustained by this removal, as the Cherokee Nation Still claims her rights to the lands on that Side of the Blue Ridge had the boundary line been run according to the meaning & Spirit of the Treaty of the 27th February 1819. (4th) You will first begin at Ellejoy Town to take the names of the Heads of families who reside perhaps above this old Town who have removed from the ceeded land, from North Carolina, from thence on by Cabbin Village to Potatoe Mine Creek and about Skeenee or Devil Town from thence to Currokee Dicks & your Services will Commence on the day you Start at Two Dollars pr [per] day and your expenses allowed and advance you fifteen Dollars for This object & should it fall Short, you will Keep an account of the Sum expended over the Allowance &c
Chas. R, Hicks

Copy of a letter of Instructions given to Messrs A. McCoy & Nathan Hicks for taking the number of the claiments for Improvements left on the ceeded lands under the provision of the Treaty of the 27th of Febry, 1819.

One would think the Cherokee would be experts on the evaluation and repayment procedure but times and circumstances change, as do procedures. The simple claims for land and improvements in 1828 and 1836 became lengthy affidavits of criminal activity by white settlers in Georgia, Alabama, Tennessee and North Carolina, perpetrated since the dawn of time, itself, with respect to the claims made from 1836-1842. Most of these 4000 claims worth about 4 million dollars were made after the Cherokee removal and before May, 1838, when it was considered over. This did not stop Indians from including losses taken as far back as the Redstick War, so that many claims were from a lifetime of hardship living near the white settlers.

The nature of claims made changed from year to year. They began after the Redstick war and included items taken by U.S. soldiers on their way to or from the War of 1812 and were of the nature of logistical things, horses, food etc. These are summarized in a letter to the Secretary of War by Return J. Meigs, Indian Agent in Tennessee:

Highwassee Garrison
5th May 1814
 Sir.I herewith transmit a statement of claims of Cherokees who respectfully ask for indemnity for losses suffered by the wanton maraudings & depredations of the Tennessee levies on their marches & countermarches through the Cherokee County in the late expeditions against the

276

Creeks: said to be all done by the left wing or division of those levies. There has been no complaint of the conduct of the right wing of the army or the 39th Infantry Commanded by Colo. Williams. In the large detailed statement now transmitted the kinds of property lost by each claimant is described opposite to his name & no. & supported by his narative as taken by a faithfull intelligent Interpretor: from the large statement I have made an abstract that the whole may be seen at one view. These depredations may at first seem incredible: but I have no dout of the justness of the statements: they are well known to thousands. I received a letter from an officer of high rank in that army in which he says, "The return of the horse through their Country has been marked by the plunder and prodigal unnecessary and wanton destruction of property: their stock of cattle & hogs have been shot and suffered to rot untouched their horses in some instances shared the same fate, their cloathing intened to defend them from the wet & cold in the present campaign has been stolen and in some instances where they remonstrated their lives have been threatened, this conduct is well calculated to dishearten & may withhold their services which would be sincerely felt by us." I have been well informed that when in some instances applications were made by the Indians to officers they received for answer that their men felt themselves unfettered by the laws & that they could not restrain them. The task of Genl. Jackson to break down the spirit of licentiousness & insubordination of such men & turn the current of barbarity against the Creeks has been done by a kind of address and unconquerable resolution united rarely to be found & the successful termination of the Creek war aught, perhaps, to spread a veil over every vice & every expense in the prosecution of such a war since it is now impossible to place the expence on the individuals who committed those excesses. Some of the Cherokees have been deprived of all their Cattle & hogs, others nearly all. The Cherokees chearfully supplied the army with Beef & pork and nearly all the corn they had. General Jackson wrote me that on his route south of the mountains with the right wing or division of the army that the Indian let him have all their corn. The Cherokee warriors have faught and bled freely and according to their numbers have lost more men than any part of the army. They know that they have rendered great services in this Creek war and have no dout their services are properly appreciated by the Government. They are a little uneasy about the intrusion on their lands but believe the intruders will be removed as soon as troops can be spared for this part of the country: for they confide in the Government they know their standing. There are people who regret that the Cherokees have taken arms in our favor they would rejoice to have some pretext to drive them off their lands.
I have the honor to be with great respect your obedient servt
General Armstrong Secretary of War.
To the Secretary of war 5th May 1814. letter on the subject of Spoliations by the Tennessee Levies in the Creek war.

Some of the claims listed here represent foraging by U.S. troops on their way to or from the Redstick War.

Te, to, nes, kee states & complains that the Tennessee Militia encamped two days in his field in November, 1815 on the Tennessee river & that they killed fourteen of his hogs, he found their skins & heads after the Militia had gone down the river.

6 Hogs large ones at 5$ each. 30.00

277

4 do [ditto] smaller...at 3$	*18.00*
4 at smaller.... at 1$..	*4.00*
	&
	$52.00
	&

Te, to, nes, kee x mark
Cherokee Agency
29 Aug. 1816

Also:

(Undated) Sir us the troops wer on the Return from the Hore Shew Battle they took a horse from me and I want you to see me paid For him and I am your friend and Brother Giledo Coo Turtle
Colo. RJ Meigs Page 2
71 Tellecockee spoliation claim 40.00

(1820) Sir the troops left one ther march from the Creek nation they killed one cow worth six dolars $6.00 and I want you to see me paid.
Colo. Meigs
72 Lillecocker's Spoliation Claim & $6.00
[added: witness] Lewis Ross

Some waited until many years to make claims for the Creek War, like Edward and Sarah Graves who claimed the loss of hogs in 1814 in a claim dated 1837:

The claim of Edward & Sarah Graves for Spoliation committed by the citizens of the United States, and which is provided to be paid under the late treaty between the United States & the Cherokees. They the said Edward & Sarah Graves allege that during the war with the Creek Indians, about the year 1824, a body of troops under the command of General White of Tennessee, encamped in the neighborhood of the House of the Pheasant , the father of said Sarah Graves, and while so encamped, killed and used twelve Head of Hogs of two years old and valued Four Dollars a head. They allege further that the claim has never been liquidated. 12 Head of Hogs estimated at $4.00 per head $48. Edward Graves During the War with the Creek Nation about the year 1813 or 1814 I lived in Wills Valley in the neighborhood of where Mr. Bell now lives. A body of troops under the command of General White on their way to the Creek Nation, encamped at the foot of the Mountain about two miles from my house. A gang of hogs belonging to my daughter, now Sarah Graves, and her Mother, raised in that neighborhood. A day or so after the troops had passed on, I went to where they had encamped, and found the heads of 12 hogs which had been killed, strewed about the camp. I knew the hogs from the mark.They were very gentle, and two years old and valued about $4 a head. Other hogs disappeared, and were probably also killed, but I did not discover any remains of them. The claim has never before been presented.Sworn to & Subscribed before me in Committee this 18th Oct.1836 John Ridge Prest Committee

P Pheasant of Wills Valley After the troops had passed, as stated by Pheasant, on their way to the Creeks Nation, my father came home and told us that a number of Hogs belonging to Pheasant's family had been Killed by the Soldiers. A number of us went to the encampment, and discovered the remains of some hogs, such as heads entrails &c scattered about. I examined the heads & I Know from the work that they belonged to Pheasants family. My father lived a neighborhood to Pheasant Sworn to & Subscribed before me in Committee this 18th day of Oct. 1836 John Ridge.
Prest.A yee. sah, dat Skee or the man who shakes off the dew
no___ 9____ Edward & Sarah Grave
Registered Book A Page 3 allowed 13 June 1837 after Examination By the Comm.

Writing in **Souls in the Treetops (2009),** Abram sums up the losses the Cherokee claimed up until 1823, listing the types of items intruders, et al., had stolen from the Indians.

An examination of losses, including early 1823, indicates that Cherokees continued to seek redress for stolen or destroyed livestock by whites with a cumulative value that approximated $35, 687. This included swine, beef cattle, oxen, mules, horses, and milk cows. Other real property included slaves, cabins, corn, guns, canoes, beaver traps, hides, deerskins, ploughs, bells, saddles and bridles, saddlebags, kettles, pewter plates, a Dutch oven, blankets, clothing, such as coats, hats, shawls, shoes and handkerchiefs, combs, spinning wheels, a loom, and cash. These valuables conservatively totaled $7,415 (2009: 178).

A number of claims were placed before the removal, but most were made and kept in the records from districts in Oklahoma, I.T., in 1842. The Federal government had set up numerous claims committees in the past and yet another was responsible for either allowing or disallowing the claims associated with removal of the Five Civilized Tribes. Something must be said about the veracity of some of these claims however. In some cases losses due to the legal process, fi fas, foreclosures, judgements and a number of sundry legal actions against Indians were claimed by some. For example, if the sheriff and the claimant serve papers on an Indian and he lost a case, whether it has merit or not, by state law he was being judged against. Now the argument can be made that the state law is the tool of oppression of the Indians and should be listed as the perpetrator of a crime. I feel it necessary to draw a line here and leave the legal aspects to some other interpretation, since I am discussing claims against known members of the Pony Club.

In many cases a perpetrator is not listed anywhere as a member of the club, but may have been and the evidence is lost. It has been difficult indeed to follow this story with so little evidence in the archives of the Southern States. Though there was considerable literature as a result of the Pony Club, there is little evidence in state libraries. The Telemon Cuyler collection, excellent as it is mentions the Pony

Club once, and they fail to recognize the phrase at the archives. There is nothing in the printed archives for state governments in Georgia, Tennessee or Alabama that mentions the Pony Club. The newspapers of the time have numerous stories in which the Pony Club is addressed defined and redefined. Descriptions of the club are mentioned all over the country in books and articles, but there is little if any data at the local or federal governmental level. Whether this implies a basic ignorance or a cover up is anyone's guess. At any rate, we proceed with the best evidence of the crimes commited by members of the Pony Club, the Claims.

Most of the claims made both before and after removal simply listed everything owned and left behind, in most cases land and improvements. The following claim by Rattling Gourd, familiar to us in the incident involving the pony Club, is a typical claim in which theft is not indicated.

The United States for Spoliation Dr [Debtor] To Ratting Gourd of Coosoowattee District since 23rd May 1838

Eighteen head of Hogs	90.00
Ten head " Do. [Ditto]	62.00
Two head of Horses 1 Black filly 1 Bay mare	100.00
One cow and calf	15.00
Two Barrows 3 year old	10.00
Nine pots from the largest sise [size] down the small	26.00
Three pair cards 1 at 2.00 & 1 at 1.50 & 1 at 1.00	4.50
One coffee pot	.50
Three small tin cups	.183/4
Five weeding hoes	2.50
One Grubing [Grubbing] Hoe	1.50
One Handsaws	2.00
One large auger	1.00
One Jack plane	2.00
One Beading plane	1.00
One Iron square	.50
1 Gimblet and 2 small augers	1.121/2
Two Feather beds one at 12. and the other at 8.	20.00
One round shave	.50
Chickens to the worth of	1.25
Fresh pork	1.00
One axe worth	2.00
One set of Knives and forks	1.00
One sett [set] of plates	1.00

Three large plates	1.00
Six Table spoons	.50
One sett of cups & saucers	1.00
One sett of Tea spoons	1.00
One pair Drawing chairs worth	2.00
One mans Saddle	5.00
A large patch of fine cabbage	
Two water pails	1.00

This applicant affirms that he was forced by the authority of the United States to abandon the above named property and that it is worth the prices annexd according to the best of his knowedge and belief affirmed to before me this 18th of Sept. 1838 Collins McDonald Agent C.C. East Ratting Gourd Tobaco plant &Cah.soo.to.tyCame before me and solemnly affirms that the above account against the United States is just and true and that he was forced to abandon sd property by the authority of the United States according to the best of their knowledge and belief affirmed to before me this 18th of Sept. 1838.
Collins McDonald Agent C.C. East
Tobaco Plant
Cah. soo lan. ty
Spoliation Ratting Gourd Coosoowattee Dist Since May 1838 Referd through Jno Ross Pr Chief to Maj Genl Scott commanding US Army for Settlement Richd Taylor pres Committee J Jones Clk protem Committee

George Still Spoliation Claim

Then there were the claims made that include the names of perpetrators of crimes of theft. Perhaps one of the most thorough is that of George Still, who lived in the vicinity of Standing Peachtree. Still testified in 1829 on the Cherokee-Creek Boundary by the 1821 treaty and in doing so submitted a biography of his life in North Georgia. George Still served as an Assistant Conductor under Moses Daniel, Conductor of Cherokee during the removal.

George Still, a half breed Cherokee, aged about sixty years, has been born and raised in the Cherokee Nation-when he was a small boy his father and mother moved and settled a short time in the Old Hightower Town, and then moved and settled in the Pumpkin Patch Village on a creek about 10 miles from the river on the south side-they lived there one year. They then went down the country and lived with the Creeks one year, and then they returned and lived one year again in the Pumpkin Patch Village, then they moved and settled on the south side of the river opposite the mouth of Oostunnahlee and had made one crop, when Genl. Andrew Pickens of South Carolina marched an army into the Cherokee Nation down the river into the forks, and crossed the Hightower just above the forks, and destroyed all the improvements of several Cherokee families who had settled there; he recrossed the river and destroyed all the villages and improvements wherever he went-this took place in the time of the Revolutionary War. Where the Pumpkin Patch Village of Cherokees was settled, there had been a settlement, a small village of Creeks, but there were all gone before he went to the country, and has never known of any other Creeks being settled in the country since, anywhere on the waters of Hightower River. He has since then lived in several different parts of the nation, until just after the close of the late Creek War, he moved and settled at the Standing Peach Tree on the east side of Chattahoochy River, and he lived there until about two years ago. All the time he lived at the Standing Peach Tree he believed he was living on Cherokee land, the Cherokees told him so-the Creeks were living at Sand town on Creek land which is about 15 miles below the Standing Peach Tree-he always understood after he went to the Chattahoochy to live, that the Cherokees owned the land to the High Shoals of Appalachy and by the Stone Mountain-he never knew of any line between the two nations west of Chattahoochy, until the line was run from Buzzard Roost to Will's Creek-he never heard of but one place called Suwannah Old Town, and but one place called Buzzard Roost. The said George Still declares the foregoing statement to be just and true to the best of his knowledge and recollection, and has hereunto subscribed his name, the date above written.

Signed GEORGE STILL.

Robt. D. Harris.

OLD RED BANK, CHEROKEE NATION.
South side Hightower,
10th Dec. 1829

The Claim

Still summarizes several years of losses and mentions those who were responsible for taking his property. Claims like this make the case for the existence and cover up of a band of thieves preying on the Indians for a very long period of time.

The United States To George Still (of Hickory Log Dist [District]) Dr [Debtor] for:

1 Bay Horse 5 year old	estamated at $100.00
1 Brown Horse 5 year old	estamated at 70.00
1 senball Horse 8 year old	estamated at 80.00
1 Black Horse 7 year old	estamated at 80.00
1 Sorrel mare 3 year old	estamated at 40.00
1 Sorrel Horse 4 year old	estamated at 40.00
1 Grey Mare 10 year old	estamated at 70.00
1 Sorrel Mare 2 year old	estamated at 75.00
1 Bay Mare & colt 5 year old	estamate at 60.00
1 Bay colt 2 year old	estamated at 25.00
1 Black mare 7 year old	estamate at 100.00
1 Grey Mare 7 years old	estamated at 80.00
4 large steers	estamated at 80.00

82 Head of Cows	estamated at	820.00
1 forged note and Interest		37.00
1 forged note and Interest		50.00
	&	
		$1807.00

Personally came before me George Still the Claimant of the Cherokee Nation East and solemly affirmed that the above is a just account of property stolen from him by white men citizens of the United States the two first discribed horses as discribed was stolen by two white men one named **Gilmer** and the other **Beaver** done both citizens of the United States done on Standing Peach tree about 13 years ago The clamant states he saw a white man named **Binion** who told him that he saw the above discribed horses in the possession of said named white man claimant says that the said Binion was well acquainted with Himself and property claimant states he then pursued the said **Gilmer & Beaver** to Jasper County in Georgia & then heard that they had sold the horses to a white man named Speers He then went to the said **Speers** house and told him that he wanted to see his horses Speers said he should see them in the morning The next morning the said Speers said that the horses was gone.

The next senball Horses as discribed was stolen by one **Taitem** a white man citizen of the United States done at standing peach tree about 12 years ago the claimant says he employed a white man named **Jones** to persue the said Taitem. Jones persued him to Abervill Dist South Carolina Jones stated when he returned that he found the Horses in the Possesion of a white man who told him that he bought the said horse from one Taitem who lived in Georgia and that he would not let claimant have the horse unles he would come and make proof to the Horse but as it was some distance from home the claimant could not comply The next Black Horse as discribed was stolen at the same time and by the same **Taitem** and was seen in the posession of the same white man at the same time that the senball horse was seen. The next sorrel horse as discribed was stolen by **Charles Harris** a white citizen of the United States done at standing peach tree about 12 years ago claimant states he saw one **Campbell** a white man who told him that he saw the said Harris have the horse in his posession Campbell was well acquainted with claimant and his property as he lived a neibor to claimant The next sorrel as discribed was stolen by one **Gilmer** a white man done at standing peach tree about 16 year ago claimant states a month after his horse was stolen that **Thos Carol** a white man told him that he saw the said horse in the posession of a white man named **Williams** in Gwinette County Georgia in the said Carrol was well acquainted with claimant and horse. The next a Grey mare as discribed was stolen by one **Philpot** a white man done on Little River about 7 years ago claimant saw one **Poriss** a white man who told him that he saw the said mare in the posession of a white man who told him he bought her from said Philpot but short before.

The next a sorrel mare as discribed was stolen by **William Heard** a white man done at Standing Peach Tree about 12 years ago claimant states he did not see the said mare in the posessions of said Heard but that he has good reasons for so believing. The next a Bay mare and colt and a bay colt 2 years old as discribed was stolen by a white man name not recollected done at Standing Peach tree about 12 years ago claimant states that his horses was taken out of the range and that

283

there was no people but whites living near him. The next a Black mare was stolen by one **Springen** a white man done at Standing Peach Tree about 13 years ago claiment states that he did not see the mare in the posession of said Springen but that he has good reason for so believing said Springen stole her. He also says that he saw one **Kice** a white man who told him he saw the mare in the posession of said Springen Kice was well acquainted with the claimant and knew the mare.The next discribed a Grey Mare was stolen by one **Welck** a white man done at Talapoosee about 10 years ago claimant states he did not see the mare in the possession of said Welck but has good reasons for so beliefing. The 2 Head of steers as discribed was stolen by one **Brown** a white man also the 82 Head of cows was stolen by the same Brown a white man done at Standing Peach tree about 13 years ago claimant says that the said Brown took the steers & cow out of the range The next was a note forged for $27 dollars made payable to **James Barker** or Bearer dated 14th day of April 1830 claimant states that he never knew any such man as Barker nor never knew gave any such note to any person He also say that he was sued on said note and had it to pay with interest and cost amounting to $37 dollars.

The next was a note forged by a white man for $10 dollars made payable to **Ezekiel Ralston** a white man dated the 3rd day of May 1810 claimant states that he never knew any such man as the said Ralston nor never gave any such note to any person He further says that a white man named **Bogan** who had this note in his posession sued him and attached his property and caused him to pay the sum of $50 dollars for the principal interest and cost He further affirms that all the above prices for the above mentioned property are reasonable and that he has had no pay for the same affirmed to before me this day of Sept 1838 Moss Daniel Agent for collecting claims George Still.

Personally came before me Jack Still of the Cherokee Nation East and solemly affirmed that he saw the two first discribed Bay & Brown Horse in the posession of a white man who told him that he bought said Horses from said **Gilmer** and **Beaver** both white men and that they lived in Georgia He knew the horses to be the same alluded to above He further affirms that the prices are reasonable and that the claimant has had no pay for the same to the best of his knowledge & belief affirmed to before me this day of Sept 1838
Moss Daniel agent for collections & claims
Jack Still

Personally came before me Tunday of the Cherokee Nation East and solomly affirmed that he saw a white man who told him that he saw the said **Taitem** have the two horses as described a senball & a black horse in his posession and the white man said that he knew them to be the claimants horses He further says that the prices are reasonable and that the claimant has had no pay for the same to the best of his knowledge and belief.
Affirmed to before me this day of Sept 1838
Moss Daniel agent for collecting claims

Tunday Personally came before Tie,can, es, kee and Jack Still of the Cherokee Nation East and solemly affirmed that they was well acquainted with the claimant and knew his property and also knew that he had all the above discribed horse and cows stolen from him and they believe it to be done by white men citizens of the United States They further say that the prices are reasonable and that the claimant has had no pay for the same to the best of their knowledge and belief.

Affirmed to before me this day of Sept 1838
Moss Daniel Agent for collecting claims

Tie, can, es, kee Personally came before me Tally Tie, can, es, kee a white woman and solemly affirmed that she saw said sorrel mare in the posession of said **Williams** a white man and knew it to be the same alluded to above She further says that the price is reasonable and that the claimant has had no pay for the same to the best of her knowledge and belief.
Affirmed to before me this day of Sept 1838 Moss Daniel Agent for collecting claims
Tally Tie, can, es, kee
Personally came before me Thomas Woodall a white man and solemly affirmed that he saw the above mentioned steers and cows in the possession of said **Brown** a white man in a short time after they was taken and knew them to be the same alluded to above He also says that the prices are reasonable and that the claimant has had no pay for the same to the best of his knowledge and belief.
Affirmed to before me this day of Sept 1838
Moss Daniel Agent for collecting claims.

Thos Woodall Personally came before me Tie, can,es, kee and Edward Still of the Cherokee Nation East and solemly affirmed that the claimant paid the said forged notes to the said named white men and that they do not believe that claimant ever gave any such notes they further affirm that the amounts are correct and that the claimant has had no pay for the same to the best of their knowledge and belief. Affirmed to before me this day of Sept 1838
Moss Daniel Agent for collecting claims
Tie, can, es, kee
Edward Still.

Still is very thorough in his claim about dates and places and also the perpetrators of theft involved. They are names heard over and over again with respect to the Pony Club. It is difficult to trace those mentioned only by last name, unless the name is unusual enough that there is only one known person in the record. An example of this is the culprit Bogan, he is, no doubt, Shadrack Bogan, a mill owner in Gwinnett County most famous for cheating on the 1832 Land Lottery draw, where he was employed by the state to pick winners. Seems Bogan cheated by giving friends and family choice lots, and was fired for those efforts.

Of those last names mentioned, Philpot, Taitem (Tatum) and Welck (Welch) are familiar as members of the Pony Club of Carroll County. Equally familiar is William Heard, who is also mentioned in several other Indian claims, including that of Quaity Sopes, who lived on Sopes Creek near the Chattahoochee River. Listed as claim 819 in Volume C of the claims books, Heard is mentioned by name:

In a claim recorded in Vol. C #819, in the fall of 1838, Soap and an Indian named Crow of Hickory Log District told Moses Daniel, U.S. agent for collecting claims, that "a white man named William Heard" stole the following from Soap:

1 Bay Mare 5 years old 100.00
1 Chesnut Sorrel horse 7 years old 70.00
1 Gray mare 10 " old" 80.00
_____250.00

The horses were "stolen by a white man named William Heard down on Soap Creek near Chattahoochee River about 15 years ago," Soap claimed. Although he did not personally see the horses in Heard's possession, a Cherokee named Yellow Paw testified that he had been an eyewitness.

Soap testified that he "has good reasons for believing Said Herd stole Said horse."

Heard in fact returned a "Saddle & bridle and gave them to the claimant, but told him he should not have the horses untill the next day," Soap testified. "The next day (Soap) could not find the white man. He further said he has had no pay for the said horses as described above (Bishop 2009)."

Buck Hurd is also listed as Buck Heard, in a claim by Cherokee Charles Moore, which was witnessed by Noo Tan Hilla of Hightower. This is an indication Buck Hurd did operate in North Georgia at a time when the Pony Club was forming in Dekalb County. He appears mainly in Superior Court records for the early years of the county. Several times William Heard is listed on the docket for assault, riot and perjury, as is his relative Helsmen Heard.

March 1836	State	Mr. Heards and Michael Leusse	burglary
September 1838	State	Helsman Heard	Charge not recorded
September 1838	State	Helsman Heard	assault and battery
September 1838	State	William Heard	riot
March 1839	State	William Heard	riot
March 1839	State	William Heard	perjury

William Heard actually predates the arrival of the Philpots in Dekalb County, and his alias, Buck Hurd is mentioned in regard to the John Murrell shenanigans, which gives rise to more speculation about the relationship between the two gangs, the collapsing or telescoping of time and events in the 1830s and the fantastic stories attached to both.

Another Dekalb County resident Charles Harris, is mentioned in the claim. Or is this just the nearest "Charles Harris" to Standing Peachtree? Likewise there is a

Kicy in the 1820 Habersham County Census records. Who these people were, who stole so cavalierly from the Indians, is always going to be questioned because so few records state with clarity the full names and counties they lived in.

Gilmer, Beavers, Binion, Speers, Jones, Campbell, Porris and Brown—what are the chances of ever discovering who these parties are? Was there ever a man named **James Barker,** who was reported to have signed notes; was this an alias or a bogus name? These are the kinds of questions which may never be answered because of lost information. We rely solely on tips given in other accounts and claims to draw any conclusions on the matter.

The horses were the prime target of the Pony Club. They represented quick assets that could be sold in far away counties or states and the Cherokee could not testify against those stealing them (Remington 1891).

2009 Abram, Susan Marie, **Souls in the Treetops: Cherokee War, Masculinity, and Community, 1760-1820.**
@http://etd.auburn.edu/etd/bitstream/handle/10415/1828/SusanAbramDissertation Final.pdf?sequence=1Cherokee claims

November 24, 2009 Bishop, W. Jeff, **Chief Soap: Fact Vs. Fiction**, Georgia Trail of of Tears Association, @http://trailofthetrail.blogspot.com/2009/11/chief-soap-fact-vs-fictionhtml.

1837 Graves, Edward, Sarah Graves, **1837 Jan. 13, Spoliation Claim**, University of Tennessee Libraries (Knoxville, Tennessee). @http://digilab.lib.utk.edu/cgi/t/text/yext-idx?c=vvt;rgn=main;view=text;idno=0012 000570 000281 0000&q1=1814&op2=&q2=&op3=&q3=&rgn=main.

1820, Meigs, Return Jonathan, **1820 United States to Lillecocker,** @htp://idserver.utk.edu/?id=200800000003120.

Undated Meigs, Return Jonathan, Giledo Coo Turtle, **Cherokee Claim Letter to Return J. Meigs. @http://idserver.utk.edu/?if=200800000003101.**

10-2-1824 McCoy, Alexander , **1824 Oct. 2, [to] Alexander McCoy and Nathaniel Hicks**, @ http://ideserver.utk.edu/?id=200800000003094.

1993 McLoughlin, William Gerald, **After the Trail of Tears: the Cherokee's Struggle for Sovereignty, 1839-1880,** Univ. of N. Carolina Press: Chapel Hill.

1816 Ross, John, **PA0220** 1816 Aug. 29, Cherokee Agency Tetoneskee, Univ.of Tennessee Libraries (Knoxville, Tennessee). @ http://digilab.lib.utk.edu/cgi/t/text/text-idx?c=vvt;cc=vvt;rgn=main;view=text;idno=0012 000570 000273 0000&q1=spoliation&op2=&q2=&op3=&rgn=main.

Claims and Perpetrators

Based on Newspaper articles, county histories in both Georgia and Alabama and a sample of Indian claims (Clark, 2004, Johnson, 2007, Sanfilippo, 2009).
I have come up with the following list of Pony Club members; where they originate from and where they go after the club is dissolved.

The small sample of the 4,000 or so claims of the Cherokee that I read indicates that the Pony Club was extremely large, some estimating hundreds of people involved and that perpetrators were chased into neighboring states like South Carolina, Alabama and Tennessee. Many of its members are mentioned in these claims, not just the leaders, like the Leathers, Philpots and Yorks, but some of the relatives and known members from the different lists we have. The diverse origins of this crime clan are noteworthy and beg the question: did other clubs exist at this time in other counties?

Pony Club Member	1820	1830	1840	
Richard Blackstock	Jack	Hall	Lump	
Thomas Blake	Tenn	Carr	Alabama	
Calloway Burke	S. Car	Carr	**Killed 1832**	
James Cannon	Hall	Hall	**Penitentiary**	
James Cartwright	Tenn	"	Carr	
Wilson Cartwright	"	"	"	
John Craddock	S.Car	"	-	
Henry Curtis	Gwin	"	-	
Jonas Dawson	Rich	"	**Texas**	
Allen Fambrough	Monr	"	Monr	
Joshua Gay	Gwin	"	**Alabama**	
John Gilley	Habr	"	Pldg 40	
Willis Gilley	Habr	"	"	Pldg 50
John Goodwin	Gwin	Dekb	Dekb	
William Hitson	-	permit	**Alabama**	
Thomas Hogan	Tenn	"	Pldg 37	
Jesse Humphreys	Jack	-	Chrk 40	
James Johnson	Tenn	"	Pldg 37	
John A. Jones	Bald	Carr	"	
John Killian	Gwin	"	**Penitentiary for murder**	
Garret Langford	Tenn	"	**Texas**	
Abram Leathers	Hall	"	-	
Joel Leathers	Hall	"	Chrk 34	
John Leathers	Hall	"	"	
Samuel Leathers	Hall	"	Pldg	
Looney	Tenn	Tenn	Tenn	
Hiram Mahaffey	"	Carr	**Alabama**	

289

Name				
James Mahaffey	"	"	"	
Wright Majors	"	"	**died 1830**	
Thomas Medaris	N.Car	"	Carr	
James Philpot	Tenn	"	Pldg 37	Ark
Jesse Philpot	"	"	"	"
Martin Philpot	"	"	"	Ala/Miss
Reuben Philpot	"	"	Pldg 37	Tenn
Richard Philpot	"	"	"	Ark
William Philpot	"	"	Pldg 40	**Killed 1844**
Alexander R. Ramsey	S.Car	"	Ala/Miss	
Henry Reatherford	Gwin	Gwin	Lump	
William Reatherford	"	"	"	
Roberts	Hall	Hall	Hall	
John Sappington	Wilk	Wilk	Wilk	
William Shipley	Habr	"	Pldg 37	
Joshua Smith	Hall	Hall	Hall	
Edward Tatum	Elbt	Carr	Lump 34	
John Tatum	"	"	"	
Hugh Tatum	"	"	"	
Thomas Tatum	"	"	"	
Thurmond	-	-	**Killed 1835**	
Asa Upton	Tenn	"	?	
Nathan Upton	"	"	Carr	
Edward Watts	-	Dekb	Dekb	
John Watts	-	Carr	**Killed in Ala 1832**	
John Welch	Gwin	"	-	
Pinkney Welch	"	"	-	
Thomas Welch	"	Carr	-	
Jack West	-		**Charged with Murder**	
Jim West	-	"	"	
Crawford Wright	Gwin	"	Pldg 40	
James Wright	"	"	Pldg 40	**Died mysteriously**
John Wright	"	"	Pldg 37	"
William Wright	"	"	Pldg 40	"
Allen York	Tenn	"	Pldg 37	Arks
Josiah York	"	"	Pldg 40	
Thomas York	"	"	Pldg 37	Arks
William York	"	"	Cobb 34	"

Richard Blackstock is listed in Blackstock family records as one of its black sheep. He came from Jackson County Georgia and shows up in Hall County in the 1830s. He won a lot in the 1832 Lottery and from then on appears in Lumpkin and Forsyth County records. In 1834, he accompanied Pony Club leader Joel Leathers to the home of a Cherokee named Child Toter, where he and Leathers stole a horse worth $80.

While still in Tennessee, Josiah York married Sarah Blake, daughter of **Thomas Early Blake** and Elizabeth Owen Blake. Thomas Blake moved along with 50 or more members of several related families to Georgia about 1826. These families made their way to Carroll County in 1827 and represent the core of the Pony Club. Though he is not mentioned in any of the Indian claims discussed here his presence in other capacities was well known. He was listed as the object of an Alabama slick company bent on destroying the Pony Club in Carroll County. The Columbus, Ga. *Enquirer* said of this endeavor:

About the last week of April, a party from Tarapin Creek in Alabama, broke over the State line, and being joined by some of the white citizens, and a few Cherokee Indians, settlers and residents of Cherokee county, formed themselves into an association under the denomination of Regulators, proceeded to take up and whip, (without warrant), in the course of one or two days, five persons, namely, John and Edward Watts, John Sappington, John Gilly, William Wright and Thomas Blake (Aug. 4, 1832: 2/4)...

When the Pony Club was first run out of Carroll, then Paulding county, Blake and several members of the original family moved to Alabama.

John and Rachel Burke moved to Georgia from South Carolina around 1820 and by 1830 John was living in Fayette County while Rachel and the children, including **Callaway Burke,** were living in Carroll County. Callaway is mentioned in inferior court minutes of Carroll, winning a bid to move the Carroll County jail. As we saw in an earlier chapter he became involved in the Pony Club and precipitated its downfall in Carroll County. His death at the hands of John Goodwin, Hawkin Phillips, Frances Adams and Nethaniel Black, as well as other "slicks", enrolled in both Georgia and Alabama, led to the ouster of the Pony Club by William Springer and the Carroll Grand Jury.

Callaway Burke's inferior court records concerning his estate include the names of persons he had business ties to. Most are known as members of the Pony Club, and it includes some Indians: **Indian Harry, Indian Black-bird, House Boy (bugg), J. Charley** and **Choeageky.** Others mentioned in this record include the following and those in bold are known Pony Club members:

J. Baxter	Ulysses Boswell	**Wiliam Burke**
Thomas Blake	Mr. Brooks	Thomas Chandler
Ransom Boswell	**Caswell Burke**	James Collins

William H. Davis	**James Philpot**	**Alexander Ramsey**
Micaja Deason	**Jesse Philpot**	Mr. Slaggs
A. Greene	**Martin Philpot**	John Talent
John Killian	**Reuben Philpot**	**Asa Upton**
Charles Lawry	**Richard Philpot**	**James Upton**
Mr Mcbride	**William Philpot**	James Witcher
Mr. McCoogin	Larkin Powell	George Whisenhunt
Daniel McRae	**Henry Reatherford**	**Jesse Wright**
William McRae	**William Reatherford**	**Woods Wright**

Though Burke was a proven member of the club, his parents continued to live in Carroll County through the 1840 census.

James Cannon was member of the club listed by The Columbus Enquirer as living near one of Gen. Coffee's stands in the Indian Territory. The newspaper noted that the result of the Callaway Burke affair caused many members to be captured and whipped and run out of the country (this usually means the state).

…In Cherokee county, Gay, Cannon, Philpot and Roberts and another whose name is not now recollected were whipped (Col.Enq. Aug. 4, 1832)…

James Cannon later ended up in the Georgia Penintiary.

James and **Wilson Cartwright** also came to Carroll County from Tennessee though it is not clear what relationship they had with the Philpots and Yorks in Tennessee. Acting as a Justice of the Peace or in some dubious capacity, one of the Cartwrights accompanied a man named Mehaffee into Indian Territory to levy on a horse belonging to the Lee family. The *Cherokee Phoenix* noted:

…Mehaffee told Cartwright to levy on him, he did so; yet when attempting to take him away the widow Lee caught the bridle and George Lee coming to her assistance, took the horse from Cartwright, supposing him to be one of the Pony Club. Cartwright returned to Georgia and obtained two warrants, one for George and one for Johnson Lee (Jan 1, 1831: 2/4)…

One of the Cartwrights found themselves on the wrong end of the "slicks" and according to the Enquirer, received lashes:

…On the day Wright was whipped, Cartwright was whipped and on the next day Gilley was whipped (Aug. 4, 1832, 3/2, 3)…

The Cartwrights were able to overcome their relationship to the Pony Club and remained in Carroll County through 1840.

Another member of the Pony Club was **John Craddock,** who is listed as a land lot winner in the 1827 land lottery for Carroll County, while a resident of Taylor County. He appears in the 1830 Census of Carroll County and is mentioned in an incident involving the death of one William Young of Carroll County.

De Kalb County Gao. 12th November 1830

To his Exellency George R. Gilmer

Sir, I have Just learned from unquestionable authority, that on Friday morning the 5th. Inst, Just before day, **John, A. Craddock,** *his two sons and William Young, being on their return from the Cherokee Country to Carroll County, Was overtaken and fired on by Johnston Lee, and Sam Scott, and Jim Lee, When William Young fell desperately wounded, a pursuit then ensued, but no further damage done, on their return Young not being yet dead, Sam Scott, stamp'd him in the face and breast, until he Expir'd, - said Scott and Lee's being Cherokees...*

Your Excellences Obt, Servant
Jacob R. Brooks

Craddock was implicated in the theft of 6 horses from Grit, a Cherokee Indian, in the fall of 1830.

...Affiants had been out Turkey hunting about 6 miles from where the horses were stolen, and were on our way back when we met 3 white men citizens of the United States, two of them called **Craddock,** *the name of the other unknown, having Claimants horses in possession, -- riding bare backed, with pau pau bark tyed in the horses mouths in lieu of bridles, and running the horses off a pathway towards Cedar Town -- when they discovered affiants, they turned off the path through the woods & gallopped around affiants -- They had approached within a short distance of affiants before we were discovered. Affiants saw the horses distinctly & were well acquainted with them, and know them to belong to the Claimant Grits -- affiants never heard of Grits recovering any of said horses or any thing for them --.*

Sworn to and Subscribed before me 5th Sept. 1838} Jay Hicksone of the Committee
Eli Scott his X mark
Con noo ta ya his X mark

Craddock is mentioned by name in the July 30, 1831 issue of the ***Cherokee Phoenix*** in association with the known members of the Pony Club:

293

...Who has not heard of the "notorious olde Dick Philpot" and his generation; the Craddocks, Langfords, Yorks, Ramseys, Johnsons, Shipleys, Uptons and etc. (page 3, column 3)...

Craddock and his family disappear after the demise of the Pony Club. So many of them moved to Alabama, Mississippi or Arkansas, and others simply vanished.

Henry Curtis was one of the Commissioners of Carroll after the act of 1829 setting up Carrollton as seat of the new county. He served on the Board of the Carrollton Academy and was the sheriff of Carroll County during the reign of the Pony Club. A native of Gwinnet County in 1830, Curtis developed a reputation of ruthlessness against the Indians in the February, 1830 assault on four Indians resulting in the death of **Chuwoyee**. The Cherokee had cleaned out intruders from along the Alabama Road; so the sheriff and 24 others from Carroll County retaliated by going into Indian Country and arresting four of the raiding party members. One of the Indians was killed in the incident (***Cherokee Phoenix***, Feb. 10, 1830: 2/4, 5). Curtis was also involved in an incident with Thomas York and Giles Bogges which resulted in the theft of two Cherokee horses (***Cherokee Phoenix***, Feb. 12, 1831, 2/3). While Bogges was later associated with the efforts to destroy the Pony Club, Henry Curtis was not and he left Carroll County along with the rest of the Club after 1832.

Jonas Dawson is listed on the 1830 Census of Carroll and came there from Richmond County. The ***Cherokee Phoenix***, on March 24, 1832 (1/2) accused Dawson of several crimes:

An intruder, by the name of Dawson, has settled himself on the Hightower River, and forcibly, taken possession of a ferry belonging to a Cherokee. He has built houses for his accommodation and publicly vends liquor. A Post Office has been established and he has appointed himself Postmaster!

After The fall of the Pony Club, Dawson like many others, moved to Texas.

Allen G. Fambrough was a member of a well known Monroe County, Georgia family who moved to Carroll County, where he became a state representative. Fambrough was an old friend of Wilson Lumpkin and a long time supporter of Cherokee Removal. He was the person who proposed renting the property of emigrating Cherokees to Georgia Citizens. He was accused by William Springer, head of the Carroll County, with being a leader of the Pony Club "feed council" or legal arm of the criminal operation. In a rousing response, Fambrough called Springer a "flagacious liar and poltroon" (Aug. 18, 1832, page 3/6). When the dust cleared, Fambrough lost his seat and moved back to Monroe County.

Joshua Gay moved from Gwinnett County to Carroll County before the 1830 Census. He is listed in the ***Columbus Enquirer*** of August 4th, 1832 as one of four men whipped for horse theft in the aftermath of the Callaway Burke affair. He moved to Alabama after the demise of the Pony Club.

John and Willis Gilley were long time members of the Pony Club. Willis, from South Carolina was chosen by the Ga. Legislature to act as commissioner involved in the elction of early officials in Rabun County. With brother John he ended up in Habersham County in 1820 and Carroll in 1830. Willis is remembered for his riding a horse through the new Hotel in Carrollton challenging all comers to race (Carroll Free Press 1907).

John Gilley was whipped along with Philpot, Watts, Sappington, Wright and Blake according to the ***Enquirer*** (Aug. 4, 1832). Willis is mentioned in William Springer's article in the Federal Union (Aug. 3, 1832) concerning his defense council, Jones and Fambrough:

Willis Gilley, having committed many depredations, was, by some six or eight citizens, seized and SLEEKED. He admitted the justice of the whipping, but complained they had given him five lashes too many. Jack (Jones) and his colleague (Allen) Fambrough, volunteered their services to Gilley, and presented for his signature two twenty five dollar notes. On stating his inability to pay such a sum, they told him that recompense was never expected (3/4)…

John Goodwin of Dekalb County is not the John Goodin or Goodwin of Alabama who formed the slick company to deal with the Pony Club in Carroll County. This John Goodwin came from Gwinnet County, moved to Dekalb County where he remained through the 1840 census. This Goodwin appears in the record as someone who aided one of the Philpots and:

used forged accounts to seize estate ($3170), as well as horses, cattle, hogs and a Negro slave (worth $600) belonging to **Chenaquah**, *deceased (Johnson 2007, Clark, 2004).*

Goodwin is another example of a member not living in Carroll County. The lines and borders of this club are so remote in history it is almost impossible to determine whether the bevy of thieves living in counties other than Carroll are members; or do they have their own club?

William Hitson is one of those mysterious people that appears now and then but not in any census or official documents. It is apparent he had a permit to live in Cherokee Territory, presumable hired as a laborer by one of the Indians. He and the Philpots were excoriated in an article of the *Cherokee Phoenix,* dated May 7, 1831.

...Hitson has been caught in a dark, rainy night shelling corn in the crib of Mr. John Martin of Coosawaytee, and after being caught he obtained permission to stay all night. In the morning Mr. Martin, not being willing to have stolen property about his house, insisted that he should take his corn with him, which he accordingly did...

To this Elias Boudinot, editor of the *Phoenix* added:

This Hitson was a miller and came into the nation in that capacity a number of years ago. He resided in the nation under a permit, until lately, when taking advantage by the laws of Georgia he took the oath of allegiance and obtained a permit from the governor's agent to continue his residence. Thinking probably that there was no more constraints on him, and that he was now fully, to all intents and purposes, under the protection of Georgia, he commenced to steal from his former benefactors. He was, however, detected in his first attempt upon Mr. Martin, and by means of the very lenient and peculiar treatment he received, he became so ashamed of his conduct, that immediately on his return and delivering his stolen corn to his family, he left the Nation. In a few days he returned and removed his family and effects. A good way to get rid of a thief—Ed. Cher. Phox (3/3,4).

Hitson's wife and children later appear in Pike County, Alabama records though he does not.

Thomas M. Hogan (b. ca 1810 at SC - d. 08-12-1872 at Houston,TX), whose father-in-law was James Upton was one of the original Pony Club members who left Tennessee and came to Carroll County about 1826. He became involved in the criminal activities that led to later claims by the Indians. Hogan accompanied the Philpots and other club members on a horse stealing raid on Jesse Sanders and Jack Wright on Sweet Water Creek. They stole 12 horses worth some $500 and secreted them back to Carroll County. In 1831, John A. Jones recommended to then Governor Gilmer that the Hogan's residence be used as a polling place during upcoming elections. When the 1832 Carroll Grand Jury made its presentments, Thomas Hogan was sited for "...assaulting and violently beating Absolom Adams on election day in the 649th District..." and also for "...threatening to beat...Thomas Wynn and having pistols and rocks to annoy the good people of the 649th District (Bonner 1971: 34).

Like many of the club members, Hogan moved to Paulding County where he appears in the 1837 census. The club continues for a few years there, the area becoming Polk County, when it is formed from Paulding in 1851.

Jesse Humphries is a shadow of a person who infrequently appears in censuses or any other documents. He appears in the Jackson County 1820 Census then disappears until 1840 when he is listed in the Cherokee County Census. Humphries accompanied Hogan and several others on the raid on Jesse Sanders and Jack Wright on Sweet Water Creek which resulted in 12 horses being stolen.

James A. Johnson was rumored to be the son-in-law of Richard Philpot. He originated in Tennessee and moved to Georgia with the rest of this extended clan. Lawyer John A. Jones of the Pony Club feed council recommends the house of James Johnson to be a polling place for the upcoming 1832 election, in a letter to Governor Gilmer. After the fight with the slicks of Carroll County in 1832, Johnson moved to Paulding County with most of the Pony Club family, where he became a Justice of the Inferior court. In 1837 he took property from a Cherokee Indian named James Downing. This according to a claim made in Oklahoma in 1842.

An interesting story is recounted by Dr. Henderson, writing for the **Cedartown Record,** in 1875. While he didn't like to accuse or name members of the Pony Club he did let on about something that happened to James Johnson during the 1832 election in Paulding:

They had counted out a sufficient number of votes to ascertain who was elected, and a very prominent candidate of the Cleantown persuasion, for Judge of the Inferior Court was decided to be elected. He and his friends were rejoicing in a big way when suddenly all was sad -- Slicks are coming. Men commenced running, hiding, and dashing in every direction and in a short time, Captain Cunningham and Lieutenant May charged over the yard fence horseback, with sixty Alabama Slicks, and formed in line before the door of the house in which the election was held, and Captain Cunningham called aloud for this prominent Cleantown candidate to come out of his house. At this time about a hundred guns were cocked and presented. Slicks and all others were in madness. Officers were hollowing "I command the peace, don't shoot." Captain Cunningham continued calling for him to come out. Someone told him he was just elected Judge. The Captain replied that he had come over to ___ him, at the same time took a large ___ rope from his saddle, and ordered the Judge to cross his lands. The Judge drew his pistol and said the first man who laid hands on him he would shoot a ball through. The Captain followed him up, rope in hand, the Judge backing, until he got in the corner of the fence, and said if he had taken any man's property he had the money to pay for it. One of the Alabama Slicks said that was what they came for, you or your money, and further said, "when I track my cows and horse to your house, you threatened to shoot me if I didn't leave, and now, sir, nothing will satisfy me but you or the money." The matter was finally compromised, the Judge paying fifty dollars, all the money he had, and gave his note and security for the balance. At this time the most of the Cleantown gentry had left or had hid in the bushes. The Slicks retired for camping, and the crowd left, and by dark every thing was still and quiet, except a few who had been drunk and asleep. They retired to some Indian hut for quarters for the night (June 26, 1875)...

Lawyer **John A. Jones** was the head of the "feed council" of the Pony Club. He hailed form Baldwin County, where his family was well established. Like so many who ran for office in Georgia, he had to move in order to run for office in Carroll County. He is one of the club members mentioned by name in the Grand Jury presentments for 1832. Jury head William Springer was quick to point out during the presentment that John A. Jones had been named in the confession of one of the Watts boys, dying from a gun shot from Creek Indians in Alabama, as a fence for stolen property. The evidence obtained by no greater witness than Gen. Thomas S. Woodward of Alabama (Federal Union Dec. 13, 1832, 3, 4). The cornered lawyer took the opportunity to respond to charges by impugning those who rose up against him. He recalled Springers size (said to be 400 lbs) and insolvency in the past. For others he had accusations:

Again the Grand Jury has presented Edmund Holland and Joel Hicks for keeping a gambling house. The night before the presentments were read was spent by Wiliam G. Springer, foreman of the Grand Jury and Justice of the Inferior Court, in a gambling room, to which he was conducted by Giles Bogges, the owner of the house. When the Foreman went to the room the card players were considerably confused and evidenced a disposition to break up the party, but were reassured by the foreman who promised to take no notice of them. But I am forced to acknowledge that I am not Jesuit enough to say what he did with his oath to the country, unless as a disciple of Hudibrass he believes that it is he who makes the oath that brakes it not he who for convenience takes it (Federal Union Nov. 22, 1832: 3/6).

Fearing a whipping in some remote place in the dead of night, Jones went so far as to ask the Governor for Gen. Coffee's Militia to step in and charge down on his Carroll County tormentors. It was with some surprise that the Government failed to send anyone or respond in any manner and Jones must have taken this to heart and absconded back to Paulding County.

John Killian's story is memorialized in Dr. Henderson's **History of Polk County** (The Cedartown Record June 19, 1875):

A murder was committed in the valley, near the big spring, in the spring of 1833. John Killian killed a man by the name of Prior, a citizen of Carroll county, who was there hunting stolen property. Killian had been whipped by the Slicks, and two or three of his brothers in law, the Rathorfords had all been desperately whipped. The difficulty between them was in relation to them all being whipped. They were both drinking. The particulars of the evidence I don't now remember. Killian stood his trial and was sentenced to five years imprisonment in the penitentiary by his Honor, Judge Hooper, at the first court held in the new county of Paulding in the fall.

The same source indicates Killian came to Paulding County in 1832 and settled in the Euharly Valley at "Cleantown", one of several places known as a Pony Club Headquarters. Where he comes from and where he ends up after his conviction remain a complete mystery.

Garret Langford is from McMinn County, Tennessee, as was the core of the Pony Club. His exact relationship to the extended family is uncertain as he married one Martha Watts in 1829, in Carroll County, according to **Inferior Court Minutes.** The *Cherokee Phoenix* on July 30, 1831 mentions Langford by name as "one of his (Dick Philpot's) generation (3/3)".

In an article in the Dec. 13, 1832 *Federal Union*, William Springer excoriates John Jones for his support of Pony Club Member Langford:

Garret F. Langford was one Sunday , found playing chuck-luck with negroes. The overseer of the mining company who detected him, made the negroes whip him forthwith. Jack (Jones) hastened to the place , linked arm with the rascal, took him away, and commenced and continued a vexatious prosecution, without the most distant hope of pecuniary remuneration, except what could be produced by theft; for Jack Knew that Langford and the other members of the Pony Club had no other resource but stealing (3/5).

When the Pony Club was dismantled in Carroll County, Langford fled and remained in Texas.

Joel Daniel Leathers was considered a leader of the Pony Club, both in Carrol County and later when he moved his operation to Cherokee County. Personal communications indicate the whole family was involved in the club (Lewis Oct. 9, 2009). His extended family first appeared in the 1820 Hall County Census. By 1830 the family had moved to Carroll County and Joel began gold mining in Cherokee Country on the Chestatee River. Leather's Ford, a crossing there is named after him, and is the scene of some difficulties involving the Georgia Guard and intruders. In 1831, Governor Lumpkin signed a bill to allow Robert Ligon to build a bridge across the Chestatee at Leather's Ford to allow easier access to Cherokee Territory.

Tracing the family history of Joel Leathers, Jerry Clark (2004) found that his early aspirations included clearing the intruders out of Carroll County:

In 1829 Joel Leathers of Carroll County, GA wrote to Col. Hugh Montgomery, US agent to the Cherokees, that he was "frightened" of 400 families of intruders who had settled in

Carroll County (recently ceded by the Creek Indians). Leathers warned that these intruders were a lawless and unruly bunch of land grabbers.

Leathers had a place located at Leather's Ford on the Chestatee River near Dahlonega, GA where the "Gold Digger's Road" crossed the river. He had another store on Salaquoya Creek in the Cherokee Nation. The Cherokee towns of Sixes and Dahlonega were in the area where gold was discovered in 1828, resulting in America's first full-blown gold rush. This event became the main reason for Cherokee removal. According to Cherokee claims, Leather's stores frequently served as storage areas for many horses, cattle, and hogs stolen from the Indians (Clark 2004).

Joel Leather's many crimes, according to Clark and other sources include:

Joel *stole 6 hogs ($18) from* Suwucha *of Hightower.*

Joel *stole 25 hogs ($135) from* Susannah Tarapin *of Hickory Log*

Leathers *stole 2 horse, a wagon, and hogs from* Thomas McDonald *(a Cherokee).*

Joel Leathers *("a noted thief") took a horse from* Bear Meat.

Joel Leathers *stole from* Polly Vann.

Joel *lived 15 miles from* Ned Crittenden *(Cherokee), & took Ned's hogs to Carroll County.*

1829 Joel *had cattle (worth $72) belonging to* Rachel Baldridge, *Salaquoya Creek.*

1830 Joel *had hogs belonging to* Nanny, *Hightower River.*

1831 Joel *had hogs belonging to* Arnulla *and* Bill Vann *to the Sixes gold fields.*

1831 Joel *took cattle of* Nancy Baldridge *(Cher.) to Carroll County.*

1832 Joel *took cattle ($26) of* Tekancesky.

1832 Leathers, *"a captain of the noted pony club" stole the great coat (worth $20) of* George Blackwood *(Cher.) at Sixes Town.*

1834 Joel Leathers & Richard Blackstock *stole a horse ($80) from* Child Toter *of Hightower Town and in 1835 26 hogs ($78) from* Child Toter.

1834 Joel *took 2 hogs ($12) of* Sawney *of Hickory Log to Sixes.*

1834 Joel *killed 2 hogs ($36).*

There is no record of his being either whipped or taken into custody and he appears in the Houston County, Texas Census of 1840.

It is uncertain which of the **Looney** family were members of the Pony Club. What is certain is that the Yorks and Looneys were intermarried. Mary Polly York Married Moses Looney and Sally Looney married Thomas York. The Looneys lived in Tennessee and John Ross mentions one of them being involved in an assassination attempt by two men, one named Looney and one Harris.

…He said his name was Looney, that he lived in Rhea County and the state of Tennessee, about sixteen miles from the town of Washington (Cherokee Phoenix Jan. 21, 1832: 1/3-6)…

That Looney and Harris, probably Charley Harris, a suspected Pony Club member, intended to kill Ross that day is made clear by Ross' statements:

…And Looney remarked, "Harris, now I am gonna tell the whole truth about this business"…I looked around and saw Harris dismounted, at the same time heard him say, "Ross I have been for a long time wanting to kill you and I'll be damned if I don't now do it."

Having fled, Ross picked up more information about Looney the following day. He questioned the Indian with the two, who had had a fight with them after the assassination attempt.

…Looney is the brother-in-law of James Philpot, and that he had accompanied Harris from Philpot's house to the place he was stationed on the hill—that the pony on which Harris rode, belonged to Philpot. Upon Reuben Philpot representing the rifle gun for the property of Saul Rately and that it had been left in his care…

Exactly which Looney was involved in this is uncertain from the Newspaper article, but only one Looney ever appeared in Georgia records concerning the Pony Club. In 1838, **Joseph Looney** is enrolled in the Paulding Militia along with William Philpot and served under the tarnished captaincy of John Witcher. Looney appeared in this militia unit despite never having appeared in any Georgia Census before or since.

Hiram and **James Mahaffey** were well familiar with the club core before leaving Tennessee. Hiram married Martha Hogan of the Thomas **Hogan** clan, while, Elizabeth Mahaffey married Crawford **Wright** in Carroll County. Sister Nancy Wright married Isaac Mahaffey and Lucinda Wright married John Mahaffey. After the club ended the family accompanied many others who fled to nearby Fayette County, Alabama and later to Pontotoc County, Mississippi. According to family history, Alexander Hogan led the family wagon train from Mississippi to Texas.
301

One of the Mahaffeys is mentioned in the **Cherokee Phoenix** in an incident involving one of the Cartwrights and some Indians of the Lee family. Of course a horse was involved, which Cartwright and Mahaffey were attempting to "levy upon."

...Mahaffey told Cartwright to levy upon him, he did so; yet when attempting to take him away the widow Lee caught the bridle and George Lee coming to her assistance, took the horse from Cartwright, supposing him to be one of the Pony Club. Cartwright returned to Georgia and obtained two state warrants one for George and one for Johnson Lee (Jan. 1, 1831: 2/4)...

Wright Majors is another long time friend of the core members of the Pony Club. He married Susan Upton of the James Upton clan in Tennessee and moved to Carroll County with them. He was born in 1801 and died in 1830 in Carroll County, so he does not leave much of a print on history. However, his probated will lists his friends, acquaintances and those with whom he did business. Like the probate papers of Callaway Burke, it is a treasure trove of information about those intimately involved in the Pony Club. The will lists the following people involved in his estate, many of whom are Pony Club members:

James Brantly	Martin Jones	Jonathon Sanders
James Bromley	**Garret F. Lankford**	**William Shipley**
James Bryce	**John Leathers**	Neil Stone
William Bryce	**Hiram Mahaffey**	David Striplin
Callaway Burke	**James Mahaffey**	Larkin Turner
W.D. Collins	**James Majors**	**James Upton**
Jacob Cotrell	**William Majors**	Thomas Weatherby
Edward Dyer	Bunell Mathis	Solomon Wise
Nathan Gann	Daniel May	Riley W. Wilkin
Baylis Gilley	Dancil McDowel	Isaac Wood
John Gilley	Elijah McPherson	**Crawford Wright**
Jonathon Hayes	Daniel McRae	**James Wright**
Henry Headrick	James Mical	**Jesse Wright**
David Hiden	Sidney Mulwee	**John Wright**
Alexander Hogan	**Richard Philpot**	**Woods Wright**
E.P. Hogan	**William Philpot**	**William York**
William Jackson	John Robbison	John Young
Thomas Johnson	Russell	

William Majors appeared in the 1840 Paulding County Census and others end up in Mississippi and Texas.

Thomas Medaris, who came to Carroll County from North Carolina was included in the presentments of the 1832 Carroll County Grand Jury and cited for disrupting the 1832 election.

In the same presentments the grand jury indicted Thomas Medaris for keeping a drunken and disorderly company about his house, allowing "fiddling and dancing" and for making whiskey on the Sabbath and "for menacing voters" in the 682cd District (Bonner 1971: 34).

After the Pony Club left, Thomas Medaris invested in a farm near Buckeye, on the Chattahoochee. He deeded this land to his kids and moved to Campbell County where he remained.

The leaders of the Pony Club were the **Philpots,** who, according to family records, left Tennessee in a wagon train of some fifty people, possibly just ahead of local law enforcement. Reuben, Richard, William, James, Martin and Jesse Philpot were related to the Yorks by intermarriage. William Married **Elizabeth York** while James married Delilah York.

The Cherokee Phoenix mentions the Philpots almost every time the Pony Club is mentioned and anyone associated with "Dick Philpot" or "Old Man Philpot are suspected of being club members. Their crimes against the Indians are many; this list represents that put together by Jerry Clark and a combination of sources, The ***Ga. Geneology Society Quarterly***, Don Shadburn's book **Unhallowed Intrusion** and loose spoliation claims found in the Telamon Cuyler and Penelope Allen collections.

Jesse Philpot, Jim and Jack West *stole from* **Dick Scott.**.

James Philpot stole from **John Fields.**

1830 **Jim Philpot, Reubin Philpot, Asa Upton** *and other unnamed persons attacked two Cherokees (***John Ridge** *and* **John Fields***) with clubs and knives near Vann's Old Place. The Indians were searching for missing horses.*

*Feb. 1830 a gang of 30-40 intruders kidnapped four drunken Cherokees (***Daniel Mills, Rattling Goard, Chuwoyee,** *and* **The Waggon***). Chuwoyee was killed, Rattling Goard was put in the Carroll County jail, Mills escaped, and The Waggon also escaped after being stabbed in the chest with a butcher knife by "Old Man"* **Richard Philpot***. In 1842 The Waggon submitted a claim for his medical costs ($50) and pain & suffering ($5000).*

1830 the **Philpots** *stole 3 horses ($130) of* **Ailsy Ketchum** *of Vann's Valley.*

1831 **Philpot** *stole a grey mare on Little River from* **George Still.**

303

...A Grey mare as discribed was stolen by one Philpot a white man done on Little River about 7 years ago claimant saw one Poriss a white man who told him that he saw the said mare in the posession of a white man who told him he bought her from said Philpot but short before(Still claim)...

1832 Philpot's sons *killed a cow of* Ground Mole *near Major Ridge's place, and drove other cattle to Carroll County.*

1832 members of the Philpot family *took horses of* Swan *of Oothcaloga Valley*

1832 the brothers Reuben and James Philpot *took a horse ($150) of* Archy Downing *of Racoon Town. James was "a notorious rogue" belonging to "a slick company."*

1832 stolen cattle ($91) belonging to John Fields *was tracked to the* Philpot *neighborhood in Carroll County.*

1833 Philpots *of Carroll County took horses ($120) of a woman named* Larney *of Coosawattee Town.*

1835 Philpots *took cattle ($55) of a woman named* Setahna *of Etowah Town.*

1835 a Philpot *stole a horse of* William Pritchett.

1834 Kolkahlosky *of Head of Coosa lost 3 horses ($260). He was informed that they were stolen by* "the Philpots," *but the Indian did not pursue because "I was afraid of them."*

1836 Jim Philpot *took horses & cattle ($140) of* Harry Scott. *Jim was "a man of bad Character and generally believed to be a rogue."*

1837 Philpot & John Goodwin *used forged accounts to seized estate ($3170), as well as horses, cattle, hogs and a Negro slave (worth $600) belonging to* Chenaquah, *deceased.*

1837 Jim Philpot *stole horse ($100) of* Satahnee.

1837 Reubin Philpot *of Clean Town stole rifle ($25) of* Naucheah *of Pettit's Creek.*

1837 James Philpot *and his brother "Ahquahuste" [meaning "Ribbon" in Cherokee] were sons of "Old Man Philpot" and stole the household goods of* Nancy Ketcham *of Vann's Valley.*

Reuben "Phillips" [Philpot] *had possession of stolen objects belonging to* Betsy Cade *near Vann's settlement.*

Reuben Philpot *took horse & saddle ($115) of* Edegungnahe *of Running Waters, during a Cherokee ball play [i.e. lacrosse] game between Etowah Town vs Cedar Town.*

James Philpot *("a very bad character") took or killed 70 hogs ($225) of* Bear Paw *on the Tallapoosa River (taken on 3 separate occasions).*

James Philpot, Reuben Philpot, Jack and Jim West, Thomas Hogan, and Jesse Humphrey *stole 12 horses ($500) of* Jesse Sanders *and* Jack Wright *on Sweetwater Creek.*

On Aug. 12, 1831, The **Cherokee Phoenix** carried a story of the Georgia Guard and how it ignored the activities of the Pony Club. In it the Philpots were described as "bad Men":

…A short time since a detachment consisting of 28 men head by Col. Nelson made a military tour through a part of the country and passed the very doors of some of these "bad white men"; for instance several families of the Philpots about three miles south of the head of Coosa (2/1-5)…

When the Slicks defeated the Pony Club in Carroll County in 1832, Reuben went back to McMinn County Tennessee to avoid a warrant initiated by Springer's Grand Jury. The other Philpots moved to Paulding County and resumed their pillaging of the Cherokee. In 1838 many of them moved to Alabama but only for a short time.

Between then and 1845, Richard, his sons and families then moved to Calhoun county, Miss prior to 1845. They all lived in that area for the remainder of their lives except for Jesse Robert who moved to Cherry Hill (Polk County), Arksansas about 1870 or 1871. Family notes from members of Jesse Robert's family say that 39 of them left Mississippi by wagon train and crossed the Mississippi at Memphis before moving on westward to Polk County on the border of Oklahoma Territory (P.C. Lester Oct. 27, 2009).

William Philpot remained in Paulding County until 1844 when he was murdered by an acquaintance from Tennessee. According to the **Georgia Black Book** (1982)

InCarroll County on the 31st March last, William Philpot was murdered by Eli Thurman. Thurman is about 5 feet 10 or 11 inches tall, fair complexion, 21 or 22 years old, light hair, and blue eyes(April 1844) .

Family genealogist Bill Lester recalls:

… about 15 years ago a 90-something year old cousin of mine, who was a teenager when some of William Philpot's children were still living, told me that he was always told that William was "involved" with Thurmon's wife and that Thurmon bushwhacked him not far from home and that William's horse came trotting into the yard with his body draped over the saddle.

William is buried in a small cemetery on a hill overlooking the Tallapoosa River about 3-4 miles north of Buchanan (Oct. 17, 2009).

…William was 46 at the time so, if the love triangle rumor is true, he was interested in a young lady about half his age. I do know he left a widow, Elizabeth York Philpot, with eleven children to raise, one of them just three weeks old at the time of his passing (Oct. 19, 2009).

Alexander R. Ramsey was born in 1802, presumably Edgefield District, South Carolina. He appeared for the first time in the Georgia record in Carroll County living amongst the other members of the Pony Club. Ramsey appears early in the record of the Pony Club in the area of Sandtown.

1826 *Allen York, Alexander Ramsey, members of the Welch family, and Philpot clan stole cattle of* **Archy Rowe** *(Cher.) on the Tallapoosa River. The cattle were traced to Buzzard's Roost.*

After the defeat of the club in Carroll County, the Ramseys move to Fayette County Alabama, where other Ramseys live, later they moved on to Pontotoc County, Mississippi.

Henry and William Reatherford are mentioned late in the history of the Pony Club and mainly in relation to Polk County history. The Reatherfords or Rutherfords appear in the 1830 Gwinnett County Census, and they are mentioned in the History of Polk County as brothers in law of John Killian of the Gwinnet County Killians.

A murder was committed in the valley, near the big spring, in the spring of 1833. John Killian killed a man by the name of Prior, a citizen of Carroll county, who was there hunting stolen property. Killian had been whipped by the Slicks, and two or three of his brothers in law, the Rathorfords had all been desperately whipped (Cedartown Record. June 19, 1875)…

The *Columbus Enquirer* of Aug 4, 1832, identifies a man named **Roberts,** who lives in the Cherokee County near one of Gen. Coffee's stations, who was whipped along with "Gay, Cannon and Philpot." An illusive character to history, it is uncertain who this is, tho the paper identifies him as:

…Roberts was several years doorkeeper or messenger to the House of Representatives and one year a member from Hall County (page 3 col. 3)…

John Sappington was the son of Caleb Sappington of Wilkes County, who was intimately associated with the Georgia Guard, the State funded agency sent to protect the Cherokee from the Pony Club. Caleb was actually 2cd Sargeant, behind

1st Sargeant Jacob R. Brooks. An August 4th account of whippings associated with the Callaway Burke affair in the *Columbus Enquirer* indicate:

…regulators, proceeded to take up and whip (without warrant) in the course of one or two days, five persons, namely John and Edward Watts, John Sappington, John Gilley, William Wright and Thomas Blake (page 3 col. 2)…

William Shipley came to Carroll County from Habersham County, though he had won a lot in Lee County during the 1827 Lottery. Shipley lived among the core group of the club in Carroll and when it moved to Paulding, he became sheriff there. Shipley was one club member who did not run away after the fall of the club. He spent the remainder of his days in Floyd County. He is not mentioned very often in the record of the club but appeared on two Indian claims:

1830 **Tom York** *and* **William Shipley** *of Pumpkin Creek stole horses of* **Jim Godwin** *of Ioctatee Creek.*

1830 **Asa Upton and (William) Shipley,** *"Two noted thieves of the pony club" stole a horse named Tiskeenee ("a famous foal getter") from* **Owl Murphy.**

His activities garnered the distaste of the editor of the Cherokee newspaper and he is mentioned in the July 30, 1831 *Cherokee Phoenix* along with other members of the Pony Club:

…Who has not heard of the "notorious olde Dick Philpot" and his generation; the Craddocks, Langfords, Yorks, Ramseys, Johnsons, Shipleys, Uptons and etc. (page 3 column 3)…

The August 4th, 1832 *Columbus Enquirer* indicated William Shipley and Allen York were whipped by the regulators that included John Goodwin, Hawkins Phillips and Nethaniel Black.

Edward, John, Hugh and Thomas Tatum were very active members of the Pony Club. The Tatums came to Carroll County by way of Elbert County, on the South Carolina border. They lived in the Philpot neighborhood between John Craddock and Joshua Gay. Their names appear on many of the Indian claims made after the removal, sometimes by first name, other times just as "tatum." One such claim was that of George Still, a bundled claim from the teleman Cuyler Collection. Made in 1838, still lists a dozen horses stolen from him over a number of years. Two of them were taken by one of the Tatums:

…The next senball [added: and Black] Horses as discribed was stolen by one Taitem a white man citizen of the United States done at standing peach tree about 12 years ago the claimant

says he employed a white man named Jones to persue [pursue] the said Taitem. Jones persued [pursued] him to Abervill Dist South Carolina Jones stated when he returned that he fund the Horses in the Possesion [Possession] of a white man who told him that he bought the said horse from one Taitem who lived in Georgia and that he would not let claimant have the horse unles [unless] he would come and make proof to the Horse but as it was some distance from home the claimant could not comply The next Black Horse as discribed was stolen at the same time and by the same Taitem and was seen in the posession of the same white man at the same time that the senball horse was seen...

A claim made in 1842, mentions Thomas Tatum: Taking his sorrel horse worth seventy five dollars (Shadburn 1993: 650). Likewise, Dick Proctor accuses Hugh Tatum of taking "a bay horse and colt worth eighty dollars (648). Too Na Wee's claim in 1842 noted:

...that in 1834 a white man named Tatem stole a brown horse from my mother and he sold the horse to a white man who lived in the settlements in Ga., and in 1838 he stole the gray horse also and threatened to steal all of my mothers horses. And afterwards he attempted to steal a mare from my mother by breaking the stable door. He got the mare but my brother took the mare away from him before he could get away (648, 649)...

In 1834, after the trouble in Carroll County is over, the Tatums move to Lumpkin County to continue their devious ways, at least until the Indians are removed.

Thurmon a club member mentioned only once in the record, is not the same Thurmond responsible for the murder of William Philpot. The only thing known of this person was reported in the Federal Union, Oct 3, 1835, page 2 col.3.

> We learn that a party of citizens of this county, started last week in pursuit of a man by the name of *Thurmon*, who was supposed to have stolen several horses, from the neighborhood of Ama Calola. They overtook him in the night, on Cottokay, in Gilmer county; he, upon seeing them, immediately fled; they hailed him and ordered him to stop, but refusing to do so, he was fired on; he died immediately. Thurmon was a man of notorious bad character, and strongly suspected of belonging to a gang of "Poney Club men," who have for some time infested our section of country.—
> *Miners' Recorder.*

Asa and Nathan Upton were core members of the club, having come from Tennessee with the original wagon train. James, Sr. was very active in Tennessee, appearing in several deeds with the Philpots and majors.

Rhea County Tenn
PG. 110 (page 99 (E-106) (14 June 1817) (Registered 11 Sept 1817): Deed of Conveyance, Richard Philpot to William Floyd for $600, 117 acres on Camp Creek including place where Floyd now lives. Beginning some distance below the boiling spring on each side of Spring branch which is beginning corner of 600-acre tract granted by NC (No. 223) to Stockley Donelson and dated 20 Sept 1787, etc; corner James Upton. Teste: Jesse Thompson and Elias Majors

State of Tennessee} July Session 1816 - There was this deed proven in Open Court of Rhea County . Oath of Richard Philpot and James Upton. Let it be registered {LS} Given under my hand and private Seal (not having an official seal) the 22 July 1816.

A. *Rawlings Clerk*

James had two sons who were listed as members of the Pony Club: Nathan Jr. and Asa and both were mentioned numerous times in claims by Indians who had been robbed.

1830 **Nathan Upton** *of "Philpot's clan" stole cattle of* **John Fields, Jr.**

1830 **Jim Philpot, Reubin Philpot, Asa Upton** *and other unnamed persons attacked two Cherokees (***John Ridge** *and* **John Fields***) with clubs and knives near Vann's Old Place. The Indians were searching for missing horses.*

1830 **Asa Upton** *and (***William) Shipley**, *"2 noted thieves of the pony club" stole a horse named Tiskeenee ("a famous foal getter") from* **Owl Murphy.**

Writing in the *Carroll County Times* of June 8, 1883, a reader wrote a letter to the editor remembering the Callaway Burke killing. Identified only as G. A. S. the author recalled seeing the club members involved:

The killing of Caloway Burks in 1834 is probably remembered by few. Hawkins Phillips, John Goodin and five Indians spent the night at my father's and inquired for stolen cattle. I had seen the cattle driven by Burk, Upton and others in the direction of Almon's cane brake, near the present site of Buckhorn tavern where by my direction, the cattle were found the next morning, and driven back to Alabama by the Indians, Goodin and others, going on to hunt thieves.

Through fear of the Pony Club, Almon would not allow them to stay all night, but loaned them a gun and they started to Hickstown, now Villa Rica. After crossing the Tallapoosa near where

Mr. Hart afterward settled, they met Burk and others, all armed. Goodin's party were on the alert and each party soon detected the character of the other. Burk leveled his gun and Goodin shot him dead.

I have frequently seen Goodin in Carrollton since and served in the Seminole War with him three months in 1838. About the time of Burk's death, the Slicks were organized as an antidote for the Pony Club. The Slicks lynched several of the Club and were prosecuted for it, Jones for the prosection and Thos. Chandler for the defense.

The smiling, prosperous Carroll County stands out in striking contrast with the wild battle ground of the Pony Club and the Slicks of 1831. G.A.S.

Under this state of feeling. a combination from Alabama, Cherokee and Carroll, commenced a raid:—Went to the house of James Upton, took Crawford Wright from his family—tied him to a tree—stripped him—struck him 90 or 100 lashes—extorted a promise that he would not law them and that he would leave the State in 20 days.

Excerpt from the August 4, 1832 Columbus Enquirer.

While James Upton Sr. stayed in Carroll County after the Pony Club's demise, many of his kin went to Alabama, and Texas. His daughters had married Wrights and Hogans and accompanied them west. Asa Upton may have been killed as he completely disappears from the records and a sister names her son Asa Upton Wright, perhaps in memory. Nathaniel also disappears but is rumored to have moved to Texas with the other members.

Edward and John Watts are shadowy figures in records of Georgia. Edward can be found in the 1830 census records of Dekalb County and John in the census of Carroll County. John lives between the house of Reuben Philpot and that of Garret Lankford according to the Census. During the Callaway Burke affair, the *Columbus Enquirer* reported both Edward and John Watts had been whipped by regulators for offenses in Alabama and Georgia. William Springer, chairman of the 1832 Carroll County Grand Jury, in a December 13, 1832 account in the Milledgeville *Federal Union* indicated the Watts were leaders of the club and brought up the troubling news that one of the Watts boys had been killed by Creek

Indians in Alabama. Gen. Thomas S. Woodward had been on hand to take the Man's dying confession, which cast aspersions not only on the Pony Club, but also the feed council made up of Jones and Fambrough (3: 4-6).

John and James and their mother flee Carroll, ending up in Benton County Alabama.

John, Thomas and Pinckney Welch: Thomas moved to Carroll in time for the 1830 census and all three are mentioned in Indian claims. George Still mentions them in his 1838 spoliation claim:

…The next discribed a Grey Mare was stolen by one **Welck** a white man done at Talapoosee about 10 years ago claimant states he did not see the mare in the possession of said Welck but has good reasons for so beliefing…

Arkalookee's wife singles out Thomas Welch as the thief who stole her property.

 The Welches appear to have been members from the start, appearing in the earliest claim against the Pony Club on record:

 1826 Allen York, Alexander Ramsey, members of the Welch family, and Philpot *clan stole cattle of* Archy Rowe *(Cher.) on the Tallapoosa River. The cattle were traced to Buzzard's Roost.*

Where the Welches originate from and where they go after the club's downfall remains a complete mystery. They seem to be swallowed up by time itself.

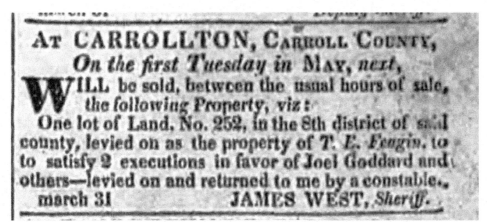

AT CARROLLTON, CARROLL COUNTY,
On the first Tuesday in MAY, *next,*
WILL be sold, between the usual hours of sale, the following Property, viz:
One lot of Land, No. 252, in the 8th district of said county, levied on as the property of T. E. Feagin, to to satisfy 2 executions in favor of Joel Goddard and others—levied on and returned to me by a constable.
march 31   JAMES WEST, *Sheriff.*

Macon Telegraph, Mar. 31, 1828 -- page 3/5

Jim and Jack or John West were another mystery pair. They spend their brief time on the stage of this drama and are heard from no more. Exactly how they

311

come to be in the Pony Club is unclear. It is not even certain where they lived in the 1830s. Several times they are mentioned in claims made after the Indian Removal.

James Philpot, Reuben Philpot, Jack and Jim West, Thomas Hogan, and Jesse Humphrey stole 12 horses ($500) of Jesse Sanders and Jack Wright on Sweetwater Creek. Jim and Jack West stole from Dick Scott.

The Wests are more famous for the crime of murder which causes them to run in 1832 and therefore end any trace of their existence in the historical record. Evidence indicates the familiar format: a man is looking for stolen property in Carroll County; he is murdered by someone from the club. On 21 November 1830,

Federal Union, Mar. 22, 1832 -- page 1 col. 2

John West and James West murdered James Lockoby of Dekalb County. On March 12, 1832, Governor Lumpkin issued a proclamation offering a 400 dollar reward for the capture of the Wests.

The **Wrights** included all the sons and daughters of Jesse Wright, who came to Carroll County from South Carolina.

William Wright
Theana Wright Hightower
John Wright mysterious death
Elizabeth Wright **Upton**
Crawford Wright who died mysteriously sometime after moving to Paulding.
Elizabeth Wright **Mahaffey**
Lucinda Wright **Mahaffey**
James Wright who died mysteriously
Martha Wright Wilson
Jesse Woods Wright
Sally Wright
Nancy Wright **Mahaffey**
Thomas Wright
Melinda Wright

Elizabeth married John Upton and had a son Asa Upton, evidence indicating Asa had been killed or hung by the slicks. The sudden disappearance of Crawford and James seems to bear out the claim by the letter of G.A.S. in the Carroll paper that slicks "…lynched several of the Club and were prosecuted for it, Jones for the prosection and Thos. Chandler for the defense (Carroll Free Press, June 8, 1883)."

Several of the Wrights married Mahaffeys as well, lending credence to the view the Pony Club was indeed a family affair while it lasted. William Wright may have been the person who was involved in the 1831 survey of the Cherokee Country and paid for services according to Mary Bondurant Warren's **Whites Among the Cherokee** (1987: 138). Don Shadburn's **Unhallowed Intrusion,** mentions one of the Wrights in regards to thefts from BearPaw of Forsyth County.

Bear Paw, a former resident of Hightown (or Etowah) District, removed to Indian Territory in 1838 in Stephen Foreman's Detachment. His account totaled $158.50 for 27 head of "stock hogs," a rifle gun, 20 bushels of corn, a "Round Log house," a "dirk knife," and 13 chickens. Bear Paw's oath before Clerk Few of Goingsnake maintained that his hogs were taken in 1831 "by John Wright, a white man, without caus or provocation, and my Rifle Gun was *taken from me in 1835 was taken from me in 1835 by Jack a white man without any cause whatever (1993: 645)...*

After the Pony Club left Carroll, many ended up in Paulding County, as did several of the Wrights. In Charles Henderson's **History of Polk County,** which appeared in the *Cedartown Record*, a tussel between Jonathon Long and one of the Wrights is mentioned:

I must not forget an old scar worn veteran who fought, bled, and died in the trying days of the Pony Club, Jonathan Long, who done gallant service. He was good on a chase, and never failed to bark when he treed, while many other men were good in a chase, but failed to bark. He treed an old fox in the shape of a Wright, and caught him, but he was very hard to handle. They had it up and down, over and under, buckle and tongue, and finally the other foxes pitched on him, all going for Jonathan, over the head and eyes, back and front, and the result was, Jonathan came out only second best and badly hurt. Nothing daunted, he was soon up and ready for another chance. He was ready to denounce wrong and defend the right, contending strictly for his own rights, but no more (June 26, 1875)...

When the Pony Club was defeated in Paulding County, most of the Wrights moved to Texas.

The family of **Josiah York** came to Carroll County with the Philpots, Uptons and other Tennessee members of the Pony Club. Mary "Polly" York was married to Moses Looney Feb. 27, 1817 in Roane Co, Tenn., Thomas York married Sally Looney, while Elizabeth and Delilah York married William and James Philpot, respectively. Josiah married the daughter of Thomas Blake and these families were related to the Johnsons and rumored to be related to the Ramseys. Family history indicates they all moved to Carroll County for two possible reasons:

...The reasons why this area was chosen is a mystery since Josiah's father, William, was not awarded land in this lottery, however the choice of area was possibly dictated by their affiliation with the notorious Pony Club (Sanfilippo P.C. Aug. 8, 2009)...

It is my belief that members of the 'club' were involved in the murder of another Indian in Washington Co., although I am not sure where the Philpot men lived except in E. Tennessee and it had to be near the York home (Oct. 20, 2009)...

The family history also includes some insight into the early days of the club. Diane Sanfillipo indicates and it is her suspicion that the families were intruders in Carroll County before it was formed. As such they faced the recriminations not only of the State and Federal governments, but also the Indians:

314

Anyone living there before 1825 were living on Creek land... and since it is known that the York and Philpot families had to 'fight' Indians when they arrived, then I would think they were there before the survey... Bill Lester told a wonderful story told by Elizabeth York Philpot carrying a rusty sword, holding her newborn baby, while she could hear the yells of the Indians fighting the men after dark. Gives me shivers to think about it (Aug. 12, 2009)!

The Yorks began appearing in Indian claims very early in the record:

Josiah York *of* **Sand Town** *took cattle & hogs (worth $144) belonging to* **Nelly** *(a Cherokee), near Sally Hughes' Ferry on the Etowah [or Hightower] River.*

1826 Allen York, Alexander Ramsey, members of the Welch family, and Philpot *clan stole cattle of* **Archy Rowe** *(Cher.) on the Tallapoosa River. The cattle were traced to Buzzard's Roost*

These two claims indicate that the club may indeed have begun at Sandtown on the Chattahoochee River and that the Yorks, Philpots, et al had arrived by 1826. If the claim is correct, this was before Carroll County was established. Buzzard's Roost Island is only a half mile or so north of Sandtown and the topography there on both sides of the river is conducive to cattle herding as it is flat; what were called "old fields" and had been treeless for as much as a thousand years.

Thomas York *burned down log house ($30) of* **Bear Paw** *of Etowah, and took his corn, chickens, and dirk knife ($3.50).*

1830 **Tom York** *and* **William Shipley** *of Pumpkin Creek stole horses of* **Jim Godwin** *of Ioctatee Creek.*

1830 **Thomas York and his son** *had possession of hogs stolen from* **Nainne** *(Cher.) of Allatoona. The hogs were taken into the gold mining area.*

1836 a man named **York** *stole horses and cattle ($195) of* **Ailsey Scott** *(Cher.)*

The August 4, 1832 Columbus Enquirer, reporting the sordid Callaway Burke affair, mentions that Allen York was whipped, along with fellow club member William Shipley by Alabama slicks led by John Goodwin. Responding to charges made against himself, John A. Jones of the "feed council" attempted to make the case for his own innocence in the Ga. Journal:

On Thursday, the 3rd of May, Col. Allen Fambrough and myself started from my residence in Carroll County, for Van's Valley, in Cherokee County, in consequence of a message from Allen York and Wm. Shipley (two men believed to belong to the Poney Club) informing us that *they were held in confinement by a number of armed men, having (as they believed) no authority to detain them; that they feared violence to their lives or persons; requesting our legal advice and assistance, and leaving the fees to our discretion...*

Upon traveling, the two lawyers met a group of the slicks and asked about York and Shipley.

...They informed us that they had given York fifteen or twenty lashes. Before we met them, they had whipped several others, most if not all of them tenants of Georgia settled on places left by emigrating Indians and rented to the state (July 5, 1832: 3/3).

When the Carroll Grand Jury finally got rid of the Pony Club there, the Yorks moved on to Paulding County with the rest of the Pony Club. Josiah, Allen and Thomas are shown there in 1837 and 1840, but soon thereafter only Josiah remains. He became a magistrate of Paulding and later Polk County and Yorkville is named after him.

The case against the members of the Pony Club is very strong. There are many many consistent claims made against this same group of people who migrated from Tennessee to become tenants of the new ceded lands in Northwest Georgia. But they were not the only people involved in crimes against the Indians. There seems to have abeen other versions of the club in other counties surrounding the Cherokee and Creek Nations.

Lost Businesses: James Vann's tavern (Ga. DNR).

October-December 1967 *Ansearchin News Quarterly,* The Tennessee Geneology Society: Memphis.

1971 Bonner, James Calvin, **Georgia's last frontier: the development of Carroll County,** Univ. of Ga. Press: Athens.

1830 Brooks Jacob R., **Letter to Governor George R. Gilmer, 12 November 1830**; original records, Record Group 4-2-46, Box 17, File II Names: Georgia Archives: Morrow, Georgia.

Feb. 10, 1830 **First Blood Shed by Georgians**, *Cherokee Phoenix*, : page 2 col. 4, 5.

Jan. 1, 1831 **Hightower, Cherokee Nation**, *Cherokee Phoenix*, page 2 col. 4.

Feb. 12, 1831 **Head of Coosa, *Cherokee Phoenix,*** page 2, col. 3.

May 7, 1831. **A. Freeman letter, *Cherokee Phoenix,*** page 3 col. 3, 4.

July 30, 1831 **Matters and things as they are**, *Cherokee Phoenix*, page 3 col. 3.

Aug. 12, 1831, **Matters and Things as They Are**, *Cherokee Phoenix,* page 2 col.1-5.

Jan 21, 1832 **To Satisfy the Reported Inquiries, *Cherokee Phoenix,*** page 1 col. 3-6.

March 24, 1832 **Cherokee Memorial, *Cherokee Phoenix***, page 1, col. 2.

2/13/2002 Clark, Jerry L, **Richard, Reuben, & James Philpot.** @http://genforum.genealogy.com/Philpot/message/673.html.

Aug. 4, 1832 **For the Enquirer, *Columbus Enquirer,*** page 3, col. 2, 3.

Aug 18, 1832 **For the Enquirer, *Columbus Enquirer***, page 3 col. 6.

Winter 2002 Davis, Jr., Robert S., **Some Cherokee Indian Spoliations 1836-1837, *Georgia Geneoligical Society Quarterly***, Vol. 38 no.4.

Mar. 22, 1832 **Proclamation,** *Federal Union*, page 1 col. 2.

Oct 3, 1835 **Miner's Recorder,** *Federal Union*, page 2 col.3.

Nov. 22, 1832 **The Grand Jury of Carroll County,** *Federal Union*: 3/6.

Dec. 13, 1832 **To the Public,** *Federal Union*, page 3 col. 3-5.

July 5, 1832: **For the Journal,** *Georgia Journal,* 3/3.

1982 Davis, Jr. Robert Scot, **The Georgia Black Book Morbid, Macabre and Disgusting Records of Genealogical Value,** Southern Historical Press: Easley, S. Carolina.

June 8, 1883 **G.A.S., Letter to the Editor,** *Carroll County Times* .

June 19, 1875 Henderson, Dr. Charles K., **Early History of Polk County,** *Cedartown Record*.

June 26, 1875 Henderson, Dr. Charles K., **Early History of Polk County,** *Cedartown Record*.

Sun, 20 May 2007 Don Johnson, **Joel Daniel Leathers & The Pony Club,**@<http://genforum.genealogy.com/leathers/messages/729.html>

1907 **Mrs. Joseph Kingsberry,** *Carroll Free Press.*

1819-6/1829 **McMinn Co., TN. County Court Minutes** Vol. 11.

2002 Motes, Margaret Peckham, **Blacks Found in Deeds of Laurens & Newberry Counties, SC: 1785-1827,** Clearfield Co., Inc.: Baltimore.

1974 Register, Alvaretta Kenan, Index to the 1830 Census, Clearfield Co., Inc.: Baltimore.

20 Jun 2007 Sanfilippo, Diane Stark, **Josiah Cowan York, Sr. and His Family, Updated**, @http://files.usgwarchives.net/ga/paulding/bios/york929gbs.txt.

1993 Shadburn, Don L., **Unhallowed Intrusion: A History of Cherokee Families in Forsythe County, Georgia,** W.H. Wolfe associates: Alpharetta.
318

PA0274 Spoliation claim [of] Grits, 1838 Sept. 5 repository: Hoskins Special Colections Library, University of Tennessee, Knoxville
collection: MS2033 Penelope Johnson Allen.

2033, **1838 Sept. United States to George Still of Cherokee Nation East**
Penelope Allen Collection, 1801-1984, Box 1, Folder 166, The University of Tennessee Libraries (Knoxville, Tennessee) is the digital publisher.

1989 Wilkins, Thurman, **Cherokee Tragedy: The Ridge Family and the Decimation of a People,** Univ of Okalhoma Press: Norman.

Personal communications:
Diane Sanfilippo: August 8, 2009
August 12, 2009
October 20, 2009

William Lester: October 9, 2009
October 17, 2009
October 19, 2009
October 27, 2009

Many of the ferries were originally Cherokee improvements (Edwin Lamasure 1907).

Other possible members

Since the New Echota Treaty already had provisions in it for the repayment of claims for spoliation and loss, many officials of the federal and state governments cast a blind eye on what was happening to the Cherokee. They recommended any Indian who was stolen from or experienced any loss to use the spoliation section of the treaty for redress, rather than belabor the point before removal. One good example of this is the experience of Cherokee John Ridge in Alabama.

The trouble had begun a year before while Ridge was in Washington. A swaggering white man named John H. Garret, who had been elected a Major General in the Alabama Militia and who liked to talk of dueling and "the code", forcibly ejected William Childers, Ridge's tenant and ferryman, and seized possession of the farm and ferry. In Ridge's absence Sarah, his wife, appealed to Major Curry, who ordered Garrett off in turn appealed for justice to the governor of Alabama. Garrett was still in possession of the property in the Summer of 1836, having put up structures on the opposite side of the Coosa from Ridge's buildings. Ridge now took the matter to General John E. Wool, who had just been sent with American troops to police the Cherokee Nation and disarm the Indians while they prepared to remove under the New Echota Treaty. The general sent troops to oust Garrett, and Childers was reinstalled as tenant and ferryman. Garrett soon returned with a large force of men; he had, moreover, secured a writ of possession and an injunction from the chancery court of Cherokee County, Alabama forbidding Ridge and Childers further use of the ferry and farm. Childers was ejected a second time, and when ridge appealed once more to General Wool, the general advised that Garrett could not be removed without bloodshed and that it would be sensible to submit to force and look to the United States for spoliation under the Treaty of New Echota. That was the course which Ridge elected to follow (Wilkins 1989: 295).

An example of some of the claims and those accused follows. These are from bundled claims made between 1836-38 (Ga. Geneology Society); claims in Forsyth County, Ga. (Don Shadburn) and loose claims in the Telemon Cuyler and Penelope Allen collections. Those known to be **Pony Club** members are in bold print.

George Still,
Cherokee

Gilmer	
Beaver	Williiam Heard
Joe Binion	Springen
Speers	**Welch**
Tatum	Brown
Charley Harris	James Barker
Williams	Ezekial Ralston
Philpot	Shadrach Bogan

John Vann	Thompson	Lizzy Sanders	William Lay
	Thomas		William Baker
	Williams		Daniel Bird
	Willis Bobo		
	John Franklin	Peacheater	James Wilson
			Sam
Grits (Ala)	**John Craddock**		Winn
			Samuel Jones
William Reid) (N Car)	Pickle Simon Moss		Hufftutter
		Thomas Sourjohn	**Soloman Rately**
Polly Vann	John Hagans **Joel Leathers**		
		Ca see la wee	Plum
Soap	William Heard		Bolen
	Pleasant Jones		**Thomas Tatum**
	Thos. Copeland		
	George Hinckley	Su wu chu	**Joel Leathers** Thompson
John Ratliff (Ala)	David J. Hooks		
		Jesse Raper	John Reeves
Bear Paw	James D. Sutton		
	Mat Sutton	Jacob Harnage	John Stancel Sr
	John Wright		John Stancel Jr
	Jack		
	Thomas York	David Van	Moses Hendrix
Black Fox (Tenn)	Soloman Davis	Cynthia Ledbetter	George McDuffie
Dick Eiskey	Bart Bailey		
		Davis	David Timson
Arley Hornet	John Price		Peter Kent
	Beth Quillian		
		Kulkeeloskee	Andrew Johnson
Bumgarner	Oliver Strickland		
		Dick Scott	**Jesse Philpot**
Brice Martin	Berry Atkinson		**Jack West**
			Jim West
Dick Proctor	William McKinney		
	Hugh Tatum	Anoren Ross	John Boyd
Too na wee	**Tatum**	Jonathon Mulkey	John Coleman
Lizzy Sanders	James Wilson		

Spring Frog	James Hughes		
James Fields	Bob Weir	Sally Hughes	William Greene
Major Ridge	John Ownstead	Charles Moore	**Buck Heard**
John Fields	**James Philpot**	David Sanders	John Westbrooks
Richard Scott	John Holsenback	Arkalookee's wife	**Thomas Welch**
Robert Brown (Ala)	William Brazeale James Wilcox		

What about those people not mentioned as members of the club? Who are they? Are they members we just can't prove or do they have their own pony clubs? The factors I used to determine who was a club member include mention by newspaper articles, evidence in books and Indian claims…but guilt by association in claims, in other words when someone is mentioned *with a known member*. One thing that can be said about the Club is that some members did not live in Carroll or Paulding County. Some lived as far away as Gwinnett County and operated in the same area as the rest of the club. Still others returned to far away counties after the club was disbanded. In many cases members or their families won draws in the 1832 Land Lottery and moved into the Cherokee area.

Alexander Hogan, 7-1-142 * (Union)
William York 26-2-190 * (Murray)
James Philpot 8-3-106 * (Murray)
James Upton 18-3-741 * (Paulding)
Thomas Welch 3-27-2 * (Gilmer)
Abraham Leathers 5-2-81* (Gilmer)

The Club was defined by its complex membership and strategy of hiding horses in far away places and selling them in other states or counties. The concept wasn't new and there was evidence clubs like this existed in Savannah in the 1760s. Indians were expert at this and many like Menawa had names that meant "horse thief." So it is not unlikely that the Club had some competition from other places.

To define someone as a horse, cow, or hog thief, one need only be mentioned as charged. However, after the Indian removal many bogus claims were made by Indians who either couldn't remember the names of perpetrators or made them up. In some cases the names were of other Indians and in still other cases the transactions they called theft were legitimate. We have to also remember that in the climate created by Governors Gilmer and Lumpkin, local officials as well as hardened criminals found themselves doing the same jobs: dispossessing the Indians. The Cherokee claimed even before they were removed that forged documents were being used to seize Indian properties to satisfy fake *fi fas* and other judgements. A good example of that is the claim by Indian Margaret Baumgarner, who claimed **Oliver Stricklin'** stole "taking it for the benefit of another person. (Shadburn 1993: 646)." At the time Strickling was Clerk of Superior Court in Cherokee County and probably serving a levy. Another example is that by Lizzy Sanders, claiming **Daniel Bird** levied upon her because she "owed him for things out of his store (649)." At some point it becomes certain that some claims were not spoliation but were legitimate actions by officials, but, because of the nature of the event, the length of time past since many of these events took place and the attitude of the Federal Government of promoting the claims process, they were paid. Some claims were turned down outright and some discounted, but most were paid out of the vast fund set aside for them..

FRACTIONS TO RENT.

I WILL rent, at public outcry, on Thursday, the 14th February next, at the house of Mr. M'Afee, formerly Gates' Ferry, all the IMPROVED FRAC- TIONS below the mouth of Sewauna in the counties of Cobb and Forsyth, until the first day of January, 1834; —on Saturday, the 16th February next, at the house of Oliver Strickland, formerly Scudder's, all the IM- PROVED FRA TIONS lying below the county line of Forsyth and Lumpkin in the county of Forsyth;-- on the 18th of February next, at Leather's Ford, all the IMPROVED FRACTIONS below the mouth of Te- sentee in the county of Lumpkin;--and on the 20th of February next, at M'Laughlin's store, all the IMPROV- ED FRACTIONS from the mouth of Tesentee to the North Carolina line in the counties of Lumpkin and U- nion. Terms made known on the renting days.
Jan 24–31   W. N. BISHOP, *commissioner.*

Federal Union, Feb. 14, 1833 page 1 col. 5.

If we digress to the beginnings of these problems with the Indians and the Club, we assume it began in Dekalb, formerly Fayette, District 14, in the neighborhood of Sandtown. This is probably true for the Carroll Club, but it was not the first indication of trouble. In 1828, in Habersham County, the Grand Jury indicted several men for attacking an Indian and stealing his horse:

We also present Jas. D. Sutton, Edward Townsend, Madison Sutton, Henry Bramlett and Joseph Bramlett, did with force of arms, on the 22cd day of September, take from the Bear's Paw, a Cherokee Indian, a certain horse. We also present Henry Bramlett for striking Ache, the Bear Paw's wife with a gun (Southern Recorder Dec. 06, 1828: 3/5)...

In the 1832 Presentments for Habersham, attention to these types of crimes is still a major topic. The **Federal Union** notes:

...We also recommend extension of penitentiary confinement, by a close adherence to which we believe our country will be shortly relieved of all those villains who are enlisted under the counterfeiting and Poney Club banner, say, for example, horse stealing or passing counterfeit money, the first crime shall be punishable with ten years confinement, the second twenty and the third ninety nine and so on proportioning all other crimes of greater or less magnitude accordingly (Nov. 15, 1832: 3/4).

Several of the Pony Club members and many others accused of crimes against the Cherokee were operating from Habersham County or moved from there to either Carroll or the Cherokee County (county and year).

Henry Bramblet	Fors 34
Joseph Bramblet	Fors 34
Soloman Davis	claim by Black Fox in Tenn.
John Franklin	claim by John Vann, Union34
John Gilley	--
Willis Gilley	--
Joel Hasley	mentioned in the Cherokee Phoenix
Samuel Jones	claim by Peacheater, Gilmer inf ct
William Shipley	Pldg 37
Jesse Stancel	Lump 34
John Stancel	Cher 34
John Stancel	Murr 34
James D. Sutton	Lump 34
Mat Sutton	Lump 34
Edward Townsend	Cher 34

324

The Stancels are one of the most notorious set of thieves to plunder the Cherokee. They are mentioned in several articles of the Cherokee Phoenix concerning stolen horses and the father-son team of John Sr. and Jr. undergoing justice in the Indian Territory by receiving lashes. The Stancels are also mentioned by Shadburn in his **Unhallowed Intrusion** (1993) with respect to a claim filed by Jacob Harnage, who claimed:

…Compensation for two horses, worth $120, stolen by white men. Harnage's statement before the clerk reveal that he emigrated to Indian Territory in 1828 and settled on the Grand River. 'He lived at Frog Town on the Chesta'tee [river] where he had two horses stolen by young John and Old John Stansel [also Stancil]; they owned to the claimant that they took his horses, but it was out of his power to get redress from them—as they were white men of Habersham County, Georgia (653, 655).'

Quite a few Club members as well as other thieves were from or operated out of Gwinnett County. Like Habersham it had jurisdiction over a great portion of Indian land and a broad border with it along the Chattahoochee River. Some of the notorious ones include:

Gwinnett		Later county
William Baker	claim by Lizzy Sanders, Cher 32	
Job Binion	claim of George Still	Dekb 40
Willis Bobo	claim by John Vann	Murr 37
Shadrack Bogan	claim of George Still	Cass 34
Thomas Copeland	claim of Sopes	Cobb 34
Gilmore	claim of George Still	
John Goodwin		Dek 30
William Greene	claim of Sally Hughes	Lump 34 Cass 34
John Holsenback	claim of Richard Scott	
John Killian	penitentiary	
William Lay	claim of Lizzy Sanders	Cher 32
John Ownstead	claim of Major Ridge	Gwin 30
Henry Reatherford		Lump 34
William Reatherford		Lump 34
John Reeves	claim of Jesse Raper	
John Welch		Gwin 30
Thomas Welch		Gwin 30
John Wright		Gwin 20

I believe the story of the Pony Club would be incomplete without the history of Gwinnet and Dekalb Counties. The club relied heavily on those willing to squat or intrude on either Indian land or government land won by cession. The original return of Hugh Montgomery for intruders in Gwinnet seems to foreshadow what is to come until the Indians are removed. Those intruding into Gwinnet and living among the Indians are reviled by Montgomery and later, in Gwinnet County Presentments as well. A short history of Shadrack Bogan is a good example of how things were back then:

…William Shadrack Boggan-Bogan was born 1787 Anson County, North Carolina, and died May 1857 Cedar Bluff, Alabama; son of William Patrick Boggan/Bogan and the former Elizabeth Denson. He married 3 March 1815 Ann Foster Fee in St Paul's Episcopal Church, Augusta, Georgia, by Rector John Garvin. They left for Gwinnett that same day. Both are buried in Cherry Creek Cemetery, Cherokee County, Alabama.

Ann Foster [F]ee (1798-1866) was born in Augusta, daughter of George and Elizabeth (Foster) Fee, both of whom were born in Liverpool, England, where they married in 1790. While in Augusta, Shadrack Bogan was issued a drayage license in [1805].

Shortly after moving to Gwinnett in 1816, they settled at Hog Mountain, where they stayed until 1835. There he set up a store or trading post where Indian trails converged from all directions. Fur-trading with the Indians became brisk. A Mr. Gilmore and Shadrack Bogan were two of the chief buyers. The Indians called Mr. Gilmore "Open Hand" and Mr. Bogan was called "Santalanks" which meant "trader" in Indian language. Mr. Bogan traded whiskey ("firewater") to the Indians for furs. One day, fur trading was very brisk and they kept coming back with more furs until "Santalanks" was out of "firewater." Upon investigating his supply of furs, Bogan discovered only three furs in his stock. There was a hole cut in the wall beside the furs where the Indians had retrieved them for resale for more "firewater."

In 1821, along with John Winn and Patrick L. Dunlap, Shadrack Bogan was ordered to lay out and mark a road along the nearest and best route from Gwinnett County Courthouse toward Hall County Courthouse as far as the county line. The road that was laid out passed by the hotel and tavern known as the "Hog Mountain House" of Shadrack Bogan.

The Bogan family lived at Level Creek Church community in Suwanee 1816-1835.
Bogan built a water mill which was located near the present intersection of I-85 and State Road 20. This mill was known at the time as Bogan's Mill and later was called "Woodward's Mill." The mill was destroyed by fire in January 1978. Bogan Road enters Highway 20 near there.

Shadrack Bogan drew 40 acres of land in Cass County in the Gold Lottery and moved there in 1835. This land was located north of Rome. The family moved from there to Alabama, settling at Cedar Bluff in Cherokee County by the 1840 census.

On the 1850 census of Cherokee County, Alabama, he is listed as merchant, farmer, and innkeeper. He owned a bauxite bank there and served as justice of the peace and constable. William Shadrack Bogan left no will at his death, believed to have been 15 April 1857 (Margaret Bogan Bray and Carolyn Pirkle 2006)…

Bogan's friend was also mentioned in a claim by George Still, although it was spelled Gilmer. During the 1832 Land Lottery drawing, Bogan was charged with fixing the outcome of several draws and relieved of duty. He maintained his innocence and placed an ad in the Georgia Journal asking Georgians to wait til the lottery was over to judge his innocence or guilt.

A CARD
TO THE PEOPLE OF GEORGIA.

THE citizen who addresses you, values reputation more highly then fortune, or life; but he is aware, that to attempt at this time, to vindicate his character as an honest man, would be a fruitless labour. Rumour, with her thousand tongues, has scattered falsehoods over the country : and after a trial by an august tribunal, he has been pronounced guilty. He does not impeach the purity of motive of any member of the senate constituting the court of impeachment ; but that honorable body has condemned him on suspicion alone, and has erred in its judgment. He is guiltless of any fraud against his fellow-citizens; and his duty as a lottery commissioner, he has discharged with zeal and fidelity. The drawing of the land lottery, in the management of which he is charged to have practised a fraud, will be closed in a few weeks; and the condition of the wheels, at the termination of the drawing, will bear conclusive evidence, of his guilt, or of his innocence. He awaits the development, with the confidence inspired by conscious integrity : to the examination of this result, he earnestly solicits the attention of his fellow-citizens: and after it shall have been ascertained, for the vindication of his character he will appeal to the justice of a generous, and magnanimous people.

SHADRACK BOGAN.

Dec. 27——25-1t.

Georgia Journal, Dec. 27, 1832 page 3 col. 6.

Dekalb County was the site of the origin of the original Pony Club, on the river at Sandtown. Most moved on to Carroll or other counties in search of new victims. One who stayed was William G. "Buck" Heard. Mentioned previously with respect to blackbirding and reportedly as a member of the Murrell gang, Buck was a famous frontier outlaw. He is mentioned in slave journals and social science discourses on slavery almost as a fixture. According to Donna Weed (2010), a Heard family genealogist, Buck was born about 1801 and married Rebecca Gill. His criminal career started about 1826, when he was charged with stealing a horse, a modus operandi that would identify him for many many years. George Still claimed William Heard had stolen his sorrel horse in 1826 and perhaps this is where the charge originated.

Soap also claimed Buck Heard stole from him:

In a claim recorded in **Vol. C #819** *in the fall of 1838, Soap and an Indian named Crow of Hickory Log District told Moses Daniel, U.S. agent for collecting claims, that "a white man named William Heard" stole the following from Soap:*

1 Bay Mare 5 years old - 100.00
1 Chestnut Sorrel horse 7 years old - 70.00
1 Gray mare 10 years old - 80.00
_____ 250.00

The horses were "stolen by a white man named William Heard down on Soap Creek near Chattahoochee River about 15 years ago," Soap claimed. Although he did not personally see the horses in Heard's possession, a Cherokee named Yellow Paw testified that he had been an eyewitness. Soap testified that he "has good reasons for believing Said Herd stole Said horse."

Heard in fact returned a "Saddle & bridle and gave them to the claimant, but told him he should not have the horses untill the next day," Soap testified. "The next day (Soap) could not find the white man. He further said he has had no pay for the said horses as described above."

Buck Heard also stole from Indian Charles Moore, which was witnessed by Nootanhilla of Hightower (Davis 2002).

Buck was mentioned several times in Dekalb County Grand Jury presentments, posted in the *Federal Union* beginning in 1834:

…We present Henry Cupp, senior, John Worthy, Samuel Worthy, William Heard, Woolf and Henry Stowers for an affray at the house of John Austin in this county on the 13th day of September, 1834 (3/6)...

Later, in the 1838 presentment, Dekalb charged Buck with perjury for lying about the destruction of a wagon, for firewood we can only assume:

We present William Heard for the offence of perjury; for that the William Heard did, on the 22nd day of March, in the year 1833, in the county of Dekalb, before the Hon. Hiram Warner, judge of the Superior Court, take his corporeal oath, by laying his hand on the Holy Evangelist of

Almighty God, did then and there, in a certain issue between hasting D. Palmer and James Thompson; commit willful and corrupt perjury (Southern Rocorder: 3/3)...

Heard is listed in Dekalb Superior Court records for numerous charges in the 1830s:

March 1836	State	Mr. Heards and Michael Leusse	burglary
September 1838	State	William Heard	riot
March 1839	State	William Heard	riot
March 1839	State	William Heard	perjury
September 1838	State	Helsman Heard	Charge not recorded
September 1838	State	Helsman Heard	assault and battery

#795; WILLIAM G. HEARD; Simple larceny; 5; 7 April 1840; 7 April 1845; Cobb

In Vivian Price's **History of Dekalb County** 1822-1900 (1997), she cites a payment made to Buck Heard for painting at the jail house in one of the many "sundrie times while in jail" (189). Franklin Garret, in **Atlanta and It's Environs** (1954), notes: "...It would appear that Mr. Heard was a regular user of the jail facilities (64)..."

Helsman Heard (Hillsman?) may be related to Buck and he also appeared in the seedy side of Dekalb County history. Another Heard, by the name of George is listed in the Dekalb 1830 census. He is prosecuted in Cherokee County for stealing an Indian's horse and sentenced to four years in the Penitentiary (*Federal Union* Sept. 24, 1834: 3/3)

Buck Heard's notoriety continues up until the Civil War in Dekalb County records. He leaves an indelible mark on history as a man some thought may have been an alter ego of John A. Murrell. He is also associated with the Pony Club in other circles. No doubt Heard gravitated to "Snaketown" and "Murrell's Row" in Atlanta, where most of the miscreants on that side of the river tended to converge.

The Dekalb version of the Pony Club seems to have included:

Job Binion
John Goodwin
George Heard
Helsman Heard
William Heard

As we nave noted, after 1832, many Pony Club members moved to Paulding County. A large number, though, also relocated to Cherokee County. Early on Joel Leathers had relocated to the gold mines near Auraria and settled on the Chestatee near "Leather's Ford." Another Cherokee Countian mentioned in Indian claims is James Wilson. Lizzy Sanders claimed he took, in 1832: **"…One bay horse, a bay mare, and 40 head of hogs estimated to be worth $330 (Shadburn 1993: 649)…"** Likewise he was cited by Peacheater, who claimed Wilson, in 1834, finagled him out a horse **"…for false charges which he held against me (469)…"** In fact many of the claims made against Cherokee Countians were against officials of that county serving fi fas etc for alleged debt. Lizzy Sanders also accused William Lay, William Baker and Daniel Bird of theft. Lay and Baker were judges of the Inferior Court at the time and although this sounds like the set up the Pony Club had in Carroll County, these officials are not ever prosecuted or slicked. Does that prove their innocence?

William Baker	claim of Sanders	Cher 32
Daniel Bird	claim by Sanders	Cher 34
William Greene	claim by Hughes	Cher 34
Charles Harris	claim of George Still	Cher 32
George Hinckle	claim by Soap	Cher 34
William Lay	claim by Sanders	Cher 32
Joel Leathers		Cher 34
William McKinsey	claim by Proctor	permit, Cher 34
John Stancel Jr	claim by Harnage	Cher 34
Oliver Strickland	claim by Bumgarner	Cher 32
James Wilson	claims of Sanders, Peacheater	Cher 32

There are many other perpetrators listed in claims from different counties in Northwest Georgia these include:

John Boyd	claim by Anoren Ross	Lump 34
William Brazeale	claim of Brown (Ala)	Camp 30
John Franklin	claim by John Vann	Union 34
Moses Hendrix	claim of David Vann	Jack 30
John Price	claim of Hornet	Lump 34
Bethel Quillian	claim of Hornet	Lump 34
John Westbrooks	claim of David Sanders	Henr 28
Richard Winn	petition of William May	Jack 30

Mentioned in claims but not found in the record:

Bart Bailey	Plum
James Barker	Roberts
Jack	Sam
Andrew Johnson	Thomas
Pleasant Jones	Thompson
Peter Kent	Bob Weir
George McDuffie	James Wilcox
Moss	Williams

Out of State:

Hufftutter (Tenn.)
James Hughes (Tenn)
Looney (Tenn.)
John H.Garret (Ala)
David J. Hooks (Ala)
Lathom (Ala)
William Stone (Ala)
Moss (N. Car.)
Pickle Simon (N.Car.)

With permits:

Soloman Rately	permit, license, Lump 34
Michael Doudy	permit, license
Ezekial Ralston	poor white married to an Indian on the Chestatee.
John Coleman	settled on rented improvement (Joe Wickett)
William Hitson	employee of Thom McDaniel, license

Unknown:
Springen
David J. Hooks
James Speers

1993 Shadburn, Don L., **Unhallowed Intrusion: A History of Cherokee Families in Forsyth County, Georgia,** W.H. Wolfe associates: Alpharetta.

Dec. 06, 1828 **Presentments, Habersham County, *Southern Recorder*,** page 3 col. 5.

Nov. 15, 1832 **Presentments, Habersham County, Federal Union,** page 3 col. 4.

1988 McCabe, Alice Smythe (Editor), **GA: Gwinnett County, Georgia, Families 1818-1968 (with supplement),** Gwinnett Historical Society, Inc.: Lawrenceville @http://kfgeorgia.net/genealogy/showmedia.php?mediaID=177&medialinkID=1398

Dec. 27, 1832 **To the People of Georgia, *Georgia Journal*,** page 3 col. 6.

Winter 2002 Davis, Jr., Robert S., **Some Cherokee Indian Spoliations 1836-1837, *Georgia Genealogical Society Quarterly*,** Vol. 38 no.4.

Oct. 15, 1834 **Presentments Dekalb County, *Federal Union*,** page 3/6

Nov. 06, 1838 **Presentments Dekalb County, *Southern Recorder*,** page 3/3

Sep. 24, 1834 **The New Counties, *Federal Union*,** -- page 3/3

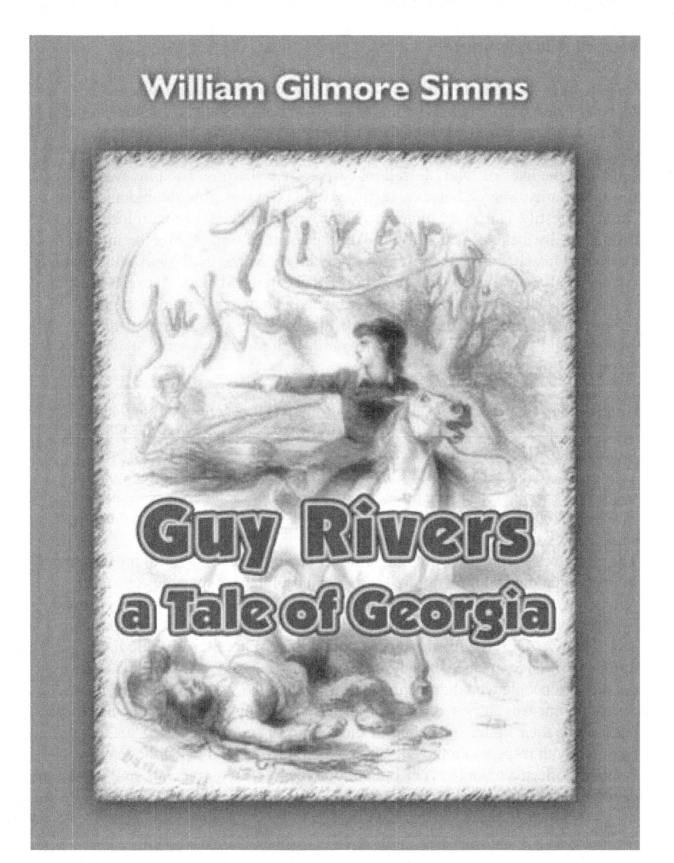

Pony Club in Literature

The 1830s in Georgia and Alabama were as tenuous as the late 1700s had been in Florida. There was an immense border in which runaway slave, enemies of the United States and fleeing criminals were able to pass. Jacksonians contended with Clarke men and Nullifiers with Union men. Abolitionists were agitating in the south and the likes of John Murrell made everyone nervous. The time was also ripe for opportunity: Slaves, horses and cattle could be stolen from the Indians, who could not testify against a white man. Their land could be taken with forged legal documents by men deemed "officials" of the counties surrounding the Indians. Corruption reached from the intruder along the Alabama Road, or at White Path, in Alabama, all the way up to the governor's office in the State of Georgia. Most of fault for this lay with the Federal Government, who had promised Georgia to remove the Indians back in 1802, when all the land west of Georgia, namely Alabama and Mississippi were sold. Regardless, it took 36 years to alleviate Georgia's "Indian Problem."

None of this occurred in a vacuum. The northern states, free of any Indian influences or dangers, due mainly to the strategy of pushing "undesirables" into Indian lands bordering their states, now opposed Indian removal in Georgia, Tennessee, Alabama and North Carolina. Northerners now thought it appalling southerners would repeat what they had done a generation before: Indian removal by force. To make matters worse for the Cherokee, the tribe split into feuding camps, one for emigration to Oklahoma, Indian Territory and another against it. The latter, under John Ross, fought removal beyond the 11th hour to the detriment of many who died on the Trail of Tears. The absolutely despicable acts of the removal were propounded by the outlandish belief that it could all be overturned by the Federal Government. Ross should have known from previous experience how tentative the U.S. government was on Indian affairs. Ramshackle forts, unfunded or undermanned expeditions, cosmetic fixes and etc. were the modus operandi of people who didn't care and deferred to the states to solve problems. Surely no one was surprised when Jackson told the Supreme Court that he would not enforce their finding on behalf of the Cherokee and against the State of Georgia, with respect to removal. Yet Ross plodded on and when the removal came he collected 65 dollars per Indian for expenses, an outrageous sum for the dead or the living.

The agony did not end in Oklahoma Indian Territory either. The murders of Ridge and others from the "treaty party" who favored and signed the New Echota Treaty in 1835, created a civil war that lasted for some time. Pinheads and Golden Knights would fight through the American Civil War as well. Men like Stand Watie found themselves facing Zeke Proctor and other former Southern neighbors who had volunteered for and against the Confederacy.

The Pony Club dissolved like salt in water. Once the Indians were gone new faces began arriving to take their land. These new people weren't crackers and gougers or former intruders. They were people familiar with law and order and demanded it from the beginning. New vagrancy laws, fresh faces and no border meant things were going to settle down in Georgia, Alabama, Tennessee and North Carolina. By 1840, the wild-west had moved on beyond the Mississippi. The frontier bravado of the Pony Club was now only found in dime novels, paperbacks and issues of *Police Gazette*.

Many Americans were kept abreast of the happenings and events in Georgia and the south because of the novels of William Gilmore Simms. He traveled the south, even went to Auraria to find out about the workings of the Pony Club. The earlier frontier violence novels were giving way to a new genre in literature, the "border romance." Simms wrote very popular books like **Guy Rivers, Richard Hurdis** and **Border Beagles.** They dealt with frontier violence and romance, from the point of view of the yeomanry, but certainly with the values of the Planter society. Simms, writing in *The Literary World* (1852), explained his interest in the Pony Club and related issues on the frontier. Growing up in Charleston he heard the stories at the local Bull's Head Tavern:

…King street, where it stands, was then the great place for the cotton and tobacco merchants. I have seen the street impassable a thousand times with the enormous long trains of wagons from Georgia, North Carolina, and the mountain region of our state, loaded with cotton, and alternating with the massive tobacco hogsheads, which, working in yokes, and drawn by mules or horses, constituted their own vehicles of carriage. The Bull's Head brought up all these teamsters at night. A vast inclosure, in the rear of the building, received the wagons, and, at their fires, as at a camp, I have lingered, when a boy, to listen to the wild narratives which they told of their far forest and wild experience. I have a thousand times meditated a series of legends of "The Bull's Head," which I shall yet, at some future day, if time is allowed me, put on record. The picturesque effect of the great fires blazing in the open area, the huge, athletic forms of the backwoodsmen grouped about them, their bronzed and swarthy faces,—their rude dialect, the novelty of their stories, the quaint force of their remarks, sensibly and strongly impressed my boyish imagination. On various pretexts, I contrived to hang about

them and to listen; and the pleased attention which I betrayed, raised me greatly in their regards, and made me a favorite among them. I squatted down along with them, and partook heartily of their corn bread and venison, of which they usually brought with them plentiful supplies; and, more than once, I meditated running off with them, to partake of that wild experience of which they told with such effect. Had they given me any encouragement, I might have done so. As it was, but one thing restrained me,—and that was the recollection of my poor old grandmother. What would be her loneliness without me! I thought of that! I was the only remaining promise—feeble enough, for my childhood was a sickly one—of a once goodly and numerous stock. My heart failed me— or rather my heart strengthened me against it— when I meditated to run away. But I still lingered in the dangerous vicinity. It was full of temptations, such as had their frequent effect upon me later in life, and have prompted many of my wanderings. It was here that I first gathered from Georgia wagoners, the information which I subsequently made use of in my novel of "Guy Rivers," touching the famous "Pony Club." They described the chief leaders of this Banditti. They detailed many of their adventures; and the history which I subsequently put on record had been registered in my memory more than ten years before (1852: 3)…

In **Guy Rivers,** Simms introduces the hero Ralph Colleton (Colleton is a prominent South Carolina family name), who meets the antagonist Guy Rivers, a lawyer turned leader of the infamous Pony Club, on a trail in the back hills of Georgia. Rather than give up his horse to this highwayman, he out maneuvers him and speeds away, but is wounded in the process. The ensuing chapters embroil women and grog houses and goings on around the mining districts of Cherokee County Georgia. Many of his other books follow the same formulaic prose, good and evil in the back country of what was then called the Southwest.

Literary critic Michael Price discussed the significance of the book, in his **Stories with a Moral** (2000):

…Simms called Guy Rivers a "tale of Georgia- a tale of the miners- of a frontier and wild people." Widely regarded as a haven for embezzlers, runaway slaves, horse thieves, and cattle rustlers, the region around Auraria had acquired a well deserved reputation for lawlessness. Moreover, Guy Rivers and his band of outlaws had a contemporary parallel in real life. The Sandtown community in modern Fulton County is on the eastern side of the Chattahoochee River and derives its name from the Sandtown Indians, who migrated there from the Alabama territory following the Creek war of 1813-14. According to John H. Goff, the premiere student of Georgia place names, Sandtown was a crossing point on the river for trails leading to gold diggings in the region, as well as a hang out for a band of marauders called the Pony Club or the Pony Boys (2000: 62).

Mary Winisatt, in **The Major Fiction of William Gilmore Simms,** also stresses the impact John Murrell had on Simms' novels, the Pony Club….

Specialized in terrorizing luckless settlers and stealing their horses; among the features connecting it to Murrell is that branches of the organization existed, so a contemporary writer claimed, in every state then in the Union (1989: 123)...

While the idea that the Pony Club was a Murrell offshoot or that it was prevalent in many states is not born out by the facts, but represents a general range of thought on the subject that included most northerners, who claimed Murrell was nothing more than an anti abolitionist gone wild; to the particularly Indian point of view that the Pony Club was the arm of removal in the State government in Georgia. It is easy to see how categories and events collapse, between 1828 and 1838, so that Murrell and the Pony Club and damn near anything else that happened in those years were all connected or even one event. Any horse thief was "with the Pony Club" any slave stolen was "Murrell's work." A person like Buck Heard takes on almost legendary status these 180 years later and all thanks to the **border romance**, sketchy reporting and faulty memories. This is how the Club is remembered; Indian antagonists in one county "Guy River's cave" in another county.

The view purveyed in Britain received even more contrivance with the 1841 edition of **The Romancist and Novelist Library,** whereby the Club has the power of Kingdom:

...the Pony Club is the proprietor of everything and everybody throughout the nation, and in and about this section. It is the king, without let or limitation of power, for sixty miles around. Scarce a man in Georgia but pays in some sort to its support, and judge and jury alike contribute to its treasuries. Few dispute its authority, as you will have reason to discover, without suffering condign and certain punishment; and, unlike the tributaries and agents of other powers, its servitors, like myself, invested with jurisdiction over certain parts and interests, sleep not in the performance of our duties; but, day and night, obey its dictates, and perform the various, almost laborious, and sometimes dangerous functions which it imposes upon us. It finds us in men, in money, in horses. It assesses the Cherokees, and they yield a tithe, and sometimes a greater proportion, of their ponies in obedience to its requisitions. Hence indeed the name of the club (1841:8)...

A good example of this sheer fantasy is the writing of Charles Dickens, who, in 1846, took a shot at border romance with his **The Pony Club: A Tale of the Backwood Settlements of Georgia.** Here, all the elements collide with astonishing results:

Some twenty years ago there existed in the upper part of Georgia, on the border of the Indian Territories, a small band of desperadoes, whose wild deeds and daring robberies rendered them the terror of the early settlers. This fraternity , which bore the appellation of "The Pony Club"- probably because they confined themselves to the stealing of horses and cattle, consisted of seven members, whose names were so scrupulously concealed, whose meetings were so secret, and whose robberies so skillfully conducted that the borderers could never discover by whom they had been deprived of their property. Possessed of large and fertile tracts of land quietly "located" in the midst of their neighbors, they seemed to be wholly absorbed by their agricultural and mining pursuits. At a distance rumor had reported them rich; and in their immediate neighborhood, in spite of the rudeness of their houses and attire, they bore the character of respectable men and thriving farmers; and not unfrequently were they solicited to aid in searching for the horses which they themselves had stolen, and the Cattle they had driven away and sold (Dickens, Ainsworth, Smith 1846: 363).

The more serious side of the topic received some note in Law Reviews of the time. The issue involved guilt by association and committing slander by inferring someone was a member of the Pony Club. The **Georgia Reports - Charleton -65 Ga.** recalled an 1833 case from Muscogee County, Cooper vs. Perry, wherein "you are a member of the Pony Club" was deemed actionable as slander by counsel

A String for the Poney.

I PERCEIVE by an advertisement inserted in the Herald of the 10th inst. that I am charged by Thos. S. Woodward, with roping certain Ponies therein described. If by roping, he means stealing, I do not know where the gentleman has found ground for his assertion, as he knows I am not a member of the Poney Club. I should be sorry to have roped ponies to one tenth the extent that he has ponies and Indian Lands both. For his information, I will state that a very particular friend of his, Mr. Paul H. Tiller, arrived at this place, not long since, with their joint interest in ponies, a snake-tailed one, such as he describes among the number. If the Club have been cheating each other, I beg they will not trouble me with their matters, as I do not belong to the concern.   WILEY G. ROPER.

March 16   7 tf

April 6, 1837 Columbus Enquirer (Ropers were related to the Gilleys).

because it implied the accused stole a horse (1903: 487). After the Callaway Burke affair many issued statements in the newspapers indicating they were not members of the Pony Club. After Gen. Thomas Woodward of Alabama made statements about Pony Club men in the local papers, one man wrote a personal disclaimer in the ***Columbus Enquirer,*** letting everyone know he had no part of the club.

The Pony Club, from time to time has been mentioned in both fiction and humor, as in Eugenia Price's **To See Your Face Again** (1997); Cohen and Dillingham's **Humor of the Old Southwest** (1994); Michael Wallais' **Pretty Boy Floyd** (1994) and Charles Frazier's **Thirteen Moons** (2007).

Any student of the history of the Cherokee has heard of the Pony Club, because every book on the Cherokee recounts what they did. There is little or no information in the Government of the United States or the State of Georgia. Even the Serial Set 197, the compilation of claims against club members is buried in less than a dozen libraries **IN THE ENTIRE UNITED STATES**. Without the work of Indian groups, the Trail of Tears Organization and people like Don Shadburn and Marybelle W. Chase, and others, information on the Pony Club could have been lost forever.

January-June 1852 Simms, William Gilmore, **Home Sketches or Life Along the Highways and Byways of the South,** *The Literary World – A Journal of Science, Literature and Art, Antiques & Collectibles*, E.A. and G.L. Duyckinck: N.Y.

2000 Price, Michael E. **Stories with a Moral: Literature and Society in Nineteenth-Century Georgia,** Univ. of Ga. Press: Athens.

1989 Winisatt, Mary Ann, **The Major Fiction of William Gilmore Simms,** La. State Univ. Press: Baton Rouge.

1846 Dickens, Charles, William Harrison Ainsworth, Albert Smith, **The Pony Club: A Tale of the Backwood Settlements of Georgia,** *Bentley's Miscellany,* vol. 20, Richard Bentley: London.

1841 Hazlitt, William, **Guy Rivers the Outlaw, By William Gilmore Simms,** *The Romancist and Novelist's Library: New Series*, Vol. 2, John Clements, Little Pulteny Street: London.

April 6, 1837 **String for a Pony,** *Columbus Enquirer*, page 2 col. 4.

1997 Price, Eugenia, **To See Your Face Again**, Martin Press:

1994 Cohen, Hennig, William B. Dillingham**, Humor of the Old Southwest,** Univ. of Ga. Press: Athens

1994 Wallis, Michael, **Pretty Boy: The Life and Times of Charles Arthur Floyd,** St. Martin's Press: N.Y.

2007 Frazier, Charles, **Thirteen Moons**, Random House: N. Y.

Bart Bailey	288, 321, 330	J. Baxter	291
Eli Bailey	270		
Joshua Bailey	270	James Beamer	31
Bailey's Mills	226	Bean	31, 59
William Baity	21	Joseph Beanstick	230, 231
Baker	59	Bear Meat	300
General Baker	109	Bear Paw	4,
William Baker	110, 188, 232	313, 315, 321	
	321, 325, 329,330	Bear's Paw	324
Nancy Baldridge	300	Beavens	56
Rachel Baldridge	300	Beaver	283, 287, 320
John Ballard	176	Beckett	56, 57
Banks	57	Bee	56
Isaac Bankston	171	Bell	59
Amanda Bannoris	90	Mr. Bell	170, 278
Richard Bannoris	90	Bell, John	32
Gaspard Barber	118	Bella	256
Jacob Barclay	110	Bernard	19
John Barclay, Captain	110	Timpoochee Bernard	34
James Barker	320, 330	Thomas Bernard	111
James Barker	284, 287	Berry	57
Moses Barker	111	Berry	59
Timothy Barnard	136, 138	Michael Berry	111
Barnes	176	Thomas Berry	111
Judge Barnes	192	Ben	50
David Barnwell	1, 212	Benn	31
Thomas Barry	111	John Benge	265
Henry Barton	90	Richard Benge	170
Holly Barton	90	Grandpa Benjamin	254
JOHN BARTON/BOSTON? 192		LEVI BENSON	191
John W. Barton, 2nd Sgt.	270	William Benson	86
William Bartram	105	Best	57
Thomas Bates	111	Bettyneck Plantation	113
Peter Batoe	111	Bibbin	57
Bass	56	Bill	20
Mr. Bassam	170	Buffalo Bill	65
Margaret Baumgartner		John Billings	111
(nee Vickery)	232, 323	Bingham	56

Binion	283, 287	Shadrack Bogan	285, 325
Joe Binion	320, 325, 329		326, 327
Bird	56	Shadrack Bogan	285
Daniel Bird	188, 321, 323, 330	William Shadrack	
John C. Bird	197	Boggan, Bogan	326
Abraham Birdwell	198	William Patrick	
Elijah Bishop	111	Boggan, Bogan	326
Col. Wm. N. Bishop	245	William Bogan Ensign	110
W.N. Bishop	323	William Bogan	116
William Bishop	111, 117	Giles Bogges	294, 298
E.E. Bissel	243	Jiles G. Bogges	230, 231
George Black	50	Jiles Boggus	233
Nethaniel Black	291, 307	Major Bogus	230
Indian Black-bird	291	_____ Bolen	189
Blackburn, Lewis	32	Bolen	321
Richard Blackstock	188, 289	Simon Bolivar	161
	290	Charles C. Bolton	180
George Blackwood	300	Robert Bolton	111, 117
Blair	56	Militia Major	
Blake	295	James C.Bonner	232
Elizabeth Owen Blake	291	Thomas F. Booker	176
Ruel Blake	86	David Booker	176
Sarah Blake	291	THOMAS BONNER	189
THOS. BLAKE	191	WM. R. BOON	192
Thomas Blake	88, 210, 212	Daniel Boone	65, 72
	289, 291, 307, 314	Thomas Booth mate	110
William Blevins	31	Louis Borges	90
LUKE BLIVINS	191	Johann Bornemann	167
Blizzard	57	Ransom Boswell	291
Governor Blount	13, 98, 136	Ulysses Boswell	291
John Blount	252	Elias Boudinot	199, 203, 236
William Blount	43, 73		296
Blundon	56	Boudinot	208
Blythe	56	JONATHAN BOX	190
Willis Bobo	321, 325	WILLIAM B. BOX	191
Bogan	284	John Bowden	117, 190
Bogan Road	326	Uriah Bowden	123
Shadrach Bogan	320	JOHN BOWERS	190

Bowles	132, 135, 139	George Brown	111
	152, 167	Hugh Brown	110
Mr. Bowles	139	James Brown	110, 265
William Bowles	108, 132	James C.Brown, Adj.	110
William Augustus		R. Brown	176
Bowles 107, 108, 120, 124, 132		Robert Brown	321
	136,138	Thomas Brown	31
Bowlegs	252	Thomas Brown, Col.	110
Billy Bowlegs	248	James Bromley	302
Jim Boy	148	James Brook	110
Boyd	56, 59, 86	Elisha Brooks	240
General Boyd	113	Jacob R. Brooks	176
John Boyd	321, 330	James Brooks	110
Captain Boyer	138	Thomas Brooks	110
Roger Boyle	110	Allen Brooks	270
Bechel Bradley	176	Mr. Brooks	291
George Brakor	118	Jacob R. Brooks	293, 307
Henry Bramblet	324	Bruce	59
Joseph Bramblet	324	Bruinton	56
Henry Bramlett	324	JAMES BRUMLEY	190
Joseph Bramlett	324	Bruner	59
William Brazeale	321, 330	Bryant	59
Brandon	56	Hawkins Bryant	111
James Brantly	302	William Bryant	110
Lewis Brantly	171	James Bryce	302
A Braswell	171	William Bryce	302
Sam Braswell	171	Hawkins Bryson	110
Braveboy	57	Capt. Buffington	269
Brewer	59	Buckner	59
William Brewer	111	William Bull	104
WILLIAM BRICE	189	Tyler Bulware	102
Bengamon Briges	171	Bunch	56
Brim	134	Ralph Bunch	54
Brown	57, 59, 135, 284	Bunch, Bench or Benge	31
	285, 287, 320, 330	Bunn, Jesse	32
Caroline Brown	180	Robert Bunning	31
Col. Brown	113	Bunyan	31
Colonel Thomas Brown	102	John Burch	111

Carolina	59	Cheesekau	42
Caroline	180	Chenaquah	295, 304
Carr	59	Bailey Cheney	119
Paddy Carr	34	Chigilly	134
Tom Carr	34	Joseph Childers	171
William Carr	111	Michel Childers	171
Thos. Carrol	283	William Childers	320
John Carroll	111	E.D. Chisolm, 4th Cpl.	270
John Carrson	170	Chisholm, James	32
Carson	59	John D. Chisolm	130
Kit Carson	65	Thomas Chivers	56
Carter	56, 59	Choate	59
Thomas Carter	270	Choeageky	291
Cartwright	21, 302	Johnny Chopoe	255
James Cartwright	188, 289	Choowalooka	265
	292	Col. William Christian	40
Wilson Cartwright	191, 231	Chulowee	229
	289, 292	Benjamin Church	65
William Alexander		Chuwooyee	199, 200, 201
Caruthers	92		230
Ca see la wee	308, 321	Chuwoyee,	303
Secretery of War Cass	242	Chuyowee	294
The Cat	152	John H. L. Claiborn	88
Causey	57	Matthew Clanton	86
Chambers	59	Clark	59
Chambers, Masfield	32	Angus Clark	118
Thomas Chandler	291	Daniel Clark	31
Thos. Chandler	310, 313	Gen. Clark	252
Charity	57	George Rogers Clark	120
J. Charley	291	Jerry Clark	299, 303
Charles	59, 254	John Clark Surg.	110
Marybelle W. Chase	339	Clarke	333
James Chatworth	118	Elijah Clarke	120, 123
Benjamin Chavez	54	Gen. Elijah Clarke	40
Chavis	56	Clay	59
Elizabeth Chavis	56	Governor Clay	246
JAMES CHECK	191	Judge Henry Clayton	198
JAMES R. CHECK	190	James Clemmons	111

William Cleghorn	235	George Cook	123
James Cleghorn	240	David Cooke	110
Ephraim Clibborn	110	Cooper	59
Gen. Clinch	255	Cooper vs. Perry	338
Gen. Duncan Clinch	161	ROBERT COOPER	189
Cline, Thomas A	32	William and Joseph	
Gavin Cochrane	5	Cooper	31
Robert Cochrane	111	Copes	56
Admiral Cochrane	159	Copeland	32
Admiral Cockburn	159	Thomas Copeland	325
Coffee	182	Thos. Copeland	321
Gen. Coffee	210, 213, 292	FREDERICK	
	298, 306	CORDAMAN	191
Coffel	102, 105, 106	Corn	56
Joseph Coffel	105, 106	Cornplanter	248
James Coffield	108	James Cornelius	180
Cohee	59	Cornells	102
Cohen	338	Davy Cornells	35
Colbert	59	Joseph Cornells	31, 35
William Colbert	31	Vicey Cornells	124
Cole	59	John Cornish	111
John Coleman	321, 331	Margarett Cornish	56
Colemen, William	32	Cornwallis	110
Parker Collens	20	Jacob Cotrell	302
Ralph Colleton	91, 336	Cotter	268, 269
Collins	56	Reverend William J.	
James Collins	291	Cotter	266
Collins, Parker	32	Cotton	86
W.D. Collins	302	Joshua Cotton	85, 86
William Collins	119	Cox	59
Judge Walter T. Colquitt	233	John T. Cox	176
Colly	59	John Crawford	111
Captain William Cone	252	Tarrant Crawford	242
William Cone	112	John Craddock	289, 293
Conner, ____	32		307, 321
Bengamon Conner	171	Craddocks	293, 307
Hair Conrad	265	Col. S. D. Crane	245
Arthur Coody	130	William Crane	171

HARREL FELTON	189	James Foreman	251, 252
Joseph Fenner	118	Stephen Foreman	313
John Ferguson	111	Ben Forrester	255
Fernando	56, 57	Mr. Forrester	255
Clerk Few	313	Sandy Forrester	256
Col. Few	113	A. Forrester	255
William Few	135	E. R. Forsyth	240
John Fiddler	111	Governor Forsythe	197, 229
Fields	59	Foster	59
Charles Fields	110	Mrs. Foster	231
James Fields	321	Drury Fort	10, 117
John Fields	130, 321,303, 309	Lt. Fowler	230
Old Field	231, 265	R.T. Fowler	176
George Fillet	123	Black Fox	320
Joseph Fillet	123	Francis	56
Findley	56	David Francis	34
James Finley	270	James Francis	31
John Findley	72	John Francis	111
Jonathon Finlay	111	Josiah Francis	34, 252
William Finley	270	Prophet Francis	148, 163, 164
Fisher	59	Francisco	56
Andrew Fitch	111	Franklin	59
Euhar Fixico	255	John Franklin	321, 324, 330
Benjamin Fletcher	3	Joseph Franks	111
Henry Flicks	117	EBINEZAR FRASIER	192
Flint	59	Frazier	59
George Flora	123	Charles Frazier	338
Floyd	148, 149, 252, 269	Freeman	59
Gen. Floyd	150	Freeman, George	32
General John Floyd	148	Thomas Freeman	40
William Floyd	309	French	60
Folsom	59	Robert French	111
Montgomery Folsom	246, 247	BENJAMIN FREW	190
John Forbes	31, 133	Spring Frog	321
John Forbes and co.	159, 160	Charles Fuller	270
Ford	59	Henry Fuller	270
James Ford	78, 79	Fulsum	60
Jim Ford	80	William Fuz	111

JOHN GADEN 190
Gen. Gaines 161
Henry Gaither 120
Major Henry Gaither 136
George Galphin 21, 50
Galphinton 136
Robert Gandey or Gowdy 31
Robert Gamble Esqr 160
Nathan Gann 302
Garcia 161
S. Garden 256
Captain Gardner 242
William Garner 20
Garnier 101
Garret 60
Franklin Garret 87, 329
John H. Garret 320, 331
Caleb Garrison 212
JAMES A. GARRISON 190
James F. Garrison 212
Rector John Garvin 326
Antonio Garzon 119
Gate's Ferry 323
John Gathard 21
Gay 211, 188, 292, 306
Joshua Gay 289, 295, 307
JOHN GAYDEN 191
Foreign Minister Genet 120
Gentry 60
George 56, 100
George Guess, Guest, Gass 31
Henry George 111
King George 72
Lord Germain 142
Gibson 56, 60
Edward Gibson 50
Lieutenant Governor
Edward Gibson 105

Sutherland Gibson 111
Joshua Giddings 253
JOHN GILBERT 189
Robert Gilbert 123
Rebecca Gill 327
WILLIS GILLERY 192
JOHN P. GILLASPY 191
Gillet 56
Baylis Gilley 302
Gilley 292
John Gilley 188, 210, 289, 291
295, 302, 307, 324
Willis Gilley 188, 211, 289, 295
324
JOHN P. GILLISPIE 189
Gilly 211
Gilmer 283, 284, 287, 320
G.R. Gilmer 235
George Gilmer 203, 297
Governor Gilmer 193, 205
212, 214, 235, 243, 269, 323
Governor George Gilmer 177
Gilmore 325
George R. Gilmore 269, 293
Mr. Gilmore 326
JOHN E. GILON 190
Gipson 56
Girthy or Girty 150
Simon Girty 150
Nathaniel Gist 31
JOHN E. GITON? 190
Givens 60
Governor Glen 225
Glover 60
Joel Goddard 311
THOS. GODDARD 191
Godett 57
William Godfrey 117

Jim Godwin	307, 315	James Greyham	212
John H. Goff	336	Grierson	31
Mary Sue Going	61	Robert Grierson	50
Norman Goings	61	Griffin	57
Thomas Goldsby	111	Griffin	60
Phillip Goodbread	111, 117	Davis Griffith	170
Goodin	210, 213, 309, 310	Hines Griffith	170
Isaac Goodin	209	Cornelius Griffiths	123
John Goodin		Grimmet	60
(Goodwin)	208, 232	Grit	293
Goodwin	211, 230	Grits	321
Francis Goodwin	123	John Grizzle	111
John Goodwin	187, 188, 289	Ground Mole	304
	291, 315, 295, 304	Grubbs	252
	307, 325, 329	Andrew Gums	111
John Goodin	295, 309.	Gunn, Thomas	33
Jomes Gormon	111	Edward Gunter	130
Goulding party	99	John Gunter	31
Gowen	56	William Gunter	111
John Gowen	56	Gussal	56
Graham	60	Jasmine Guy	54
Grant	60	Button Gwinnett	66
Ludovick Grant	31, 225		
B. Gravely	270	James Habersham	19, 49
Edward Graves	278, 279	John Hackney, 1st Sgt.	270
Sarah Graves	278, 279	Robert Hackney	270
Gray	60	Assune Hadjo	255
John Gray	118	Billy Hadjo	254
Jonathan Gray	21	Charlo Hadjo	255
Samuel Gray Lieutenant	110	Columma Hadjo	255
Grayson	60	Hathlo Hadjo	255
Wm Graystock	118	Hillabee Hadjo	256
Green	56, 60	Spoak Oak Hadjo	255
A. Greene	291	Talloa Hadjo	255
Alston Greene	235	James Hagan	110
William Greene	321, 325, 330	John Hagans	321
Edmund Grey	226	Hague	150
Mr. Samuel Grey	203	John Hague	150

Jesse R. Johnson	270
Thomas Johnson	170, 302
Johnsons	187, 293, 307, 314
Edward Johnston	111
William Johnston	111
Josiah	187
Joseph Judge	61
Thos Justin	118
Katy	255
Kelly	56
Ailsey Ketchum	303
Herbert Ketcham	61
Nancy Ketcham	304
John Pendleton Kennedy	91
THOMAS KENNON	192
Peter Kent	321, 330
Kersey	56
Frances Scott Key	244
Keyes House	88
Kice	284
Kicy	287
8 Killer	170
John Killian	289, 292, 298
	306, 325
King	56
King Fisher	43
Robbin King	117
Robert King	111
Solomon King	111, 116, 123
Wallace King	111
Tsu la Kingfisher	37
Jack Kinnard	136
JOHN KIRBY	245
Col. Kirkland	152
Rachel Klein	102
CARINGTON KNIGHT	192
George Knolls	124

Henry Knox	136, 169
Martin Kolb	235
Kolkahlosky	304
Secretary of War	
P. Kroft	179
Kulkeeloskee	321
Lewis Kuykendall	80
John C. Ladson	117
Jean Lafitte	157
William Lafton	171
Edwin Lambard	171
Eligay Lambard Se	171
William Lambard	171
William Lambard Jun	171
Landrum	56
Landrum, James	32
Lane, Daniel	32
Pierce Lane	123
William Lane	121, 123
Lang	121
Ricardo Lang	122
Richard Lang	120, 124, 144
Langfords	293, 307
Garret Langford	188, 289, 299
	302, 310
Moses Langford	111
James Langham	111
Britt Langworth	100
Garret Lankford	211
Langley, John	32
Noah Langly	21
Langley, Ozell	33
Larney	304
Lantern	56
Lathom	331
George Latimer	111
Simon Lavine	111
John Lawrence	111

William Love	110	John Mahaffey	301
Lovina	56	Mahardy	60
Lowe	60	James Wright Major	110
Lowry	56, 60	Majors	187
George Lowrey	31, 35	Elias Majors	309
Major Lowery	35	James Majors	302
William Lucas Lieutenant	110	William Majors	302
Lt. Lucky	149	Wright Majors	189, 191
Lumpkin	236, 237		290, 302
Governor Lumpkin	213, 244	Malachee	134
	257, 299, 323	Richard Malpas	123
Mr. John Lumpkin	237	the Man-slayer	152
Wilson Lumpkin	193, 203, 240	William Mangum	117, 119
	294	Manly	56
Governor Wilson Lumpkin	312	Manning	56
JOHN LUNA	190	Kaspar Mansker	44
John Lyman	111	JOHN MAREDITH	190
Lynch	57, 60	Margaret	256
James Lynch	111	GEORGE MARLER	189
Joseph M. Lynch	251	John Marshall	110
John Lynn	111	Martin	31, 60
		Brice Martin	321
Mackey	60	E.B. Martin	212
Thomas Maderis	233	EMANUEL MARTIN	192
Madison	146	Governor Martin	135
President Madison	144	Mr. John Martin	296
John Magee	171	Jese Martin	21
Maggie	247	John Martin	21
Elizabeth Mahaffey	301	Steve Martin	54
Elizabeth Wright Mahaffey	313	John Martindale	111
Hiram Mahaffey	289, 301, 302	Gen. Francis Marion	112
Isaac Mahaffey	301	Maria	256
James Mahaffey	290, 301, 302	Mary	180, 256
Lucinda Wright Mahaffey	313	Maskill	56
MARLIN MAHAFFEY	192	Mason	21, 56
Mr. Mahaffey	231	Isaac Mason	78
Nancy Wright Mahaffey	313	Samuel Mason	78
Mahaffeys	187	Matthews	56

Pinckney Treaty	137	Robert Prine	50, 105
Redding Pinson	176	Prior	298, 306
Mr. Pitt	226	Edward Prichett	112
William Plowden	120, 124	Pritchard	57
Plum	189, 321	William Pritchett	304
RUBEN H. POGUE	190	Proctor	330
WILLIARD H. POGUE	191	Dick Proctor	308, 321
Polhemus	61	Edward Proctor	112
R.W. Pollard, 1st Sgt.	270	Philip Proctor	112, 117
Pompey	56	Zeke Proctor	335
Pone	56	Edward Prue	112
Joseph Ponse	112	Pryber	226
John C. Pope	176	Dr. Christian Pryber	225
SHEROD PORCH	190	Governor Queseda	120, 121
Porris	283, 287, 304	Beth Quillian	321
Porter	60	Bethel Quillian	188, 330
DANIEL POSEY	192	SAMUEL QUINTON	190, 191
John Potatoe	198		
Potter	56	HODGE RABUN	191
Powell	60	Rae	31
Captain Richd Power	124	Cornelius Rain	123
Larkin Powell	292	Joseph Rain	123
William Powell	270	Robert Rain	124
Richard Powers	133	William Rain	123
Jesse Prescott	112	Ralston, ____	33
Elvis Presley	54	Ezekial Ralston	
ROBERT PRESSLEY	190	284, 320, 331	
Prevost	136	Alex Ramcy	117
G.M. Prevost ensign	110	Alexander Ramsay	212, 236
General Prevost	109		292
Price	56, 60	David Ramsay	103
Eugenia Price	338	Alexander R. Ramsey	290
Edward Price	112		306, 311, 315
John Price	188, 330	Alexander Ramsey	187, 229
Michael Price	336	Ramseys	187, 293, 307, 314
Vivian Price	329	Jesse Raper	321, 325
John Prichard	112	William Rapids	112
Primus	255	Saul Rately	205, 301

William Strahan	112
DRURY STRICKLAND	192
Irvin Strickland	21
Lazeras Strickland	21
Oliver Strickland	188, 232
	321, 323, 330
Simon Strickland	21
Sion Strickland	21
David Striplin	302
John Stuart	31
John Stuart	39
Alison Stuart	118
John Studars	171
Benjamin Sturges	243
Summerlin	57
Jos. Summerlin	112
Joseph Summerlin	116, 123
Sunaffe Tustenukke	
(Abraham)	51
Sutton	32, 60
James D. Sutton	321, 324
Jas. D. Sutton	324
Madison Sutton	324
Mat Sutton	321, 324
Su wu chu	300, 321
Swan	304
Caleb Swan	169
Sweat	56
Henry Sweeny	123
Sweetwater	266
John Swords	112
Moses Symonds	112
Taborn	56
John Tait	135
Taitum	283, 284, 285
John Talent	292
Tallesee King	135

Tarleton	136
Tarrepin	170
Tate	56
Jeremiah Tate	112
William Tate	112
Tatum (Taitem)	307, 308, 320
	321
Edward Tatum	188, 190, 290
	307
J. WESLEY TATUM	192
John Tatum	188, 290, 307
Hugh Tatum	188, 290, 307
	308, 321
Thomas Tatum	188, 290
	307, 308, 321
WESLEY TATUM	190
Taylor	60, 180
JOHN J. TAYLOR	190, 191
Judge Taylor	219
Mr. Taylor	179
Richard Taylor	112, 130, 265
	281
Tecumseh	42, 148
Gov. Telfair	136
Susannah Terapin	300
Gen. Henry M. Terrell	245
HENRY M. TERRELL	245
Terrell, John	33
G.B. Terry	243
Testenuggee	248
Tetoneskee	277
Tekancesky	300
Thaxton	56
Thomas	56, 60, 187, 321
Evan Thomas	112
Governor Thomas	36
Tephilo Thomas	124

Finest Watley 171
Watts 56, 212, 295, 298
Edward Watts 210, 290, 291
307, 310
Chief John Watts 42,43
James watts 311
John Watts 31, 210, 290, 291
307, 310, 311
Jno Watts 170
LITTLEBERRY WATTS 189
Martha Watts 299
SEABORN WATTS 189
WILLIAM WATSON 189
Washington 60
George Washington 4, 135,136
Margaret Wauton 255
Ed Wauton 255
General Wayne 73
Webb 56
JOHN WEBB 190
Rachel Webb 181
John Wealt 112
Thomas Weatherby 302
Weatherford 148
BillyWeatherford 150
William Weatherford 31, 34
150,153
Weatherford 102
Weatherfords 125
JAMES WEATHERLY 192
Jon. Weaver 112
Weaver 57
Donna Weed 327
Bob Weir 321
WILLIAM WELBORN 199
Welch 229, 285, 306, 320
John Welch 188,290, 311, 325
Mark Welch 188

Pinkney Welch 188, 290, 311
Thomas Welch 31, 236, 290
311, 321, 325
Welck 284, 311, 315
Wellibey 163
Wells 150
Edward Wells 50
JOHN WESIENHUNT 190, 191
HENRY WESENHUNT 190
GEORGE WESENHUNT 190
PHILLIP WESENHUNT 190
PETER WESENHUNT 190
191, 192
Jack (John) West 187, 290
303, 305, 311, 312, 313, 321
JAMES WEST 192
Jim West 290, 305, 311, 312
313, 321
John West 187
Mr. West 200
John Westbrooks 321, 330
G.H. Whatley 271
Joel Wheeler 170
Wheeler, John F 33
Whetchel 176
Ensign Isaac Wheyler 121
George Whisenhunt 292
White 60
General White 278
James White 172
Whitfield 106
Colonel Whitley 44
Whitmore, Stephen 32
Joe Wickett 331
Eleazar Wiggans 31
Henry Wiggington 157
James Wilcox 321
Wildcat 248

CPSIA information can be obtained
at www.ICGtesting.com
Printed in the USA
BVOW04s0011241217
503152BV00033B/218/P